COLLECTED WORKS OF ERASMUS

VOLUME 19

THE CORRESPONDENCE OF
ERASMUS

LETTERS 2635 TO 2802

April 1532–April 1533

translated by Clarence H. Miller †

with Charles Fantazzi

annotated by James M. Estes

University of Toronto Press

Toronto / Buffalo / London

The research and publication costs of the
Collected Works of Erasmus are supported by
University of Toronto Press

© University of Toronto Press 2019
Toronto / Buffalo / London
utorontopress.com
Printed in Canada

ISBN 978-1-4875-0458-8

Printed on acid-free, 100% post-consumer recycled paper
with vegetable-based inks.

Library and Archives Canada Cataloguing in Publication

Erasmus, Desiderius, –1536
[Works. English]
Collected works of Erasmus.

Includes bibliographical references and indexes.
Contents: v.19. The correspondence of Erasmus: Letters 2635 to 2802
ISBN 978-1-4875-0458-8 (v. 19: hardcover)

1. Title.

PA8500 1974   199'.492   C740-06326x

University of Toronto Press acknowledges the financial assistance
to its publishing program of the Canada Council for the Arts
and the Ontario Arts Council, an agency of the Government of Ontario.

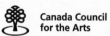

Canada Council   Conseil des Arts
for the Arts   du Canada

ONTARIO ARTS COUNCIL
CONSEIL DES ARTS DE L'ONTARIO
an Ontario government agency
un organisme du gouvernement de l'Ontario

Funded by the   Financé par le
Government   gouvernement
of Canada   du Canada

Collected Works of Erasmus

The aim of the Collected Works of Erasmus
is to make available an accurate, readable English text
of Erasmus' correspondence and his
other principal writings. The edition is planned
and directed by an Editorial Board, an Executive Committee,
and an Advisory Committee.

Contents

Illustrations

Preface

This volume comprises Erasmus' correspondence for the period 1 April 1532–30 April 1533. On the whole, the letters reflect his continued preoccupation with public and private matters that had been much on his mind since at least 1529. At the forefront in the public sphere were the twin dangers of religious civil war in Germany on the one hand and the renewed threat of Turkish invasion on the other. The danger of civil war between the forces of armed Protestantism and Catholicism, already apparent at the Diet of Speyer in 1529,[1] had become acute following the disastrous failure of the attempt at the Diet of Augsburg in 1530 to reach a negotiated religious settlement. Leaving Augsburg with good reason to believe that the emperor and the Catholic estates meant to make war on them because of their 'disobedience' in matters of faith and religion, a group of Lutheran princes and cities quickly formed the League of Schmalkalden (1531) to defend themselves against such an attack.[2] The initial membership was small, but in the following years the league expanded rapidly and was soon a potent force in the politics of the Empire. Meanwhile, in the autumn of 1529, the Turks had come perilously close to capturing Vienna, success at which would have opened the door to further penetration into the Empire.[3] As expected, a new campaign to take Vienna was launched in late April 1532. Both the internal and the external danger, however, receded more quickly and for much longer than anyone could have predicted.

Emperor Charles v considered it his supreme duty to eradicate heresy from Germany (as well as from his other dominions) and to defend Christian Europe against the Turks. His brother and imperial viceroy, Ferdinand, was

* * * * *

1 See CWE 16 xii–xiii.
2 See Ep 2403 nn10–11.
3 See Ep 2211 n10.

not only an equally zealous opponent of heresy but also, as archduke of Austria and claimant to the throne of Hungary, determined to defend his hereditary lands and the soil of the Empire against the Turks. It was not possible, however, simultaneously to crush the German Reformation and defeat the Turks. So to secure the aid against the Turks that the Lutheran estates had refused to vote at the Diet of Augsburg in 1530, Charles, with the encouragement of Ferdinand, was now prepared to grant temporary, limited recognition to the religious changes that the Lutherans had thus far introduced.

To this end Charles summoned an imperial diet that was supposed to meet at Speyer in September 1531. Postponed to January 1532 at Regensburg, the diet did not actually convene until 17 April. While the diet, which lasted until 27 July, wrestled with the question of who would contribute what to the defence of the Empire against the Turks,[4] representatives of the emperor and the Lutheran estates, meeting first at Schweinfurt and then at Nürnberg (1 April–24 July), negotiated the terms that would secure the support of the Lutherans for that defence. The resulting agreement stipulated that no imperial estate would be permitted to make war on another over matters of faith and religion and that all proceedings against Lutheran estates in the Imperial Supreme Court (*Reichskammergericht*) arising from their reform measures (the appropriation of church properties and other violations of ecclesiastical jurisdiction) would be brought to a 'standstill' (*Anstand*). Known both as the Nürnberg Standstill (*Nürnberger Anstand*) and as the Religious Peace of Nürnberg, the agreement was essentially a truce between the emperor himself and the Lutheran estates. Because the Catholic majority of the diet would surely have rejected it, the text of the Standstill was neither published nor presented to the diet for its approval. Instead, the emperor, acting in virtue of his own 'plenitude power' and omitting all mention of the 'standstill' of legal cases, issued a mandate (3 August) proclaiming a religious peace in the Empire valid until the outcome of a general council or until the contrary decision of a future diet.[5] Though intended as a temporary measure of limited scope, the Nürnberg truce was renewed as the Frankfurt truce in 1539, in which the numerous estates that had become Lutheran since 1532 were included. Reaffirmed by the Diet of Regensburg in 1541, the truce remained

* * * * *

4 Erasmus received at least one eye-witness report of the relevant decisions of the diet; see Ep 2654.
5 Although Erasmus must have known about the emperor's mandate proclaiming a religious peace, he never refers to it by name, and his references to it are a matter of guesswork; see Epp 2702 n2, 2713 n7, 2751 n2.

in force until the outbreak of war between the emperor and the League of Schmalkalden in 1546.

The truce of 1532 succeeded in its immediate aim of securing the support of the Lutheran estates against the Turks, whose renewed advance on Vienna had commenced in late April 1532, only to become bogged down in the siege of a border town in Hapsburg Hungary that was abandoned at the end of August. In the remaining months of the campaigning season the Turks captured a few forts in Hungary but did not make it to Vienna. In June 1533 King Ferdinand signed a truce with Sultan Suleiman I that managed to last until 1541.[6]

During the long months of uncertainty and anxiety between the cancellation of the diet at Speyer and the opening of the one at Regensburg, Erasmus was prey to his old fear that the emperor, in his piety, would yield to the pope's demand for harsh measures against the heretics, thus hastening the outbreak of a religious war in the Empire.[7] The conclusion of the Nürnberg truce did not dispel this fear: Erasmus perceived no real peaceful intent on the part of pope or emperor.[8] The fear of war was justified, but Erasmus had no way of knowing that the day of reckoning would be postponed until a decade after his death. It was against this background that he wrestled with the question of whether or not he should remain in Germany.

Ever since moving from Basel to Freiburg im Breisgau in April 1529 Erasmus had wondered if he should not have moved somewhere further away. Freiburg, after all, seemed dangerously close to likely scenes of religious civil war in Switzerland and Germany. Was he safe there? By the autumn of 1531 the danger that religious war in Switzerland would overflow into the neighbouring Breisgau had disappeared with the conclusion of the Peace of Kappel, which put to rest the armed conflict between the Protestant and Catholic cantons. But, as noted above, the danger of religious war between the Protestant and Catholic estates of the Empire was still very much present and showed no signs of abating.[9] So, despite having gone to the trouble and expense of purchasing and refitting a new house in Freiburg, Erasmus continued to explore his options for moving elsewhere.[10]

* * * * *

6 Epp 2699 n5, 2780 n9
7 See Ep 2645:35–8 with n6.
8 See Ep 2702:8–10.
9 See CWE 16 xi–xii, 17 xvi–xvii, 18 xi–xiii.
10 See CWE 18 xiii–xiv.

What Erasmus sought was a refuge that was, first, safely remote from Germany and yet not so distant that a frail old man could not face the journey, and second, free of hostile theologians. These requirements seriously limited his choice among the destinations where he knew he would be welcome. Poland and Italy were too far away, while Paris, to which he had an open invitation from Francis I (Ep 1375), was home to the theological faculty that had accused him of being a 'clandestine Lutheran' and had formally condemned a long list of propositions drawn from his works.[11] Faced with this situation, Erasmus gave renewed consideration to two destinations that had long been on his list of possibilities: his native Netherlands (usually referred to as 'Brabant' or 'Brabant and Flanders') and the city of Besançon (which was then part of the Hapsburg Franche-Comté). The move to the Netherlands was the one that came closest to fruition.

In 1523 Margaret of Austria, regent of the Netherlands, wanting to lure Erasmus into returning to the Netherlands from Basel, had made the resumption of his long-unpaid imperial pension conditional on his doing so. Queen Mary of Hungary, who succeeded Margaret as regent in 1531, imposed the same condition.[12] In February 1532, moreover, her secretary, Nicolaus Olahus, invited Erasmus to return to his native land, pointing out that he was in a position to secure favourable terms.[13] In the correspondence that followed, Erasmus, who trusted Olahus' discretion, was frank with him about the considerations that had so far prevented him from yielding to pressures to 'come home.' He nursed a sense of injury over the non-payment of his pension. He had bitter memories of the Louvain theologians, who had denounced him as a heretic, had tried to persuade the emperor that he was responsible for the Lutheran heresy, and had abandoned none of their hostility. He feared that the burdens of life at a court that had issued harsh edicts against heresy would both inhibit his scholarly production and subject him to pressure to abandon his mediating position between ardent papalists and Lutheran zealots. He fretted that Brabant was too far from the source of the Burgundian wine that he considered essential to his health, that he would have to sell his new house at a loss, and that his fragile health would make the journey impossible. Despite all this, however, he indicated his eagerness to explore the possibility of his return.[14]

* * * * *

11 See n44 below.
12 See Ep 1380 introduction.
13 Ep 2607
14 Epp 2646:3–13, 2762, 2792:3–45, 64–73

Thus encouraged, Olahus enlisted the support of Jean de Carondelet, archbishop of Palermo and president of the privy council of the Netherlands, in the effort to lure Erasmus back to his homeland. In letters of July 1532 both Olahus and Carondelet assured Erasmus that his demands would be more than generously met but insisted somewhat impatiently that they could not intervene effectively with Queen Mary on Erasmus' behalf until he came to a firm decision to return and stipulated his conditions for doing so.[15] It appears that these letters were long delayed en route to Freiburg. As of 31 January 1533 neither Olahus nor Carondelet had received a reply,[16] and indeed Erasmus did not write again to Olahus until the first week of February 1533 (see below). Meanwhile, unsure of how things stood regarding Brabant, Erasmus had taken steps towards moving to Besançon.

During a visit to Besançon in 1524 Erasmus had been received with great hospitality by the city fathers and other prominent figures. In 1529 he had seriously considered moving there from Basel before finally deciding to move to Freiburg. And he continued to use his connections at Besançon to procure supplies of Burgundian wine.[17] In July 1531 he wrote the city council, asking if it would be possible for him to settle in Besançon should it become too dangerous to remain in Freiburg.[18] At some point thereafter the city fathers responded with a letter of invitation, which Erasmus acknowledged with gratitude in October 1532.[19] There appears to have been a second letter of invitation as well.[20] But he remained undecided between Brabant and Besançon until he learned that while the city fathers were eager to welcome him, the clergy (despite his good friends among the cathedral canons) were not.[21]

By January 1533 credible reports that Erasmus intended to move to Besançon had reached Olahus and Carondelet.[22] Their dismay at Erasmus' apparent change of mind was dispelled by the receipt of the letter to Olahus of 7 February 1533 that was Erasmus' long-awaited response to their letters

* * * * *

15 Epp 2689, 2693
16 Ep 2759:3–8
17 See Ep 2733 n4.
18 Ep 2514
19 Ep 2733:1–3 with n1
20 Ep 2761:29–31
21 The invitation is first mentioned in a letter of 19 April 1533 (Ep 2792:34–6). On 5 February 1533 a move to Besançon still seemed a real possibility (see n20 above).
22 Ep 2759:17–27

of July 1532.[23] Stating that his heart yearned for his native land, Erasmus asked for two things: a formal letter of invitation from the queen or her chancellor, so that he could leave Freiburg with honour and without seeming to act out of antipathy; and money to cover his travel expenses.[24] In the last week of March 1533 both Carondelet and Olahus informed Erasmus that they had successfully petitioned the queen to recall him to the Netherlands but that the emperor's approval was needed before the decision could be implemented.[25] That is where matters stood at the end of the period covered by this volume. A few months later, on 13 July 1533, following receipt of the emperor's permission to proceed, Queen Mary issued the letter of invitation. It was carried to Freiburg by Erasmus' former servant Lieven Algoet, who also brought money for Erasmus' journey. By this time, however, Erasmus' health was such that he really could not undertake the journey, and he never recovered sufficiently to do so.[26]

Thoughts of illness and death are seldom far from the surface in the letters of this period. It was not just that Erasmus himself was old, frequently ill, and facing the prospect of his own death,[27] but also that good friends were dying with alarming frequency. Foremost among these was his great friend and patron William Warham, archbishop of Canterbury. The news of his death in August 1532 elicited from Erasmus deeply felt tributes to his memory,[28] as well as unfounded fears that the income from the livings that Warham had bestowed on him would cease.[29] The deaths of a trio of other good friends (Alfonso de Valdés, Krzysztof Szydłowiecki, and Zacharius Deiotarus) contributed to the feeling that he was having a 'bleak' year.[30] The death of Bonifacius Amerbach's infant daughter Ursula and her father's profound grief added to the general gloom.[31]

Although no death was involved, the news that in May 1532 Sir Thomas More had resigned as lord chancellor, an office that he had held for less than three years, was nonetheless unsettling. In the letter informing Erasmus of his

* * * * *

23 Ep 2785:2–11
24 Ep 2762:16–35
25 Epp 2784–5
26 See Allen Ep 2820 introduction.
27 For the painful illness that plagued him in the spring and summer of 1533, see Ep 2770:1–6 with n3.
28 Epp 2726:35–62, 2758:35–79, 2776:28–51
29 See Epp 2761 n10, 2783:6–10.
30 See Ep 2776 n4.
31 Epp 2678, 2684

resignation More discreetly refrained from criticism of Henry VIII. Indeed, he wrote of his gratitude to the 'gracious sovereign' who had granted him permission to retire to private life and attributed his decision to do so entirely to poor health and the desire to devote his remaining days to his family and his studies.[32] The immediate occasion of the resignation, however, was the so-called Submission of the Clergy, a major step in the course of events that in 1534 would result in the declaration of royal supremacy in the English church.[33] In the encomium of More's legal career that was his public reaction to the news of the resignation,[34] Erasmus accepted More's version of events and did not mention his suspicion that More had been motivated by the fear of falling into royal disfavour because of his opposition to Henry VIII's divorce from Queen Catherine.[35] He knew that a distinguished career had come to an unexpectedly early end. He did not yet know, of course, how close he had come to divining the real reason, or that More's imprisonment (1534) and execution (1535) would soon follow.

In the midst of all this preoccupation with illness, death, and a contemplated change of residence, Erasmus had to turn his mind to some still simmering controversies as well as some continuing scholarly projects. It is the controversies that appear first in the letters included in this volume. When Julius Caesar Scaliger's *Oratio pro Cicerone contra Erasmum*, which attacked Erasmus' religious orthodoxy as well as his literary judgment, was published at Paris in September 1531, Erasmus jumped to the conclusion that the real author of the work was his old adversary Girolamo Aleandro writing under a pseudonym.[36] He also believed that Aleandro had been behind the publication of Alberto Pio's final book against him, the *Tres et viginti libri* of March 1531, and that Aleandro had gone to Paris to encourage the publication in July 1531 of the *Determinatio*, the formal censure of the errors in Erasmus' works that the Paris faculty of theology had adopted in 1526/7.[37] In April and July 1532 Aleandro, writing from Regensburg where he was attending the diet as special papal legate to the imperial court, wrote three letters to

* * * * *

32 Ep 2659
33 See Ep 2659 n2.
34 Ep 2750
35 Ep 2735:42–4
36 Ep 2564 n2
37 Ep 2565:4–7 with n3

Erasmus defending himself against the latter's charges.[38] Pointing out that he had had no personal contact and scarcely any correspondence with Alberto Pio since the sack of Rome in 1527, that he had never even heard of Scaliger until learning from Erasmus of the existence of the book published under that name, and that he had not visited Paris for eighteen years, he argued that he could not possibly be guilty as charged. Adopting a conciliatory tone, Aleandro suggested the restoration of good relations on the basis of the 'forgetfulness of injury' to which they had agreed at Louvain in 1521 during their last face-to-face encounter.[39] Back then the reconciliation had been brief; now there was none at all. Erasmus was not persuaded by Aleandro's 'very weak' arguments and predicted that he would continue 'doing exactly as he always does at every opportunity.'[40] Even after François Rabelais, who knew Scaliger personally, informed Erasmus that he was a real person,[41] Erasmus refused to absolve Aleandro from responsibility for the *Oratio*, insisting that that 'well educated but thoroughly wicked Italian' had incited Scaliger to attack him.[42]

Despite his resentment of the *Oratio*, Erasmus had not deemed it worthy of a public response. He had, however, responded to Alberto Pio and to the Paris theologians. His vituperative *Apologia adversus rhapsodias Alberti Pii*, though published after Pio's death in July 1531,[43] had not brought the controversy to a conclusion. In 1532 Pio's friend Juan Ginés de Sepúlveda came to his defence in the *Antapologia pro Alberto pio comite Carpensi in Erasmum Roterodamum*, a copy of which he sent to Erasmus with Ep 2637. Since both the letter and the *Antapologia* were courteous and respectful in tone, Erasmus sent Sepúlveda a conciliatory letter (Ep 2701) and decided not to pursue the controversy any further. As for the *Determinatio* of the Paris theologians, Erasmus' response to it, the *Declarationes ad censuras Lutetiae vulgatas*, was

* * * * *

38 Epp 2638–9, 2679. In these letters Aleandro does not in fact mention specifically the charge that he had encouraged the publication of the censure of the Paris theologians. But the language of Ep 2679:22–4 (*ut eos animarem qui in te scripserunt* 'to encourage those who were writing against you') suggests that he was aware of the charge.
39 See Ep 2679:39–42 with n7.
40 Ep 2644:9–15, 21–3
41 See Ep 2743.
42 See Allen Epp 3005:25–9, 3127:40–3.
43 Ep 2486 n10

in print by January or February 1532.[44] Almost immediately he set to work
on a revised and expanded edition, for which he solicited the advice of his
neighbour in Freiburg, the Dominican Ambrosius Pelargus.[45] Its publication
in September 1532 elicited no response from the Paris theologians, so the
long, acrimonious controversy between them and Erasmus had at last come
to an end.[46]

To this list of works growing out of old controversies one might add
the long letter of 9 August 1532 to Karel Uutenhove (Ep 2700) that was published in the *Epistolae palaeonaeoi*. The greater part of it is a renewed assault
on the Observant Franciscans reminiscent of the *Epistola ad gracculos* of 1530
(Ep 2275). Erasmus takes aim at two antagonists whom he had already lampooned in the *Colloquies* – the Franciscan preacher Medardus, who had attacked him publicly at Augsburg in 1530 during the diet, and Alberto Pio,
who had been buried in the garb of a Franciscan – and comments at length on
the ways in which the current behaviour of many of the 'seraphic brethren'
contradicts the spirit and the letter of the rules of their order.

As was the case in other spheres of his activity in the period covered
here, Erasmus' literary productions were, with some exceptions, a continuation or a revisitation of earlier projects. In the order in which they are
mentioned in the letters, they were as follows:
1/ Erasmus' Latin translation of St Basil the Great's *De Spiritu Sancto*,[47] a
by-product of the Froben Greek Basil that, after years of preparation under
Erasmus's supervision, had been published in March 1532 (see Ep 2611 introduction, and cf Ep 2648 introduction);
2/ prefatory letter for Johann Herwagen's edition of Demosthenes, provided
reluctantly as a favour to Herwagen (Ep 2695);
3/ second edition of the *Apophthegmata*, with two new books added (Ep 2711);
4/ eighth edition of the *Adagia*, enlarged by 488 new entries (Epp 2726, 2773);
5/ third, revised edition of the *Opera omnia* of St Jerome (Ep 2758);
6/ introductory letter for the Froben *editio princeps* of the Greek text of
Ptolemy's *Geographia* (Ep 2760);

* * * * *

44 Ep 2552 n10
45 See Ep 2666 introduction.
46 For a lucid summary of that controversy, see the introduction to the *Declarationes*
    in CWE 82 ix–xxxiv.
47 Ep 2643

7/ prefatory letter for a psalm commentary attributed to the ninth-century abbot of Fulda, Haymo: *Pia brevis ac dilucida in omnes Psalmos explanatio* (Ep 2771); the contents of which are a reflection, not of Erasmus' abiding interest in the Psalms, but of his persistent readiness to castigate monks whose vices bring discredit to the ideas of monasticism;

8/ *Explanatio symboli apostolorum sive catechismus* (Ep 2772), Erasmus' catechetical treatment of the Apostles' Creed, a long and erudite expansion of ideas first adumbrated in 1524 in the brief colloquy *Inquisitio de fide* 'An Examination Concerning the Faith';

9/ *Aliquot homiliae divi Joannis Chrysostomi*, Erasmus' translation of eight sermons by St John Chrysostom (Ep 2774), the latest in a long series of editions of works by Chrysostom, including the Latin *Opera omnia* of 1530 (Ep 2359).

Of the 166 letters in this volume, 90 were written by Erasmus and 75 were addressed to him. One of those by Erasmus (Ep 2698), the so-called *Tragoedia Basiliensis* 'Tragedy at Basel,' is not a letter at all but rather the account of a shocking murder-suicide that Erasmus enclosed with several letters to friends. One further letter (Ep 2777), written by Juan Luis Vives to Erasmus' secretary Gilbert Cousin, was included by Allen because 'it is so closely concerned with Erasmus.' These surviving letters include approximately ninety references to letters that are no longer extant. Since some of these references are to an unspecified number of letters, no exact total of letters known to have been written during the period covered by this volume can be determined, but 285 would be a cautious estimate. Of the surviving letters, 26 were published by Erasmus himself. Of these, 9 appeared in the *Epistolae palaeonaeoi* of 1532, 8 in the epistolary appendix to *De praeparatione ad mortem* of 1534, and one was printed with *De puritate tabernaculi* in 1536. Another 7 were prefaces to works or editions by Erasmus, and 2 were prefaces to the works of others. The remaining letters were published by a variety of scholars in the period from 1531 to 1941. Twenty-two of them were first published by Allen. To allow the reader to discover the sequence in which the letters became known, the introduction to each letter cites the place where it was first published and identifies the manuscript source if one exists. Allen's text and his numbering of the letters have been followed. Three of the letters have been redated. One of them, Allen's Ep 2680, redated to the year 1521, has already appeared as Ep 1241A in CWE 8. The other two appear here with considerably less drastic changes of date: Epp 2710 and 2764 have become Epp 2730A and 2766A.

All of Erasmus' correspondents and all of the contemporaries of Erasmus who are mentioned in the letters are referred to by the version of their name that is used in CEBR. Wherever biographical information is supplied in the notes without the citation of a source, the reader is tacitly referred to the appropriate article in CEBR and to the literature there cited. The index to this volume contains references to the persons, places, and works mentioned in the volume, following the plan for the Correspondence series in CWE. When that series of volumes is completed, the reader will also be supplied with an index of topics, as well as of classical, scriptural, and patristic references.

As with all the other volumes in this series, the basis for translation and the starting point for annotation is the edition of the *Erasmi epistolae* that was founded by P.S. Allen. This is, however, the third of the volumes in the CWE Correspondence series to be based on volumes IX–XI of Allen's edition, which were completed after his death (1938) by his widow, Helen Mary Allen, and H.W. Garrod, who had been his collaborators on earlier volumes. At the time of his death Allen had, with few exceptions, collected and provisionally arranged all the letters for vols IX–XI, but had done the notes for only 27 of them. The remaining work of annotation had to be done by Mrs Allen and Garrod. In many cases, therefore, 'Allen' is used in the notes as shorthand for 'the Allen editors.' Where their work has needed to be corrected, updated, or expanded – far more often in their case than in that of Allen himself – I was able to rely on the advice and assistance of distinguished colleagues here in Toronto and elsewhere. The great majority of the classical and patristic references that were not supplied by Allen were supplied by Charles Fantazzi. Amy Nelson Burnett and Timothy J. Wengert both read the entire manuscript and offered comments that led to important additions and corrections to the notes. In addition, Hans Trapman, Robert Sider, Bert Hall, George M. Logan, James Tracy, Paul Grendler, James Farge, and Erika Rummel responded generously to requests for help with difficult matters of history, bibliography, or interpretation. The notes on coinage were contributed by Lawrin Armstrong. The volume was copyedited with typical thoroughness and care by Mary Baldwin.

When in the early stages of annotation the translator, Clarence H. Miller, found it necessary to withdraw from further participation in the project, responsibility for the final revision of the translation fell to me. Since that was something I could not possibly do by myself, I sought and found help from Charles Fantazzi. He kindly read the entire manuscript, found answers to the many questions concerning the translation that Professor Miller and I had raised, and made helpful suggestions for further changes and corrections. He also provided his own translation of Ep 2772, which had not been included in Professor Miller's text. Without his help, this volume could not have been brought to publication. Sadly, the process of publication could not be completed until several months after Professor Miller's death on 21 June 2019.

As ever, two libraries were of special importance in the preparation of this volume: that of the Centre for Reformation and Renaissance Studies at Victoria College in the University of Toronto, and that of the Pontifical Institute of Mediaeval Studies on the campus of St Michael's College in the University of Toronto. To Natalie Oeltjen, Assistant to the Director of the Centre for Reformation and Renaissance Studies, and to William Edwards, reference librarian of the Pontifical Institute, I am indebted for a degree of support and assistance that amounts to special treatment.

JME

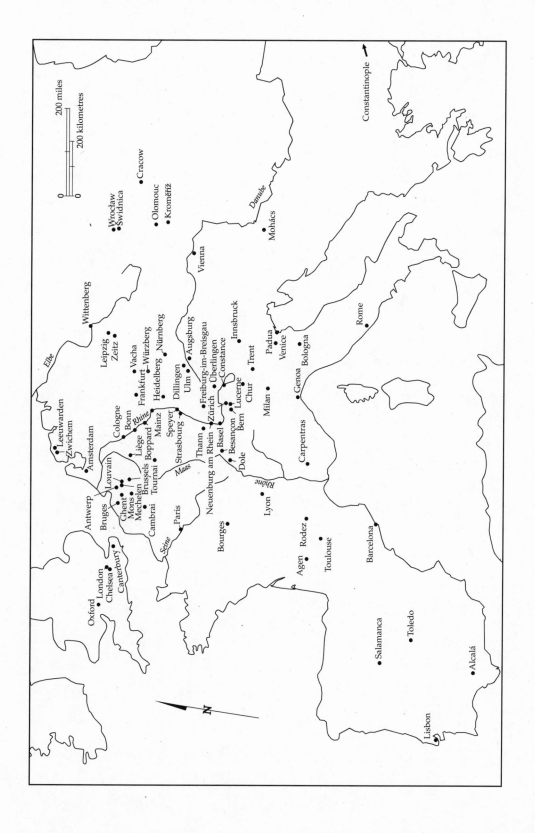

200 miles
200 kilometres

Constantinople

Cracow

Wrocław
Świdnica

Olomouc
Kroměříž

Danube

Mohács

Vienna

Wittenberg

Elbe

Leipzig
Zeitz

Vacha

Frankfurt
Würzburg
Nürnberg

Rome

Augsburg
Innsbruck

Heidelberg
Dillingen
Ulm

Freiburg-im-Breisgau
Überlingen
Constance
Trent

Padua
Venice
Bologna

Leeuwarden
Zwichem

Amsterdam

Cologne
Bonn

Rhine

Boppard
Mainz
Speyer

Strasbourg

Zürich

Lucerne
Bern
Chur

Milan

Genoa

Liège

Antwerp
Bruges
Louvain
Ghent
Mons
Mechelen
Brussels
Tournai
Cambrai

Maas

Thann
Neuenburg am Rhein
Basel
Besançon
Dole

Carpentras

Paris

Seine

Rhône

Lyon

Oxford
London
Chelsea
Canterbury

Bourges

Agen
Rodez

Toulouse

Barcelona

Salamanca
Toledo

Alcalá

Lisbon

N

THE CORRESPONDENCE OF ERASMUS

LETTERS 2635 TO 2802

2635 / To Jean Morin   Freiburg, [March–April?] 1532

This letter was first published in the *Epistolae palaeonaeoi* (September 1532). Like
Ep 2636, it lacks a month-date. For the sake of convenience, Allen placed the
two letters together at the beginning of his volume x. Jean Morin was the official who in September 1531 granted the royal licence for the publication in
Paris of Julius Caesar Scaliger's *Oratio pro Cicerone contra Erasmum* (Ep 2564
n2). Erasmus had written Ep 2577 to him to protest the publication of the work.
Morin sent a reply (see n2 below) that pleased Erasmus greatly and elicited this
letter from him.

ERASMUS OF ROTTERDAM TO THE MOST RENOWNED GENTLEMAN
HIS LORDSHIP THE ROYAL BAILIFF OF PARIS, GREETINGS
Jacobus Omphalius,[1] most renowned sir, in his letter to me related many
things about your extraordinary natural endowments and upright character,
and also about a certain special and favourable attitude you display towards   5
the reputation of Erasmus,[2] so much so that when certain people there maliciously sought to prevent my works from being published among you, you
very justly stopped them from doing so. Since I believe this to be so and am
delighted by it, I was all the more amazed at their trickery in palming off
under your name a book absolutely swarming with scurrilous insults and   10
impudent lies, nothing but raging madness,[3] and in so doing not only dis-
gracing a most renowned university but also endangering the young people
studying there. Although no established procedure there specifically forbade
such temerity, no one ever appeared who dared to do anything so criminal and barbarous; a human sense of shame took the place of any law and   15
sufficed to deter everyone from such wanton scurrility. Now the law itself
brings forth such monstrosities. And they say that the perpetrators of such
barbarous villainy are certain theologians, especially that lover of discord
whom Prudentius seemed to foretell when he said:

    O tortuous serpent,   20
    Threading a thousand ways

* * * * *

2635
1 Teacher of Latin authors at the Collège de Lisieux; see Ep 2311 n14.
2 Omphalius' letter is not extant; it appears to have conveyed Morin's response
  to Ep 2577.
3 Ie Scaliger's *Oratio*; see introduction above.

With sinuous fraudulence,
Disturbing peaceful hearts![4]

And he even threatens the displeasure of the Parlement if there is no subser-
vience to his malice.[5]   25
    Either I know nothing at all about the Parlement or I think I am right to
believe that it will be immensely displeased if it learns about this absolutely
shameful and pestilential example. I think the same would be true of his most
Christian Majesty. As for the opinion of the Holy Father, I am quite sure that
in his wisdom he perceives what a curse the madness of such books is to reli-   30
gion and learning. For what could be easier than under a false name to make
up any accusations whatever against anyone whomever? But far be it from
me to imitate the madness of others so as to become quite mad myself. This
monstrous fetus was conceived at Venice and was fathered by an Italian.[6] But
since they did not dare to publish it there, they found a publisher at Paris,   35
instigated by the theologians and with the added allurement of your name. It
would be very easy for me to get letters of injunction from the emperor and
King Ferdinand, and even from Pope Clement, but it seemed to me inappro-
priate to interrupt with such complaints princes of the highest rank who are
engaged in matters of the greatest importance that give them little joy.   40
    I find it hard to believe that Noël Béda approves of this transgression,
but some nonetheless report that he not only approves but even adds some
poison of his own to particular items. If this is true and he has actually gone
to such lengths in his madness, he is not far from being possessed by the
devil. It would be a splendid contest if I were to repay him tit for tat,[7] which   45
would be good and advantageous for me. I have printers quite ready to do
my bidding, and I could paint the mad begetter of this book in his true colours without stretching the truth in the least. But I would rather look to
what befits me than to what he deserves.

* * * * *

4 Prudentius *Cathemerinon* 6.141–4; cf *Adagia* II x 51. This is clearly a reference to
  Noël Béda, syndic of the Paris faculty of theology and Erasmus' most relentless
  adversary in France (Ep 1571 introduction). Someone, perhaps Omphalius, appears to have informed Erasmus of his role in finding a publisher for Scaliger's
  Oratio. Cf lines 41–3 below.
5 Erasmus refers to the *Senatus*, which was his usual word for the Parlement of
  Paris, the highest court in France.
6 Girolamo Aleandro (Ep 2638), to whom Erasmus attributed authorship of the
  book, deeming 'Julius Caesar Scaliger' to be a pseudonym
7 Literally 'render like for like'; see *Adagia* I i 35.

But now let us have an end to such quarrels. As for you, most renowned   50
sir, I am most grateful for the support you give me and I beg you to maintain
your favourable opinion. You do indeed promise to do so on your own, but
under the stipulation that I write nothing against the Christian faith or against
his most Christian Majesty. I have no doubt you have heard some complaints
about my beliefs. But time after time men of integrity, once they examined   55
the matter closely, perceive that these are mere slanders. How vigorously I
have taken up arms here against the sects and continue to do so, I leave for
others to say. I am surprised that you think any admonition concerning the
king is necessary. For how, I beg you, could it ever have entered my mind to
take up my pen against a king who is the most flourishing and lauded of our   60
times? I am beholden to him for the kindnesses he has bestowed on me, and
they have often been most generous.[8] I praised him in published books,[9] even
when he was still the enemy of the emperor.[10] What would have happened
to me if I should now rail against one who is a friend, neighbour, and ally?
My thoughts on other matters you will learn from Omphalius, just as you   65
wanted him to inform me of your opinions. Farewell.

Given at Freiburg im Breisgau, in the year 1532 after the birth of Christ

2636 / To Jacopo Canta   Freiburg, [March–April?] 1532

Like Ep 2635, this letter was first published in the *Epistolae palaeonaeoi* with no
month-date. Again like Ep 2635, Allen placed it here at the beginning of the
volume for the sake of convenience.

Jacopo Canta (dates unknown) was the chamberlain of Cardinal Lorenzo
Campeggi, papal legate at the court of Charles v; see Ep 2570:55–8. Apart from
that, scarcely anything is known of him.

* * * * *

8 See, for example, Ep 1375, Francis' handwritten invitation to Erasmus to settle
  in France under his royal patronage.
9 Above all in the paraphrase on St Mark, which was dedicated to Francis; see
  Epp 1400, 1403.
10 Ie before the Peace of Cambrai (August 1529), which brought a temporary
   halt (until 1536) to the warfare in Italy between Charles v and Francis i; see
   Ep 2207 n5.

DESIDERIUS ERASMUS OF ROTTERDAM TO MASTER JACOPO CANTA,
GREETINGS

Your servant Aegidius Vannonius[1] has, most distinguished sir, inspired in
me the warmest feelings towards you, singing the praises of the admirable
programme by which you seek to revive studies which, through some quirk   5
of fate, have languished in many circles, and to devote all your resources,
all your endeavour and effort, to that one goal. This convinces me that you
are not only a good man but also a magnanimous one. For if literary culture,
which is declining in many circles, should die away completely, what would
this life of ours be, I ask you, or what should we expect but to degenerate   10
into Turkish barbarism? And just as I very highly endorse your efforts, so
I pray that Christ Greatest and Best will vouchsafe to favour what you are
doing. I pray that from now on you will consent to add Erasmus' name to
the list of your friends. Give my respectful greetings to the most reverend
Cardinal Campeggi. I know how much I am indebted to him and indeed I   15
am happy to be so, and I wish to owe him more. I am extremely busy but I
stole a few minutes to greet you, having obtained this young man, greatly
devoted to you,[2] whom I would willingly have taken into my household,
except that he already has such an obliging master. I need faithful servants
more than anything else, but in that matter things do not always turn out as   20
I wish. Farewell.

At Freiburg im Breisgau, in the year 1532 after the birth of Christ

2637 / From Juan Ginés de Sepúlveda   Rome, 1 April 1532

This letter was first published in *Sepulvedae epistolae* folio A.

Born in Pozoblanco, near Córdoba, Juan Ginés de Sepúlveda (c 1490–1573)
studied initially at Alcalá and Sigüenza, and then (1515–23) at the Spanish
College at Bologna, earning a doctoral degree in arts and theology. He then
joined the household of his friend and patron Alberto Pio, humanist scholar,
papal diplomat, and formidable antagonist of Erasmus (Epp 1634, 1987). A
prolific scholar, Sepúlveda won fame for his translations of Aristotle as well
as for original works. Among the latter were his *De fato et libero arbitrio* (1526)
an attack on Luther's *De servo arbitrio*. Following the sack of Rome by imperial troops in 1527, Pio moved to France, but Sepúlveda remained in Italy and
by 1529 had entered the service of Cardinal Francisco de Quiñones (Ep 2126

* * * * *

2636
1 Apart from his name, nothing is known of Vannonius.
2 Ie as a messenger

n3), whom he accompanied in 1529 on his mission to prepare for the corona-
tion of Charles v as emperor at Bologna in 1530 (Ep 2198 introduction). In 1536
Sepúlveda left the papal court to become the official chronicler and chaplain
of Charles v, whom he accompanied to Spain. Of the many works published
after his return to Spain, those for which he is best known are two polemics in
defence of the Spanish conquest of America and the enslavement of the natives.
He died in Pozoblanco and was buried in his parish church.

Sepúlveda appears to have attracted Erasmus' attention in the mid-1520s,
probably as author of the treatise on free will against Luther (see above).
Erasmus mentioned him briefly in the *Ciceronianus* as a writer of considerable
promise (CWE 28 429). By the beginning of 1530, however, Erasmus had heard
rumours (Epp 2261:75–7, 2329:94–8, 2375:74–81) that Sepúlveda was assisting
Alberto Pio in the preparation of his *Tres et viginti libri in locos lucubrationum
variarum D. Erasmi Roterodami* (1531), a compendium of all the passages in
Erasmus' works that could be interpreted in support of the view that Erasmus
was the source of Luther's heresies. Even though Pio died in January 1531, two
months before the publication of the book, Erasmus published a savagely vituperative reply, *Apologia adversus rhapsodias Alberti Pii* (July 1531); see Ep 2486
n10. Sepúlveda came to the defence of his deceased friend with the *Antapologia
pro Alberto Pio comite Carpensi in Erasmum Roterodamum*, a copy of which he sent
to Erasmus with the present letter (see n1 below). As the text of the letter makes
clear, Sepúlveda was eager for Erasmus to understand that the treatment of
him in the *Antapologia* was intended to be courteous and respectful. Erasmus
responded with a conciliatory letter (Ep 2701). After this initial encounter, the
two men engaged in a further correspondence on scholarly matters that is best
described as professional in tone (Epp 2729, 2873, 2905, 2938, 2951, 3096).

JUAN GINÉS DE SEPÚLVEDA SENDS CORDIAL GREETINGS
TO DESIDERIUS ERASMUS OF ROTTERDAM
I have included with this letter to you my *Antapologia in Favour of Alberto
Pio*, which was printed some time ago at Rome.[1] I had intended to send it at
the very first opportunity, so that you would become aware of it, preferably   5
through me, and would understand that I undertook the task of writing it as
a duty, not with any hostile attitude or any desire to take advantage of your

* * * * *

2637
1 The *Antapologia* was first published at Rome (Antonio Blado) in January 1532.
   A second printing followed at Paris (Antoine Augereau) in March 1532. As the
   balance of this paragraph shows, it was a hand-corrected copy of the Rome
   edition that accompanied this letter.

Juan Ginés de Sepúlveda
From *Retratos de Españoles illustres* (Madrid 1791)

ignorance of it in order that the book might be more freely and more widely disseminated. But my will was hindered and my plan blocked by some very respectable people who were favourable to both of us but were too cautious and wanted to avoid anything that might cause a quarrel between us. When they had read the book it seemed to them that some expressions should be softened or even deleted because they thought, contrary to my opinion, that you might be offended by them, even though I tried throughout the whole book to do no more than to employ the utmost moderation in dealing with you. On the other hand, there were a few places here and there where they wanted to appease the feelings of the Italians, who they claimed might be offended if I did not take such precautions. Thus, through their efforts, it happened that the book, which was already printed, was not published until it had been corrected in some places according to their notions, as you will see. I did not want you to be unaware of this lest, if the Paris edition should come into your hands and you were to see there the original readings,[2] you be surprised when you saw the corrections and noticed the new and different readings here.

As for the Observations of Zúñiga,[3] which I mention in that little work, you should know that they are in the possession of Francisco de Quiñones, Cardinal of the Holy Cross, who wishes to concur with the wishes of Zúñiga, who, when he was dying, directed that this book should not be issued in its unfinished and unpolished state but that it should be sent to you in excerpted and summary statements. I would willingly have undertaken this task of excerpting at the desire of the same prelate if heavy duties had not prevented me. But if I understand that such a gesture would be pleasing to you, I will give it the highest priority and I will see to it that a copy be sent to you as soon as possible.[4] There are, if you are interested in knowing, eighty notes altogether on the second edition of your annotations on the works of Jerome,[5] and more than a hundred on the fourth edition of your translation and annotations on the New Testament.[6]

Farewell. From Rome, 1 April 1532

* * * * *

2 The corrections to the Rome edition were not made in the Paris edition.
3 Diego López Zúñiga, one of Erasmus' earliest and harshest Catholic critics (Ep 1260 n36)
4 In his last years (1524–31) Zúñiga continued to compile notes on Erasmus' editions of St Jerome and the New Testament, with the aim of refuting Erasmus' errors. He bequeathed the notes to Cardinal Quiñones with the request that they be sent to Erasmus in summary form. Given responsibility for the task by Quiñones, Sepúlveda turned it over to Iñigo López de Mendoza y Zúñiga; see Ep 2705.
5 Basel: Froben 1524–6
6 Basel: Froben 1527

2638 / From Girolamo Aleandro   Regensburg, 1 April 1532

This letter, as well as Epp 2639 and 2679, were first published by Jules Paquier
in the *Mélanges d'archéologie et d' histoire* of the École française de Rome 15 (1895)
363–74. The manuscript is a volume of copies of Aleandro's letters made by his
secretaries under his direction (Vatican MS Lat 8075 folios 70 verso–73 recto).
Aleandro, Erasmus' one-time friend turned enemy (Ep 1553 n9), was currently
attending the imperial diet at Regensburg in his capacity as special papal legate
to the imperial court (see lines 28–9 below with n5).

   Both this letter and Ep 2639, which is a postscript to it, respond to Erasmus' reported accusation that Aleandro had been responsible for the publication of both
Alberto Pio's *Tres et viginti libri in locos lucubrationum variarum D. Erasmi Roterodami*
and Julius Caesar Scaliger's *Oratio pro Cicerone contra Erasmum*. Erasmus' letter
is not extant, but Aleandro mentions it in a letter of 28 January 1531; see Paquier
Mélanges (as above) 365 n1. For Erasmus' accusations of Aleandro in letters to
others, see Epp 2371 n22, 2564 n2. Erasmus' response to this letter, not extant,
was courteous; Aleandro answered it with Ep 2679.

TO ERASMUS OF ROTTERDAM
For the last ten years I have not spoken to Alberto Pio more than three or four
times, and even then it had nothing to do with you, and for the past seven
years I have not written to him even once, so far as I can remember. This I
know for sure: I have not seen the man for the past five years. After I had,   5
by the grace of God, fortunately escaped the slaughter at Rome, and after
the pitiful fall of the city a few days later, I learned nothing about him until I
was presented with a huge book which, it seems, he had written against you
in the meantime at Paris, and a little after that his death was announced.[1]
Thus it is absolutely clear that I could not have seen those very letters which   10
have caused such a flare-up between us before they were published in that
large volume.[2] Observe the plausibility of what you wrote to some of my
friends, specifically naming me, and what you enigmatically insinuated in
many places in your books, namely that I was the source and the abettor of

* * * * *

2638
1 Pio died on 10 January 1531; his *Tres et viginti libri* was published on 9 March.
2 Ie the correspondence between Erasmus and Pio in the period October 1525–
   March 1529, printed at the beginning of the *Tres et viginti libri*: Ep 1634 (Erasmus
   to Pio), Pio's *Responso paraenetica* (Ep 1987 n2), and Erasmus' *Responsio ad epistolam paraeneticam Alberti Pii* (Ep 2080 n4)

what Alberto wrote against you.[3] As for that little book which was published,   15
falsely I think, under the name of Julius Scaliger and which you suspect is
an egg laid by me, so help me God I had not even heard the name of it until
you wrote me about the matter: as if indeed I had such leisure and such a
fertile brain that I would be able, or were so mad as to wish, at great risk to
my health and to the neglect of my household, to hatch eggs daily for others,   20
which would earn universal praise for the false authors and cause you to
hate me – and whatever detriment I might gain from it would go on forever!

I swear by all that is holy that what I write here is the absolute truth. But
if you do not think so and persevere in the suspicions that you seem to have
thus far entertained, may the one who has lied about us come to no good   25
end.[4] But if you believe what I am telling you, as in all justice you both can
and ought to do, then you should take it as an established fact that up to now
I have never plotted against you and during this legation have not so much as
dreamed of doing so,[5] whatever anyone may have written or spoken against
me, and especially the one who was the worst of all and fittingly came to   30
the worst end in the sack of the city; he was punished for his other crimes
but most of all because he continually attempted to set us at odds with one
another.[6] And in order to let you know how sincere my feelings towards you
have been, the breve sent to you by Pope Adrian, which you call 'golden,' and
which you so often boast about and fling in the faces of your enemies,[7] was   35
(in case you don't know it) my creation and was conceived at a time when
you did not cease to deserve ill of me. I still have in my possession the original
version of it, which is fuller and more ample in its praises than the one that
was sent you to you.[8] And even now I am so far from having the hostile attitude towards you about which you write that if you merely cancelled a few   40
passages or changed the parts in your books that are less than satisfactory, not

* * * * *

3 Aleandro had doubtless seen Epp 1719:36–47, 1987:4–11, 2077:54–60, 2329:99–
   104; cf Epp 1479:147–8 with n57, 2198:25 with n5, 2371:35–40, 2375:81–2,
   2379:110–12, 2682:45–54. In the *Responsio ad epistolam paraeneticam* Erasmus, ad-
   dressing Pio, refers to Aleandro as 'the Bullbearer, the better part of your soul,'
   and 'a large part of this disaster' (CWE 84 87; cf CWE 84 16–17). In the *Apologia adversus rhapsodias* Erasmus, referring to those who had urged Pio to write against
   him, reiterates the old charge that Aleandro was 'a Jew, a group of people with
   whom I have never been on good terms' (CWE 84 114 with n33).
4 Aristophanes *Lysistrata* 1037, cited in Greek
5 On Aleandro's current legation see Ep 2565 n2.
6 Unidentified
7 Ep 1324, from Pope Adrian VI, which Erasmus liked to call his *Breve aureum*
8 Aleandro's draft of the *Breve aureum* is Ep 1324A.

only to me but to any true friend of yours, and if, moreover, you corrected
that utterly false opinion about me which you have impressed on the minds
of our friends, even now I declare that any enemy of yours is an enemy of
mine. Surely you know, my good man, that anyone who wants to suppress   45
you also wants to suppress the cause of languages and good learning. And
once they are suppressed, what will become of Aleandro? If I have done
anything to deserve some reputation and renown in this sort of learning –
though the measure of my own abilities, of which I am quite aware, prevents
me from believing it – still your testimony in my favour moves and delights   50
me a great deal, since everyone considers your approval to be the colophon
of judgment.[9]

I assure you that after we stopped seeing one another face to face, I
devoted myself intensely to the study of Holy Scripture: not content with the
early, holy Fathers, Greek and Latin, many of whose works, even those of the   55
least known, lined my shelves, I also added to them the greatest masters of
modern theology and examined very carefully writings by Thomas, Scotus,
Ockham, Gabriel and all the rest of that calibre,[10] so much so that those who
are most famous for such learning affirmed that I was proficient beyond the
ordinary level. But if you consider Holy Scripture apart from skill in lan-   60
guages (and in our times you have taken the lead in providing a happy combination of the two), then Aleandro would rank among the scholastics just as
barbarous as would a wretched scholastic among those truly learned in the
humanities, that is, like a goose among swans.[11] And so put an end at last to
these quarrels, these suspicions, by which you have stirred up the hatred of   65
many learned and high-ranking men. And as for our friendship, which I have
always thought to be intact and unimpaired, if you think it has been somewhat contaminated, we can easily repair it by the best remedy, forgetfulness
of injury, and by restoring former courtesies. Let us both endeavour that we
not become laughing stocks to the whole world because of these dissensions   70
and hatreds and that our efforts, which ought to be strenuously devoted to
promoting literary studies and to pacifying and augmenting Christian piety,
not be turned to defamatory books, vitriolic orations, ferocious hostilities,
and abominable contentions among Christians and friends.

* * * * *

9 See *Adagia* II iii 45, 'He added the colophon,' ie he added the finishing touch,
  without which a bit of business cannot be concluded.
10 Thomas Aquinas, Duns Scotus, William of Ockham, Gabriel Biel
11 Cf Virgil *Eclogues* 9.6, cited in *Adagia* I vii 22 ('A jackdaw among the Muses').

My affection for you and my desire to restore, or rather to continue, our   75
friendship, has caused me to write more than I hoped to do when I began and
more than my public duties allowed. Hence I will bring my writing to an end
by adding this: all the irritation that your letter caused me, or at least most
of it, was dispelled by the ten lines written in your own hand at the end of it,
from which I learned that the most upright and learned gentleman Ludwig   80
Baer was both alive and in your company when you wrote.[12] Nothing could
have delighted me more than this message. In a manner of speaking your
letter brought to life for me the dearest of all my friends. Just as I was once
refreshed by his very holy companionship, and now by the mere recollection
of him my spirits are revived, so for a long time I have been very worried be-   85
cause I was uncertain whether he, like so many of my other friends, had left
here to join the heavenly hosts, since I had heard absolutely nothing about
him for so many years. As for the letter which you say he sent to me a while
ago, if I had received it I would have answered it with great pleasure, and
the joy that now floods my mind because he is alive and well would have   90
seemed greater and more lasting because it would have been more timely.
     Farewell from Regensburg, 1 April 1532

2639 / From Girolamo Aleandro   Regensburg, 1 April 1532

> This is a postscript to Ep 2638, written after it was already sealed (see lines 49–50
> below). For the manuscript and the first publication of the text, see the intro-
> duction to Ep 2638.

ALSO TO ERASMUS
There was some rust in my relationship with Glapion before my departure
from Worms,[1] since we disagreed about both public and private affairs; I
also had some friction with the nephew of the bishop of Strasbourg, even

* * * * *

  12 For Ludwig Baer, Erasmus' friend, neighbour, and adviser on difficult theo-
      logical questions, see Ep 2225 introduction. His years of study and teaching in
      Paris (1496–1513) overlapped with those of Aleandro (1508–13).

  2639
   1 In 1521 Aleandro attended the Diet of Worms as papal legate. His views fre-
      quently clashed with those of Charles v's personal confessor, Jean Glapion
      (Ep 1275), as well as other members of the imperial court, whom he deemed
      too reluctant to impose the imperial ban on Martin Luther, who had already
      been excommunicated by the church.

when we were together at Paris.[2] So you can see what kind of credence can   5
be given to what they say about me.[3] And you know very well how volatile
and difficult to get along with[4] Glapion is by nature, as you yourself once
wrote somewhere.[5] As for that French bookseller who is active at Venice,[6] a
man who is quite dull and stupid both by nature and through his incessant
drinking, if I thought that you had the least credence in his words, Erasmus   10
would cease to be Erasmus in my eyes. And yet, as I gather from some of
your writings, he has gone a long way towards persuading you of something
he perhaps thought you would be glad to hear, namely that I am intent on
going through your books by day and by night, searching for something to
pick out of them that I can later attack in my writings or pass on to Alberto 15
Pio. Oh what unadulterated and incredible madness! – mine if I had done
such a thing, and yours even more so if you believed it. At that time, for
as long as I was in Venice,[7] I was suffering from a double case of quartan
fever, and if there were any brief peaceful intervals they had to be devoted
entirely to the common good and to obtaining peace between Venice and the   20
emperor, which was the task assigned to me in a letter from the pope. Half-
dead as I was and occupied with these obligations, could I have devoted
my attention to such trifles as these, from which I always thought I should
abstain even when I was well in body and mind, since I knew that there was
nothing more destructive to both literary and Christian pursuits than such   25

* * * * *

2 The bishop of Strasbourg was Wilhelm von Honstein (c 1470–1541). Nothing is
   known of his nephew.
3 In his only surviving letter to Aleandro, Erasmus says that he has learned from
   Glapion and the bishop of Strasbourg (see preceding note) about 'the monstrous account of me you gave to the emperor' (Ep 1482:20–3). One supposes
   that Erasmus had raised this matter again in the letter to which Aleandro is responding. Aleandro's point seems to be that the disagreeable things said by the
   bishop were to be discounted because he (Aleandro) and the bishop's nephew
   had been on bad terms during their time together at the University of Paris.
4 Aleandro uses an extremely rare Greek adjective (δυσεπίγνωστον) that is not
   clearly defined in the dictionaries. Its components appear to add up to the
   meaning given here, which is at least not inconsistent with the information
   supplied in the following note.
5 In the *Spongia* Erasmus defends himself against the charge, levelled by Ulrich
   von Hutten, of having disparaged Glapion; see CWE 78 79–80, where Erasmus
   admits that he 'could never entirely trust' Glapion. In a letter that Aleandro
   would not have seen, Erasmus stated that he mistrusted Glapion because of his
   Franciscan garb; see Ep 1805:181–4.
6 Unidentified
7 1529–30

dissensions among learned men – the very starting point or at least the fuel
for the fires of Lutheranism? I admit that I purchased whatever books that
had been brought from Germany to Venice when I was there – to the great
profit of that clown of a bookseller – not in order to study them (since I did
not have time for that) but to enlarge my library, which I intend to bequeath   30
greatly enriched to some religious order for public use after my death.[8] And
could such a man as you, with all your prudence, your learning – and I might
add, your age – be persuaded that I was performing either mercenary or
trivial duties for Alberto Pio and wrote about this to many friends? See how
wisely you acted, and how unlike Hercules. For he slew the seven-headed   35
hydra, which could sprout two heads when any one of them was cut off,
with one blow;[9] you, on the other hand, fighting a one-headed enemy, stir
up as enemies all those you name as collaborators with Alberto in that work
when you make me, Sepúlveda, and heaven knows how many others, including the whole University of Paris, the authors of that book, or at least   40
accomplices in it.[10] And as far as I am concerned, you can not only rest easy
but you can also sleep peacefully. Apart from being preoccupied with wholly
different matters, as God has willed for me, I am not such a busybody as to
scratch the itches of others. But I don't think that others whose names you
have mixed up with the case of Alberto Pio will be as silent as I. And as each   45
of them strives to defend his name, which you paraded there, I am afraid you
will find in the end that by your action Alberto is not yet dead but every day
sprouts up alive against you.

I decided to add these remarks to the other letter, which had already
been sealed, because by chance at the very time your letter was delivered to   50
me a mutual friend of ours also showed me what you wrote to him two years
ago, as well as some places in your books where you alluded to this matter
indirectly, but not carefully enough to keep it from being easily recognized.[11]

* * * * *

8 Aleandro's library, which he bequeathed to the church of the Madonna dell'
   Orto in Venice, was noteworthy for the very large number of Protestant writings that it contained.
9 The slaying of the hydra, a monster that dwelt in the lake of Lerna in the
   Argolid, was the second labour of Hercules. In the telling of the myth the number of heads varied greatly, but the Greek poet Alcaeus fixed it at nine. Hercules
   did not dispatch the hydra with one blow. It took a long struggle and he needed
   the help of his friend Iolaus.
10 'That book' is Pio's *Tres et viginti libri*. For it and the 'accomplices' in it, see Epp
   2329:91–104, 2371:35–40 with n22, 2486:35–9 with nn10–11.
11 Cf Ep 2679:29–38, where Aleandro again mentions this 'friend' and suggests that
   he may have been motivated by 'malevolence.' His identity remains a mystery.

But let these matters now be consigned to perpetual oblivion. And be assured of my affection, and remember also that I could, if I wished, be a formi-   55
dable adversary. But away with all of this, and let it not even enter my mind
to elevate such squabbles and absurdities above the common good, which I
recognize would gain much from your safety and our cooperation. With my
very best wishes.

Forgive me for these trifles, which I do not compose as something to   60
last forever,[12] but rather as something ephemeral, considering the magnitude
of my responsibilities, the shortness of time, and the nature of the affair –
which I want to be buried forever – like something that is merely blurted out.
But from you I expect quite a long letter, in which friends may recognize that
the scars of the wounds you have inflicted on me through that utterly false   65
accusation or suspicion have been completely smoothed over.

Regensburg, 1 April 1532

2640 / From Johann von Botzheim   Überlingen, 6 April 153[2]

This letter was first published as Ep 171 in Förstemann / Günther. The autograph, which was in the Burscher Collection of the University Library at Leipzig
(Ep 1254 introduction), had the year-date MXXXI, which someone corrected to
MDXXXI. That the actual year-date must be 1532 is clearly indicated by Botzheim's
knowledge not only of the purchase of Erasmus' new house in June 1531 but also
of the subsequent additions and renovations in the three months before Erasmus
moved in (see Epp 2506 n1, 2517 n11). For Botzheim, see Ep 1103 introduction.

Greetings. I hear that you have finally spent a fortune, putting out 600 gold
florins to buy your own house, adding also at no little expense some new
extensions to make it more comfortable for you.[1] I offer you hearty congratulations, because that leads me to believe that you will be with us for many
more years – but let Christ provide for that. I wrote you almost three months   5

* * * * *

12 As Thucydides famously said of his history of the Peloponnesian war (Greek in
   the text)

2640
1 In Ep 2512:10–11 Erasmus put the price at 'almost eight hundred gold florins,'
   a figure that may have included the cost of the extensions. In Ep 2530:1, the
   figure named was 'seven hundred gold florins.' In a letter of 12 September 1535
   he states that the actual cost of the house was '624 gold florins in proven gold'
   (Allen Ep 3056:6–7).

ago about certain matters and about those Zoiluses of yours,[2] Medardus and our Bicornis,[3] the messenger being the chaplain of Fabri, bishop of Vienna,[4] who informed me orally that you would write me very soon concerning the matters about which I had written to you, saying also that you were in the process of publishing something about them. So far I have not been able   10
to find out anything about them. If you wish, please let me know what you have done in this regard and whatever else you think I should know.[5] We are apprehensive about the imperial diet,[6] doubtless (if only it were not so!) to be frustrated in fact and in hope. Here we are struck with fear by the frequent, wrongly conducted assemblies of princes and by some fatal injustice of our   15
times.[7] Farewell.

From Überlingen, 6 April 1531[8]

With the undying devotion of your loyal servant, whatever he may be worth, Johann von Botzheim

To Master Erasmus of Rotterdam, the incomparable defender of un-   20
blemished theology and good letters, teacher and patron, most cherished and venerated in every way

* * * * *

2 The letter is not extant. Zoilus was a sophist of the fourth century BC whose books attacking Homer made his name proverbial for the kind of critic eager to belittle the achievements of his betters; see *Adagia* II v 8.
3 Medardus, a Franciscan preacher in the entourage of King Ferdinand, had pub-licly attacked Erasmus in Augsburg during the imperial diet there in 1530; see Ep 2408:5–19. Bicornis (ie 'Two-horned,' meaning the wearer of a bishop's mi-tre) was Melchoir Fattlin, suffragan bishop of Constance who, as Erasmus re-ports to Botzheim in Ep 2516:43–78, had also attacked him in public. Both took aim at Erasmus' New Testament scholarship.
4 Johannes Fabri (Ep 2750). The chaplain's name is not known.
5 Erasmus took his revenge on Medardus in the colloquy *Concio, sive Merdardus* 'The Sermon, or Merdardus,' which was first published in the September 1531 edition of the *Colloquia*. Transformed into 'Merdardus,' the name means 'Shitty'; cf Ep 2408 n7. Erasmus' only known rejoinder to Fattlin is in Ep 2516:79–120, a letter first published by Allen.
6 Ie the Diet of Regensburg, which would formally convene on 17 April 1532
7 The language here is obscure, but Botzheim seems to be voicing a pessimistic view of the many imperial diets of recent years and their failure to check the spread of religious division in the Empire. He probably also has in mind the tendency of the religious camps to organize themselves into armed alliances, as in the establishment (1530–1) of the League of Schmalkalden under the leader-ship of the two chief Protestant princes, the elector of Saxony and the landgrave of Hessen (Ep 2443 n40).
8 On the year-date see the introduction above.

2641 / From Alonso Ruiz de Virués   Regensburg, 15 April 1532

This letter was first published as Ep 171 in Förstemann / Günther. The autograph was in the Burscher Collection of the University Library at Leipzig (Ep 1254 introduction).

On Virués, a Spanish Benedictine monk and admirer of Erasmus, see Ep 1684 introduction. After being appointed court preacher to Charles v, he was summoned in the winter of 1531 to join the imperial court in Germany and went with it to the imperial diet at Regensburg, from where he wrote this letter.

Cordial greetings. After so many letters that I sent to you in the last year and a half without receiving the least jot or tittle of an answer,[1] it might seem inappropriate now to trouble you, most learned Erasmus, with a new one, except that the rules of friendship require that when I am close by I should not neglect to do what I would have done when I was much further away. 5
Here, briefly, is the reason I am writing.

The emperor sent me letters summoning me to come from Spain (I have no idea why), though I had no wish to do so; the very idea had not crossed my mind, since I have always profoundly disliked life at the court. But at this time, when the flames of evangelical piety have enkindled so many wildfires, 10
I would seem to be remiss if I did not obey the command of the emperor, especially since for three years now this Catholic prince has defended the truths of Christianity and restored the harmony of the church,[2] at the cost of being torn away from his beloved wife and children, living as it were in exile from his own home – if the emperor of the world can suffer exile anywhere in the 15
world. And so I obeyed, moving from the university (at Salamanca, where I had been resident for some time)[3] to the court, from the college to the palace, and from the cloister to the theatre. My journey was long, wearisome, and laborious to undertake in the middle of winter. What good it will do I still do not know. For the Catholic faith is now in such a state that it seems it can be 20
set in order not so much by intellectual activity as by that human transaction

* * * * *

2641
1 Virués had written to Erasmus from Spain on 20 August 1530 a letter that is not extant. Erasmus received it on 1 August 1531, and answered it on 21 August with Ep 2523. Evidently sent to Spain, it had clearly not arrived before Virués' departure to join the imperial court in Germany (see introduction).
2 Ie since his departure from Spain in the summer of 1527 to deal with the problems of Italy and Germany
3 Since the spring of 1531, as the prior of San Vicente, the Benedictine college of studies at the University of Salamanca

in which matters are usually settled by warfare. And that is not surprising, since just about everyone is looking out for himself, not for Jesus Christ. The emperor sits as an arbiter between them; and if both sides are so stubborn that he cannot achieve what he wants, he will do (I think) what he can short 25 of the danger of warfare. For such is his kindness and brotherly love that in matters that do not impinge on the essence of the faith he thinks it better to look the other way rather than to set Christians against Christians of whatever kind, Catholics against heretics, or at least schismatics.[4] Meanwhile I work hard on my sermons, so that if I do not reclaim the Germans from their 30 error, at least the Spanish will not be infected by the plague of heresy.[5]

Now you know the reason for my journey and also for my letter. And, if I may take it upon myself in my usual way to bother you with my dull little admonitions, I see that the leading figures at court circulate various (to use no harsher word) judgments about you because, while the emperor has spent two 35 years in Germany for the sake of the faith,[6] you have not even presented yourself to greet him and, at so many gatherings debating the doctrine of the Catholic church, you have not joined the forces of the church;[7] you can hardly deny that you owe the latter duty to Christ and the other one to the emperor, who, second to Christ, has always given you kind support and protection. And so let 40 me urge you, O wisest of men, that if you have a legitimate excuse you take any occasion that may arise to present an apology and do not neglect to do so any longer; but if you do not, that you atone for any fault or neglect on your part in whatever way you can while there is still time. But if perhaps you cannot accept my advice in either case, in your kindness you will certainly not condemn 45 my devotion and my good will. You will reassure me if, having now received so many letters from me, you now send one when the distance to be traversed is forty miles, though you did not when it was four hundred miles.[8] Farewell.

From Regensburg, 15 April in the year 1532

* * * * *

4 Ever since the Diet of Augsburg in 1530 the German Protestants had been persuaded that the emperor in fact intended to make war on them because of their religion. Their fears would be allayed by the conclusion of the Religious Peace of Nürnberg in July 1532; see Ep 2702 n2.
5 Virués preached in Spanish to the court.
6 From the Diet of Augsburg in 1530 to the Diet of Regensburg in 1532
7 A reference to Erasmus' failure to attend the Diet of Augsburg, as many friends on both sides of the religious divide had urged him to do; see CWE 16 xiii–xiv, CWE 17 xii–xiii. The scolding tone of these comments did not please Erasmus; see Ep 2644:18–20.
8 Virués is doubtless thinking of German miles, which were nearly five times the length of English miles. The figures are still not accurate, but they serve the purpose of indicating the contrast between relatively close and far away.

Sincerely yours, Brother Alfonso Virués   50
† To the most distinguished gentleman, Desiderius Erasmus, professor
of evangelical philosophy, at Freiburg

2642 / To Bonifacius Amerbach   [Freiburg], 20 April [1532]

This letter (= AK Ep1626) was first published in the *Epistolae familiares*. The autograph is in the Öffentliche Bibliothek of the University of Basel (MS AN III 15 28).
Bonifacius' reply is Ep 2649.

    The background of the letter is the call to a professorship of civil law at Dole
that Bonifacius had received (preliminary inquiry in early March 1532, formal
offer from the rector a month later); see AK Epp 1611, 1617, and cf Epp 2630:43,
2631:55–60.

Cordial greetings. My baker[1] delivered your earlier letters.[2] Since then I have
not had anyone to take a letter to you. 'You will neither do nor say anything
Minerva would not approve of.'[3] Let your mind be your best adviser. Unless
you are repelled by the court, a professorship at Dole would be an outstanding position, but to be a professor there would not be without strife, since   5
your temperament, unless I am mistaken, would be as averse to quarrels as
to the court.[4] You are a domestic animal and tame. To fight against the gods
may well not yield a happy ending.[5]
    Whether this freedom of action of which you speak will last long I do
not know. I am afraid that when the emperor sets out, things will return to   10
what had been given up, or rather what was pretended to have been given
up.[6] But only God foresees the future. For that reason, in order to enjoy the

* * * * *

2642
1 Allen's text has *Pistor*, which makes it appear to be a surname, though the editors thought it might be a simple common noun. We follow AK in reading *pistor*
   (a miller, baker, or pastry chef).
2 Erasmus had last written to Bonifacius on 25 March (Ep 2631).
3 Ie you will not act contrary to reason and in defiance of nature. See *Adagia* I i 42,
   citing Cicero *De officiis* 1.31.110 and Horace *Ars poetica* 385.
4 Dole was the administrative capital of the Hapsburg Free County of Burgundy
   (Franche-Comté). It appears that the professorship of law there involved official
   duties as legal adviser to the court and perhaps as a judge. Cf Ep 2649:18–20.
5 To fight against the gods is to 'fly in the face of nature or struggle against the
   decrees of destiny.' See *Adagia* II v 44.
6 This appears to be a reference to the situation, either in Dole or in Basel, as it
   affected Bonifacius' decision to accept or reject the offer of the professorship at
   Dole. But we have no information concerning the role of the emperor or what
   'they' had 'given up.'

PICTA LICET FACIES VI
VAE NON CEDO SED INSTAR
SVAI DOMINI IVSTIS NO
BILE LINEOLIS
OCTO IS DUM PERAGIT
PIETH SIC GNAVITER IN ME
ID QVOD NATVRAE EST
EXPRIMIT ARTIS OPVS

BON. AMORBACCHIVM.
10. HOLBEIN. DEPINGEBAT
A. M. D. XIX. PRID. EID OCT.

Bonifacius Amerbach by Hans Holbein the Younger
Kunstmuseum Basel

home and hearth of your native land,[7] you will have to think up some pretext that will satisfy the people at Dole. You have given the excuse that you do not know how things stand there. They have been reported to you as not at all   15
bad, so you must think up some new reason to decline their offer.

Like a spoiled child you can give up your mother's breast,[8] but a wife and children, together with the affection of your father-in-law,[9] will be considerable hindrances.[10] Therefore make up your mind firmly about what you will do. For to be hanging in suspense is a miserable thing.   20

Farewell. 20 April

Cordial greetings to Basilius[11]

To the most renowned gentleman Master Bonifacius Amerbach. At Basel

2643 / To Johannes Dantiscus   Freiburg, 30 April 1532

This is the preface to Erasmus' Latin translation of St Basil the Great's *De Spiritu Sancto* (Basel: Froben 1532), a by-product of Froben's Greek Basil (Ep 2611). For the Polish diplomat and churchman Johannes Dantiscus see Epp 2163 n34, 2563A introduction.

TO THE REVEREND FATHER IN CHRIST AND THE MOST WORTHY
MASTER JOHANNES DANTISCUS, BISHOP OF CHEŁMNO,
AMBASSADOR OF THE KING OF POLAND TO THE EMPEROR,
DESIDERIUS ERASMUS OF ROTTERDAM SENDS GREETINGS
I was eager indeed to make your acquaintance, and behold how completely   5
and ungrudgingly you have revealed yourself to me, most distinguished prelate. For in your letters and poems we see an extraordinary mirror image of your mind and character, that is, of your uprightness, integrity, devotion, and extraordinary learning;[1] and the features of your countenance (and also

* * * * *

7 Basel
8 Ie Bonifacius, born and raised in Basel, could choose to leave it
9 Leonhard Fuchs, burgomaster of Neuenburg am Rhein (midway between Basel and Freiburg)
10 His wife was reluctant to leave Basel, and her father was reluctant to be deprived of her close proximity. See Ep 2649:12–14.
11 Basilius Amerbach, Bonifacius' older brother

2643
1 How many letters Erasmus and Dantiscus had exchanged over the years is not known. This is the only surviving letter of Erasmus to Dantiscus. Dantiscus' only surviving letter to Erasmus, unknown to Allen, was first published as

the character that largely shines through it) are wonderfully represented in   10
this artful plaster image,[2] which makes me more tolerant of the affairs of the
court and the truly lively play that you have had to take part in for so many
years,[3] which up to now have kept me from enjoying the face-to-face association with you that I longed for and from 'hearing and responding to living
words.'[4] Certainly my longing for you has not yet been completely satisfied,   15
but it has been allayed in great part. Still, lest it seem that reciprocal favours
do not balance one other, I send you, in return for the golden heart portrayed
in plaster that you gave me, a writer portrayed on paper but in fact truly
gemlike – except that he appears to be somewhat inferior through the fault
of the modeller. You have sent me the perfect king,[5] unquestionably the fore-   20
most among the monarchs of this age. I send in return the truly great Basil,
whom everyone recognizes as a prince among Greek writers,[6] portrayed by
my pen on paper, not in plaster. How well I have done it is up to you to
judge, since you have mastered the literature of both languages.

The subject matter is the Holy Spirit, whom the viperous posterity   25
of Arius tried to subordinate as a minister to the Son, whom they do not
consider to be God as Basil does, but to be a created substance, so that in

* * * * *

Ep 2563A in CWE 18. Dantiscus was an accomplished Latin poet, known for
his verses celebrating military victories and occasions of state, as well as epi-
taphs and epigrams. For his works (published at Cracow and Rome) celebrating the achievements of Poland and King Sigismund I, see Jacqueline Glomski
Patronage and Humanist Literature in the Age of the Jagiellons (Toronto 2007) 35,
118, 130–3, 135–7.
2 Dantiscus had apparently sent Erasmus a plaster medallion of himself and of
King Sigismund I (the 'perfect king' of line 20 below).
3 Erasmus' term for 'a lively or bustling play' is *fabula motoria* (literally 'a play
characterized by motion or movement'). In Roman theatre a play so described
was the opposite of a *fabula statoria*, a quiet play with little or no action. The allusion is to Dantiscus' years (1519–32) as Polish ambassador at the imperial court,
which was constantly on the move as the emperor wandered from one place to
another in his far-flung dominions: from the Netherlands to Spain, and thence
to Italy, Germany, the Netherlands again, and then once more to Germany before Dantiscus went home to Poland following the Diet of Regensburg (cf n25
below). For other examples of this use of 'taking part in a lively play,' see Epp
2644:24, 2745:4.
4 *Aeneid* 1.409
5 Sigismund I. His image was evidently on the obverse of the medallion of
Dantiscus; cf line 20 above.
6 Erasmus writes τὸν πάνυ βασιλέα 'the perfect king' and τὸν ἀληθῶς μέγαν Βασίλειον
'the truly great Basil' in Greek, punning on the Greek word for king, *basileus*.

IOANNES DANTISCS EPISCOPVS CVLMENSIS.
Prælia deſcribis victriciaque arma Poloni;
Et quantis ſcateant tempora noſtra malis:
Salicet in terras vbi atrocia frigora regnant
Pierius vatum ſit penetrare calor.

Johannes Dantiscus

the ranking of the three persons they granted the third and lowest place to the Spirit.[7] Throughout that period this question came to a violent boil and, as tends to happen, from one serpent many heads suddenly emerged, and 30 the strife of many discordant opinions became a whirlwind. The ship of the church was buffeted about by sectarian waves no less than it is today, as we see to our sorrow – Christ is in a deep sleep in the souls of men in general, but especially in those who ought to be most vigilant. Since I saw that this work by a most respected doctor was highly praised in a monody by Gregory of 35 Nazianzus,[8] and that it had not yet (so far as I know) been translated into Latin, I gladly undertook this task, because I had got whiffs of the progeny of that viper obliterated so long ago secretly trying to come to life again and striving once more to deprive two persons, the Son and the Spirit, of being called truly divine.[9] In that way Christians would now be no better than 40 Jews and Turks,[10] who, whenever they pretend to make a profession of piety,

* * * * *

7 Arius (c 250–c 336) was the founder of Arianism, the principal heresy that denied the divinity of Christ, maintaining that though he was the Son of God he was created by the Father from nothing and was therefore not God by nature. Arius and his views were condemned at the Council of Nicaea (325), but Arianism continued to thrive, in part through the patronage of Arian emperors, until the final victory of Trinitarian orthodoxy at the Council of Constantinople in 381. The original Arians, however, had said little about the Holy Spirit. It was a closely related fourth-century sect known variously as the Pneumatomachi or the Macedonians (after their supposed founder Macedonius [d c 362], bishop of Constantinople), who specifically denied the divinity of the Holy Spirit. They too were condemned at the Council of Constantinople.

8 Ie the *Panegyric on St Basil* (Oration 43), the funeral oration delivered a few years after Basil's death in 379. Gregory of Nazianzus (329–89), archbishop of Constantinople, and his friend Basil the Great (c 330–790), bishop of Caesarea, were two of the three 'Cappadocian Fathers' (the third was Gregory, bishop of Nyssa [c 330–c 395]), whose defence of the Nicene doctrine of the Trinity led to its triumph over Arianism at the Council of Constantinople.

9 Cf Ep 2615:339–42, where Erasmus takes note of the publication in July1531 of Michael Servetus' soon-to-be-infamous antitrinitarian treatise *De trinitatis erroribus libri septem*. Servetus' views would eventually cause him to be tried and executed in Calvinist Geneva (1553). Erasmus may also have had in mind Johannes Campanus (c 1500–74), a Netherlander who in 1530 was arrested in Wittenberg primarily for his antitrinitarian views. He not only made the Son subordinate to the Father, but also understood the Holy Spirit to be not a distinct person but simply the power or the effect of the Father and the Son; see OER I 249–50 and cf Ep 2728 n6.

10 For people of Erasmus' era and location, 'Turk' was the word for a Muslim as well as for a native of Turkey.

readily allow Christ to be called a prophet, or even divine, if you press the point, but only in the same way as Moses and the other prophets. If someone takes exception to making Moses equal to Christ, they grant that God gave richer gifts to Christ than to Moses.[11] Those who are more moderate[12] profess   45
that the Holy Spirit is an excellent creature but still subservient to Christ. Those who are more shameless say that the Holy Spirit is not a substance but only the excitation of a good mind.[13] But God forbid that the hissing of these vipers blow upon anyone reborn in the name of the Father, the Son, and the Holy Spirit!   50

I will not exert myself in the praises of Basil, lest some one ask me, 'Who says anything against him?' But I will not pass over in silence something that occurred to me in the process of translating. I thought I detected something in this work that we see and deplore in some of the most celebrated and praiseworthy authors, such as Athanasius, Chrysostom, and   55
Jerome.[14] 'What is that?' you will say. After I had completed half of the work without boredom, the phrasing seemed to reflect a different writer and a different character. Sometimes the style swelled up to the level of tragedy; then again it sank into colloquial speech. Sometimes it seemed rather vain, as if the author wanted to show that he had learned what Aristotle handed down   60
in his books *Enunciation* and *The Predicaments* or what Porphyry treated in his booklet *The Five Predicables*. Moreover, he sometimes wandered away from his initial intention and returned awkwardly from his digression. Finally, many things seemed to be included that had little relevance to what he was discussing, while certain things are repeated more out of forgetfulness than   65
judgment. In contrast, Basil is always sound, straightforward, clear, consistent, but also insistent, never making reckless departures from the matter at hand, never mixing worldly philosophy into the divine mysteries unless he is forced to do so by his adversaries, and with scorn when he does. He is

* * * * *

11 This is a fair statement of the Muslim understanding of Jesus as described in the Qu'ran. Jews, however, do not recognize Jesus as a prophet.
12 Here Erasmus abruptly switches back to 'the viperous posterity of Arius.'
13 We have not been able to trace this exact phrase, but the reference may be to Campanus; see n9 above.
14 Erasmus had published editions of works by all three authors: the *Lucubrationes aliquot* of Athanasius in 1527 (Ep 1790); several works of St John Chrysostom, including the Latin *Opera* of 1530 (Ep 2359); and two editions of the *Opera omnia* of St Jerome, in 1516 and 1524 (Epp 396, 1465). In all three cases he complained of having to contend with texts falsely attributed to the author or genuine works corrupted by later interpolations.

always calm and proceeds with a sort of virginal modesty, far removed from 70
any ostentation, never departing from his inborn gentleness, not even in the
heat of battle. These things led me to suspect that someone who was eager
to make the volume larger had mixed in many elements, either excerpted
from other authors (for this subject has been treated carefully by many Greek
authors), or devised by himself. For some are learned but inconsistent with 75
the character of Basil; then again some are such that they reveal their author
as someone who has woven his own wordy but lame trifles into the very
learned books of Athanasius on the Holy Spirit and who strove to be thought
of as Chrysostom on the Second Epistle to the Corinthians and on the Acts of
the Apostles. Moreover, it is a criminal sort of contamination to stitch one's 80
shreds and patches onto the noble cloth of these outstanding men, or, to put
it better, to ruin fine vintage by adding to it their own wine that has gone flat.
That this unbearable sacrilege has happened to Jerome's explanatory commentaries on the psalms is so obvious that it cannot be denied. There was a
ready remedy to such an affront to the church: princes and bishops should 85
have taken care that archetypal copies of books that they considered worthy
of being read were placed in reliable libraries.

So it is that in these translations I confess I have been overtaken by
such weariness that from time to time I have whispered to myself that line of
Virgil, 'Do you not sense that the strength belongs to someone else and that 90
the gods have turned against you?'[15] since in other translations there was
nothing that offended my sensibilities. But I will consider this suspicion of
mine to be merely a dream if you disagree with it. At the end of the work,
like a boatswain crying out the oar strokes, he digresses into a description
of a naval battle, decked out with tragic language, in which he places before 95
our eyes a marvellous picture of the church of that time, wretchedly tossed
about, not all that different from its condition in our times, when the clash
of opinions is so blind that sometimes we strike our friends as if they were
enemies, and there is no charity or harmony, and if there is any, it is produced
by a conspiracy of error, that is, a shared disease. And amidst such a diversity 100
of teachings, in such a corruption of morality, in such a confused uproar of
vociferations, when there is almost no distinction any longer between men
and things, anyone might rightly wonder what troop he should join. There
is no honesty, but rather a prodigious mange, not to say a raving madness,
of calumniation has taken hold of many, who either savagely criticize the 105
errors of others or wrongly interpret what is rightly said. A scorpion sleeps

* * * * *

15 *Aeneid* 5.466

under every stone.[16] What a huge storm one syllable stirred up against such an incomparable man! Because in the usual formula at the end of a prayer or a sermon, he said 'with the Spirit' once or twice instead of 'in the Spirit,'[17] Basil was stoned by the words of his calumniators throughout all the cities,   110 all the towns, all marketplaces, all assemblies. Neither his blameless morals, nor his rare learning joined with matching eloquence, nor his high office, nor a certain wonderful courtesy and kindness towards everyone could protect him from the poisonous hissing of his detractors.[18] Hence I, who am a nobody, not comparable in any way to such a man, could quite rightly be   115 considered too thin skinned if I were unable to bear the insults of some loquacious detractors.

At the same time, this discussion clearly illustrates what St Jerome said: Arianism, Eunomianism, Origenism,[19] and other errors concerning the divine persons take their origin from human philosophy – not that philosophy itself   120 is wicked, but that the heavenly philosophy which springs from the breast of

* * * * *

16 *Adagia* I iv 34, a warning to 'beware of speaking heedlessly in the presence of fault-finders and slanderers.'

17 See *De Spiritu Sancto* 1.3: 'Lately when praying with the people, and using the full doxology to God the Father in both forms, at one time *with* the Son *together with* the Holy Spirit, and at another *through* the Son *in* the Holy Spirit, I was attacked by some of those present on the ground that I was introducing novel and at the same time mutually contradictory terms' (translation from *The Nicene and Post-Nicene Fathers* Second Series ed Philip Schaff and Henry Wace VIII [Edinburgh 1896; repr Grand Rapids MI 1989] 3, but substituting 'Holy Spirit' for 'Holy Ghost'). The point was that in Greek both 'in' (ἐν) and 'through' (διὰ) were used to indicate an instrument or a means, which seemed to imply that the Holy Spirit was simply an instrument or a means in the hands of the Father and/or the Son rather than a Person of equal status: uncreated, eternal, fully divine. In the treatise Basil defended the propriety of his formulation while condemning those who denied the divinity of the Holy Spirit (see n7 above).

18 Basil's defence of what came to be the orthodox view of the Trinity earned him the enmity of the champions of Arianism in its various forms, including Emperor Valens (364–78). Their defeat, at the Council of Constantinople (see n7 above), did not come until after his death.

19 Eunomians, also known as Aetians and Anomoeans, were fourth-century exponents of a doctrine much like that of the Arians (see n7 above), holding that the Son is unlike the Father in essence. Their ideas met with little lasting success, but they are remembered for having elicited vigorous defence of orthodox doctrine from the Cappadocian Fathers (n8 above). Origenists were named for the biblical exegete Origen (c 185–c 254), whose unclear language and uncertainties about the relationship of the Holy Spirit to the Father and the Son made him seem to some to be unorthodox on the subject of the Trinity.

the Father through the Son neither wishes nor ought to be explained by the standards of such philosophy.[20] For how can divine mysteries be perceived by men who are no more than human, who have no idea even about many natural phenomena? But those who took Basil to task at that time were actu- 125 ally philosophasters rather than philosophers. Before the unlearned multi- tude they passed themselves off as consummate philosophers because they had tasted (but not truly learned) the meaning of enumeration, genus, spe- cies, substance, accident, quantity, quality, what is opposite to what and in how many ways opposites are said to be so, in how many ways something is 130 predicated as either *in* or *from* something else. These are the elements taught nowadays to mere boys who are coming to the threshold of philosophy, so that the impiety of such people should be attributed to erroneous opinions, not to philosophy. What storms they would have raised in the world if they had also tasted what Aristotle taught about the forms of the syllogism, about 135 demonstrations, about topics, fallacies, what belongs to nature, and what is beyond it? But I am being carried away, beyond the limits of a preface.

And so to come to an end, whatever this little effort of mine may be, I have wished to dedicate it to you, O most distinguished prelate, not only be- cause the enticement of your name will make it more attractive to students, 140 but even more because your sharp eye will polish and revise it, for I am sending you only a first draft. If someone should indict me for recklessness in doing this, the only defence I can bring forward against such an accusation is my own nature and – even more valid than that – long-standing practice. It is very difficult to reshape nature, but it is even more difficult to unlearn 145 what long practice has deeply ingrained, and when both are joined together, I think it is quite impossible for a man to change. But the gods are all power- ful.[21] This, you will say, is to accuse rather than excuse oneself. What can one do? Often the honest confession of a mistake gains pardon from a merciful judge. If, however, I should try to evade some of the blame, I would shift 150 it to the printers, who always want me to lay the egg before it is ready to be laid. And when something has been conceived, they do not allow the fetus to mature; instead they force me, against the will of Lucina, to abort it.[22] I know

* * * * *

20 Jerome was firmly of the view that 'the true profession of the mystery of the Trinity is to own that we do not comprehend it' (*De mysterio Trinitatis recta con- fessio est ignoratio scientiae*); *Commentarii in Isaiam* xviii proem (PL 24 627A).
21 Cited in Greek, a direct quotation from Homer's *Odyssey* 10.36. See *Adagia* iv vi 11.
22 Lucina was the Roman goddess of childbirth.

very well what would be worthy of you, distinguished sir, but like the poor
little Greek, I take a few coins from a meagre wallet, and 'not according to   155
your worth, your Reverence, for if I had more I would give more.'[23]

I pray that the lively drama in which you have played for so many years
will have a happy ending,[24] both privately for you and publicly for the kingdom of Poland, and that King Sigismund, who is more amply endowed than
anyone with all the ornaments worthy of such an extraordinary prince, will   160
soon restore you to your sweet homeland and your beloved flock, to whose
care you remain devoutly faithful through all the waves of your troubles.[25]

Given at Freiburg im Breisgau, 31 March in the year of our Lord 1532

2644 / [To Conradus Goclenius]   Freiburg, 3 May 1532

> This letter was first published in the *Vita Erasmi*. The identity of Goclenius,
> professor of Latin at the Collegium Trilingue in Louvain (Epp 1209, 1994), as the
> recipient is evident from the contents, particularly the references to the lawsuit
> over the canonry at Antwerp (lines 31–2 below).

Cordial greetings. The two Dutchmen who visited you live here, but both
have lost their money belts.[1] The younger one was marvellously eager to
become my servant.[2] For one of my servants went home to Burgundy, but

* * * * *

23 Cited partly in Greek. According to the story, the poor Greek in question had
   repeatedly offered Emperor Augustus an epigram in his honour, but in vain.
   Eventually Augustus sent an epigram of his own to the Greek, who praised it
   highly and offered Augustus a few coins from his poor wallet, acknowledg-
   ing that it wasn't enough but saying 'If I had more I would give it.' Everyone
   laughed, and Augustus ordered his steward to pay the Greek a munificent sum
   for his epigram. See *Apophthegmata* 4.176, citing Macrobius *Saturnalia* 2.4.31
   (CWE 37 393–4).
24 See n3 above.
25 Summoned back to Poland in February 1532, Dantiscus attended the Diet of
   Regensburg in the following summer (see Ep 2687:85–6) and then went home
   to Cracow.

2644
1 Ie they are penniless and willing to do anything; cf Horace *Epistolae* 2.2.39–40.
2 This was doubtless Quirinus Hagius, who entered Erasmus' service at about this
   time; see Ep 2704 n6, and cf Franz Bierlaire *La familia d'Erasme* (Paris 1968) 93.

he returned.[3] I am waiting for Bebel to come back from England;[4] if he does
not have any certain information, I plan to send off one of my servants to   5
England.[5] What I most expected was lacking in your letter, since I have been
waiting eagerly to hear for certain that you have the canonry.[6] Such a large
flock of vultures keeps me from being free of worry about it.[7]

I wrote to Aleandro, complaining about the book by Julius Caesar.[8] In
order to escape being branded with a stupid misdeed, he excuses himself in a   10
letter which is carefully composed, but the arguments he uses are very weak.
I am sending you a copy. As I see it, he almost persuaded you; but I, having
lived in the same residence and also shared the same bedroom,[9] know him
inside out, and I am as sure as I am alive that he laid the egg. But we must go
along with the times. Words will be repaid with words.   15

The monk Alonso Virués has been summoned to the court.[10] He wrote
seven disquisitions about me; to put it in a nutshell, they are thoroughly
monkish.[11] It is said they are now being printed at Paris.[12] He himself wrote
to me from the court, in a friendly way but also not without threats (as is
characteristic of monks).[13] The bishop of Augsburg told me through his own   20

* * * * *

3 Gilbert Cousin; see Ep 2381 n1.
4 The Basel printer Johann Bebel was away on the second trip to England (the first
   having been in 1531; Ep 2487 n9) during which he was to deliver letters to Erasmus'
   friends and gather information on the state of Erasmus' English pensions.
5 It was Quirinus Hagius who was sent; see n2 above.
6 Ie the canonry of St Mary's at Antwerp, Goclenius' appointment to which in
   1525 had resulted in a prolonged legal battle that lasted more than eight years;
   cf Ep 2552 n5.
7 The 'vultures' were the opponents of Goclenius' appointment.
8 The book was the *Oratio pro Cicerone contra Erasmum* of Julius Caesar Scaliger.
   Erasmus' letter to Aleandro is not extant, but Aleandro's reply (see following
   lines) is Ep 2638.
9 In Venice in 1508, when both were working at the Aldine press; see Epp 256,
   1195 n14.
10 Ie to the imperial court; see Ep 2641:7–9.
11 In 1526 Virués circulated in manuscript seven *Collationes ad Erasmum*, commentaries on points in Erasmus' writings that he thought might have been expressed more cautiously, so as to avoid provoking the wrath of the monks. He
   dispatched two copies to Erasmus, who initially interpreted the *collationes* as
   the prelude to an underhanded attack and had to be persuaded by others that
   Virués was in fact a trustworthy friend; see Ep 1684 introduction.
12 They were never published anywhere.
13 Ep 2641

messenger that he would write me about what is going on at the diet.[14] I have no doubt that Aleandro will be doing exactly as he always does at every opportunity.

Jan van Campen is acting in the lively drama.[15] He is now printing some work or other at Nürnberg.[16] Johannes the Dane has offended the bishop of Chełmno by passing around my letter.[17] Master Gilles is worried about the College, not without reason.[18] They were half asleep when they admitted Rescius with his wife.[19] They should have stuck to their principles. Everybody who is well educated here loves the gospel.[20] Otherwise I would not have failed in my duty.[21]

Farewell, 3 May 1532

I am still building on the verge of the grave.[22] See to it that you put an end to the suit. It may be that Aleandro did your cause no good.[23] He is a

* * * * *

14 There is no extant letter of Bishop Christoph von Stadion to Erasmus reporting on the diet at Regensburg.
15 Again Erasmus uses *fabula motoria* (cf Ep 2643 n3) to describe the life of the court, forever on the move. Jan van Campen had recently resigned from his post as professor of Hebrew at the Collegium Trilingue in Louvain to enter the service of Johannes Dantiscus, Polish ambassador to the imperial court; see Ep 2629.
16 His psalm commentary, dedicated to Dantiscus; see Ep 2570 n30.
17 Erasmus mistakenly calls Jakob the Dane (Jakob Jespersen; see Ep 2570) 'Johannes.' He makes the same mistake in Ep 2736:14. Erasmus' accusation was that Jespersen had offended Dantiscus by showing one of Erasmus' letters to him to Girolamo Aleandro; see Epp 2646:14–15, 2693 146–7, and Allen Ep 2849.
18 Gilles de Busleyden. For his worries about the Collegium Trilingue at Louvain, see Epp 2573:37–52, 2588.
19 Rutgerus Rescius (Ep 546) was the first professor of Greek at the Collegium Trilingue. In 1525 he married a local woman and moved out of the college, thus inviting charges that he had violated the terms of the founder's will by not living in the college (which he could not do as a married man), and that he was neglecting his duties. At the time Erasmus came to his defence, while urging him to strive to give satisfaction to the executors and to continue his successful teaching at Louvain. See Epp 1768 n10, 1882.
20 'Here' presumably means Catholic Freiburg.
21 Presumably by moving elsewhere
22 Literally 'next to the sepulchre' (*sepulchro proximus*). The reference is to continued work on the renovation of his new house despite his age and poor health; cf Ep 2646:5–7.
23 Nothing is known of any intervention by Aleandro in Goclenius' suit over the canonry in Antwerp.

clever artificer of clever artifices! Forgive me, I did not reread it.[24] Give my   35
greetings to Master Joost, the president,[25] and to Rescius.[26] Resende has
remonstrated with me about the publishing of the poem. But I thought he
was a free man. Otherwise I would never have published it.[27] But I wonder why you did not want me to know about it. Once more, farewell, my
dearest friend.

2645 / To Joost Sasbout   Freiburg, 3 May 1532

This letter was first published in the *Epistolae palaeonaeoi*. Joost Sasbout (1487–
1546), native of Delft and lord of Spalant, matriculated at Louvain in 1506, and
subsequently went elsewhere to study canon and civil law, receiving his doctorate in or before 1513. In 1515 he was appointed to the council of Holland,
and in 1527 he was sent as an imperial commissioner to Friesland. In 1543 he
became chancellor of Gelderland. Otherwise, little is known of him. He and
Erasmus appear to have known one another slightly. Erasmus sent him greetings in letters to friends (Epp 1092:19, 1188:49, 2644:35–6). This letter and
Ep 2844 are the only ones that survive from their direct correspondence. Three
others are mentioned in Allen Epp 2851:43, 2923:7, 3052:2–3, 3061:39.

ERASMUS OF ROTTERDAM TO THE VERY DISTINGUISHED MASTER
JOOST SASBOUT, COUNCILLOR AT THE HAGUE,[1] GREETINGS
There was once a saying that whoever was honest at Athens had to be ex-
traordinarily honest indeed.[2] Now, however, it would not be absurd to say
that anyone who is a friend of Erasmus in our times has to be a genuine   5

* * * * *

24 This usually means 'forgive me for not having reread the letter and made
    corrections.'
25 Joost Sasbout (see Ep 2645), who was not the 'president' of anything. In 1527
    he had been seriously considered for the presidency of the council of Friesland,
    and Erasmus may have thought that the appointment went through.
26 See n19 above.
27 For André de Resende and his poem satirizing his fellow Dominicans in Louvain
    and their hostility to Erasmus, see Ep 2500 introduction and n3. Erasmus, to
    whom Resende sent a copy of the poem, published it without his permission,
    believing that Resende was 'a free man,' ie that he had left the order.

    2645
 1 Erasmus was evidently unaware of Sasbout's appointment in Friesland (see
    introduction).
 2 *Adagia* IV i 53

friend indeed, since flattery, slanders, and lies are seething and raging everywhere and everything is inflamed, so that it is not safe to say anything
even against an enemy or to let it be known who one's friends are. Still, it is
my experience that in this tumult there are not a few who sincerely wish me
well. I hold them dearer because they are few. But I prefer a few outstanding   10
friends to a crowd of untried people from the common multitude.

It has been some years since I learned (from some friends who are not
to be taken lightly) that you have a genuine regard for my pursuits and say
favourable things about them. From a letter of Quirinus Talesius,[3] who was
once my famulus, I have recently learned that your affection for me has not   15
yet cooled. For that reason, my very dear Sasbout, I declare that I am most
beholden to you, and glad to be so. Would that it were as easy for me to do
something good for you to match your affection as it is for me to wish to respond to your affection with mine. When I hear how our native land Holland
is harrassed with so much warfare, plundered by so many depredations, tor-   20
mented with so many invasions, torn apart by both friends and enemies,
I am sorely grieved to hear it, as I should be.[4] Most of these evils spring
from the ambition of the rulers, than which nothing can be more deadly if
it lacks the genuine wisdom befitting a king. When greedy merchants covet
new properties, they either treat ancestral lands as if they were abandoned   25
or consign them to the vagaries of chance. Once upon a time it was an altogether splendid thing to be the count of Holland. But this roiling of human
affairs is ceaseless, and in fact almost no place in the world has been struck
by a more enormous storm. And just as the skill of a helmsman becomes apparent in great storms, so too it seems to me that it requires an extraordinary   30
measure of both uprightness and prudence to keep a firm hold on the helm in
such violent storms and such total turmoil. Whether we have accomplished
that I do not know, but certainly we have tried, and continue to try very hard.

I look forward to what we are going to get from the Diet of Regensburg.[5]
Certainly I have good hope, but I would be more confident of a favourable   35
outcome if the emperor in his piety did not place so much stock in clerical

* * * * *

3 Not extant; perhaps that answered by Ep 2647
4 The Hapsburgs and France were not at war at this time, nor is there any indication of the old hostility between Holland and Gelderland. So this seems to be
  a general reference to conflicts in the recent and not-so-recent past. But see Ep
  2798:76–8 with nn12–13.
5 The Diet of Regensburg, in session since 17 April, would reach its conclusion
  on 27 July. For an eye-witness report on what was happening at the diet, see Ep
  2654:9–24; see also Ep 2702 n1.

dignitaries;[6] I would not wish to challenge their authority, of course, but there is no end to the ambition of some of them. Queen Mary, the most praiseworthy lady of our times, is calling me back to Brabant,[7] but afterwards I would still have to go on living – if indeed I would have any desire to live at all. I want   40 to die at my studies;[8] I do not wish to pass away in the business of the court.

I was going to write to Master Abel van Colster and Master Gerrit van Assendelft,[9] both very notable gentlemen, but the physician Gerardus Henricus,[10] who was returning from Italy, encountered me here when I was worn out with my studies and with writing letters, and I did not want to   45 hold him up any longer, since he was hurrying back to home and hearth after a long trip. Thus I beg you to play the part of a letter from me for those celebrated men until I get a bit of free time. For I do not want to address them in a shabby or vapid letter. In the meantime persuade them that this letter is written also to them.   50

Farewell. At Freiburg im Breisgau, 3 May in the year after the birth of Christ 1532

2646 / To Nicolaus Olahus   Freiburg, 3 May 1532

This letter was first published in Ipolyi page 234. The manuscript is page 211 of the Olahus codex in the Hungarian National Archives at Budapest (Ep 2339 introduction). For Nicolaus Olahus, secretary to Mary of Hungary, regent of the Netherlands, see Ep 2339 introduction. His reply to this letter and to Ep 2613 is Ep 2693.

* * * * *

6 For Erasmus' fear that the emperor, in his piety, was too eager to do the pope's bidding by crushing the Reformation with force, cf Ep 2472:33–5 with n9.
7 See Ep 2646.
8 Horace *Epistles* 1.7.85. Cf Epp 2646:9–10, 2651:27.
9 For Abel van Colster see Ep 2800 introduction. Gerrit van Assendelft (1488– 1558) was probably the 'heer van Assendelft' mentioned in Ep 1044:32–4 as an avid reader of Erasmus' books, and was possibly the addressee of Ep 1166. A member of the council of Holland since 1515, he became its president in 1528. Erasmus sent greetings to him again in April 1533 (Ep 2800:102). Meanwhile, in October 1532, he addressed to Assendelft a letter of extravagant praise that included clear hints of financial need (Ep 2734), whereupon Assendelft helped arrange a handsome gift of cash from the estates of Holland (Ep 2819).
10 On his way home from Italy, where he had taken a degree in medicine, Gerardus Henricus of Amsterdam (documented 1532) paid a visit to Erasmus, who entrusted him with the delivery of this letter as well as of Ep 2646, in which he recommended Henricus to Nicolaus Olahus. In Ep 2693:9–10, Olahus confirmed that Henricus had delivered the letter to him in Ghent. Nothing else is known of Henricus.

ERASMUS OF ROTTERDAM TO NICOLAUS OLAHUS,
SECRETARY TO HER SERENE MAJESTY

I have received the letter in which you urge me to return to Brabant,[1] and
I have answered it by the same master of the letter carriers who had delivered it.[2] I stay here unwillingly, but nevertheless I am engaged in building.[3] 5
In hiding here at home, I hardly hold back my frail spirit, which is already
on the verge of departing.[4] Because I do not have any wine from Burgundy
now, the change from that wine puts me in peril.[5] The smallest cold snap or
unfavourable breeze confines me to bed. I do not see what use I could be to
her serene Majesty. And I am afraid that if I go back, the court will not allow 10
me to take care of my frail little body. I will not be loath to die at my studies.[6]
And yet I would be pleased to spend the little time I have left (hardly more
than a hand's breadth) in the service of such a lady.

The bishop of Chełmno is somewhat annoyed with Jakob the Dane for
circulating everywhere the letter I sent to him.[7] I recommend my Lieven to 15
you; I wish you could persuade him to engage in a way of life in which there
would be some opportunity for his talent and his learning. For he was born
for literary studies, in which he has been diligently occupied, and not without good results.[8] I hear that you are also learning Greek,[9] and that Lieven
might be of some use to you. 20

I am sending you this letter by Gerardus Henricus of Amsterdam, who
is returning from Italy after getting his medical degree.[10] I would not want
recommending him to be a burden to you, nor is he looking for anything
definite. As for you, my dear Olahus, continue to follow your own bent, and
whenever you get the chance give me the pleasure of a letter from you. Best 25
wishes to her serene Majesty.

Farewell. Freiburg, 3 May 1532

* * * * *

2646
1 Ep 2607
2 The answering letter is Ep 2613.
3 Ie in the renovation of the new house that he had occupied in the autumn of
   1531; see Epp 2506 n1, 2517 n11.
4 Cf Ep 2644:32.
5 For Erasmus' dependence on wine from Burgundy, see Epp 2348:9–16, 2397:3–17.
6 See Ep 2645 n8.
7 'Jakob the Dane' is Jakob Jespersen; see Ep 2644:25–6 with n17.
8 Erasmus' former famulus Lieven Algoet was, with Erasmus' strong support,
   currently seeking an appointment at the court of Queen Mary; see Ep 2567,
   2583:32–40, 2587:71–4, 2693:16–99.
9 Erasmus writes 'Hellenizing' in Greek. Jakob Jespersen, who had recently entered the service of Olahus, was teaching him Greek; see Ep 2570:27–9.
10 See Ep 2645 n10.

2647 / To Quirinus Talesius   [Freiburg], 7 May 1532

This letter, no longer extant, was one of several to Talesius, probably autograph, which in 1625 were in the possession of Pieter van Opmeer. See Opmeer's *Historia martyrum Batavicorum sive defectionis a fide maiorum Hollandiae initia* (Cologne: Gualther & Henning 1625) 104, where the letter is described as one congratulating Quirinus on his appointment as pensionary of his native city of Haarlem (cf Ep 2389:12–38). Opmeer did not print any of the letters.

2648 / From Jacopo Sadoleto   Carpentras, 8 May 1532

This letter was first published in *Sadoleti epistolae* page 164. It is a letter of thanks for the dedication of the Froben Greek Basil (Ep 2611), written before Sadoleto had seen the work; a supplementary letter of thanks followed on 7 June (Ep 2656). At the beginning of March 1532, Bonifacius wrote to Sadoleto that, following instructions from Erasmus (cf Ep 2612), he was sending him a copy of the Greek Basil 'dedicated to you,' along with several other 'recently published' works of Erasmus: the *Declarationes ad censuras Lutetiae vulgatas* (Ep 2552 n10); the *Enarratio psalmi 38* (see n7 below), the *Dilutio* against Josse Clichtove (Ep 2604 n12), and the *Apologia adversus rhapsodias Alberti Pii* (Ep 2486 n10). See AK Ep 1610:35–41.

JACOPO SADOLETO, BISHOP OF CARPENTRAS, SENDS CORDIAL
GREETINGS TO DESIDERIUS ERASMUS OF ROTTERDAM
I am thoroughly annoyed that my letter was delivered to you so very late. I would have liked it to be delivered on time, not so much to please you (and you are friendly and kind enough to write that it does) as to make you 5 quickly aware of my obligation to you. In fact I received your letter dated 27 February at the beginning of March.[1] I am glad to accept your congratulations on my sound health, which I take as bearing witness to your extraordinary affection for me. But still you should know that from the middle of November till the end of April I was not in very good health. And so during 10 that whole time my studies were interrupted, and I could not accomplish anything worthy of a true man.

* * * * *

2648
1 Not extant; the letter of dedication for the Basil edition (Ep 2611) is dated 22 February, and contains no congratulation to Sadoleto on his good health (see following sentence).

But now I have returned to my former area of studies, about which I wrote you before, namely, to write a commentary on the Epistle of Paul to the Romans. This is extremely difficult, as you are aware and as I also know from 15 my own experience, but I am not discouraged. May God grant a favourable outcome to my plans, for no effort or labour will be lacking on my part.[2] But I had the good fortune, very opportunely, to acquire a complete printed edition in Greek of Chrysostom's commentary on all of Paul's epistles, which was sent to me as a gift by the bishop of Verona;[3] I think you have heard of 20 it or even acquired the volume itself. I certainly hope that it will make up for what, as you write, was lacking to you when you first undertook the task, if by some chance you are now willing to carry through what you began long ago. I will not exclude the Froben press when the time comes for printing, especially if such a scholar as you were taking care that it be done right. But 25 more than that, my dear Erasmus, I need your opinion, which I have always considered, and always will consider, to be most valuable. It is an arduous undertaking, and I come to it with difficulty and late in the day. I have also found new meanings, and not just a few of them. As to whether they are right or not, I do not trust my own judgment; I must seek out the opinion of 30 men like you (if there are any), and especially your own judgment, since you are preeminent in this kind of writing and in it you have provided not only learning (which in your case is at the highest level) but also abundance and a dignified style. I am delighted that you have brought out Basil the Great, speaking his own language, so that he has passed into the hands of a large 35 audience. That you have dedicated it to me reveals that you have a higher opinion of me than I had expected or that I think I deserve. But your benevolence and kindness are such that you take into account not what I deserve to receive but what it behooves you to give. Certainly I thank you and extend to you my deepest gratitude; I will repay the favour if the occasion arises. 40

I find it surprising that so many people attack you, and so frequently, and it is most annoying to me. I do not see any reason for it except perhaps the one I wrote to you about a while ago, namely, that you are held in such high esteem that your preeminence seems to expose you to all the blasts of

* * * * *

2 The commentary was finally published in 1535: *In Pauli epistolam ad Romanos commentariorum libri tres* (Lyon: Gryphius).

3 The complete edition of Chrysostom in Greek that was organized by Gian Matteo Giberti, bishop of Verona, did not get past the first three volumes, which were devoted to the epistles of Paul (Verona: Sabii, 28 June 1529).

ill will.⁴ For those who set out to get a reputation in the wrestling arena of   45
theology choose some very famous name to attack so as to get from the very
outset something that will recommend them to the mob; the contention itself then intensifies the fight. But if I were in this position I would respond
to all such opponents with one single defence: partly by excusing as the actions and opinions of youth whatever I might have written too freely when   50
I was at that age; partly by modestly and carefully retracting anything that
might seem (not actually be but merely seem) to give a handle to slanderers
(for we see that was done by the greatest and holiest doctors); and finally, by
explaining my meaning about Christian doctrine in such a way that no one
could have any doubts about what I meant. After I had done this, I would   55
react to my opponents with complete silence, since their insolence and malevolent slanders would be refuted by the very facts of the case, and also by
your extraordinary reputation and virtue. But I say such things not so much
to advise you (for you do not need any advice) as to testify to my feelings
and attitude.⁵   60

Would that one could rightly mourn the death of Oecolampadius, for
that is what the writing and the teaching of the man deserved, even if he had
not shown himself to be destructive in other ways.⁶ I am eagerly awaiting
your Psalm and I want to read through it.⁷ I have heard that a volume of your
letters has been published and is available at Lyon.⁸ I have sent some people   65
to buy it. In the meantime, my dear Erasmus, if you love us, take care of your
health and sustain this stage of your life in your usual manner, by the highest
intellectual pursuits and your awareness of good counsel. And I, who love
you very much, will never ever fail to promote your fame, your praises, and
also your wishes. Farewell.   70

Carpentras, 8 May 1532

* * * * *

4 See Ep 2385:40–3.
5 This paragraph is essentially a repetition of advice already given in Epp
  2272:39–51, 2385:43–54.
6 Johannes Oecolampadius, leader of the Reformation in Basel and an estimable
  humanist scholar, died on the night of 22/3 November 1531.
7 Ie the commentary on Psalm 38; see Ep 2608.
8 The *Epistolae floridae*, published by Herwagen at Basel in September 1531 (Ep
  2518). A pirated edition was published by Chrétien Wechel at Paris in November
  1531. Either or both might have made it to the bookstalls of Lyon.

2649 / From Bonifacius Amerbach   .   [Basel], 15 May 1532

> This letter (= AK Ep 1642) is Bonifacius' answer to Ep 2642. The surviving
> manuscript, an autograph fair copy that has no address, is in the Öffentliche
> Bibliothek of the University of Basel (MS C VIa 73 5).

Cordial greetings. If ever at any other time, in your last letter you gave me
very clear evidence of your good will towards me; by answering my inquiries in such a friendly fashion you changed me from debtor to an indentured
servant. I know, my incomparable Erasmus, how much I owe you and I am
not unaware how far behind I am in repaying you. If anything is accom-   5
plished by devotion and gratitude, for I am capable of nothing more, I will
pay what I owe, and I will without doubt be your faithful debtor, for my
memory of the good deeds you have done for me will never fade away.

  I have finally answered the people at Dole;[1] I tried as hard as I could to
thank them for offering me such an honourable position. Moreover, I did not   10
want to offer any excuse apart from the actual reasons that kept me from going. Since I was aware that my wife was not very enthusiastic about leaving,
and my father-in-law was most reluctant to be separated from his daughter
and was therefore hesitant, and the magistrates here were no more favourable and also reminded me of my commitments to my native land, what   15
was I to do, or what more reasons did I need? As for me, I did not think it
right to damage my reputation for keeping agreements or to go against my
father-in-law's affection for his only daughter; though still hesitant, I finally
extricated myself all the more easily because I am not at all attracted by the
goal to be aimed at, namely the court.[2] Actually, by my inborn temperament   20
I prefer to live as a private person, and from childhood on I have considered
life at court to be no more than splendid misery. Otherwise, so far as either
my profession or my native land is concerned, here I could satisfy my own
inclinations; there I would somehow have had to swallow as best I could the
hatred, or rather the weariness, of fierce contention, even if other things suit-   25
ed me. But more concerning these matters sometime when we are together.

          * * * * *

2649
1 Ie he turned down the offer of a professorship of law at the university. His letter
  of refusal is AK Ep 1640 (dated 'sometime before 15 May 1532').
2 See Ep 2642 n4.

If Polyphemus goes on acting the way he has decided to do, the last two syllables of his name can be changed to form Polypotes.[3]

Farewell, most illustrious Erasmus

15 May 1532   30

Devotedly yours, Bonifacius Amerbach

2650 / To Bonifacius Amerbach   [Freiburg], 15 May 1532

This letter (= AK Ep 1643) was first published in the *Epistolae familiares*. The autograph is in the Öffentliche Bibliothek of the University of Basel (MS AN III 15 89). Allen notes that 'the watermark of the paper points to 1532 or 1533. AK accepts Allen's dating.

Greetings. I have read your secrets, but by mistake. At any rate, I would have believed the letter was written to me if it had not made mention of the remedy.[1]

* * * * *

3 Bonifacius uses the Greek word Πολυπότης, meaning 'big drinker.' Erasmus' wayward famulus and letter carrier Felix Rex (Ep 2130 introduction), nicknamed Polyphemus ('many-voiced' or 'much spoken of'), had recently visited Erasmus; see Epp 2661:14–15, 2663:5. Towards the end of February 1532 he had set out from the court of Elector John Frederick of Saxony, bearing letters to Erasmus; see Epp 2609–10. According to Erasmus' account in Ep 2728:60–80, he went first to Cologne, where 'he drank away several months' in the home of Tielmannus Gravius. Then he proceeded to Freiburg, where he proposed to become 'the steward' of Erasmus' house. Erasmus got rid of him by sending him on an embassy to the Diet of Regensburg, where 'he drank away six weeks.' Erasmus' own nickname for Rex was 'Cyclops,' because he was 'hardly more intelligent' than Homer's one-eyed giant, 'and as big a drunkard.' See Ep 2121:4–6 with n4. In the Basel autograph Bonifacius erased Πολυπότης and substituted the following as an alternative to the sentence: 'Πολυπότης, nay rather Polyphemus, has carried on vigorously in his usual fashion and has not yet changed his ways.'

2650
1 The word translated as 'of the remedy' is *pharmaci*, which is the genitive singular of either the neuter *pharmacum* or the masculine *pharmacus* (from the Greek *pharmacon* and *pharmacos*). In classical Latin *pharmacum* meant 'poison,' and *pharmacus* meant 'poisoner' or 'sorcerer' (someone who makes magic potions). By the sixteenth century, however, *pharmacum* had come into frequent use as 'remedy' or 'medicine,' and *pharmacus* (or some variant of it, like *pharmacopoeus* or *pharmacologus*) meant 'apothecary.' Without the text of the letter to which Erasmus is referring, or of Bonifacius' answer (if any) to this letter, we cannot know what 'secrets' Erasmus unintentionally read; nor can we know whether he was referring to a poison or a remedy, a poisoner or an apothecary.

Farewell. 15 May
You will recognize the hand.
To the renowned Doctor Bonifacius Amerbach. At Basel   5

2651 / To Bernhard von Cles   Freiburg, 19 May 1532

This letter, the reply to one no longer extant, was first published in the *Epistolae palaeonaeoi*. For Bernhard von Cles, cardinal-bishop of Trent and faithful patron of Erasmus, see Ep 1357.

ERASMUS OF ROTTERDAM TO THE REVEREND LORD BERNHARD,
CARDINAL AND BISHOP OF TRENT, GREETINGS
Those who claim to understand the nature of spirits tell us that good spirits usually evoke cheerfulness, bad ones terror and disgust. If what they say is true, then you and King Ferdinand must have some inborn spirit which is fa-   5
vourable and friendly to me. For no letter ever comes to me from his Majesty or your Eminence that does not bring an extraordinary comfort to my mind, even if the subject matter is hardly cheerful. On the other hand, there is a different sort of person who never writes a letter, however friendly and soothing, that is not mixed with some bitter poison.   10
   How much pleasure I felt when I read what you write in your last letter,[1] namely, that Ferdinand, the most serene king of the Romans, speaking to a large audience, extolled my name with such great honour that I do not need a recommendation to him from anyone else at all. What would such a kind prince do if I had really earned something from his Majesty by perform-   15
ing some duty for him? My burdensome age and my even more burdensome ailments are especially irksome to me precisely because they keep me from serving so devoted, so upright, so friendly a prince. But since, according to Greek proverbs, youth is a time for deeds, middle age for plans, old age for prayers,[2] the thread of my life has come to such a length that for so great a   20
prince I can do no more than pray that all goes very well for him, which I constantly do. Hitherto your kindness has admonished me in your letters to ask for something specific from a prince who is so friendly to me; you say that you will see to it that I get what I hope for. Would that Christ, the greatest

* * * * *

2651
1 Not extant
2 *Adagia* III v 2

monarch of all, had prescribed such a thing for me! There are many things I   25
would ask of him, but nothing more than a mind worthy of him. From King
Ferdinand I hardly see anything to ask that his extraordinary kindness does
not already provide. Except for studies, in which it is agreeable to die,[3] I am
useless for any function in life. To bestow a lofty position on me would be like
loading goods on a horse already collapsing after he has run the course of his   30
life. Nothing could be more absurd than to give more provisions to someone
who has already completed his journey. Frugality, which gets by on little,
has always been pleasing to me, but now it is also necessary. Nevertheless,
I would hope to have a peaceful old age, even if I am denied the cheer and
prosperity which I see that many have when they are old. To fend off old age,   35
to preserve health, neither the pope nor the greatest of princes, the emperor,
can possibly achieve. But since both of them wish me well, I only wish that
they could at least stop the mouths of those who rail at me. But not even that
is in their power.

For apart from those who openly snarl at me from all sides, there is no   40
lack of those who seek my downfall by nefarious devices and hidden snares.
I know that what you, in your kindness, say in order to console me is very
true: glory won through virtue is always subject to envy, and it is not only in
our times that disturbances have been thought up and carried out by wicked
men. I remember how viciously Jerome's detractors snarled at him, but his   45
extraordinary virtue either overwhelmed their malice or at least counterbal-
anced it and rendered it more bearable. But what am I compared to such
men? If you consider teaching and piety, I am unworthy to wipe off their
sandals;[4] if you consider the magnitude of the ill will, I am leagues ahead of
them. I frankly confess, however, that it is owing to the clemency of princes   50
that I have thus far held out against such serpents.

At present I have nothing to ask from King Ferdinand except that, if my
envious enemies stir up tragic commotions, he would continue to be what he
has been: I am confident that he will even increase what his royal beneficence
has done up to now, on his own initiative and through your recommenda-   55
tion – or rather admonition. The piety of his most holy Majesty has made him
worthy always to enjoy prosperity and peace. But since our own wickedness

* * * * *

3 See Ep 2645 n8.
4 Cf Matt 3:11, Mark 1:7.

has earned us warfare, I pray that by the favour of God victory in war should fall on his side and also in favour of all of us.[5]

Henricus Glareanus sends to Ferdinand, the renowned King of the   60
Romans, a specimen of his studies,[6] not at all seeking any sort of reward except the favour of this greatest of princes, which he has already experienced to such a degree that by so fulfilling his duty he has not so much gained as given thanks. If anyone is, he is a man of upright and unstained character, whose learning is manifold, profound, and accurate, far different from some   65
people who want to be considered consummate scholars when they have managed to write ten verses. This man has combined philosophy with poetry, historical knowledge with the discipline of mathematics. He lectures here publicly, with a regular salary;[7] nevertheless, he privately instructs some well-born young men, so that his house is truly a workshop of the most ad-   70
vanced academic studies and he is the foremost ornament of this academy. What more need I say? He is worthy to become better known and dearer to the king by the recommendation of your Eminence. He will be motivated to promote such studies all the more eagerly if he knows that this dutiful offering has not been displeasing to his royal Majesty.   75

Farewell. On Pentecost 1532

2652 / To Bonifacius Amerbach   Freiburg, 31 May [1532]

This letter (= AK Ep. 1651) was first published in the *Epistolae familiares*. The autograph is in the Öffentliche Bibliothek of the University of Basel (MS AN III 15 60). The year date is confirmed by the reference to Sepúlveda's *Antapologia*. Bonifacius' reply is Ep 2653.

Cordial greetings. I have twice received the little book by the self-important Sepúlveda, the first time from Paris (where it was printed), and soon

* * * * *

5 Ie in the struggle to defend the Empire against the Turks, which was the principal item on the agenda of the Diet of Regensburg (April–July 1532); see Ep 2654:9–20.
6 For Henricus Glareanus, the preeminent Swiss humanist of the day, much admired by Erasmus, see Ep 440. His edition of the *Roman Antiquities* of Dionysius of Halicarnassus (*Dionysii Halicarnasei Antiquitatum sive originum Romanarum libri XI* [Basel: Froben and Episcopius 1532]) was dedicated to King Ferdinand. For its presentation to Ferdinand and Glareanus' reward, see Ep 2801 n1.
7 In 1529 Glareanus had settled in Freiburg, where he would remain for the rest of his life, and had received an appointment as professor of poetry.

afterwards from Rome (where it was first printed).[1] It is mere nonsense; I do not think it deserves any response.[2] I have more important things to do.

I had hoped that you would come, but it didn't work out. If everything 5 is going exactly as you want, I am immensely pleased.[3] Best wishes to you and to your dear ones.

Freiburg, the day after Corpus Christi

Today my Cacabus came to me,[4] saying that the person to whom you had ordered the letters to Alciati to be given was nowhere in the world to 10 be found. Wondering about this, I ordered him to show me your note to Cacabus. For 'Bernlardus' he had read 'Burcardus,[5] and for 'Melin,' 'Meliti.' I told him to go to the secretary of the city council and look for Bernardus Melin, and he was found.[6] It was really smart of you, to be sure, to commit anything to such a blockhead! That same Bernlardus has not changed his 15 plan but says that he will wait for Anton Bletz,[7] who will arrive (I imagine)

* * * * *

2652
1 The little book was *Antapologia pro Alberto pio comite Carpensi in Erasmum Roterodamum* of Juan Ginés de Sepúlveda. For Sepúlveda and the printings of his book, see Ep 2637 introduction and n1.
2 Erasmus did not publish a response, but he did send Sepúlveda a conciliatory reply to Ep 2637 (Ep 2701).
3 Bonifacius had turned down the flattering but unattractive offer of a professorship at Dole (Ep 2649:9–26), and now, following the death of Oecolampadius in November 1531, there was a respite in the official pressure on him in Basel to take communion according to the reformed rite; see Ep 2519 introduction.
4 The reference is to Erasmus' servant Jacobus (documented 1532–3), a somewhat disreputable character whom Erasmus eventually accused of theft. He is mentioned in Epp 2653:1, 2694:1, 2696:1–2, 2697:8–14, 2735:52–5, 2788:40–1. Here Erasmus transforms 'Jacobus' into 'Cacabus' ('Shittybus'); for 'Jaco' he substitutes 'Caca,' with its echo of the Greek κακός 'bad,' 'evil,' but more directly of the Latin verb *cacare* ('to shit'), the Dutch word *kak* 'shit,' and its German cognate *kacke*. He had done this to a number of other names as well; see Epp 2261 n30, 2441 n4, 2580 n2, and cf Ep 2408 n7.
5 Bonifacius must have written 'Bernhardo,' which to Erasmus looked like 'Bernlardo.' His deadpan reading of it that way even though he knew perfectly well that the reference was to someone named 'Bernardus' (see line 12) was probably his way of teasing Bonifacius for his dreadful handwriting.
6 He has not been identified. Alfred Hartmann offers no adequate documentation for his suggestion of Bernhard Rumelin (AK Epp 1651 n4, 1914).
7 The professional Swiss courier who regularly carried letters between Freiburg, Basel, and Paris (Ep 1784 n1).

at the Greek calends.[8] I added these things while the physician Albanus was waiting.[9] Farewell yet once more, my dearest friend.

To the most renowned gentleman Master Bonifacius Amerbach

2653 / From Bonifacius Amerbach   Basel, [early June 1532]

First published by Allen, this letter (= AK Ep 1657) is Bonifacius' reply to Ep 2652. The autograph is in the Öffentliche Bibliothek of the University of Basel (MS C VIa 73 10). Allen describes the letter as 'apparently not sent.' There is no address, and the verso was used for the rough drafts of other letters.

Cordial greetings. Thank you for instructing Jacobus when he was stuck by my writing.[1] It is nothing new for you to give evidence of your concern for me; since I have perceived how ready you are to help me in more important matters, why would you not also follow your usual bent in more trivial matters? And I am in your debt down to the last penny, and any time I can I will   5
respond as is my duty. You are right to scorn the trifles of those who speak ill of you.[2] Most of them seem to aspire to live in the highest infamy with posterity, seeking the petty sort of glory attained long ago by the one who set fire to the temple of Diana.[3] Anton Bletz recently said that he would come back here within a month and then would go straight to Paris.[4] If you want   10
to write something, get it ready in the meantime. Farewell, most eminent Erasmus. At Basel

* * * * *

8 Ie never
9 Albanus Torinus (Ep 2084 n1), who was evidently on a visit to Erasmus at Freiburg and carried this letter to Basel

2653
1 Reading 'in literis meis' as a reference to the letters of the alphabet rather than as a letter to someone. Jacobus (Ep 2652 n4) had been unable to decipher Bonifacius' handwriting; see Ep 2652:11–14.
2 Bonifacius uses a Greek word frequently found in the New Testament: *kakológon* 'speaking ill of.'
3 The temple of Diana (Artemis) at Ephesus was one of the wonders of the ancient world. In 346 BC, shortly after it had been completed, it was set on fire and destroyed by a young Ephesian named Herostratus, who was desperate to have his name go down in history. His fellow citizens were so shocked that they issued a decree imposing the death penalty on anyone who even mentioned his name.
4 See Ep 2652 n7.

2654 / From Johann von Vlatten   [Regensburg, c June 1532]

For Johann von Vlatten, chancellor of the duke of Jülich-Cleves, see Ep 1390.

This letter was first published by Allen. He listed as his manuscript source a rough draft in 'the Archives at Cologne, Harffer Archiv. I. Reichsangelegenheiten,' but Paul Oskar Kristeller found that no such volume existed in any archive at Cologne (*Renaissance News* 14 [1961] 17). Dr Hans-Werner Langbrandtner of the Vereinigte Adelsarchive im Rheinland has kindly informed us that the letter in question is in the private archive of the counts of Mirbach-Harff (accessible via the LVR-Archivberatung, Pulheim-Brauweiler): Bestand Vlatten, vol 20 ('Briefwechsel Johann von Vlatten ... in verschiedenen Reichsangelegenheiten, 1525–1562') page 1. Allen described the manuscript as 'full of perplexing corrections and alterations in the middle and at the end, making it not always easy to determine the writer's intention.' The apparatus of his text, however, gives no alternative readings. The approximate date is assigned on the basis of the reference (lines 7–8) to the proposed second edition of the *Apophthegmata* (Basel: Froben 1532). This means that the diet in question has to be that at Regensburg (17 April–27 July 1532), where Vlatten would have been present as a member of the delegation from Jülich-Cleves.

Greetings, Erasmus, most learned of all mortals. The reason the most excellent boy prince, etc, who is extremely fond of you, replied to you so late and did not send his thanks sooner was not any defect in his integrity or in your imperishable scholarship but rather a certain stupid negligence in those who have charge of him.[1] Nevertheless, if there was any fault in this delay, it can   5
be happily healed in the course of time.

The prince will be greatly pleased that you have enlarged your *Apophthegmata*.[2]

Whether we like it or not, those ferocious enemies of Christianity, the Turks, will put an end to our diets and endlessly prolonged deliberations.   10
The present evil must be countered by a present remedy, for what is needed to strike fear into such an enemy is arms, not deliberations. To protect Germany the emperor has promised 5,000 horsemen and 20,000 foot soldiers

* * * * *

2654
1 The prince was William V, son of John III, duke of Cleves (Ep 2189 introduction). The thanks owed were presumably for the first edition of the *Apophthegmata*, which had been dedicated to him (Ep 2431).
2 See Ep 2711.

from his own estates.³ The Germans have in fact provided the emperor
with 8,000 horsemen and 40,000 footsoldiers.⁴ I can hardly believe that the   15
Bohemians and the Austrians would fail to live up to their great valour.⁵ The
pope offers encouraging words.⁶ The French king denies us any sort of help
whatever.⁷ The English king has not yet decided what he is willing to pro-
vide.⁸ The voivode stirs up factions with amazing schemes,⁹ and it is thought
that the king of Poland will be the spectator at a miserable tragedy.¹⁰ The   20
religious business will be settled not by arms but by a general or a national
council. If the pope refuses to call a council, I hope that in a matter so sacrosanct and so utterly necessary the emperor will make use *ex officio* of his
extensive imperial authority.¹¹

* * * * *

3 In his effort to secure financial aid from the imperial diet for defence against the
   Turks, Charles v had offered to hire his own troops with subsidies voted by the
   estates of his hereditary lands outside the Holy Roman Empire. Most, if not all,
   of the money would have come from the estates of the Netherlands. The army
   thus raised (as distinct from the army of the Empire) included troops recruited
   in the Netherlands, Germany, Italy, and Spain, in approximately the numbers
   indicated here; see RTA 10/1 171–2.
4 'The Germans' means the imperial diet, which did indeed make this offer and
   refused to consider a higher figure; see RTA 10/1 457–60.
5 For the figures on the funds and troops raised in the Austrian hereditary lands,
   as well as in Bohemia, Moravia, Silesia, Hungary, Croatia, and Slovenia, see RTA
   10/1 172, 458 n2.
6 Clement VII in fact made good on a promise to contribute the cost of 10,000 Hungarian cavalrymen; see RTA 10/1 170.
7 Francis I made preparations to defend his own interests in Italy and in Lorraine
   but offered no help to Charles; see RTA 10/2 937:35–8.
8 In late August/early September, Charles v was still negotiating with Thomas
   Cranmer, Henry's ambassador at the imperial court, in an unsuccessful attempt
   to secure Henry's aid against the Turks; see RTA 10/1 155 n40.
9 John Zápolyai, voivode of Transylvania, Ferdinand of Austria's rival for the
   kingship of Hungary and ally of the Turks
10 Sigismund I
11 The imperial diet, which had a long history of airing its grievances against
   Rome, had since 1522 been calling for a general council or, failing that, a national council, to settle the religious divisions of Germany, and its members
   knew full well the historical precedents for an emperor's summoning a council
   against the will of the pope. It was a demand advanced by both the Catholic
   and the Protestant estates, though they had quite different ideas about how a
   council should be constituted and conducted. The emperor had several times
   (eg at the Diet of Augsburg in 1530) promised to secure from the pope the
   convocation of a general council 'within six months,' but Pope Clement VII,

2655 / From Bernhard von Cles   Regensburg, 5 June 1532

This letter, Cles' response to Ep 2651, was first published as Ep 172 in Förstemann / Günther. The manuscript, written and signed by a secretary, was in the Burscher Collection of the University Library at Leipzig (Ep 1254 introduction).

Venerable in Christ, eminent sir, sincerely beloved by us. Although we learned from your letter sent on Pentecost,[1] the last one that we have received, that you have reached an age when you are not able to undertake any function apart from your studies, nevertheless it seemed desirable for us to send you a letter and, putting side any possible scruples, to encourage you once more to 5 do what we recommended in our most recent letter,[2] because we think that there is no one, of any age whatever, who does not always have something that he can conveniently and honourably request. Thus if there is any request from his royal Majesty in which we can gratify you, you need do no more than ask us, and we will act in such a way that you will know how dear your 10 interests are to us.

There may indeed be no lack of schemers who set snares for you, but let this be your one and only solace: you have laid your foundations on rock and the hardest marble, and this solid foundation of yours will make all their attempts absolutely futile.[3] 15

Finally, we have read what you write about Henricus Glareanus, a most learned man; whether the work which he has recently revised has reached the hands of the king, for whom it was intended, we do not know;[4] but as soon as we have any certain knowledge about it, we will recommend (as you

* * * * *

fearing the diminution of papal authority, had withheld his cooperation. Emperor Charles was at this stage in his career reluctant to exert his independent authority in the matter. At the diet in Regensburg, he responded to the insistent demands of the estates for a council, national or general, with or without the pope, by agreeing once more to work with the pope to procure a council, but turned aside the demand to act independently if the pope did not cooperate. See RTA 10/1 392, 595, 597–600, 608–9.

2655
1 19 May
2 See Ep 2634:18–21.
3 Cf Matt 7:24–7.
4 The work in question was Glareanus' edition of Dionysius of Halicarnassus; see Ep 2651 n6.

wish) the work of this person to his Majesty, for his respectful consideration   20
as well as our own. By this letter we send you good wishes.

Regensburg, 5 June 1532

Bernhard, by the mercy of God, his most reverend Eminence, cardinal
and bishop of Trent

To the venerable in Christ Master Erasmus of Rotterdam, eminent gen-   25
tleman, sincerely beloved by us, professor of sacred theology. At Freiburg

2656 / From Jacopo Sadoleto   Carpentras, 7 June 1532

This letter was first published in the *Sadoleti epistolae* page 167. It supplements
the thanks already rendered in Ep 2648 for the edition of St Basil. In the interim,
however, Sadoleto had also received copies of other books by Erasmus, including the *Declarationes*; cf Ep 2648 introduction. The first paragraph of the letter is
an introduction for a person unnamed who has not been identified.

JACOPO SADOLETO, BISHOP OF CARPENTRAS, SENDS CORDIAL
GREETINGS TO ERASMUS OF ROTTERDAM

The man who has delivered this letter to you is certainly not well known to
me, and I have not examined his behaviour or character. But since he came to
me and said he was moved by your far-flung fame and a love, as it were, of   5
your renown, to travel to you in order to pursue genuine learning under such
a master, I could take no exception to such a determination; for it seemed to
me that he had set his mind on a splendid goal and a most outstanding teacher. Accordingly, when he asked me for a letter of recommendation, I was
glad to follow my usual practice in cultural matters like these, and I readily   10
granted his request. Thus I recommend him to you, with this proviso, that
when you yourself have reached a judgment about him and have decided to
accept him into your friendship, you then take him on and kindly welcome
him in such a way that, without any inconvenience to you, he himself might
gain some benefit from such high-minded enthusiasm.   15

As for me, two or three days after I wrote my last letter to you,[1] I received your little books, of which I have read a good part. I was especially
delighted by your refutation of those carping critics.[2] Your responses are per-
meated by remarkable learning and – what especially pleases me – moderation of spirit. For the Basil I thank you once more, over and over again,   20

* * * * *

2656
1 Ep 2648
2 *Declarationes ad censuras Lutetiae vulgatas* (Ep 2552 n10)

because you have deigned to include me in the number of those whom you have been willing to honour in the monuments of your genius. And if you have not been repaid with a matching effort on my part, certainly my wishes for you are equal to those extraordinary wishes of yours for me.

Farewell, my dear Erasmus, and give my greetings to our friend 25 Amerbach. Once again farewell.

Carpentras, 7 June 1532

2657 / From Viglius Zuichemus   Padua, 8 June 1532

This letter was first published in Van Heussen page 112, and subsequently as Ep 30 in vze. For Viglius Zuichemus, at this time lecturing on civil law at Padua, see Ep 2101. His most recent letter to Erasmus was Ep 2632. Erasmus' response to it and to this one is Ep 2682.

TO ERASMUS OF ROTTERDAM

When I went to Venice for the Ascension of the Lord, which (as you know) is celebrated solemnly there,[1] Ephorinus most opportunely arrived there with your letter to me.[2] At the same moment I also received a second one via Giambattista Egnazio,[3] to which you merely added a note saying that 5 you were sending once more a letter you had previously sent via a certain Cyprius. But Cyprius never showed up here,[4] and Egnazio said that the letter

* * * * *

2657
1 From the year 1000 the feast of the Ascension has been a special holiday in Venice. It began as a commemoration of the Venetian conquest of Dalmatia and featured a procession of boats into the Adriatic, with prayers that it would remain calm and quiet for all those who sailed upon it. In 1177, Pope Alexander III, grateful for Venetian help in his conflict with Emperor Frederick I, participated in the procession, giving the doge a ring to be cast into the sea as a token of the marriage between the republic and the sea, and bidding him do the same each year. The ceremony continues to this day, on a smaller scale, and with the mayor replacing the doge.
2 Ep 2604. For Anselmus Ephorinus and his arrival in Venice at this time, see Ep 2539 introduction.
3 The second letter was a copy of Ep 2604. For Egnazio, Venetian humanist and longtime friend of Erasmus see Ep 2105 introduction.
4 Petrus Cyprius is known only as the 'young man of sound judgment' who had stayed with Erasmus for several months before setting out by 10 March 1532 for Italy, carrying a copy of Ep 2604, the original of which Erasmus feared had gone astray; see Allen Ep 2604 introduction. Cyprius is mentioned again in Allen Ep 2871:20.

had been delivered to him by a servant of Bebel.[5] In any case, I had answered the first letter long ago.[6] Since, however, I could not enjoy you in person, I was delighted to have Ephorinus in your stead, and was also very grateful to you because through your letter you prepared the way for my acquaintance with him. For my part I will do everything I can to cultivate that acquaintance. I have taken Ephorinus to Padua and thus far have offered him every service I can. And indeed I shall attach myself to him all the more closely because he seems to agree with me in my affection and sincere regard for you. Hence my spirits are frequently lifted by his references to you.

Your guess about that German was not wide of the mark.[7] It is not at all surprising that we do not get along, since he cannot control himself even with Anselmus, who shares the same native land with him and whose judgment he ought to value more than mine. I recently laid down the conditions under which I would get along with him. So far he has somehow managed to comply with them in my presence and has abstained from recriminations. Recently I goaded him a bit by showing him your dedicatory letter to Bishop Thurzo for the commentary on Psalm 38.[8] For he has long been supported by the bishop's beneficence, and even now he asks the bishop for travelling money every year. His opinion about the Italians is so deeply implanted that it cannot be uprooted: he always wants them to be thought incomparable. When others are present I keep my opinion to myself; and they do not dare to say what they really think, and tend to rely on him as the final authority.

I recently promised you something about the Amphitheatre, and now at long last I could write you about it at length, except that I am afraid to offend your serious ears with such trifles.[9] To keep you up to date, your Viglius also visited the Amphitheatre and inspected everything carefully. It is a wooden construction adorned with many images and outfitted on all sides with many boxes. It also has many sections and levels. The builder has put each of the figures and ornaments into its proper place, and he showed me such a huge mass of written sheets that, even though I had always heard that Cicero was the most ample fountain of eloquence, nevertheless till then I could never have

* * * * *

5 From letters of Bonifacius Amerbach to Ephorinus and Viglius we know that Johann Bebel, the Basel publisher, had made a trip to Italy at about this time; see AK Epp 1652–3, both dated '[May/June 1532].'
6 With Ep 2632
7 'That German' was Georg von Logau, native of Silesia, ardent Ciceronian, and critic of Erasmus; see Ep 2568:14–23 with n4.
8 Ep 2608, to Stanislaus Thurzo, bishop of Olomouc in Moravia, Logau's patron
9 For the strange project of the 'theatre of memory,' see Ep 2632:160–83 with n20.

been brought to believe that one author covered such a vast domain or that
such a great number of volumes could be stitched together from him. I wrote   40
you the name of the builder; he is called Giulio Camillo.[10] He stammers badly
and can hardly speak Latin, giving the excuse that by perpetually occupying
himself with writing he almost lost the ability to speak it. He is said to have
some proficiency in the vernacular, which he is reported to have taught pro-
fessionally for some time at Bologna. When I asked about the method of the   45
work, its purpose and actual success, as if I were filled with religious awe by
such a miraculous phenomenon, he exhibited some pages and recited from
them so as to express all the rhythms, the metrical endings, and the entire
ingenuity of it in the Italian manner, but wholly inadequately because of his
language impediment. The king is said to have urged him to come back to   50
France, bringing his magnificent contraption with him.[11] But since according
to the king's command all the Latin had to be translated into French, he hired
a translator and an amanuensis for that purpose, and he was forced to put
off his departure in order to keep from displaying his work half finished. The
maker of this theatre calls it by many names: sometimes a man-made mind   55
and spirit, sometimes a mind equipped with windows. For he imagines that
everything that can be conceived by the human mind but that we cannot see
with our bodily eyes can nevertheless be woven together by careful thought
and then expressed in certain bodily signs so that everyone can immediately
perceive with their eyes what is otherwise sunken in the depths of the human   60
mind. And because of this corporeal viewing he called it a theatre.

When I asked him whether he had written anything in defence of his
opinion, since many nowadays reject this enthusiasm for imitating Cicero, he
replied to this effect: that he himself had written a good deal but that none
of it had yet been published except a few things in Italian,[12] at the request of   65
the king. But he is of a mind to publish his own opinion on the subject whenever he gets some free time and has completed the work to which he has
entirely devoted himself,[13] and on which he himself has spent, as he claims,
1,500 ducats, while the king has still only donated 500 ducats; but he still

* * * * *

10 Another ardent Ciceronian; see Ep 2632 n17.
11 Francis I, to whom Camillo had explained his project, had taken interest and
   given Camillo 500 gold ducats in anticipation of the delivery of the amphitheatre; see Ep 2632:175–7, and cf lines 67–9 below.
12 Camillo's *Trattato della imitatione*, a polite criticism of Erasmus' *Ciceronianus*,
   was not published until after Camillo's death, and only in incomplete form; see
   Ep 2632 n18.
13 Ie the amphitheatre

expects ample contributions from the king when he becomes aware of the   70
benefits of the work.

I cannot get as well acquainted with Bembo as I would like,[14] for I do
not yet know Italian well enough, and he is not very willing to use Latin.[15]
Whenever I meet him I get an interpreter or I follow like a shadow someone who can speak to him in Italian. He does not get along very well with   75
Egnazio. I do not know the reason for their disagreement, but Bembo is very
careful to deny any blame for it. Recently however, I came to understand the
reason for the disagreement quite well. For Alciati recently wrote to me that
the plague had broken out again in Bourges and that he was looking for a
position somewhere else. Since he especially wanted to go to Padua,[16] I asked   80
some people, and among them Bembo, to help him achieve his goal by writing to Venice, to those who are in charge of hiring at the university, and also
by urging Egnazio to help, since he was the one especially singled out for the
task by Alciati himself. Bembo offered to help in all other ways, but he said
he could not write to Egnazio, excusing himself by asserting that Egnazio   85
hated him. And he advised me, if I wanted to do any good for Alciati, to say
nothing to Egnazio.

Sucket wrote to you the same thing he has already often written to me
from Turin, where everything has gone so well for him that no letter from me
could get him to come here.[17] Lazzaro Bonamico is thinking of going back to   90
Bologna,[18] I imagine because the son of Cardinal Campeggi, whom Bonamico
privately tutored here, has become the bishop of Bologna.[19] Moreover, some
of Bonamico's students have tried very hard to get a position for him, to

* * * * *

14 After his arrival in Padua, Viglius had made the acquaintance of the great
   humanist Pietro Bembo and visited him a few times; see Ep 2594:44–6.
15 After receiving this letter, Erasmus wrote to Bembo recommending Viglius to
   him (Ep 2681).
16 Andrea Alciati (Ep 1250 introduction), with whom Viglius had studied law at
   Avignon and Bourges, would return to Italy in 1533, but to Pavia, not to Padua.
17 Viglius' friend from their time together as students of Alciati, Karel Sucket (Ep
   2191) had been appointed to a lectureship in law at Turin, where he flourished
   until his unexpected death in November 1532. Cf Epp 2682:60–2, 2700:163–5,
   2753:26–30.
18 The eminent Ciceronian Lazzaro Bonamico of Bassano (Ep1720 n10) had been
   lecturer in Latin and Greek at the University of Padua since September 1530.
19 Alessandro Campeggi (1504–1554), son of Lorenzo Campeggi, was elected
   bishop of Bologna in 1526 as replacement for his father, who continued to ad-
   minister the diocese until 1541, by which time Alessandro was old enough to
   receive holy orders and be consecrated as bishop.

replace Romolo Amaseo,[20] and because Amaseo refuses to resign, some of
Bonamico's young students are being instigated to intercede for him with the   95
prefect at Bologna.[21] And so we expect more Longolian activity.[22] Farewell,
best and greatest of masters.

Padua, 8 June 1532

2658 / From Jan Boner   Padua, 8 June 1532

> This letter was first published as Ep 173 in Förstemann / Günther. The manu-
> script, apparently autograph, was in the Burscher Collection of the University
> Library at Leipzig (Ep 1254 introduction).
>
> For Jan Boner, the Polish youth who with his tutor Anselmus Ephorinus
> and his companion Stanisław Aichler had paid an extended visit to Erasmus at
> Freiburg on the way to Italy, see Epp 2533, 2539 introductions.

Greetings to you, sir, most learned beyond all others known to world. My
tutor and I do not wish to seem ungrateful. We often planned to send you
greetings in a letter, which you would have deigned to receive with favour
even though it would have been far removed from the Muses and unworthy of such a great personage. I have nothing to write except to give you   5
immense and undying thanks for your recommendations to learned men
everywhere on our behalf, which have been of great service to us. For when
I showed Fugger your letter,[1] he immediately embraced us most heartily,
spoke to us with a kindness that could not be surpassed, and showed us all
the rooms in his house, including the ones he has prepared for you, which   10
are certainly very elegant and in my judgment very comfortable. He desires
nothing more than your actual presence.[2] Master Koler honoured us in every

* * * * *

20 Romolo Quirino Amaseo of Udine (1489–1552), was appointed lecturer in Latin
   and Greek at the University of Bologna, a position he held until 1544.
21 It is not clear what 'prefect' (*praefectus*) means here. Appointment to the university was in the hands of the city council.
22 Ie more advocacy of Ciceronian purity, as advocated by Christophe de Longueil
   (Longolius), the initial target of Erasmus' *Ciceronianus*; see Ep 1948 introduction.

2658
1 Erasmus' letter of introduction, not extant, to the Augsburg banker Anton
   Fugger
2 Fugger had repeatedly invited Erasmus to settle in Augsburg at his expense;
   see Epp 2525, 2561:15–17.

way that he could.³ Master Viglius received us most kindly,⁴ but he couldn't
give us lodging in his own house. Nevertheless we were hospitably taken
in by some learned and honourable men, Germans and Dutchmen, all of   15
whom are your fervent admirers. Stanisław sends his most fervent greet-
ings.⁵ Farewell, and do not cease to embrace me, together with Anselm, with
your customary affection.

Padua, 8 June 1532
Your most entirely devoted servant, Jan Boner   20
To the most renowned and learned gentleman Master Erasmus of
Rotterdam, foremost among theologians, his teacher most cherished in every
way. At Freiburg im Breisgau.

2659 / From Thomas More   Chelsea, 14 June 1532

This letter was first published in the epistolary appendix to *De praeparatione ad
mortem* (Basel: Froben 1534) 103–8. It was written in the wake of More's resignation as lord chancellor of England (16 May 1532). In Ep 2750:13–14, Erasmus
reports that the letter, having been 'held up in Saxony,' took several months to
reach him.

THOMAS MORE SENDS GREETINGS TO ERASMUS OF ROTTERDAM
There is something, most dear Erasmus, that I have desired from my childhood to this very day, to wit: that what I am glad has always been your lot
I might also be glad one day to have for myself, namely, to be free of public
duties and to be able to have time to live only for God and for myself. Now fi- 5
nally, Erasmus, through the kindness of God, in his goodness and power, and
through the beneficence of a most indulgent prince, I have achieved it at last.
But I have nevertheless not achieved it exactly as I wanted it. It had been my
wish, in the final period of my life,¹ during whatever years were left to me, to
be hale and hearty, at least as free of sickness and pain as is compatible with 10

* * * * *

3 Johann Koler, canon of St Moritz in Augsburg (Ep 2195 introduction)
4 In Venice, whence he took them with him back to Padua; see Ep 2657:12–13.
5 Stanisław Aichler, Jan's companion on his journey from Poland to Italy and
  back (Ep 2545).

2659
1 More writes *vitae colophonem* 'the colophon of my life,' an allusion to *Adagia* II
  iii 45, *Colophonem addidit* 'He added the colophon,' ie he added the 'finishing
  touch' to something, or 'set a cap or a crown on something.'

old age. Now however, whether I shall one day be granted that wish, which is perhaps too presumptuous, is in the hands of God. But in the meantime I had some malady in my chest. I am not so much afflicted by the perception and pain of it as I am concerned by uncertainty and fear of the outcome. When this illness had continued to afflict me unchanged for several months, 15 I consulted the physicians, who replied that the persistence of maladies is dangerous and claimed that it was not possible to effect a quick cure in this case. It would have to be remedied gradually, over a period of time, by diet, medications, and rest; and they would not predict any end to the treatment nor even give any certain prognosis of its cure.   20

And so, turning these things over in my mind, when I saw that I would either have to give up my office or be deficient in fulfilling it, and when I realized that I could not perform the tasks demanded without being in danger of death and that if I were to die I would have to abandon my position and my life at the same time, I finally decided that it was better to renounce the 25 office than to give up both life and office together.[2] And so, in order to take into account both my public duties and my health, I made humble entreaty and obtained my petition through the kindness of my renowned and generous prince, who mercifully deigned to accept my resignation from a burdensome office, which is (as you know) the highest in our land, with which he 30 had honoured me through his incredible generosity, an office as far beyond my merits as it was beyond what I hoped for or wished to have. Therefore I beg all the saints above and God, who alone has the power, to grant suitable recompense for this most fond indulgence of my renowned sovereign. And I pray that God will keep me from spending the time I have left in an inert 35 and indolent idleness and will grant me not only the mental resolve but also the physical strength to spend my hours well. For when I am in poor health I cannot do anything at all – such is my indolence.

* * * * *

2 More had in fact resigned in direct consequence of the Submission of the Clergy (15 May 1532), ie the surrender of the clergy in Convocation to King Henry's demand that henceforth no Convocation be assembled except by royal writ, that no canons be enacted without royal assent, and that all existing canons be examined by a royal commission, half the members of which would be lay and half clerical. It marked the end of the legislative independence of the clergy and was a major step towards the formal proclamation of royal supremacy in 1534, something that More could not in good conscience support. For the time being, however, there still remained something of the old cordiality between Henry and More. See J.J. Scarisbrick *Henry* viii (Berkeley and Los Angeles 1968) 297–300.

Moreover, my dear Erasmus, we are not all Erasmuses, nor would it be fitting for all of us to expect what God has graciously granted to you almost alone among mortals. For who else besides you would dare to promise what you perform? In the face of the growing burdens of old age, afflicted with ailments that would wear down and crush even a healthy young man, you have for many years never ceased to give a good account of all your time by constantly publishing outstanding books to the whole world, as if the weight of advancing age or bad health robbed you of nothing. While this seems miraculous to anyone who considers it, it is to their amazement doubly miraculous that the carping critics who have sprung up everywhere against you – who might overcome even the courage of a Hercules – do not deter you in any way from writing. Such enemies are continually stirred up by envy of your incomparable talent and your learning, which surpasses even so great a talent. For they easily see that they will never be able to rise to the level of your natural endowments and your industry. In their inflated pride, almost ready to burst, they cannot bear that they should sink so low beneath you; so they conspire together, each scheming as best he can, to turn your glory to their inglorious advantage by unceasing slander.

But while they roll their Sisyphean stones year after year,[3] what do they finally accomplish by this vain and nefarious labour except to have the stone always fall back on their heads while you emerge ever more exalted and illustrious? For if at times there should be something that disturbs some people who are neither evil-minded nor unlearned, something that they perhaps might have wished you had treated in a more temperate style, why make so much of it? For this sort of thing happens to every writer; and they themselves, while they were finding fault with you, could also have done so more temperately, so as to avoid committing the same fault and doing so more flagrantly than becomes men of their status and more frequently than should be done in any sort of book whatever. In this matter it is harder to forgive them, because they cannot be unaware that you yourself quite openly confess that you treated some subjects in this way before the emergence of these pestilential heresies which, creating havoc everywhere, destroy everything; and that if you could have guessed that such enemies and betrayers of religion would ever appear, you would have treated these subjects more gently

* * * * *

3 In Greek mythology, Sisyphus, king of Ephyra, was punished for a lifetime of deceit and trickery by being forced to spend eternity pushing a huge stone up a hill only to watch it roll back down again. 'Sisyphean labour' and 'to roll stones' became proverbial for exhausting and useless toil (cf *Adagia* II iv 40).

and temperately; what incited you to be so forceful was that certain vices of
some people were being embraced as virtues.[4] If someone wants to make this
courage of yours into a vice, he will surely have to sweat profusely before   75
he can find a way to justify all the ancient Doctors of the church. Certainly I
have no doubt that if they had seen our times as well as they saw their own,
they would all have presented some things to their own times more cautiously and more clearly. But since they did not do this, precisely because they
were remedying the evils of their own age, future evils did not occur to their   80
minds; the same thing for which these calumniators now reproach you happened to them, namely, that heretics who sprang up later boasted that they
had derived certain things from their writings. This you have in common not
only with those holy Fathers and defenders of the true faith, but also with
the apostles and evangelists themselves, and even with our Saviour himself;   85
for it is principally, indeed almost solely, from their words that all heretics
attempt to establish their false doctrines.

And so, my dear Erasmus, go on with your good work, but if occasionally something you have written troubles or bothers some good person, even
if his feelings are groundless, do not be averse to adapting some things to   90
his devout feelings. Otherwise pay no attention to the yapping and yowl-
ing of malevolent enemies. Proceed calmly, do not be held back at all. Go on
advancing studies and promoting virtues.

Concerning the man whom you recommended to me very circumspect-
ly and politely, in view of his literary attainments, though not of his religious   95
views,[5] I have been advised by friends to make sure that he not make a fool
of me.[6] Indeed I will take care of that as well as I can. For I am not unaware
how dangerous it is to admit these new erroneous sects. Even though they
have thus far been diligently suppressed here, by the care of the bishops
and the authority of the prince, it is still amazing how they try to insinuate   100
themselves, at first by crafty tricks, and then stubbornly strive to break in.
One or two of them here never cease to introduce into our country all sorts
of heresies from Belgium (to which they withdraw, as if to a safe harbour) by

* * * * *

4 See Ep 1887:1111–15; 2312A:306–12.
5 Simon Grynaeus (Epp 1657, 2433), a partisan of Zwingli and Oecolampadius,
   had visited England in the spring of 1531, carrying letters of introduction from
   Erasmus (Epp 2459–60; cf Ep 2487 n9). Cf Allen Ep 2878:21–2, where Erasmus
   reports that he had intervened to prevent Grynaeus from dedicating his edition
   of Plato to More.
6 Literally 'not smear my face,' ie '[not] give [me] empty words and make a fool
   of [me] by some form of trickery' (*Adagia* I v 48)

translating Scripture badly and interpreting it even worse in books written in our language.[7] I myself have responded to many of them in such a way 105 that I have no fear about someone who has read both them and me carefully,[8] except that some people read new things out of fickleness and pernicious things out of malice, not because they believe that what they are reading is true but because they wish it were true. But that sort of people, who are passionately inclined to be evil, you will never satisfy with any reasoning. My 110 aim is to protect as best I can those who do not depart from the truth on their own but are led astray by the seductive fallacies of clever men. Farewell, most learned Erasmus, champion of good studies.

From my manor house at Chelsea. 14 June in the year of our Lord 1532

2660 / From Gabriel Verinus
16 June [1532]

> This letter was first published as Ep 102 in Enthoven. The autograph is in the Rehdiger Collection of the University Library at Wrocław (MS Rehd 254 158). The year-date is confirmed by the reference in lines 44–6 to the *Declarationes*. Nothing is known of Gabriel Verinus other than that he wrote this letter, which indicates (lines 50-2) that he was perhaps in the service of Cardinal Campeggi.

* * * * *

7 This is clearly a reference to the reformer William Tyndale (1494?–1536). Rebuffed in his request for episcopal approval to translate the Bible into English, he went to the continent, going first for a time to Wittenberg. By 1525 he had translated the New Testament from the Greek, using Erasmus' text. After securing its publication at Worms in 1526, Tyndale found refuge in the community of English cloth merchants at Antwerp, where several of his theological and polemical works, as well as the first instalment of his translation of the Old Testament, were published in the period 1527–31. Rejecting attempts to call him back to England to place his literary skills in the service of Henry VIII, Tyndale remained in the Low Countries, where he was betrayed to the authorities, found guilty of heresy, and burned at the stake near Brussels in 1536. See the article on Tyndale by Donald Dean Smeeton in OER IV 189–91.
8 In 1528 Cuthbert Tunstall, bishop of London and More's friend, commissioned him to undertake the refutation of heretical books published in English. Tyndale was the principal target of this effort, though by no means the only one. The *Dialogue concerning Heresies*, More's million-word denunciation of Tyndale's Lutheran doctrines and his translation of the New Testament, was published in June 1529 (second edition May 1531). In 1532–3 More responded to Tyndale's *Answer to Thomas More's Dialogue* (1531) in a two-part *Confutation of Tyndale's Answer*. For these works and the others that made More the chief defender in England of the traditional church and faith, see the article on More by J.B. Trapp in OER III 88–91.

If this is the case, it is possible that Verinus and Erasmus met at some point during Campeggi's legations in Germany (1524–5, 1530–2). Lines 52–4 indicate that Verinus had earlier written to Erasmus without receiving a reply. If Erasmus wrote a reply to this tactless, pretentious, and badly written letter, it did not survive.

GABRIEL VERINUS SENDS GREETINGS TO HIS FRIEND ERASMUS

To what lengths will the fight go on with bitter hatred, my dear Erasmus? Will there never be an end to these quarrels? When I was thinking about peace, the university suddenly attacks from the rear, from the front, from both sides, under the name of a faculty, but not a faculty of eloquent dis- 5
course – from which it is as far removed as Erasmus is from their distorted slander. You have France as a fierce enemy who has discovered a poulterer,[1] that Delian one, who knows how to identify eggs.[2] But apart from some little barbed sophistries – for that is what his petty conclusions should be called – he has not a grain of salt, that is of modesty, which was always the seasoning 10
of piety, the sister of charity, in which he could be your equal, or better, your superior if he had chosen to contend with you in private writings instead of assaulting you with slanders, especially as one who is absent, who should never be convicted of a crime.[3]

But the university looked askance, and when it sees things it does not 15
like (which should be attributed to the times, not to you) it thought they were heresies. Nothing is wrong with their eyes: if they had not looked sideways they would have seen Erasmus, not the Beguards,[4] who very clearly deserve

* * * * *

2660
1 There is a play on words here that cannot be duplicated in English: *Gallia* (France), and *gallinarius* (a poulterer).
2 See Cicero *Academic Questions* 2.18.58 and 2.26.86, where Cicero observes that although it is proverbial that every egg is like every other, 'we are told that at Delos (when it was a flourishing island) there were many people who used to keep large numbers of hens for the sake of profit; and that they, when they had looked upon an egg, could tell which hen had laid it.' A Delian poulterer was thus someone who could make fine distinctions, or see differences where there were none.
3 The reference is clearly to Noël Béda and the publication of the Paris faculty's *Censurae* against Erasmus; see Ep 2552 n10.
4 At several places in the *Declarationes* Erasmus had to defend himself against the charge of the Paris theologians that he was in agreement with the heretical Beguards (CWE 82 106 n364), particularly with their claim that 'ecclesiastical laws do not need to be observed by the perfect.' See CWE 82 106–8, 133 n480, 183–4, 230, 281–2, 321, 323.

to be sown up in a thousand sacks.[5] You had forseen these accusations long
ago, as through a fog. Christian hope, which can have no fear, had sharpened   20
the perception of your mind. Now this fog has dispersed. Hence those who
fear everything and reject such hope as yours are astounded by your moderation and patience.

I might have wished that you had more leisure for such writings, for I
would value your leisure far more than the activities of the theologians.[6] But   25
for a wise man can anything not be incomplete that can still be corrected?[7]
Everyone can make mistakes, but no one except a fool persists in his error.
Afterthoughts, as they say, are usually wiser.[8] If our hope has gone astray, the
best haven for hope is to change plans. And we read that Augustine, even
when he had held some opinion for many years, changed his mind when he   30
saw it was wrong.[9] In this way you would free yourself from invidious attacks and me from the fear that this warfare would issue in Erasmus' going
from our side to that of Luther, which is perhaps what they have wished.
And even the overly fearful would have had no fear of you as an enemy if
you had fought on their side.   35

Furthermore, anyone who has great insight into these studies would
be angry at Budé, foremost of the French,[10] since in his annotations on the
Pandects he denies that Jerome is the translator of the New Testament as we
have it.[11] Oh, if only these fine minds would at last skulk in the safety of their
colleges! But if they read in Jerome's preface to Matthew that John's break-   40
through to the Word of God was not so much a felicitous as an audacious

* * * * *

5 Sewn in a sack and thrown in the river, a punishment that, according to Cicero
   (*Pro Roscio* 11.70), was imposed by the Romans and the Athenians on those
   guilty of particularly horrendous crimes like parricide
6 The Latin plays on the usual contrast between *otium* (withdrawal from business, leisure) and *negotium* (business, work, labour).
7 The Latin of this sentence is oracular.
8 *Adagia* I iii 38
9 A reference to Augustine's *Retractationes*, which, as Erasmus was wont to insist,
   were not 'retractions' at all but 'reconsiderations'; see Epp 2424 n31, 2466:206–
   17, 2690:17–20.
10 The text says 'Budé *and* the foremost of the French.' The 'and' is clearly a
    blunder.
11 Allen cites a 1551 edition of Budé's *Annotationes in XXIIII Pandectas* (Lyon:
    Gryphius) 150. Budé was perfectly correct to say that Jerome was not the trans-
    lator of the Vulgate New Testament. Jerome revised the Old Latin version of the
    Gospels but Acts, the Epistles, and Revelation all remained in the older version.

temerity,[12] they could not pardon Jerome for connecting the words reckless and audacious with the gospel.

Enough on these matters. But since the book in which you cleverly re-   45
spond to the academic questions[13] is so brilliant that it ought to be memo-
rized word for word,[14] I incorporate the entire discussion into a dialogue, so
as to preserve your ability to speak. You will fight with the university in the
person of Eloquence, and Jerome, whom you have always enthusiastically
praised, will be the third speaker in the interchange. If this labour comes
to a good birth, that is, if it deserves to be read, I will dedicate it to Lorenzo   50
Campeggi, an enthusiastic supporter of yours, to whom I am completely devoted. The letter that I wrote to you a while ago I am now sending to him.[15]
Since I do not know if it was ever delivered to you, I am begging him to take
care that it is properly carried to you, so as to elicit a letter from you.

Farewell. 16 June [1532]   55

To Desiderius of Rotterdam, either the Cicero or the Erasmus of our
times, at Freiburg, or wherever he may be

2661 / To Bertram von Damm   [Freiburg, c 17 June 1532]

This letter was first published in the *Epistolae palaeonaeoi*. The date is supplied
by that of the letter of introduction to Bonifacius Amerbach that Udalricus
Zasius provided to Damm at the end of his visit to Freiburg: AK Ep 1658 (to
Bonifacius Amerbach, 17 June 1532).

In 1513 Bertram von Damm (d 1542) of Braunschweig matriculated at Erfurt,
where he became a friend of Helius Eobanus Hessus (Epp 874, 2446) and won
his first recognition as a poet. Attracted to the cause of Luther, he moved to
Wittenberg, where he matriculated in January 1521. By 1523 he had returned to
Braunschweig and was a practising physician. In 1532, shortly before this letter

* * * * *

12 What Jerome actually says in the preface to his Commentary on Matthew is that
   the apostle John 'was compelled by nearly all the bishops of Asia to write more
   profoundly about the divinity of the Saviour and to break through, so to speak,
   to the very Word of God, through a temerity that was not so much audacious as
   felicitous' (PL 26 19A).
13 Throughout the letter Verinus' word for 'University [of Paris]' is *Academia*,
   which allows him to characterize the questions raised by the faculty of theology
   in their censure of Erasmus as *academicae quaestiones*, a clear (if not particularly
   apt) allusion to Cicero's treatise of that name; cf n2 above.
14 Ie the *Declarationes*
15 The letter is not extant.

was written, he visited Freiburg hoping to see Erasmus, who, however, dismissed him abruptly. Leaving behind a poem that he had composed in praise of Erasmus, Damm proceeded to Basel, carrying the letter of introduction mentioned above. After his return to Braunschweig via the Netherlands, where he published at Louvain a verse paraphrase of the Epistle to Titus (1533), Damm produced his major work, a translation into 'heroic verse' of St Paul's Epistle to the Romans, published as the addendum to a reprint of Melanchthon's *Dispositio orationis in epistola ad Romanos* ([Schwäbisch Hall: Peter Braubach] 1539).

ERASMUS OF ROTTERDAM TO THE MOST ACCOMPLISHED YOUNG
MAN BERTRAM VON DAMM, GREETINGS
I have not yet decided, my dearest Bertram, whether I ought to be more displeased by your immoderate modesty, which made you into someone of less rank and ability than you really are, or by my thoughtlessness, which caused 5
me to be so distracted with other cares that I perceived too late what a treasure had been offered to me. But at last I beheld in your poem the whole Bertram as if imaged in a mirror, which afforded me much pleasure of mind.[1]
For it reveals you as sober and sensible, displaying a certain charming modesty, a rare quality among the learned and an even rarer one among men of 10
noble rank.[2] My only fear is that in your country it will be read, not without some disgrace to me, that my hospitality is praised to the skies for having admitted a man like you, who had made such a long journey to see me, to no more than a brief conversation, whereas I invited the Cyclops to my table for so many days.[3] Heavens above, what a benefit I lost, either because of your 15
modesty or my negligence! But if you should ever have occasion to sojourn here, be assured that this house, and the master of this house, are completely and rightfully at your disposal. If, on the other hand, your affairs call you elsewhere, Bertram will occupy a special place among those for whom I have true affection and exceptional esteem. Farewell. 20

I fear that we have had opposite experiences: you found coals instead of a treasure,[4] while I, thinking I had found coals, lost a treasure.

* * * * *

2661
1 The poem was never published.
2 The 'von' in Damm's name is a sign of noble birth. The same qualities of good sense and modesty are praised in lines 17–22 of Zasius' letter of introduction to Bonifacius (see introduction above).
3 'Cyclops' was Erasmus' favourite epithet for Felix Rex, known as Polyphemus (Ep 2649 n3), who had visited him recently.
4 *Adagia* I ix 30

2662 / From Polidoro Virgilio   London, 19 June 1532

This letter was first published as LB III/2 1752 *Appendix epistolarum* no 367. The autograph is in the Rehdiger Collection of the University Library at Wrocław. For Virgilio, Italian diplomat and historian in the service of Henry VIII, see Ep 1175 introduction.

Cordial greetings. Since I have found this man, who says he will be going to you, I wanted to greet you in a letter even though he allows me no time to write. Your defence against the Parisian scoundrels has arrived here among us.[1] Good God, how everyone is moved to laughter by the folly of those doctors without doctrine, who so cleverly dared to find a knot in a rush.[2] You should therefore be glad that you have found a safe harbour, for these dogs would bite if they could.

We are doing well. Our friend Master More recently resigned the high office he held, so that he could find some relief and spend his old age more peacefully.[3] Bebel was recently here among us;[4] he took care of my business energetically.[5] I have given him instructions about my affairs and my recall to Italy; hence, as I have written you so often, I will finally have occasion to see you. But I am deliberately putting that off, since Erasmus will not journey to the Elysian Fields until he has seen his Polidoro.[6] Farewell.

London, 19 June 1532

Your Polidoro

† To Master Desiderius Erasmus, a most learned gentleman and a highly respected friend

* * * * *

2662
1 *Declarationes ad censuras Lutetiae vulgatas* (Ep 2552 n10)
2 To 'seek a knot in a rush' is to find fault where there is none, or to quibble over words; see *Adagia* II iv 76.
3 See Ep 2659.
4 On 3 May, Erasmus was expecting Bebel's return from England; see Ep 2644:4.
5 In 1532 Bebel, who had already published Polidoro's *De prodigiis* in 1531, published a new edition of his *De inventoribus* and the third edition of his *Adagia*. In 1534 Bebel would publish the first edition of the work for which Polidoro is best remembered, the *Anglica historia*.
6 Polidoro drew up his will at Urbino, his birthplace, in 1534. So it is possible, though unconfirmed, that he visited Bebel at Basel and Erasmus at Freiburg on the way to Italy or back to England.

2663 / To Wilhelm von Isenburg   Freiburg, 22 June 1532

This letter was first published in the *Epistolae palaeonaeoi*.

Wilhelm, count of Isenburg and Grenzau (documented c 1470–1532), belonged to an old noble family in the area of the middle Rhine. By 1491 he had joined the order of the Teutonic Knights in Prussia, and over the years repeatedly held high office in the order, represented it on diplomatic missions, and led attempts to reorganize it. In 1519 he visited Luther at Wittenberg, and during the next decade, while in command of the order's Bailiwick of Koblenz and residing in Cologne, he wrote a series of pamphlets and books in German on justification and related topics. Though he refused to leave the Catholic church, he advocated a doctrine of justification by faith alone that was indistinguishable from that of Luther. This earned him denunciation as a heretic by Catholic controversialists like the Dominican Jacob of Hoogstraten, inquisitor of Cologne. In 1529 the city council of Cologne, eager to calm the storm of controversy, respectfully asked Isenburg to desist from further public statements on religious matters. This letter to Erasmus is the last appearance of Isenburg's name in the historical record.

ERASMUS OF ROTTERDAM SENDS GREETINGS TO THE MOST
RENOWNED GENTLEMAN LORD WILHELM, COUNT OF ISENBURG,
OF THE ORDER OF THE TEUTONIC KNIGHTS

Illustrious sir, no less famous for your piety than for your family tree, Polyphemus delivered to me the very elegant dagger you sent me, with the   5
inscription that 'If I were not able to repel my enemies with the pen I would do so with the sword.'[1] I was pleased to recognize your courteous manners, which I have experienced once or twice here in conversation.[2] Peter had two swords, and Christ thought they were sufficient.[3] But against the ranks recruited on all sides against Erasmus the armies of the emperor would hardly   10
suffice. I am like the ass in the old proverb who has fallen among bees,[4] or

* * * * *

2663
1 No such dagger is listed in the inventory of Erasmus' possessions.
2 The language here implies that Erasmus and Isenburg had actually met and talked to one another in Freiburg. There is, however, no other evidence that such a thing ever happened. It may be only that Erasmus had heard reports of Isenburg's good manners in conversations with others, perhaps Polyphemus.
3 See Luke 22:38 where, however, Peter is not mentioned. Cf lines 36–7 below with n10.
4 Said of 'someone [who] has had the back luck to fall among worthless and unmannerly people' (*Adagia* I v 42)

more exactly among wasps. Furious swarms of them gather more densely
day by day. And now at Paris[5] certain cronies set out against me with a gladiatorial intent.[6] And I see no end to it, unless perchance, sated with my blood,
they drop off of their own accord like leeches. They are stirred up against   15
me because I am weak and because I am alone. I am weak because I have
no rank to drive away the malicious; for nothing drives away wasps better
than smoke.[7] I seem to be all alone because I attach myself to no party, and
I will not do so as long as God maintains this resolve of mine. Books fly out
everywhere, from Italy, France, Spain, and various parts of Germany; they   20
have no other effect than to betray the ignorant malice of their authors and to
fan the flames of the conflicts. To be sure, I do the only thing I can do: I wish
for them a better frame of mind. For I will have to stand firm in this arena
until the last day of my life. What else can one do? This is what the Fates have
decided. But as for you, I congratulate your fortitude: you manage the affair   25
with courage and with matching success, calling the parties to a middle position, and you do so with such careful moderation that you neither encounter
Scylla nor need you fear Charybdis.[8]

Your dagger,[9] my very good friend, will not allow my mind to slip into
forgetfulness of you. In return, this letter, written with my own fingers, will   30
sometimes remind you of Erasmus, whom you can safely number among
those who pray that you may have all the good fortune and happiness that
your flourishing and vigorous old age preeminently deserves. For nature
seems to have portrayed the image of a beautiful mind in your body. You
could say that such a body gives a certain outward indication of future im-   35
mortality. But alas! you sent me the dagger of Peter, which seems suitable for

* * * * *

5 Here, as in the colloquy *Exequiae seraphicae* 'The seraphic Funeral,' Erasmus
  calls Paris 'Pelusium' (from the Greek word for 'mud') rather than the usual
  'Lutetia,' which recalls the Latin word *lutum* ('mud,' 'mire'). The idea of 'mud-
  slinging' may well be implied. See CWE 40 1014 n6.
6 Ie intent on engaging him in a fight to the death. On Erasmus' fondness for the
  image of gladiatorial combat in his battles with conservative critics, see Ep 1934
  n1. The reference here is to the Paris theologians' recently published censure of
  Erasmus' writings (Ep 2552 n10).
7 It is not clear what *fumus* (smoke or steam) has to do with high rank.
8 *Adagia* I v 4
9 Elsewhere in the letter (lines 5, 36) Erasmus uses the common Latin word *pu-
  gio* for 'dagger.' Here he uses the Greek loan-word *enchiridion* 'dagger,' 'handy
  weapon,' 'handbook,' the word used in the *Enchiridion militis christiani* (*Handbook
  of the Christian Soldier*).

cutting off ears.[10] There is more need for one that cuts off tongues, for that is the most destructive part of this species of living things.[11] But I will stop joking with you. Farewell.

Given at Freiburg, 22 June in the year 1532 after the birth of Christ   40

2664 / From Caspar Ursinus Velius   Innsbruck, 26 June 1532

This letter was first published as Ep 174 in Förstemann / Günther. The autograph was in the Burscher Collection of the University Library at Leipzig (Ep 1254 introduction). For Ursinus Velius, professor of rhetoric at the University of Vienna and official historian of King Ferdinand, see Epp 1810 n6 and 2008 introduction. This is his last surviving letter to Erasmus.

Cordial greetings. That you have not written anything since the time I left you at Freiburg[1] I take in good part, as I should. For since that time I have not asked you to write, primarily because you have so many things to do that you can hardly have the opportunity to respond to letters, much less to be entreated to perform this duty.   5

From the letter I recently sent to Glareanus, that learned and esteemed gentleman,[2] you undoubtedly learned that I had been given the wooden sword,[3] as it were, and left the arena of the busy court to return to a safe and peaceful home, having been entrusted by the best of kings with the office of tutor to the royal children, who show great promise and are extremely gifted.   10 But, of course, this leisure is not without its worries; it is an assignment not to be taken lightly, as you, a man of much reading and experience, can well judge. They should have some Phoenix or Aristotle as a tutor, not Velius.[4] But I will make every effort to show that I live up to the trust placed in me

* * * * *

10 John 18:10
11 Cf James 3:5–10.

2664
1 For Ursinus' visit to Erasmus at Freiburg in the late summer of 1531, see Ep 2543 n1.
2 Henricus Glareanus (Ep 440), friend of Erasmus and since 1529 lecturer in poetry at Freiburg; see Ep 2105:25–6.
3 Ie 'I have retired.' On retiring a gladiator was presented with a wooden sword; see Adagia I ix 24.
4 In Homer, Phoenix was the tutor of Achilles; Aristotle was the tutor of Alexander the Great.

by such a great prince in a satisfactory manner. In this matter you will be of   15
no little help to me, partly because of the useful precepts about such instruction that you published a while ago,⁵ partly by the correct and trustworthy
advice that I beg you generously and willingly to impart to me, thus undertaking this task jointly with me. For it is apparent that you desire and labour
for nothing more intently than to further the Christian commonwealth, the   20
welfare of which will depend largely on the welfare and piety of its princes.

Give my regards to Glareanus. I am very sorry I could not satisfy his
wishes. In so far as I could, I would have recommended that most worthy
and civilized gentleman to his most famous Majesty King Ferdinand; but I
think that on his own merits he will be quite acceptable and well received.⁶   25
Farewell, my most learned and also most holy Erasmus, and be assured that
your Velius is your loving and most faithful friend and will remain so as long
as he lives.

Given at Innsbruck, 26 June 1532

Concerning the man whose name is well known to those familiar with   30
the matter,⁷ and who you write is defaming you,⁸ there are many things that
I would rather tell you in person than commit to writing. But if I find someone I can trust, I will either rely on him to speak to you or I will write to you
myself. But take care not to think that he⁹ has so much influence with the
most incorruptible prince as to make him expel from his most noble heart the   35
respect and high regard he has for you. It is the wickedness of these wretched
times and not the insults of those idiots that keeps him from showing more
openly his exceptional good will towards you. I know well how much that
most holy man values and trusts those who envy the praise given to others;
and on the other hand, I am not unaware of how highly he regards you –   40
indeed most highly – and in all matters he is most resolute in his constancy.

Your Ursinus

To the excellent and most learned gentleman D. Erasmus of Rotterdam,
prince among writers and theologians, a friend to be valued among the finest. At Freiburg im Breisgau   45

* * * * *

5 *De pueris instituendis* (Ep 2189)
6 Having only recently (1529) settled down in Freiburg in the Breisgau, of which
  Ferdinand was the sovereign, Glareanus might well have solicited Ferdinand's
  attention and favour.
7 The Latin of this passage appears to be corrupt. We follow Allen's surmise of
  the intended meaning.
8 Presumably Girolamo Aleandro (Ep 2638)
9 Ie Aleandro

2665 / From Jean de Pins   [Toulouse, c July 1532]

This letter, Jean de Pins' reply to Ep 2628, was first printed by Preserved Smith
in Appendix II of *Erasmus: A Study of His Life, Ideals and Place in History* (New
York 1923; repr New York 1962) 448–50. The surviving manuscript is a seventeenth-century copy in the Bibliothèque Municipale at Nîmes (MS 215 folio 165
verso). For Jean de Pins and the circumstances of the writing of this letter, to
which Erasmus replied with Ep 2757, see Ep 2569 introduction. A precise date
is impossible, but the one assigned by Allen is a good guess in light of the
place of the letter in the sequence of those to and from De Pins.

JEAN DE PINS TO ERASMUS OF ROTTERDAM, GREETINGS
Your most pleasing and desired letter was delivered to me, my dearest
Erasmus. You cannot imagine what an uproar it caused when it first arrived.
It fell into the hands of certain men whom you consider unfriendly towards
you and among whom you also do not enjoy good repute. I felt like sniff-   5
ing around secretly to see if I could somehow divine or discover why this
is so. But I think that there is no other reason than that these men, good
in other respects, are devoted, and rather intensely, to a clique made up of
certain notable people whom you have offended in your books, or rather
have torn to pieces and utterly demolished, as they themselves have often   10
complained to me and to others. At first, because these people hoped to find
something of great importance in your letter, as if there should be nothing
in the correspondence between Erasmus and De Pins except the kingdom or
conspiracies against the kingdom, they first stirred up a great commotion,
and without my knowledge and while I was gone (for I happened at that   15
moment to have left the city to spend some time in the country), they threw
into prison some poor booksellers who had brought the letter from Paris,
because they were somewhat reluctant and seemingly did not surrender the
letter quickly enough. But those people, who at first seemed to be seized by
a fit of fury, suddenly regained their sanity and composure, and desired only   20
to open the letter in my presence and with my permission. And when I had
readily agreed and they found nothing in the letter but some writing about
a certain Josephus,[1] then indeed you can be sure that their faces fell and the

* * * * *

2665
1 Ie Erasmus' request to borrow De Pin's Greek manuscript of the *Greek Antiquities*
  of Josephus

rug had been pulled out from under them.[2] In the meantime I began to laugh
at the story, but I didn't want you to be unaware of it, so that if somehow 25
you are able, or if you think the whole business is worth the trouble, you
may regain the favour of such people, unless you think that it has been so
compromised that it would be difficult for the wound to be mended and be
covered over by a scar. You know the people I mean and so I do not speak
more openly.[3] 30

And now, to get to your letter, in which you argue the case of your
friend Froben with me: concerning Josephus, I find myself compelled to go
into the matter more deeply, so as to make it all clear to you. A few years
ago I lent my Josephus to Pierre Gilles,[4] a most learned man, for his use; he
is the close friend and servant of the bishop of Rodez, who (for many good 35

* * * * *

2 Literally 'the crows' eyes had been pierced.' To 'pierce the crows' eyes' is to
confront people with something new and unexpected and force them to admit
that they had been wrong or misinformed; see *Adagia* i iii 75.
3 This incident, which De Pins describes in such guarded language, has been interpreted as an example of the hostile French reaction to Erasmus' *Ciceronianus*
(Ep 1948 introduction); see Emile V. Telle 'Dolet et Érasme' *Colloquia Erasmiana
Turonensia* i (1969) 407–39, here 410–11. But that would hardly have involved ar-
rests and official inquiries. More to the point is that Toulouse, once the centre of
the Albigensian heresy, was notorious for conservative orthodoxy, opposition
to the new learning, and the vigorous pursuit of suspected heretics by the local
Inquisition and the Parlement of Toulouse. In 1531 three Augustinian friars had
preached Luther's doctrines at Toulouse, provoking an inquiry by the inquisi-
tors and the Parlement, as the result of which several suspected Lutherans were
arrested in the first three months of 1532. In these circumstances, the arrival of a
letter to De Pins bearing the hated name of Erasmus evidently caused the bishop to be suspected of heresy. Since De Pins' accusers reportedly could not read
the letter, he was required to read it before the Parlement, as a result of which it
became clear that there was nothing in it other than an innocent request to borrow a Greek manuscript. See Richard Copley Christie *Étienne Dolet: The Martyr
of the Renaissance 1508–1546* (London 1899; repr Nieuwkoop 1964) 67–8, 75–6.
4 Little is known of the early life of Pierre Gilles of Albi (1490–1555). Around
1521 he entered the service of Georges d'Armagnac, bishop of Rodez (Ep 2569),
to whom he dedicated his *Lexicon graecolatinum* (1532) and his translation of
Theodoret's commentary on the twelve minor prophets (1533). In 1533 he dedicated to Francis i a volume of his translations of Aelian and other classical
writers on natural history, together with his own glossary of the French and
Latin names of fishes. As his reward for this, Francis sent him to the Ottoman
Empire, where he collected manuscripts, explored antiquities, and had many
adventures. In 1553 he returned to France and subsequently rejoined Georges
d'Armagnac, now a cardinal, at Rome, where he died.

reasons) is a very good friend of mine. Afterwards, when he had faithfully returned it to its owner, I began to be harassed by letters and personal requests to send it to Lyon to be printed. Sending it was a serious matter to me, since I was quite reluctant to be deprived of a manuscript for which I had once paid a large sum in Venice, and which I knew had belonged to two of the 40 most learned men of our times, to Filelfo and then to the Venetian Leonardo Giustiniani,[5] so that I was sure that it had been thoroughly corrected. But the continuous requests and endless importunities of friends forced me, unwilling though I was, to yield the palm.[6] They had hardly taken the book away when all of a sudden there was the letter from the bishop of Rodez to 45 me, with which your letter to him[7] was also enclosed. He begged me most urgently to give you access to and free use of the book for several months. The mention of my Erasmus, the oldest of my friends and unquestionably the prince of letters, made me jump for joy, but before long the joy suddenly turned to grief. For what else could I do when I saw that I could not accede to 50 the wishes of both you and our friend the bishop of Rodez? For the book was out of my control and there seemed to be no hope of calling it back. But God, in his goodness and power, helped me and suddenly turned the affair to the good. For beyond anything I could have hoped, the book came back into my control once more. Do not ask how this happened, for if I began to tell you it 55 would be boring for you to hear and also for me to tell. I then sent the book to our friend the bishop of Rodez, who happened at that very time to come to this city, on his way to the county of Armagnac in Aquitaine, where he is the viceroy of the king of Navarre.[8] He promised faithfully that the book would come into your hands safe and sound. Also, if it seems expedient, address 60 your appeal to him by letter, but I think this scarcely necessary. For I know that he will keep his promise out of the goodness of his heart.

I come now to the last item of your letter, where you ask me about our friend Bombace, to let you know whether I can give you any certain news about him. I haven't heard anything about him for a few years now, except 65

* * * * *

5 For Francesco Filelfo (1398–1481) see Ep 23:77n. Leonardo Giustiniani (1388–1446) was a wealthy Venetian patrician, holder of high political office in the republic, patron of humanists, and a friend and contemporary of Filelfo.
6 The Latin is *herbam porrigo*, literally 'proffer grass,' meaning to confess oneself beaten and yield to the victor; see *Adagia* I ix 78.
7 Ep 2569
8 The king of Navarre was Henry II of the house of Albret (reigned 1517–55), husband of Margaret of Angoulême, the sister of Francis I. Henry was also the count of Armagnac and Rodez.

that there was a rumour (may it be false!) that he perished in that fatal sack of the city of Rome.[9] They also say that the Venetian Pietro Alcionio was killed in that massacre.[10] After that nothing certain about them has come here. And so from your letter I get more than a little comfort, since you write that you received a letter from Bombace saying that he was going to Bologna.[11] Please   70 calculate the time of the letter, I beg you, so that I can tell whether it came before or after the sack. If you received it afterwards we can hope that the rumour is baseless and that our good friend is still alive and safe. For us nothing we experience could be more welcome or delightful than that.

Farewell, my dearest Erasmus, and continue to love me, as you   75 always do.

2666 / To Ambrosius Pelargus   [Freiburg, early July 1532]

For Ambrosius Pelargus, Dominican preacher and theologian who, like Erasmus, abandoned Basel for Freiburg rather than live in a city that had gone over to the Reformation, see Ep 2169 introduction. In 1529 Erasmus and Pelargus had already had a friendly exchange of letters on the identification of the various Jameses in the New Testament (Epp 2169–70, 2181–2, 2184–6).

This letter is the first of a new sequence of twelve (the others are Epp 2667–77) largely concerned with the criticisms and suggestions that Erasmus request-ed of Pelargus before the publication of the second, augmented edition of the *Declarationes* (cf Ep 2552 n10), which was published in September 1532. For that reason, Allen placed the undated letters in early July. Like the aforemen-tioned letters of 1529, those of 1532 were first published after Erasmus' death by Pelargus in the *Bellaria* (folio B6).

ERASMUS OF ROTTERDAM TO THE VERY LEARNED THEOLOGIAN
MASTER AMBROSIUS PELARGUS, GREETINGS
I have to revise my *Clarifications*, at the insistence of the printers. Therefore I beg you to send your notes, to see if they are of any help to me. For I have

* * * * *

9 Paolo Bombace (Ep 210 introduction) had indeed perished on 6 May 1527, dur-ing the sack of Rome. It seems odd that confirmation of the rumour had not long since reached De Pins. On 24 August 1534, Erasmus was still trying to find out if Bombace was alive (Allen Ep 2963:17), and not until 19 May 1535 did he report to De Pins the news of Bombace's death in 1527 (Allen Ep 3018:2–3).
10 Pietro Alcionio (Ep 450:29n) was wounded in the sack of Rome and died later the same year, possibly as the result of his injury.
11 See Ep 2628:19–21. The letter is not extant.

no intention of intermingling anything Lutheran in my writings. If you are   5
satisfied with the notes, there is no reason for you to go to the trouble of
making a fair copy. I have servants who can read anything. But if you wish
to make a copy I will not be ungrateful. In any case, I would not want
you to undertake this task before you have had a taste of it and we have
talked together.   10
     Farewell, my dearest Pelargus.
     Your Erasmus of Rotterdam

2667 / From Ambrosius Pelargus   [Freiburg, early July, 1532]

First published in the *Bellaria* (folio B6 verso), this is Pelargus' reply to Ep 2666.

AMBROSIUS PELARGUS TO THE THEOLOGIAN ERASMUS
OF ROTTERDAM, GREETINGS
I have kept my word, noble sir, and I have carefully compared the *Censures*
of the Sorbonne at Paris with your *Clarifications*, concerning which you asked
my judgment.[1] I have added from the censures of Sepúlveda those that I   5
considered most noteworthy.[2] Furthermore, I have passed over some points,
either because you yourself have already taken care of them, or because they
have little or nothing to do with theology, or because they are so true that
not even a Momus could take exception to them.[3] If I have done anything in
this matter that has earned your gratitude, I will consider it sufficient thanks   10
if you do not cease to be fond of me and if you in your good nature take in
good part these comments of mine, whatever value they may have. But now
for the first time I see what a difficult task I have undertaken, which I would
wish that either you had not confided to me or that I had not accepted. For
while I obey you and set about evaluating your writings, I have an inkling   15
of how much ill will I shall attract and call down on my head, just as the
north-easter draws clouds.[4] For apart from the grounds for ill will and disputes that I have created for myself by this discussion, I also see that I

* * * * *

2667
1 This letter evidently accompanied a copy of the notes on Erasmus' *Declarationes*
  that Erasmus had requested of Pelargus in Ep 2666. Immediately following the
  text of this letter in the *Bellaria* (folios B7–G8 verso), Pelargus inserted the text
  of his comments under the title *Iudicium Ambrosii Pelargi de Declarationibus D.*
  Erasmi Rote. ad censuras Lutetiae vulgatas sub nomine theologorum Parisiensium.
2 Presumably taken from Sepúlveda's *Antapologia*; see Ep 2637 introduction.
3 The name 'Momus' was proverbial for a captious critic; see *Adagia* I v 74.
4 *Adagia* I v 62

shall be subject to the censure of many, especially of those who would rather stubbornly fight than surrender to the truth. Moreover, there is no way I can 20 avoid gaining the enmity of the opposing party. For when I have given a white mark to one side, it will have to be (as they say) a black mark for the other,[5] And so it happens that whichever way I turn I am stuck in the same mud.[6] But as far as you are concerned, I assure myself of a better outcome, both because I began by asking pardon for speaking freely, and because I 25 exerted myself in this task at your request. If you had not pressed this labour upon me, I would have adhered to my decision to serve my own cause by maintaining the most tenacious silence.

Farewell, most accomplished sir.

2668 / To Ambrosius Pelargus   [Freiburg, early July, 1532]

First published in Pelargus' *Bellaria* (folio H), this is Erasmus' reply to Ep 2667.

ERASMUS OF ROTTERDAM TO MASTER PELARGUS, GREETINGS
I have looked over your annotations.[1] I send you a small token of my gratitude, and wish that you could have thousands of them![2] I will tell you the rest in person, whenever it is convenient for you to have a talk with me. Farewell.

Erasmus of Rotterdam, in my own hand   5

2669 / From Ambrosius Pelargus   [Freiburg, early July 1532]

First published in the *Bellaria* (folio H), this is Pelargus' reply to Ep 2668.

AMBROSIUS PELARGUS TO HIS FRIEND ERASMUS OF ROTTERDAM, GREETINGS
For the honorarium,[1] which was neither slight nor inappropriate, I thank you. But from the Spartan concision of your letter, I sense some offence on

* * * * *

5 *Adagia* I v 62
6 *Adagia* IV iii 70

2668
1 See Ep 2667 n1.
2 We have no clue to the nature of the gift.

2669
1 See Ep 2668 n2.

your part, the reason for which I am at a loss to guess, unless perhaps the   5
booklet I sent you excited your anger. If that is the case, use a sponge or,[2] if
you want, just throw the whole thing away. For I would rather be in danger
of that than to cause the loss of our friendship. It may be that sometimes I
spoke too freely. But certainly I am confident that I never went beyond the
bounds of truth or propriety. If you are angry with me for some other reason,   10
I beg you to let me know about it via the young man,[3] so that I can either
defend my innocence or, if there is perhaps something wrong, I can soothe
your feelings. Because of a head cold and a runny nose, I cannot meet you
today. Farewell.

2670 / From Ambrosius Pelargus   [Freiburg, early July 1532]

    This letter, first printed in the *Bellaria* (folio H), continues the series between
    Erasmus and Pelargus that began with Ep 2666.

AMBROSIUS PELARGUS TO HIS FRIEND ERASMUS OF ROTTERDAM,
GREETINGS
When I met you nine days ago to talk with you,[1] you certainly seemed cooler
towards me than usual, and that gave me a strong suspicion that you were
somewhat angry with me. When I asked you why, you accused me of not   5
treating you fairly in one or two places, namely those concerning faith and
ceremonies. At that time I gave you the best answer I could on those points,
but at least what was satisfactory. But I would very much like to know
whether I persuaded you.[2] Farewell.

2671 / From Ambrosius Pelargus   [Freiburg, early July 1532]

    First published in the *Bellaria* (folio H verso), this letter continues the series
    between Pelargus and Erasmus that began with Ep 2666.

    * * * * *

2 Ie erase it
3 Ie the servant who delivered the letter

2670
1 Ie the planned meeting suggested by Erasmus in Ep 2666:9–10 but postponed
   by Pelargus in Ep 2669:13–14.
2 By the time Pelargus published his notes on the *Declarationes*, there was no longer anything in them indicating disagreement with Erasmus on these points;
   see CWE 82 77 with n233, 179 with n658.

AMBROSIUS PELARGUS TO HIS FRIEND ERASMUS, GREETINGS
During our conversation yesterday,[1] when we talked about one thing and another, my most charming Erasmus, though I was delighted by the variety of
the subjects we broached, I was especially pleased that, though we discussed
everything with utmost freedom, there was still no occasion for anger. You   5
were surprised that in the course of such a severe and thorough examination
of your *Clarifications*, I reversed the order of things and did not even touch
upon what you chose to say in the fifty-fifth clarification:[2] that the phrase 'I
believe in the holy church' follows a Hebrew idiom, just as in the gospel the
expressions 'I believe him' and 'I believe in him' are frequently used alterna-   10
tively.[3] At that point my answer was nothing more than this: one person has
sharper vision than another, and many eyes see more than one eye. But, to be
quite frank about this, I deliberately passed over that point because I knew
that one should not be too quick to judge about a problematic matter. And
even now I do not take it upon myself to say anything on that point because   15
to discuss it is not the province of just anyone at all but rather of those who
have been immersed in that sacred language from the cradle onward. To be
sure, if someone argues that this is a Hebrew idiom, I am afraid there will
be no lack of those who disagree, saying that by the same principle Christ's
saying 'you believe in God, believe also in me' is also a Hebrew idiom.[4] But   20
if their opponents deny that this is so, they will be told in response that this
phrase in the Creed should also be taken as not influenced by the Hebrew
idiom. For by a sort of analogy it can be understood in the same way as
the words of Christ just cited, so that the words 'I believe in the church' are
equivalent to 'I believe and by believing I am admitted to and incorporated   25

* * * * *

2671
1 Clearly a follow-up conversation to the one mentioned in Ep 2670:1
2 In the second edition of *Declarationes* this is the fifty-second clarification (CWE 82
   306–7).
3 In the colloquy *Inquisitio de fide* 'An Examination Concerning the Faith,' one
   of the characters, Barbatius (representing a Lutheran), will agree to the credal
   article 'I believe in the holy Catholic church' only if it is changed to 'I believe
   the church,' contending that 'believe in' should be used only with reference to
   God and Christ, not the church (CWE 39 429:1–33 with n97). In response to the
   charge of the Paris theologians that it was 'temerarious' to assert that it is not
   right to say 'I believe in the church,' Erasmus responded that 'believe in' is a
   peculiarity of the Hebrew language, that the distinction is not important, and
   that both forms are found in Scripture; see CWE 82 306–7. He had made the same
   point in his annotations on Matt 10:32 and Luke 12:8, and would do so again in
   the *Explanatio symboli* of 1533 (CWE 70 263–4).
4 John 14:1

into the body of Christ, which is the church.'⁵ This is pretty much the way in
which Berengar interpreted this article of the faith. And I vote for this interpretation, whatever sort of person Berengar may have been otherwise.⁶

I am truly grateful to you for the fish and the apples (richly spiced with
citron, if I am not mistaken, and other similar kinds of condiments), which   30
you sent yesterday just as I was going to dinner. And what was your purpose, I ask you? Just to make the dinner finer? But I had a far different idea:
I shared them with my special friends, so that this gesture of your kindness
might extend more widely. Farewell.

2672 / To Ambrosius Pelargus   [Freiburg, c July 1532]

First published in Pelargus' *Bellaria* (folio H2), this letter continues the series
begun with Ep 2666. Pelargus' answer is Ep 2673.

ERASMUS OF ROTTERDAM TO MASTER PELARGUS, CORDIAL
GREETINGS
Blessed be God! What neither princes, nor bishops, nor theologians could
achieve, a woman accomplishes! Because I know that you will like it very
much, I wanted to send you the little book.¹ Farewell.   5

2673 / From Ambrosius Pelargus   [Freiburg, c July 1532]

First published in the *Bellaria* (folio H2), this is Pelargus' reply to Ep 2672, which
accompanied the gift of a 'little book.' The outlandishly inflated rhetoric that
Pelargus lays on is perhaps a part of the joke that he and Erasmus were sharing.

* * * * *

5 Pelargus' point is that 'believe in' in John 14:1 is not generally seen as simply
   a Hebrew idiom but rather implies a trust in God that saves. If that is so, then
   one can argue by analogy that the credal statement 'I believe in the church' is
   not same thing as 'I believe the church' but has the further implication of being
   incorporated into the church by virtue of one's faith.
6 Ie a heretic on the subject of the Eucharist. Berengar of Tours (c 1010–88) is
   remembered primarily as the medieval theologian whose arguments against
   the real presence in the sacrament made him the spiritual ancestor of Huldrych
   Zwingli and other 'sacramentarians' in the sixteenth century; see Ep 2284 n4.

2672
1 Neither this letter nor Ep 2673, in which Pelargus' acknowledges the gift, provides any clue to the content of the 'little book,' except that both men treated it
   as a joke.

AMBROSIUS PELARGUS TO HIS FRIEND ERASMUS, GREETINGS
Whoever gave you such an elegant literary gift must be very fond of you.
But if it has been ordained by nature or custom that the gifts that friends
repeatedly send us are usually so pleasing (especially if the gifts themselves
are impressive, or if they are enhanced by the affection or the status of the   5
sender), if they are so pleasing, I say, that we would never bestow them, particularly the ones we have just received, on other friends, especially friends
of lower status, but rather we want to hold them always in our possession as
keepsakes, then I am very much afraid that either you did not truly bestow
such a magnificent gift on me, or certainly did not do so with a full measure   10
of generosity. But if you sent the booklet with the intention that when I had
feasted my eyes on it, I should send it back, then I have feasted and sated my
eyes to the full.
    So here is your delightful little gift, keep it for yourself. I am never-
theless grateful to you, whether you sent it as a true gift or as something   15
to be soon returned after I had feasted my eyes on it. But I send it back if
only to keep anyone from accusing you of having scorned it with ingratitude. Farewell. If I too sniff at it, I get whiffs of some Carthusian as the author of this little book, or at least a woman quite familiar with a Carthusian.[1]
Whichever it may be, I leave it to you to judge, since you have a marvellous   20
nose in such matters and are very skilful in guessing. Once more, farewell.
    From our temple of the Muses.[2]

2674 / From Ambrosius Pelargus   [Freiburg, c July 1532]

> First published in the *Bellaria* (folio H2 verso), this letter continues the series
> that began with Ep 2666. Pelargus addresses matters that are not referred to
> in the preceding letters but presumably came up in one or more of his private
> meetings with Erasmus. Pelargus' language is strange and his train of thought
> difficult to follow. Erasmus' reply is Ep 2675.

AMBROSIUS PELARGUS TO ERASMUS OF ROTTERDAM, GREETINGS
I wish, most learned Erasmus, that you would consider whether it is safe
enough for you to pass over authors whose orthodoxy is established, such
as Augustine, Jerome, and some other princes of the church, and to depend
on pagan authors, especially after the usage of the church has established   5

* * * * *

2673
1 This is no help in identifying the book; cf Ep 2672 n1.
2 Ie from the university, where Pelargus was completing a doctorate in theology

that the word 'celibacy' means a chaste life, with no sexual activity;[1] and that
is the meaning approved by Priscian as well, for whom the word 'celibate'
[coelebs] means 'leading a celestial life' [coelestium vitam ducens].[2] And Jerome
also says that a 'celibate' person is one who abstains from coition and leads a
life worthy of heaven [coelum].[3] That is also what Augustine writes.[4] In sum,   10
there is no Father of the church, as far as I know, who takes the word 'celibate' to mean anything else. I add that those who are 'celibate' are said by
the jurists to be coelites [heaven dwellers],[5] who are far removed from coition.

* * * * *

2674
1 The subject of celibacy was raised several times in the censures of the Paris
  theologians (see CWE 82 189, 206–8, 241, 260–2, 288–9); Erasmus was accused
  of disparaging clerical celibacy and elevating marriage above celibacy, chastity,
  and virginity. In their consideration of one or more of the relevant passages in
  the Declarationes, Pelargus and Erasmus disagreed over the correct definition of
  'celibacy.' Pelargus, as indicated here, took the view that in ecclesiastical usage
  'celibacy' means leading a chaste life, free of sexual activity. Erasmus, however,
  evidently citing classical authors, maintained that 'celibacy' is simply the state
  of being unmarried (a claim supported by every dictionary of classical Latin),
  which does not necessarily involve the absence of sexual activity. As he liked to
  point out, for example, a priest who has a concubine and fathers children with
  her (a familiar figure in the fifteenth and sixteenth centuries) is 'celibate' but not
  'chaste' (see for example the colloquy Concio 'The Sermon' CWE 40 950:18–21).
  The word 'chastity,' moreover, does not necessarily imply abstinence from all
  sexual activity but rather from all improper sexual activity. For the unmarried, lay or clerical, church law deems all sexual activity to be improper, but
  for married couples sexual intercourse for the purpose of procreation is not
  only proper but praiseworthy. Hence Erasmus could speak of 'chaste and pure
  marriage,' something that he occasionally said was the holiest kind of life. It
  was not Erasmus' perfectly correct understanding of the terminology that got
  him into trouble with his critics, but rather his lack of enthusiasm for clerical
  celibacy and his seeming elevation of chaste marriage above virginity and abstinence. For a much fuller discussion of Erasmus' view of these matters and
  the terminology involved, see the colloquy Proci et puellae 'Courtship' nn53 and
  67 CWE 39 272–4 and 275–6.
2 Institutiones grammaticae 1.4
3 Adversus Jovinianum 2.38 (PL 23 336A)
4 De doctrina christiana 17.25 (PL 34 65)
5 Cf Ep 2675:3–6. The 'jurists' were evidently the second-century law teacher Gaius (often cited as 'Gavius') and the third-century lawyer Herennius
  Modestinus. Erasmus and Pelargus appear to have confused them with the
  Roman grammarians Gavius Bassus, a contemporary of Cicero, and Julius
  Modestus, a later figure mentioned by Suetonius (De grammaticis 20). It was
  the grammarians, not the jurists, who derived coelebs from coelites. Quintilian
  (1.6.36) ridiculed Gavius Bassus for having done so. Cf Dilutio CWE 83 125.

But if you should perhaps seek to defend yourself, how can you extricate yourself by confusing the monastic poverty advised by Christ with that   15
which is enjoined equally on all? For the trick you play to do this is perfectly
clear. This is what you say in your *Soldier*: 'You thought that it is only to
monks that poverty is commanded and personal property forbidden. You
were wrong. Both apply to all Christians.'[6] For if monastic poverty (namely,
the kind that no longer suffers being limited to what is expected of a well-   20
disciplined spirit but rather truly rejects and renounces all inheritance in the
manner of the early church) is enjoined on all Christians, then as a result all
those who are truly Christians will have professed monasticism. But isn't
there a danger that these words of yours will also open up a way for the
Anabaptists to promote their perfidy?[7] Seek some refuge, if you can, from   25
this sea of error, from these waves that propel you this way and that. For here
I cannot offer any advice or assistance. Actually I can only hope that you are
lucky enough to disentangle yourself and finally escape.

In another place, where Jerome says that Joseph was sold for twenty pieces of gold, you think that an error has crept in by the negligence of   30
the copyists and that it should read 'silver.' Here, however, you ought to
have remembered that Jerome never used his own translation but rather
the Septuagint, although he tends to disapprove of that translation. This is
clear from his own words. In his commentary on Genesis, we read: 'They
sold Joseph for twenty pieces of gold. The Hebrew has "silver" instead of   35
"gold." And our Lord should not have been sold for a less valuable metal
than Joseph.'[8] And in his commentary on Matthew, 'Joseph,' he says, 'was
not sold for twenty pieces of gold as many think, following the Septuagint,
but for twenty pieces of silver, according to the true Hebrew reading. For the
servant could not be sold for a greater price than the master.'[9]   40

* * * * *

6 Allen, assuming that this was a reference to the colloquy *Militis et Cartusiani*
   'The Soldier and the Carthusian,' was puzzled that the words cited could not
   be found in it. The (inexact) quotation is in fact from the *Enchiridion militis christiani* (*Handbook of a Christian Soldier*); see CWE 66 98, where the two sentences
   that follow are also important: 'The law punishes you if you take something
   that belongs to another, but it does not punish you if you withhold what is
   yours from your brother in need. Christ will punish both offences.'
7 Ie the belief of many Anabaptists that Christians must hold all goods in common, as was the practice of the early church
8 *Liber Hebraicarum quaestionum in Genesim*, on Gen 37:28 (PL 23 995A).
9 *Commentariorum in evangelium Matthaei ad Eusebium libri quatuor* book 4, on Matt
   26:16 (PL 26 192D).

The question of fornication as a justification in the Gospels does not seem to me to be treated as it should be. For the ancient Fathers treat it differently than you do.[10]

In the tenth chapter of Hebrews, you attribute faith to Christ, which is clearly opposed to the truth. The passage occurs in the *Annotations*.[11]   45

Further, I would like to know what the word *insubidum* in Aulus Gellius means, and also what is the etymology of the word.[12] Petrus Mosellanus says nothing about it.[13] I think he had another copy. For the copies vary in that passage. Some have *insubide*, others *insolite* [unaccustomed]. The passage is in book I, chapter 2.[14] Farewell.   50

I can hardly comprehend how happy I am and how much I should congratulate myself for my good fortune in having you visit me now and again.

* * * * *

10 The Paris theologians took exception to Erasmus' view that when adultery is committed, the marriage bond is ipso facto dissolved and that the pair are no longer husband and wife. Pelargus feared that this would be seen as sanctioning remarriage, even though Erasmus specifically denied that in his clarification, which he left unchanged in the second edition. See CWE 82 67–9 with n198.
11 This topic presumably came up in the context of Erasmus' response to the Paris theologians' censure of his views on faith. In his discussion of the 'wide range of meanings' of the word 'faith,' he observes that there is 'a faith which Christ possesses and a faith which he does not.' Pelargus is here referring to Erasmus' annotation on Heb 10:30 ('The Lord will judge his people'), which includes a discussion of the phrase found in verse 33, 'sometimes being publicly exposed to abuse.' Erasmus comments: 'The sense is that they [who have endured sufferings] are praised on two grounds, not only because they have endured persecution on account of the faith of Christ [*ob fidem Christi*] but also because they supported and shared in [the sufferings] of others' (LB VI 1011 D–E). The difficulty here lies in the Greek genitive and its Latin equivalent *fides Christi*, which can mean either the faith possessed by Christ himself or to the faith that believers have in Christ. Erasmus here clearly intends the latter reading, but Pelargus understands the former meaning and objects that Christ could not have faith in the same way as do ordinary believers. Cf Ep 2675:14–18.
12 *Insubidus -a, -um* is a post-classical word, found only in Aulus Gellius, meaning 'stupid,' 'foolish.' Pelargus speculates on the derivation in Ep 2676:17–28. It is not known why he raised the subject in the first place.
13 Petrus Mosellanus' *Annotationes in clarissimas Auli Gellii Noctes Atticae* was published by Johann Bebel at Basel in 1526.
14 Aulus Gellius 1.2.4

2675 / To Ambrosius Pelargus   [Freiburg, c. July, 1532]

First published in the *Bellaria* (folio H3 verso), this is Erasmus reply to Ep 2674.
Pelargus' reply to this letter is Ep 2676.

ERASMUS OF ROTTERDAM TO AMBBROSIUS PELARGUS, GREETINGS
On the contrary, no Latin speaker has used 'celibacy' in any other way.[1] The
examples are numberless. For when jurists give their etymology, namely that
'celibate' is derived from 'coelites' [heaven dwellers], they are not recommending chastity but rather pointing out that it is a happiness like the life of   5
the gods not to have a wife.[2] When I wrote about poverty, I was not confused
about the monastic profession of it; I only remarked in passing that it is, up
to a certain point, a quality shared by all Christians, an idea that the ordinary crowd does not know or ignores. Your calling it absurd cannot stand
because it relies on a misunderstanding of the word.[3] The information about   10
the twenty pieces of gold was derived from some Carthusian, on whom it
seems I placed too much reliance. But I am grateful to you for pointing it out.[4]
I don't remember anything about fornication as a justification, but I will look
at the passage.[5] As far as keeping the faith is concerned, no one did so as fully
as Christ, according to his human nature. And it is not unusual in Scripture   15
to attribute to Christ the head something that pertains to his body.[6] Whether
faith does not apply to Christ in any way at all needs to be examined.[7] To me
'faith' sometimes means 'trust.' They say that *insubidus* applies to someone
who is stupid or foolish. I do not know where the word comes from.[8] For
after having left Basel, I do not have many books, nor do I have any news for   20
you apart from this letter, which I think you have seen.[9] Farewell.

* * * * *

2675
1 Ie other than in the sense of the state of being unmarried, with no necessary
  implication of sexual abstinence; see Ep 2674:5–6 with n1.
2 See Ep 2674:12–13 with n5.
3 See Ep 2674:14–23.
4 See Ep 2674:29–40. The Carthusian is unidentified.
5 See Ep 2674:41–3 with n10.
6 Ie the church, Christ's 'mystical body'
7 See Ep 2674:44–5 with n11.
8 See Ep 2674:46–50.
9 Allen suggests that 'this letter' is possibly a copy of the *Tragoedia Basiliensis*
  (Ep 2698), but if that is so, it means that the exchange between Erasmus and
  Pelargus extended into early August.

2676 / From Ambrosius Pelargus   [Freiburg, c July 1532]

First published in the *Bellaria* (folio H4), this is Pelargus' reply to Ep 2675. Erasmus in return will reply with Ep 2677.

AMBROSIUS PELARGUS TO ERASMUS OF ROTTERDAM, GREETINGS
Concerning the meaning of 'celibacy,' I quite agree with you that it is properly applied to the unmarried, even those who consort with harlots in the most disgusting way or who bear children. But I think that a prudent man should have enough skill and decorum to conform to ordinary usage, for that is the 5 fine and peaceable thing to do. Come now, tell me what sense does it make for you to stick so close to the proper meaning of the word by saying that, according to the etymology propounded by the jurists, it is not abstinence they are commending but rather the life of the gods, as it were, who are not bound to any wife. Certainly, if to be celibate means to live the happy life 10 of the gods, then why shouldn't we say that those who live outside of marriage are also leading the life of the gods, even if they give themselves over to the rankest sexual indulgence? Unless perhaps you want to say that they are happy because they are exempt and free from the burdens and troubles of marriage. When you defend what you say about monastic poverty and 15 likewise about the faith of Christ,[1] you play a similar trick, that is, in your usual way you look for a crack through which you can escape.[2] Concerning the meaning and also the etymology of *insubidus* and *insubide*, I have tried to find them in Luscinius;[3] but he provides nothing certain. He simply guesses that it is derived from filthy feelings of being in heat[4] or from being sexually 20 aroused. Indeed, what Luscinius merely guesses is expressly taught by Pico della Mirandola, a man of keen intelligence and grave morals, in his explanation of the words of Julian the Rhetorician[5] in Aulus Gellius, book 19, chapter 9: *Subidum* (he says), that is 'pleasurable,' comes from *subare*, which means 'to be sexually aroused.' *Insubidum*, on the other hand, means 'unattractive' 25 and hence foreign to Venus. Four days ago I came across the passage in Pico

* * * * *

2676
1 See Ep 2675:9–17 with nn3, 6–7.
2 *Adagia* III ii 75
3 Ie in the edition of Aulus Gellius by Ottmar Nachtgall (Luscinius) published by Knoblauch at Strasbourg in 1521: *Auli Gellii Noctium Atticarum libri Undeviginti*
4 From *subare* 'to be in heat'
5 Antonius Julianus, a Spaniard, contemporary and friend of Aulus Gellius; his writings survive only in fragments cited by others.

della Mirandola by chance, not thinking about it but rather looking for something else.[6]

In the First Epistle to the Thessalonians (on which I have lectured
for quite a while), you seem to have explained not quite correctly in your   30
Annotations a passage of Paul, ἡμεῖς δὲ ἀδελφοὶ ἀπορφανισθέντες ἀφ' ὑμῶν [We
brothers, being deprived of you],[7] which you rendered as 'Now, my brothers, we have become like orphans.' For a father who has been derived of his
children is not rightly called an orphan, but this word is correctly applied to
children who have lost their parents. Relieve me of this scruple, I beg you, if   35
you have perhaps found something more correct. Farewell.

2677 / To Ambrosius Pelargus   [Freiburg, c July 1532]

First published in the *Bellaria* (folio H5), this is Erasmus' reply to Ep 2677. It
concludes the series of letters that began with Ep 2666.

ERASMUS OF ROTTERDAM TO HIS FRIEND AMBROSIUS PELARGUS,
GREETINGS
I was so overwhelmed by the labours of my studies when I was also called
upon to reply to your letter that I thought it would be the death of me. I had
very little spare time to make guesses about the meaning or etymology of   5
words. I consulted Suidas about the passage you brought up from Paul.[1] But
what I find there is on your side. And I have not found anywhere the word
'orphan' applied to bereaved parents. Translating a Greek word by a Greek
word, I was a bit inattentive. But when I add 'deprived of you as if you were

* * * * *

6 We have not been able to identify the passage in question.
7 1 Thess. 2:17. The Vulgate of this passage used the word *desolati*, which can
   mean either 'deserted by' or 'deprived of.' In all editions of his New Testament
   Erasmus used the word *orbati*, the more appropriate word to indicate the be-
   reavement of either a parent who has lost a child or of a child who has lost
   a parent. In all editions of his annotation of the passage, Erasmus attempted
   to make the implications of the Greek clearer by using the late Latin word
   (from Greek) *orphani*, adding the qualification 'as though': 'we had become as
   though orphaned.'

2677
1 1 Thess 2:17; see Ep 2676:29–34. Suidas (or Suda) was a Byzantine lexicon (more
   of an encyclopaedia than a mere word list), compiled near the end of the tenth
   century. It contained a great deal of valuable information derived from the
   earliest and best sources of ancient scholarship.

my children,' I more or less correct the mistake.[2] And this is the reading of the   10
edition: 'For the rest, we brothers, deprived of you, etc.' But it doesn't make
much difference which reading you choose. Farewell. If it is convenient for
you to talk some afternoon, that will be fine with me.

2678 / To Bonifacius Amerbach   Freiburg, 4 July 1532

> This letter (= AK Ep 1663) was first published in the *Vita Erasmi*. The autograph
> is in the Öffentliche Bibliothek of the University of Basel (MS AN III 15 30).
> Within two days of writing it, Erasmus had expanded the letter into the elabo-
> rate letter of consolation for the death of Bonifacius' daughter that appears as
> Ep 2684. Bonifacius replied to both letters in Ep 2688.

Cordial greetings. Yes indeed, you are excessively generous, my outstanding friend, since you want everything joyful to come to your friends rather
than to you, yet if something painful happens, you hide it from your friends,
although it is justly said: 'Among friends griefs are shared.'[1] For I have no
doubt that your mind is grievously tormented by a longing for your daugh-   5
ter, whom you loved so much, who was such a delight to you.[2] But as a legal
scholar, who teaches others to obey the laws of the emperors, you should
by the same token obey the laws of nature, which 'lead the willing man, the
unwilling man they drag.'[3] For however much you magnify this loss, you
cannot deny that it can be repaired, as long as you and your wife survive   10
unharmed. What if God replaced this little daughter with a little son and
heir, who will inherit not only your wealth but also your remarkable learning together with your manifold virtues? You do not need me, I think, to
counsel you that nothing should be loved immoderately lest the sorrow of
its loss should also be immoderate. You know what happened to your most   15
estimable brother Bruno.[4] What if God sometimes snatches something away

* * * * *

2 See Ep 2676 n7.

2678
1 The saying is cited in Greek. The familiar adage (*Adagia* I i 1) says that among
  friends 'all things' are in common.
2 Bonifacius' elder daughter, Ursula, aged three and one-half, died on 20 June
  1532; see AK Ep 1661.
3 *Adagia* v i 90, citing Seneca's version of a saying by the Stoic philosopher
  Cleanthes
4 See Ep 2684:122–4.

from us precisely because we love it too much and imagine that it belongs to us by right instead of as a loan and that it is perpetually ours, not temporarily. You could say that in human affairs there is here also a sort of Nemesis.[5]

I learned of your sickness only recently and I am greatly concerned 20 about it, nor can I relieve my mind of this concern unless you tell me about it in a letter.

Three days from now I will send my own servant there,[6] and through him you will be able to write me whatever you want at your convenience. I recently sent a letter of Sadoleto,[7] and now I am forwarding three packets 25 of letters from, if I am not mistaken, Italy. They came to me from Augsburg.[8] Cordial greetings to Basilius,[9] your wife,[10] and your other dear friends.

Farewell. Freiburg, 4 July 1532

Yours, Erasmus of Rotterdam

To the renowned gentleman Master Bonifacius Amerbach. At Basel   30

2679 / From Girolamo Aleandro   Regensburg, 4 July 1532

For the surviving manuscript of this letter and its first publication, see Ep 2638 introduction.

TO ERASMUS

I send cordial greetings. Your Polyphemus[1] – indeed now mine too – will tell you how I am all but torn to pieces by huge and endless tasks, so much

* * * * *

5 The goddess Nemesis is normally represented as the 'scourge of insolence and arrogance' who punishes 'excessive hopes' (see *Adagia* II vi 38). Here the meaning is extended tentatively to include punishment for loving something or someone too much.
6 Perhaps Gilbert Cousin (Ep 2381 n1)
7 AK Ep 1636, Sadoleto to Bonifacius, 8 May 1532; cf Epp 2684:135–7, 2688:26–7.
8 Cf Epp 2684:137–8, 2686:1, 2688:26–7. Included in these packets were three letters to Bonifacius, all dated at Padua, that have survived: one from Hieronymus Anginus (AK Ep 1654, 3 June 1532), one from Viglius Zuichemus (AK Ep 1655, 3 June 1532), and one from Anselmus Ephorinus (AK Ep 1656, 8 June 1532).
9 Bonifacius' older brother
10 Martha Fuchs

2679
1 Felix Rex, known as Polyphemus (Ep 2649 n3), had just undertaken his final mission in Erasmus' service, carrying letters to and from Regensburg, where the imperial diet was meeting. He presumably carried this letter as well as Epp 2685 and 2687.

so that very often I am not allowed to eat or drink, or even sleep, at the very
time when I have most need of help from such natural reinforcements. And   5
now, when I have taken pen in hand to answer your letter,[2] Polyphemus sees
that twenty more letters from Rome and from Venice have been delivered to
me, all of them very long and full of difficulties, and that shortly thereafter
an imperial secretary arrived in order to discuss with me some points which
are to be dealt with in the assembly of princes.[3] Hence you should not expect   10
any long letter from me until I get to Italy, unless perhaps in the meantime
something should happen that I know would be of special concern to you.
In that case I would not only write you about what would be necessary but
also make sure to send a letter carrier there. On the other hand, I expect from
you the long letter you promised me, one as long as a real book, and other   15
letters, too, whenever you have occasion to write about yourself, your affairs,
or even the common good, so that, in the midst of such worries and dangers,
I may take some comfort from reading a letter from you, which brings me the
greatest pleasure.

But now, however busy I am, I cannot fail to let you know how dis-   20
turbed I was when I heard from Polyphemus that I know not what ill-
informed people had persuaded you that I went back to Paris a few years
ago, both to encourage those who were writing against you and also to give
some help to Alberto both in matter and style.[4] O Christ, our God and saviour! what monstrosities I am hearing! I have not seen Paris for eighteen   25
years, and in that time I have not written to anyone who lives there except to
our friend Cyprian,[5] and to him only about two of my benefices that are not
far from Paris and that have been badly cared for, partly through his fault
and partly because of the times we live in. After I had received your letter,
another person, who boasts that he is a great friend of yours,[6] showed me   30
some six places (I believe) in your writings where you had treated me badly,
sometimes not mentioning my name but in such a way that everyone would
know against whom you were aiming your arrows. My only answer to him
was that it is a wicked practice to read something into a text that the author

* * * * *

2 Not extant
3 Ie in the imperial diet, which Aleandro was attending as special papal legate to
   the imperial court.
4 See Ep 2565:4–7 with n3.
5 Unidentified. In the period 1510–14 he is mentioned frequently in Aleandro's
   diary as someone in Paris whom he trusted to deal with financial transactions.
   The reference to him here as 'our friend' may indicate that Erasmus knew him
   as well.
6 See Ep 2639 n11.

never expressed, and even when you mentioned my name in some places, 35
the motive for their misinterpretation had to be the malevolence of some
people (including, perhaps, the one who had pointed out these passages to
me) who used lies and slanders to make Erasmus hostile to me.

I discussed with Polyphemus a few other points like these which ought
not to be discussed here, as contravening both the public good and that for- 40
getfulness of injury agreed to between us,[7] unless I should want to be considered as one who remembers past injuries. Accordingly, my dear Erasmus, if
you want to preserve in perpetuity our reconciliation (as you consider it to
be) or else the continuation of our friendship (as I take it), see to it that your
letter (or it you prefer it, your book) lets people know either that I am not 45
the person whom they think you described in such vivid colours or that you
were alienated from me at that time by the insidious accusations of others.
But as for me, I will do everything in my power to let you know in many
ways that there is no one who is fonder of you than I, and that I will remain
so all the more gladly when I am fully aware that you are not so easily per- 50
suaded, for that is the only brief complaint about you which I have made
sometimes among friends when things you wrote that were unfriendly to me
came up in our conversation.

But you should consider, my dear brother, that there are many who
have no love for either of us and who therefore strive to set us against each 55
other. Otherwise, if they were friends to you only, they would by no means
stir up against you the hostility of men like me. You should also remember
that I am condemned by my fate, however unwillingly, to live the life of the
court, where envy rules supreme, and so it is no wonder that there are many
who do not wish me well, not because they see that there is anything about 60
me that is worthy of their envy or because they think I have offended them
in some small way, but such is the malevolence and malice of this stupid and
wicked age that I will end my letter with Catullus,[8] nor will I add any new
reasons to the many that this lazy pack of pretenders already has for thinking
that whatever reward given to me by princes for my labours and dangers is 65
stolen away from them – though they are nothing but absolute drones.

* * * * *

7 Aleandro appears to be recalling the friendly meeting in Louvain in 1521 when
   he and Erasmus evidently decided to let bygones be bygones and resume
   friendly relations; see Ep 1342:120–5. As far as Erasmus was concerned, at any
   rate, the reconciliation was brief.
8 An apparent allusion to Catullus 43.8: *O saeclum insapiens et infacetum!* 'O crude
   and stupid age!'

Farewell, and after this expect from me letters from Italy which I hope
will be more cheerful and more suitable for true friends and full brothers.[9]
Once more, farewell and give my greetings to my dearest teacher, Master
Baer,[10] in person if he is there or by letter if he is not.   70

Given at Regensburg on 4 July 1532

2680 / From Girolamo Aleandro

This letter, redated to 'Louvain? c 20–5 October 1521?,' has already appeared as
Ep 1241A in CWE 8.

2681 / To Pietro Bembo   Freiburg, 5 July 1532

This letter was first published in Van Heussen page 119. The autograph is in the
Vatican Archives (MS Barberini Lat 2158 folio 108). When he wrote this letter,
Erasmus had already received Ep 2657 (see Ep 2682 introduction), so he knew
that Bembo (Ep 2106) and Viglius Zuichemus (line 5) were already acquainted.

Fortune not only favours the bold, as the proverb says,[1] but she also em-
boldens the timid. It turned out well when I recommended to you Karel
Uutenhove,[2] a young man of good birth and standing among his countrymen, but not particularly well endowed in literary studies or especially eager
to pursue them. Now I beg you not to begrudge me a closer look at Viglius   5
Zuichemus, a Frisian who completed there[3] the legal the studies he had most
happily begun and almost brought to a successful conclusion at Dole and
Bourges under the tutelage of that outstanding gentleman Andrea Alciati;[4]
only the colophon remains.[5] I was not deceived by any predisposition to-

* * * * *

9 This is in fact the last surviving letter from Aleandro to Erasmus, whose last
   surviving letter to Aleandro was Ep 1482.
10 Ludwig Baer, who in 1529 had moved with the Basel cathedral chapter to
   Freiburg (Ep 2225 introduction). Aleandro had presumably come to know him
   in Paris.

   2681
 1 *Adagia* I ii 45
 2 In Ep 2106
 3 Ie in Padua
 4 Ep 2101 introduction
 5 Ie the final, definitive touch; see *Adagia* II iii 45.

wards him, since I did not know the young man, and only after I had an op- 10
portunity to take a close look at him did I come to favour him.[6] Wonderfully
nimble-witted, incredibly upright. Nature has combined in him so many
gifts that I sometimes secretly fear that he will not live long. For the Fates
usually 'give the earth merely a glimpse' of such wonders.[7]

His native land is devoted more to Komus than to Minerva.[8] But it 15
does produce sound talents, which carry through to maturity.[9] I think that
Rodolphus Agricola is not unknown to you.[10] If I am any judge, I think
Viglius, if he lives, will turn out to be not inferior to him.[11] And so I beg you,
my dear Bembo, to examine him closely and spur on the galloping steed.[12]
Farewell. 20

Freiburg im Breisgau, 5 July 1532
Erasmus of Rotterdam, written quickly in my own hand
To the most distinguished gentleman Pietro Bembo. At Padua

2682 / To Viglius Zuichemus   Freiburg, [c 5 July 1532]

This letter was first printed in LB III/2 1754–5 *Appendix epistolarum* no 370,
where the date is given as 1533. In light, however, of the references to the recent
publication of Scaliger's *Oratio* and to the correspondence with Aleandro, this
date is impossible. The statement in line 58 that Erasmus had recently written
to Bembo commending Viglius suggests a date close to that of Ep 2681. Allen
found confirmation of this in the collation of the letter in Van Heussen page
128, which indicates that this letter was received at Padua on 5 August 1532.
Allen also adopted from Van Heussen's collation five readings that are 'plainly
better' than those in LB.

The letter is, in the main, a reply to Ep 2657, but the passages referring to the
misfortune of Haio Herman (lines 68–70) and to Viglius' connection to Bartolo
(lines 5–6) indicate that Erasmus was also replying to Ep 2632. Viglius' reply to
this letter is Ep 2716.

* * * * *

6 During Viglius' visit to Erasmus in the autumn of 1531; see Ep 2551 introduction.
7 Cf *Aeneid* 6.869–70.
8 Ie more to revelry and merrymaking than to studies; cf Ep 2586:23–5.
9 Cf Ep 2586:25–6.
10 Ep 23:58n. For Erasmus' encomium of him, see *Adagia* I iv 38.
11 Cf Ep 2586:37–9. Viglius soon embarked on a distinguished career as a jurist
and legal scholar as well as a leading counsellor and diplomat in the service to
the Hapsburg government of the Netherlands; cf Ep 2101 introduction.
12 *Adagia* I ii 47

ERASMUS OF ROTTERDAM SENDS GREETINGS TO THE VERY
LEARNED FRISIAN YOUTH VIGLIUS ZUICHEMUS

You seem to me, my dear Viglius, to be competent to govern a huge commonwealth or to rule an enormous army; with your clever stratagems you have
discovered the plans of your adversaries and you have protected yourself 5
from their false imputations by professing to belong to the time of Bartolo,[1]
since they think that those who have been trained in the language of Cicero
have no more right to enter their own area of law than those who are accustomed to profess the Franciscan rule have to go over into another religious
rule. Indeed you have given a skilful description of the Amphitheatre, cer- 10
tainly a work worthy of such a king.[2] By now I am not at all surprised that
some people don't like my *Ciceronianus*. 'This, then, is the reason for those
tears.'[3] I do not begrudge them this glory of theirs, but I am afraid that these
entrepreneurs will stir up in literary studies tragedies no less grievous than
Luther did in religious matters. The principal weapon of tyranny is to sow en- 15
mity between citizens and the societies they form; and that archtyrant leaves
no stone unturned in the effort to confound all Christianity in dissension.

What are you saying? Our Herman got his head softened with a three-
legged chair? I am surprised he was not flogged, naked as the day he was
born, for committing such a crime as using a Latin phrase that is not to be 20
found in Cicero.[4] But what if some hitherto hidden books of Cicero should
come to light? Will that Daedalus of yours build us a new Amphitheatre?[5]
What could be more stupid than such tumults? I am surprised that there is
so little talk there about the book by Giulio Camillo;[6] after it was printed at

* * * * *

2682
1 Bartolo da Sassoferrato (1313–55) was the most famous of the medieval com-
  mentators on Roman law. For humanists his name was synonymous with barbarous Latin; cf Ep 2604 n8. For Viglius' explanation of why a jurist could not
  be a Ciceronian but had to write like the authors of his legal texts, see Ep 2632.
2 A reference to Giulio Camillo's project to build a 'theatre of memory' for Francis
  I of France; see Epp 2632:154–78, 2657:30–61.
3 Terence *Andria* 126; see *Adagia* I iii 68.
4 See Ep 2632:136–8.
5 On 'Daedalus' as the name for the 'creator of any novel technical skill which
  compels our admiration,' see *Adagia* II iii 62. Since the Amphitheatre was to
  include all of Cicero's eloquence, the discovery of any of his lost works would
  necessitate its expansion or reconstruction.
6 Learning from Viglius that Giulio Camillo (Iulius Camillus in Latin) had written
  a book critical of the *Ciceronianus*, Erasmus jumped to the conclusion (lines 42–3
  below) that it was Julius Caesar Scaliger's *Oratio*, which he believed had been
  written, at least in part, by Girolamo Aleandro; see Ep 2632:154–60 with n18.

Paris it flew forth in all directions. I didn't read all of it; I just sampled it here   25
and there. It is full from start to finish with barefaced lies and utterly insane
insults. It is neither consistent nor at all coherent. He assumes that I wrote it
to obliterate the renown of Cicero so that only my books would be read. He
says that my books were burned at Paris by the public executioner. He says
that I had the lowly job of reading proof for Aldo,[7] whereas in fact I read only   30
the final proof for Aldo, to see if I wanted to add anything. Aldo read proof
after me, and did so only for the *Adagia*, which I wrote and Aldus printed
concurrently. He says that it almost came to blows because I was sitting at
the same table as Aldo, though in fact I lived on the floor above Torresani and
Aldo,[8] and they did everything they could to keep me there for some months   35
after I had finished the *Adagia*. At one place, when he cites Aristotle he says,
'I'm not saying this to you; you have not read Aristotle,' even though I have
cited Aristotle more than three hundred times both in Latin and Greek. What
need to say more? All this goes way beyond the madness of Orestes or Ajax.[9]
There is someone in Paris named Béda,[10] whom you know, who is so mad   40
with hatred that there is nothing so stupid or insane that he would not make
sure that it be printed as long as it attacks Erasmus. Meanwhile he makes a
fool of himself to everyone. He added some poison to the book by Giulio.
The author named in the title is Julius Caesar Scaliger. He pretends to be
French and mentions some obscure place.[11] From the diction, the style, and   45
the accusation about living with Aldo, I am convinced that it is by Girolamo

* * * * *

7 Erasmus spent about a year in Venice (1507–8) as a member of the circle of
   scholars around the renowned publisher Aldo Manuzio.
8 Andrea Torresani was Aldo's business partner.
9 As punishment for having killed his mother Clytaemnestra to avenge the death
   of his father Agamemnon, Orestes was hounded by the Furies and driven mad.
   Ajax, driven mad with anger when the arms of his fallen friend Achilles were
   awarded not to him but to Odysseus, killed the herds of the Greeks, believing
   them to be the Greek leaders, and then killed himself.
10 Ep 2635 n4
11 Scaliger's preface to the *Oratio* is dated 'From Agen, 15 March 1531.' Agen (in
   the south of France, 135 kilometres southeast of Bordeaux) was the seat of the
   bishop of Agen, whom Scaliger served as personal physician (Ep 2564 n2). In
   the preface he describes the town as a cultural desert where it is difficult to get
   books. See Jules-César Scaliger *Oratio pro M. Tullio Cicerone contra Des. Erasmum*
   (1531) / *Adversus Des Erasmi Roterod. Dialogum Ciceronianum Oratio Secunda*
   (1537) ed and trans Michel Magnien (Geneva 1999). The Latin text of the preface
   (pages 92–3) indicates the page numbers in the original Paris edition (A verso–
   Aij verso).

Aleandro, at least most of it; from living with him I recognize and understand his temperament better than he himself does.[12] I immediately expostulated with him in a letter.[13] But in very friendly letters from Regensburg, he swears on all that is holy that he has always been my friend and always will be.[14] In my apologias against Pio I frequently touched on him, but without naming him. This is the injury for which he wanted to be avenged. But it would be easy to follow his example, even though I am more angry at Béda than at this madman, whoever he is.[15]

To Pietro Bembo I sent a brief recommendation of Karel Uutenhove, a young man of good family but not well educated and not even eager to be so.[16] Bembo embraced him very kindly, and I think he would have done so even more willingly if he had known him. I am now writing a few words to Bembo about you.[17]

Sucket sent me a long description of his triumph, but no one has yet come along to carry an answer to him. I do not know what he is aiming at there.[18]

I am very sorry for what has happened to Alciati, who has had to relocate so often.[19] I have written to Georg Paumgartner and Giovanni Crisostomo.[20] Give my best regards to Franciscus Rupilius, to whom I shall write on another occasion.[21]

* * * * *

12 During Erasmus' stay with Aldus in Venice (1507–8), Aleandro was there as well. The two shared room and bed for about six months.
13 Not extant
14 Epp 2638–9
15 The 'madman' is evidently the author of Scaliger's *Oratio*, whom Erasmus had identified as both Aleandro and Giulio Camillo (see n6 above) and now, still not convinced that Scaliger is a real person, has to call 'whoever he is.' Behind Scaliger's *Oratio* Erasmus sees the evil influence of Noël Béda, himself described as 'mad with hatred' (lines 40–1 above).
16 Cf Ep 2681:2–5, with n2.
17 See Ep 2681:5–14.
18 See Ep 2657:88–90 with n17.
19 See Ep 2657:77–87.
20 The letter to Johann Georg Paumgartner is Ep 2683; that to Giovanni Crisostomo Zanchi (Ep 2716 n35) is not extant.
21 Rupilius (documented 1514–41) had been Viglius' fellow law student at Bourges, and was now, it seems, his contemporary at Padua. In 1527, already possessing a doctorate in law, he had entered the service of Johann (II) Paumgartner (Ep 2603 introduction) as the tutor to his sons. He remained in the service of Paumgartner, and in 1537 wrote on his behalf to Basel concerning the planned edition of Erasmus' *Opera omnia* (AK Ep 2156:31–2). Erasmus had evidently

I am glad you have established good relations with Anselmus Ephorinus.[22] What happened to our friend Herman? For a year and a half he has written nothing, not even a grunt.[23] I have told you what I suspect, and I do not think I am wrong.[24]   70

Farewell. Freiburg, 1533

2683 / To Johann Georg Paumgartner   Freiburg, 5 July 1532

This letter was first published in the *Epistolae palaeonaeoi*. In the autumn of 1531 Johann Georg Paumgartner (c 1515–70), the second son of Johann (II) Paumgartner (Ep 2603), joined Viglius Zuichemus on his journey from Augsburg to Padua, visiting Erasmus at Freiburg on the way. He was now studying at Padua under Viglius' supervision, and would remain there until at least 1535 before returning to Augsburg to become active in the family firm. In August 1532 Erasmus addressed to him the letter (Ep 2695) that served as the preface to Johann Herwagen's edition of Demosthenes. Of the subsequent correspondence between them, only Erasmus' Ep 2809 survives.

ERASMUS OF ROTTERDAM TO JOHANN GEORG PAUMGARTNER,
GREETINGS

Your father, my most excellent Georg, first conquered me with his kindness in that he took the initiative, through that very learned scholar Zasius, in seeking me out as a friend,[1] nourishing and maintaining our friendship right   5
up to the present time with very frequent and friendly letters.[2] For my part, I consider it to be among the most prominent features of my happiness that I have acquired the good will of a man who is so upright and benevolent,

* * * * *

known Rupilius and corresponded with him for some time, but the only surviving letter to him is Ep 2867. Rupilius' only surviving letter to Erasmus is Ep 3007.
22 See Ep 2657:9–16.
23 *Adagia* I viii 3. Erasmus' most recent surviving letter to Haio Herman was Ep 2261, dated 31 January 1530. No letters from Herman to Erasmus survive.
24 The suspicion was that Herman had contracted the French pox in Italy; see Ep 2587:91–3.

2683
1 See Epp 2602–3.
2 The first surviving letter to Erasmus from Johann (II) Paumgartner is Ep 2882.

and I perceive how true a friend Zasius is to me from the very fact that he
wanted to share such an extraordinary friend with me.   10

You have increased my happiness, my dear Georg, by entering into our
bond of friendship through a letter written in your own hand.[3] In it I find very
much to admire, but especially your generous temperament and the genuine
modesty with which you think you should seek so shyly and respectfully
what you could in fact rightfully claim. Certainly Johann Paumgartner him-   15
self will be all the dearer to me because he has an heir who is provided not
only with his substantial fortune but also with his remarkable virtues, which
constitute a treasure even more splendid. And if, as I believe, this letter of
yours was written on your own, and with no outside help,[4] I have high hopes
for you, and I have no doubt that if you go on as you have begun, you will   20
fully live up to the splendour of your ancestry and the expectations of all
your friends. But you will live up to them if you combine sound learning
with an upright character. Since to this end you are amply supported by the
example of your immediate family and your relations, by the vigilance of a
learned tutor,[5] and by the abundant gifts that fortune can provide, I have no   25
fear that you yourself will not come up to the mark, especially since you have
thus far sprouted up so auspiciously.[6]

Nothing remains but for us to beg God Greatest and Best to grant you
long life and good health and to advance the mind that he has inspired. In
the midst of various occupations, I have written this so that you will have   30
a guarantee in writing not only of my good wishes but also of my devotion
to you. For if the treaty of friendship struck between me and your father
demands that we should hold everything in common,[7] then it is surely right
that I should take up the affection of a parent for you. I do so all the more
willingly because I act not so much according to the laws of friendship as in   35
keeping with what you deserve. May the Lord preserve and advance your
good character, my dearest Georg.

At Freiburg im Breisgau, 5 July 1532

* * * * *

3 None of Johann Georg Paumgartner's letters to Erasmus is extant.
4 Erasmus writes 'with your own Mars' (*Adagia* i vi 19) and 'without Theseus'
   (*Adagia* i v 27).
5 Viglius; see introduction.
6 Erasmus writes that Johann Georg is 'in the blade' (*in herba*), said of cereal crops
   when they are young and still look like grass, too young to be harvested but
   with promise for the future (*Adagia* ii ii 89).
7 *Adagia* i i 1

2684 / To Bonifacius Amerbach   Freiburg, 6 July 1532

This letter (= AK Ep 1664) was first published in the *Epistolae palaeonaeoi*. Written to console Bonifacius on the death of his daughter Ursula, it is a much expand- ed version of the letter on the same topic (Ep 2678) that Erasmus had writ- ten two days earlier. The text is liberally sprinkled with words and phrases in Greek. Bonifacius' reply is Ep 2688.

ERASMUS OF ROTTERDAM SENDS GREETINGS TO THE MOST
RENOWNED DOCTOR BONIFACIUS AMERBACH

Yes indeed, my dearest Amerbach, you are infinitely and immeasurably gen- erous and self-effacing, since you want everything joyful to come to your friends rather than to you, but if something painful happens you make every 5 effort to shelter your friends from it, even though it is rightly said that grief is shared among friends.[1] If fortune inflicts some wound on you, you wish to grieve alone. But if something tragic happens to us, you are not satisfied with simply sharing that grief; you are more deeply moved than if it were your own misfortune. Your dear little daughter has died and (what we find even 10 harder to bear) you, my dear friend, have all but died with her, and your sick- ness has no other cause than grief.

I was late in coming to know about this great misfortune, and even then not from you but from your physician, who arrived here by chance. And so I would almost have died with you without knowing it. I know, my 15 dear Bonifacius, how devoted you are, both privately to those who are joined to you by blood or by marriage, and publicly to your native land, and there- fore I can easily divine how your mind is cruelly tortured by the longing for your infant daughter, whom you loved so much, kept so much in your heart, and in whom you took such delight as the first fruits of your marriage. She 20 was the first to bestow on you the sweet name of father. She was the reason you did not regret having exchanged the sweet liberty of the single life for the bonds of marriage, for in the beginning your mind seemed so set against it that you could hardly be driven to take a wife and yielded only to two powerful forces: the desire for an heir and the persuasion of friends. For in 25 that virtuous mind of yours, pleasure (as they say of the Megarians) counts for nothing.[2]

* * * * *

2684
1 Cf *Adagia* I i 1.
2 *Adagia* II i 79

And since I knew your temperament very well, I quite expected profound suffering, but your proven strength of character in other circumstances forbade me to fear that you would not share infirmity and death with   30
others. But it was right that you, a man famed for his jurisprudence, who
teaches others publicly that they must obey the laws of the emperors, should
obey with greater resignation the laws of nature, which lead the willing but
drag the unwilling.[3] So, however much in your grief you may exaggerate
this loss of yours, you cannot deny that it is reparable, as long as you and   35
your wife are safe and sound, since both of you are of an age that is not only
unimpaired but even flourishing and in full bloom. What if your marriage
had turned out to be sterile? This happens to quite a few, and since you are a
man of experience, should you not have thought of this possibility? Whoever
takes a wife must have a mind prepared to face the ordinary disappoint-   40
ments of mankind: infertility of one's partner, loss of a spouse or children,
being left alone.

But you are not childless yet, since you have a surviving daughter.[4] Is
this experience of yours so terrible? Wasn't it merely that you added a bright
star to the chorus of heavenly virgins? She leaps and dances joyfully because   45
she has been received into eternal bliss without being contaminated by the
evils of this unhappy life, and you mourn inconsolably – no, you do not
mourn, you die with her. A sprout only – no, a little flower has been plucked
from the tree; the trunk and the roots are healthy and undamaged. What if
God wanted to test your soul with this loss, to see how much you rely on   50
him? What if he gives you, in place of the darling daughter he has snatched
away, a son and heir to inherit not only your wealth but also that well-tried
wisdom of yours, joined with all manner of virtues?[5] You are far happier,
my dear Bonifacius, in having these rather than land and money, although
these goods of fortune have also been left to you by your ancestors, enough   55
to help make you not only self-sufficient but also quite resplendent. Among
these external goods the least subject to the sport of fortune are what you call

* * * * *

3 Cf Ep 2678:6–9.
4 Faustina, born 25 November 1530. In 1562 her first husband, Johann Ulrich
   Iselin (d 1564), succeeded Bonifacius as professor of civil law at Basel.
5 Bonifacius' only son, Basilius, was born on 1 December 1533 (d 1591). He studied law (1552–9) at Tübingen, Padua, Bologna, and Bourges and then in 1564,
   on the death of his brother-in-law Johann Ulrich Iselin (see preceding note),
   succeeded to the chair of civil law at Basel. See Alfred Hartmann 'Amerbach,
   Basilius' *Neue Deutsche Biographie* 1 (Berlin 1953) 246–7; Rochus von Lilienkron
   'Amerbach, Basilius' *Allgemeine Deutsche Biographie* 1 (Leipzig 1875) 397.

'immovable goods.'[6] But if goods are 'immovable,' the honour of that name really belongs only to the goods of the mind. Apart from the horrors of war, houses are destroyed by fire and the ocean washes land away, sparing not   60 even rocky cliffs. Only virtue is not ruled by fortune.

And so, if you bear patiently this slight wound inflicted by the Lord to test your faith, I am sure that in his kindness he will replace the loss of the little girl with a fine little boy who can succeed to all this wealth of yours (surpassing that of Croesus),[7] who will give us another 'you,' who will not   65 allow you to grow old or pass away. Your mind should have been supported by this hope, my very learned friend, and you should not have kept your eyes fixed on what has been taken away (if being sent ahead to heaven can be called being taken away). You should have kept in mind how many children are still hidden within you. Imagine, if you will, that you had no children.   70 Can we call God to account because he did not give what he did not promise to the couple entering into marriage? Assume there were children, many of them and good ones, but that they were soon taken away, would we have any just quarrel with God? What he gave was a gratuity. If, when he wishes, he demands the return of what he wished to give, he has a perfect right to do   75 so. For he wished it to be not a permanent gift but rather a loan.

Among the English, I knew the mother of John Colet, a matron of rare piety.[8] By the same husband she had eleven sons, and as many daughters. Of the whole troop all were taken away except Colet, who was the first born. In her old age her husband, also advanced in years, was taken from her. She   80 lived to be almost ninety years old, so well preserved in her appearance, so spry in her bearing, that you would say she had never mourned or borne children. In the end, if I am not mistaken, she outlived Colet.[9] What gave the woman such strength of spirit was not learning but devotion to God. And you, who have learning, wisdom, and determination in other matters, are   85 going to die of grief at the death of a little girl? Since we are all born subject to this law, since wherever you turn there is no place where your glance will

* * * * *

6 For 'immovable goods' Erasmus uses the legal term *res soli*, the Latin synonym for which (*res immobiles*) is used in the next sentence. The term applies to the soil (*solum*) itself as well as to buildings and other things so attached to the soil that cannot be moved without destroying them. They are the opposite of *res mobiles*, moveable goods.
7 Croesus, king of Lydia in Asia minor (560–546 BC), was renowned for being inordinately rich. His name became proverbial for a very wealthy man.
8 Dame Christian Knyvet (d 1523)
9 Colet (Ep 106) died in 1519.

not fall on such misfortunes, what sort of wisdom is it, I beg you, when something occurs according to the human condition, to be so totally dispirited as if something unheard of or monstrous had happened? In other matters the   90
ancients thought it disgraceful to say 'I never expected this.'[10] here it is quite insane to say 'I never expected this.' What does this amount to except to say 'I never expected to be human'?

I know you will say I am very late in my consolation, or rather my accusation. On the one hand, my dear Bonifacius, you should blame yourself   95
because you did not want me to know about your domestic calamity. On the other hand, perhaps it did some good in that from now on you may be better prepared for human adversity. In Terence, Micio is surprised that anyone can cherish in his heart anything dearer to him than he is to himself.[11] And certainly love of one's family is a sign of a humane and gentle mind. But I   100
doubt that Micio himself, if some accident took Aeschinus away from him, would fall ill of grief.[12] You are not now in any personal danger, and you are courageous in the face of any harm to yourself, yet you are so cast down at the death of another that I fear you may die from it. What good, I ask you, can this do you? Can your tears bring her back to life? If God demanded your   105
own life from you, I know you well enough to know that you would comply with equanimity. He reclaimed a little girl and you pine away with grief? Do you not realize how many you would bereave by a single death if what we dread should happen: wife, daughter, brother, sister, father-in-law, we your friends – in a word, all those of like mind and vulnerable together with you?   110

Finally, what a precious treasure you would steal from your country, which you not only adorn but also protect, and which rightly takes you to be the equivalent of many other men![13] If you consider your own welfare to be worthless, at least your concern for your countrymen should motivate you to take proper care of your health. No one could give you better consola-   115
tion or advice than you yourself if you would only bring yourself to bear upon yourself and say to yourself what you would say to someone else in your circumstances. But do not bring that very tender, loving person to bear but rather that upstanding and magnanimous philosopher whom we have

* * * * *

10 Cited in Greek. See the final sentence of *Adagia* i v 8 (CWE 31 392): 'Scipio does not allow the wise man to err even once, or to say "I never expected this."'
11 *Adelphi* 1.1.38–9
12 In the play (see preceding note) Aeschinus is Micio's nephew, whom he has adopted and whom he treats with unwise indulgence.
13 Cited in Greek from Homer *Iliad* 11.514; cf *Adagia* i viii 13.

hitherto admired in you. Wise men of old rightly taught that in human affairs   120
nothing should be wondered at, that is, nothing should be loved so much
that the deprivation of it would cause immoderate grief. I am very afraid of
what happened to your brother Bruno, who perished out of longing for the
wife he had lost.[14] How much good did we lose when we lost him? What if
God sometimes snatches away something from us for the very reason that   125
we love it too much and imagine that it is a permanent and personal possession instead of a convenient loan, one which is so uncertain from day to day
that the giver of the loan can soon take back what he gave. You would say
that in human affairs there is in this matter also a certain kind of Nemesis.[15]

I was not informed about your poor health until very late and I have   130
not yet heard about your recovery. That makes me greatly anxious and I will
not be relieved of that anxiety until you bid me have no fear by sending
a letter written in your own hand. Three days from now I will send there
one of my own servants to live with you for a while; through him you can
write whatever you want at your convenience.[16] Recently I sent a letter from   135
Jacopo Sadoleto,[17] which I had received wrapped in the same cloth cover
together with letters to me. Now I am sending three bundles of letters, sent
(unless I am mistaken) from Italy. They came to me from Augsburg.[18] Cordial
greetings to Basilius, to your wife, and the others dear to you.[19] Farewell, my
most beloved friend.   140

Freiburg im Breisgau, 6 July 1532

2685 / From Bernhard von Cles   Regensburg, 7 July 1532

This letter was first published by Allen. The manuscript, an autograph rough
draft, is in the 'Corrispondenza clesiana' collection of the Archivio di Stato di
Trento: 'Minute, copie e originali di lettere di Bernardo Clesio, 1514–1539' (cf Ep
2515 introduction). For Bernhard von Cles see Ep 2651 introduction.

* * * * *

14 In September 1518 Basilius' elder brother Bruno, to whom Erasmus had been
   close, married Anna Schabler, who died in mid-May 1519 at the age of twenty-
   one. Bruno died of the plague six months later. Cf Ep 2678:15–16.
15 See Ep 2678:16–19 with n5.
16 Cf Ep 2678:23–4.
17 See Ep 2678:25 with n7.
18 See Ep 2678:25–6 with n8.
19 See Ep 2678:27 with nn9–10.

TO ERASMUS

Your Polyphemus is returning to you:[1] I have given him this letter to you.
From it you will learn that it was not his fault that he tarried here instead
of flying there more quickly. But while he was waiting day after day for the
completion of his own business, the difficult affairs of his royal Majesty kept   5
his own from being completed.[2] I wanted to let you know this to keep you
from rebuking him out of a false suspicion about this tardiness.

Regensburg, 7 July 1532

2686 / To Bonifacius Amerbach   Freiburg, 8 July 1532

> This letter (= AK Ep 1665) was first published in the *Epistolae familiares*. The au-
> tograph is in the Öffentliche Bibliothek of the University of Basel (MS AN III 15
> 40). Bonifacius' reply is Ep 2688.

Cordial greetings. From the letters I sent you recently you know, I think, how
it is with Alciati.[1] Once again the plague has driven him out of Bourges and
he wants to be hired at Padua.[2]

Sadoleto received my letter without the books.[3] Later he wrote that the
books had also been delivered.[4]   5

I am worried and eager hear about your health.[5] That is how much I am
afraid of that immoderate affection of yours.

You can write back via this servant, if that is covenient.[6] Herwagen was
angry when he left me.[7] You will hear about the quarrel. But this is how it

* * * * *

2685
1 See Ep 2679 n1.
2 It is not clear what business it was that had to be cleared up at the court of King
  Ferdinand. It may have had something to do with Polyphemus' appointment
  as archer by Ferdinand in 1529 (Ep 2130:62–75, 129–32).

2686
1 The letters mentioned in Ep 2684:137–8
2 Cf Ep 2594:26–34.
3 Probably a covering letter, not extant, intended to accompany the delivery of
  the edition of Basil dedicated to Sadoleto (Ep 2611).
4 Sadoleto first thanked Erasmus for the dedication of the Basil before the books
  had arrived (Ep 2648:34–40). He reiterated his thanks after he had received
  them (Ep 2656).
5 See Epp 2678, 2684.
6 See Ep 2684:133–5.
7 Johann Herwagen, the Basel publisher

was. In the presence of Episcopius,[8] he pleaded with me to write a preface to   10
the Demosthenes.[9] I said I had yielded too much to the printers in this and
that I no longer wanted to spoil my reputation in that way. He pressed me. I
flatly refused. In the meantime Episcopius asked for a 'Letter to Goclenius'
about Ammianus.[10] While I was writing it,[11] Herwagen kept making a fuss:
'I beg you, I beg you.' I told him goodbye, adding 'You have my decision.   15
Why say anything more?' He left, for his companions were urging him to
go. I sent a servant after them to soften my reply: I said I would think about
doing the preface. He poured out his rage at my servant, saying he had come
here at your bidding to talk with me about many matters. We chatted quite
a while but he didn't talk about anything but the preface, to which I had not   20
given any thought. For I had written to him about some other matters. And
if he wanted to talk with me, I couldn't write the letter and talk to him at the
same time. But if he is really angry, I shall bear it easily, as long as he doesn't
trouble me any more. Farewell to you and also to those who are dear to you.

Freiburg, 8 July 1532   25
You will recognize the hand.
To the very renowned Doctor, Master Bonifacius Amerbach. At Basel

2687 / From Ludolf Cock   Regensburg, 9 July 1532

First published as Ep 175 in Förstemann / Günther, the autograph of this letter
was in the Burscher Collection of the University Library at Leipzig (Ep 1264
introduction).

Ludolf Cock (Coccius, Kock), documented 1508–32, was born at Bielefeld in
Westphalia. He matriculated at Erfurt in 1508, receiving his BA in 1509 and his

* * * * *

8 Nicolaus Episcopius (Ep 2233A n4)
9 Herwagen's edition of the works of Demosthenes (Basel: September 1532), for
   which Erasmus did eventually agree to write the preface (Ep 2695)
10 Johann Froben had published the Res gestae of the fourth-century historian
   Ammianus Marcellinus in the Historiae Augustae scriptores of 1518. For that volume Erasmus had edited Suetonius with a preface (Ep 586), but the title-page
   gave the false impression that Erasmus had edited Ammianus as well. In July
   1533 Hieronymus Froben (whose business partner was Episcopius) would issue
   a new edition of the Historiae Augustae scriptores incorporating the newly discovered books 27–30 of Ammianus. The editor of that volume was Sigismundus
   Gelenius (Ep 1702 n1), not Conradus Goclenius (Ep 2644). It is likely that
   Erasmus absent-mindedly substituted one name for the other.
11 There is no letter to anyone about Ammianus in Erasmus' surviving
   correspondence.

MA in 1513. Virtually everything else that is known of him derives from this letter, written in Regensburg and carried by Polyphemus (see lines 69–70).

Greetings. Some twenty years ago, when your *Adagia* was first beginning to
make its way into the hands of learned men,[1] I left the gymnasium at Erfurt,[2]
where I had studied philosophy, and travelled to Lower Germany,[3] with the
desire to see and greet you, most desired Master Erasmus. When this hope
was disappointed, I spent some time at Middelburg under Nicolaas van   5
Broeckhoven, who was then the rector of the school,[4] until I received from
friends aid sufficient for the journey to Paris, where I learned in some fashion
the first elements of Greek under the tutelage of Girolamo Aleandro, who
was later summoned to the episcopal court and abandoned the role of teaching.[5] Then I became the private pupil of Rutgerus Rescius, whom you are   10
accustomed to call your son,[6] a truly upright man and a good friend to me,
who treated me very kindly at Louvain during the time of my travels, when I
was always on the move, just like Diana Panagaea,[7] as you once wrote about
Johann von Vlatten, chief counsellor of our prince of Cleves, etc.[8] If I gained
nothing more from that time, I consider my richest gain was the acquisi-   15
tion of friends, among whom I count Willibald Pirckheimer, a man of remarkable and many-sided learning.[9] Two years ago, when I was travelling

* * * * *

2687
1 Between the first edition of the *Adagia*, published by Aldo Manuzio at Venice in
   1508, and the first Froben edition of 1513, there had been six pirated editions by
   Matthias Schürer at Sélestat.
2 *Gymnasium* = a secondary school or academy
3 Ie to the Netherlands; see Ep 1998 n6.
4 Broeckhoven (Ep 616:15n) became rector of the municipal school at Middelburg
   in 1514. In 1517 he became headmaster of the Latin school at Antwerp.
5 In December 1513 Aleandro entered the service of Etienne Poncher, bishop of
   Paris. A year later he switched his allegiance to Erard de la Marck, bishop of
   Liège.
6 Rescius (Ep 546) studied Greek with Aleandro at Paris. After the latter's retirement from teaching in 1513, Rescius began to teach Greek privately. In 1515 he
   moved to Louvain, where in 1518 he was appointed the first professor of Greek
   at the Collegium Trilingue. Nowhere in Erasmus' letters is he spoken of with
   the warm affection indicated here. Indeed, Erasmus had recently been point-
   edly critical of him; see Ep 2644:26–8 with n19.
7 *Adagia* II ix 47
8 See Ep 2454:2–4 with n1. Cock had evidently read that letter in the *Epistolae
   floridae*. Here, as in several instances below, 'etc' stands for the omitted portions
   of the official title of the person mentioned.
9 Ep 318

from Nürnberg to the Diet of Augsburg, I cannot tell you how kindly and
generously he treated a nobody like me, talking to me as if I were his equal
in age and status. Indeed he discussed the whole state of affairs and the con-   20
dition of the times briefly and compactly. Among other things he sang the
praises of Erasmus as the lover and restorer of all studies and true piety,
saying that a Christendom almost fallen to ruins could not be restored unless most of the articles of Christianity were referred to you and men like
you to be investigated. I write only a small part of what he said, so as not to   25
seem to flatter you. Then he insisted that benefices and the rewards of virtue
and learning should be bestowed only on the learned, 'far, far different,' he
said, 'from these rapacious monsters dispatched from Rome.' Then I became
acquainted with the most reverend Lord Lorenzo Campeggi, apostolic legate,
etc,[10] who bestowed on me an honourable gift at Augsburg, munificent as he   30
is to the devotees of learning.

At the recommendation of Willibald, I was also lucky enough to gain
the friendship of Hermann von Neuenahr, count and provost, etc, who was
ill at that time in Augsburg (would that the Fates had not begrudged this
man to the Christian world, for whose soul – as for that of Willibald – we   35
ought to pray).[11] Finally I gained the friendship of Prince Franz, count of
Waldeck, bishop of Minden, and also recently called and appointed to the
sees of Münster and Osnabrück.[12] I had become something of a friend of
his because of my studies at Erfurt; that friendship was confirmed by clear
indications and has good and happy prospects. Endowed as he is with the   40
genuine gifts of a bishop, he has undertaken the administration of these sees.
May Christ in his goodness and power render his efforts good and effective,
amen. Please deign, in your prudence, to write to him sometime (for from the
time he came of age he has been guided by a special affection and longing for
you) and, when the occasion arises, remind him to pay attention to what his   45
duty and his studies demand. So far his audience at Münster has been very

* * * * *

10 Ep 2366
11 Count Hermann von Neuenahr (Ep 442), provost and archdeacon of the Cologne
   cathedral chapter, fell seriously ill while attending the Diet of Augsburg and
   died on 30 October 1530; Pirckheimer died on 22 December 1532.
12 Franz von Waldeck (1491–1553) studied at Erfurt and Leipzig in preparation
   for an ecclesiastical career. In 1530 he was elected bishop of Minden, and then
   in 1532 he acquired the bishoprics of Münster and Osnabrück as well. He is
   remembered above all as the bishop who waged successful war against the
   'Anabaptist kingdom' of Münster in 1534–5.

large, a very rare thing these days. At Osnabrück also, Charles the Great,[13] by special privilege, provided public funds to hire professors of Hebrew, Greek, and Latin literature, who were to teach in the school of St Peter, which they call 'the high school.'[14] But in our unhappy times too little has thus far been 50 done about this, and the funds have been diverted to another purpose.

A few years ago, after I left the University of Erfurt, I took a teaching position at the fairly well attended gymnasium in Osnabrück, in order to keep from wasting away in inactivity. When I became shackled with my own affairs and those of my friends, I left. There also literary matters are at the mo- 55 ment reduced to such a state that it seems nothing can be done about it unless this bishop comes to the rescue and provides help. If you are well enough to do so, most learned and estimable sir, do not consider it a burden to write to him about a plan of studies and advise him to pay attention to the plans of learned men. You see for yourself how dangerous things have become 60 for Christendom, especially in Saxony, in which I include Westphalia.[15] The bishop has at his disposal Master Thomas von Halle (provost of the Minden chapter),[16] Master Burchardus Buschius (the full brother of Hermannus Buschius and dean),[17] Master Johann von Schmising (canon at Münster),[18]

* * * * *

13 The reference is to Charlemagne, who founded the diocese of Osnabrück in c 772.
14 Presumably a school attached to St Peter's cathedral, the first version of which was built in 785. We have no information concerning a *collegium trilingue* established by Charlemagne.
15 Historically (since the twelfth century) 'Westphalia' was the common designation of the area of the old duchy of Saxony west of the Weser river. The eastern portions of the old duchy had become the electorate of Saxony. At this time the duchy of Westphalia, which was subject to the archbishop of Cologne, occupied only a portion of the region of Westphalia north of the city of Cologne; Cock is evidently referring to the whole region.
16 Of whom nothing is known apart from this mention
17 Like his older brother Hermannus Buschius (Ep 1291 n4), Burchardus Buschius (documented 1496–1541) was a native of Wesphalia. In 1519 he was appointed precentor of the Minden cathedral chapter, and in 1526 he was elected dean.
18 Johann von Schmising of Münster (documented 1517–60) was a kinsman of Hermannus Buschius (preceding note). Little is known of him except that he matriculated at Cologne in 1517, that by 1528 he was a canon at Osnabrück, and that thirty years later he was dean of the Osnabrück chapter. This is the only reference to him as canon of Münster.

Master Johann von Kerssenbrock,[19] Master Theoderich von Ghel (scholaster   65
and canon of the church at Osnabrück),[20] none of them adverse to good learning, as well as others outstanding for their learning and piety. But if the episcopal court were enriched with such men, there would be no doubt that good
learning would be restored to its pristine state.[21] Having Felix Polyphemus
available as my Mercury,[22] I wanted to write to you somehow or other, to give   70
testimony of my affection for you. And out of your kindness and gentleness I
beg you to take it in good part. Because of turbulence of spirit, which afflicts
even a wise man, I didn't want to write at greater length. A few days ago,
some wicked men stripped me of everything I had as I was returning in the
evening to my residence in Regensburg. Send a letter recommending me to   75
the bishop of Münster; you will not regret having recommended me. I would
hope that your Wisdom would deign to send me a single letter in reply, for I
would value it more than any benefices or gifts of fortune. Farewell, my dear
Erasmus, half of my soul; even against your wishes I will never cease to love
you as long as I live. I would like you to give my greetings to Bertram von   80
Damm and his whole family, if he is still staying with you.[23] Polyphemus
will tell you what has happened at the Diet of Regensburg. Rescius wrote
me that he is engaged in printing some magnificent volume by a theologian
at Louvain; it will take almost a year to finish it. You can guess who he is.[24]
Campen, who is here with Johannes Dantiscus (the bishop of Chełmno and   85
the ambassador of the king of Poland, etc),[25] said he saw it once at Louvain

* * * * *

19 The younger son of a noble family, Kerssenbrock (documented 1486–1540) was
   designated for an ecclesiastical career. He is documented as canon of Osnabrück
   in 1491. In 1540 he is documented as canon of Osnabrück and Minden.
20 Theodorich von Ghel is documented only in this letter. As scholaster he would
   have been headmaster of the cathedral school. (Citing this letter, CEBR II 257 assigns the scholaster's job to Kerssenbrock, but that is a misreading of the text.)
21 The point seems to be that if Bishop Franz (n12 above) were to gather the best
   men from his three bishoprics together into a unified administration at his
   court, something effective could be done for the cause of good letters.
22 Mercury was, among other things, the messenger of the gods. For Polyphemus
   (Felix Rex) see Epp 2649 n3, 2679 n1, 2685.
23 See Ep 2661 introduction.
24 Unidentified
25 Jan van Campen, first professor of Hebrew at the Collegium Trilingue in
   Louvain, had resigned his chair in 1531 and entered the service of Johannes
   Dantiscus, currently ambassador of the king of Poland at the imperial court; see
   Ep 2570 n30.

and that it was sheer nonsense. Farewell to your Wisdom, to whom I heartily dedicate myself.

From Regensburg, in the year 1532, on the Tuesday after the Visitation of Our Lady, the Virgin Mary   90

Most devoted to Your Most Eminent Lordship Ludolph Cock of Bielefeld

Conradus Goclenius is originally from the territory of the Count of Waldeck.[26]

To Eobanus Hessus of Nürnberg,[27] or to Otto or Johann von Falckenberg,   95
full brothers, canons of the famous church at Speyer,[28] or to anyone at Cologne.[29]

To the most thoroughly distinguished gentleman and the reviver of true piety, his dear Erasmus of Rotterdam, extraordinary theologian. At Freiburg im Breisgau   100

2688 / From Bonifacius Amerbach   Basel, 10 July [1532]

This letter (= AK Ep 1666), first published by Allen, is Bonifacius' answer to Epp 2678, 2684, and 2686. The manuscript is in the Öffentliche Bibliothek of the University of Basel (MS C VIa 73 13).

Cordial greetings. Your consolatory letter, most renowned Erasmus, brought me back to life. Indeed at the death of my dear little daughter I immediately thought that Christ was treating me very justly when he asked to have back something he had bestowed on someone subject to his jurisdiction. I also re-membered many cases where the ancients lost children and yet bore the loss   5
with the greatest equanimity. And lastly, I saw that it is not at all fitting that reason could not accomplish for an educated person what time accomplishes for the common people. And yet I made no progress in composing myself, so strong was paternal affection (how others may succeed in shaking it off I don't know) that, for me at any rate, it was impossible. Since I was incapable 10
of this, I also fell sick and have struggled with the illness for eighteen days. If

* * * * *

26 Goclenius was born in Mengeringhausen in the county of Waldeck (Westphalia).
27 See Epp 874, 2446.
28 For Otto von Falkenberg, canon at Speyer since 1517, see Ep 2439 n6. Cock was unaware that he had died on 24 June 1532. His brother Johann, apparently the younger of the two, was appointed canon in 1528.
29 This appears to be a list of suitable forwarding addresses.

you ask what kind of illness, I don't think the physician himself could give a
true diagnosis. The conjecture that the fever was caused by the plague does
not seem plausible to me, both because of what I have already said,[1] and because I never had a headache but rather – and that only in the violent onset   15
of the attack – I was seized by such a burning fever that I thought my whole
body was on fire. But by the grace of Christ, it suddenly subsided on the following day after I had taken medications.[2] Now this moderation of my tem-
perature offers a sign of the commencement of my return to good health, and
your letter was no small help in promoting it. For whether it was my love for   20
you or your authority over me or both together, I was so changed by your
deeply moving language that, if any grief remained and I had not completely
shaken it off, I at least learned to bear it with equanimity; indeed as soon as
I had read the letter I began to feel better.[3] And so I give you my unending
thanks for this antidote (that is, your letter) and all the more because, even   25
though you were more occupied with more important matters in sending
here the letters of Sadoleto and others,[4] you were not unwilling to undertake
such a task for my sake. Take care of yourself, my dear Erasmus. If I hear that
you are in excellent health, then I will be fully recovered.

At Basel, 10 July   30

Herwagen was not with me when he left here. I don't think he was
really angry.[5] I would be sorry for what happened to Alciati, except that he
was called to such a splendidly paid position in Padua;[6] for I hear that he is
offered no less than at Bourges.[7]

* * * * *

2688
1 According to Alfred Hartmann, editor of the text of this letter for AK, the words
   'what I have already said' do not apply to 'I was sick ... for eighteen days' but
   rather to a sentence at the foot of the manuscript page (not included in Allen's
   text): 'Otherwise normal appetite, no vomiting, since the first day [of the ill-
   ness] some sleepiness, but contracted from three nights of insomnia following
   the death of my little daughter.'
2 According to Hartmann. Bonifacius erased 'after I had taken medications'
   (*pharmacis sumptis*) from this sentence.
3 Here, according to Hartmann, Allen misread the manuscript, which has *protinus lectis [literis] melius habere cepi*, and made it *protinus nubes habere cepi*, which
   makes no sense. The translation follows Hartmann.
4 See Ep 2684:135–8 with nn17–18.
5 See Ep 2686:8–24.
6 Cf Ep 2657:78–86. Bonifacius' information doubtless came from the packet of
   letters forwarded by Erasmus; see n4 above. Hartmann's text reads 'Italy'
   instead of 'Padua.'
7 According to Hartmann, Bonifacius expunged this clause.

2689 / From Jean (II) de Carondelet   Brussels, 19 July 1532

This letter was first published in Ipolyi page 222. The manuscript is page 331
of the Olahus codex in the Hungarian National Archives at Budapest (Ep 2339
introduction). Erasmus' friend and patron, Jean de Carondelet (Ep 1276), long
a member of the Privy Council of the Netherlands at Mechelen, had been made
its president in 1531.

JEAN, ARCHBISHOP OF PALERMO, IMPERIAL CHANCELLOR
IN BRABANT, TO ERASMUS OF ROTTERDAM, GREETINGS
Cordial greetings, distinguished sir. Master Nicolaus Olahus, secretary and
counsellor to her most serene Majesty, the queen regent,[1] has shown me several of your letters, especially the most recent one,[2] in which you respond to   5
those that Master Olahus, secretary to her Majesty, wrote to you, but con-
fusedly and reporting nothing definite. Your Lordship says that you are having a house built at Freiburg, and that you cannot do without the wines of
Burgundy. You complain about the hardship of the journeys, the long inter-
ruption in your work, and other such things, which can easily be attended   10
to, but you have not revealed your intentions, which it is important for us
to know before we proceed any further with her Majesty concerning your
salary and other matters that pertain to you.[3] For that reason, although this
whole province, from the lowest to the highest, shares a most eager expec-
tation of your arrival, and your native land itself yearns to have you come   15
back, nevertheless there is nothing that the aforesaid Master Nicolaus and
I can announce or promise to your Lordship with any certainty until you
write us more fully about your intentions, namely whether you will come or
not, under what terms and conditions, whether you are willing to be content
with your old annual pension paid promptly thereafter from year to year or   20
whether you require more. We eagerly request that you do this, so that then
we, together with Master Olahus, and with the cognizance of the queen, can
persuade your Lordship not to be reluctant to leave Germany, to undergo the
troubles of the trip, or to accede to the wishes of such a great princess. I commend myself to you most heartily.   25

* * * * *

2689
1 Mary of Hungary, sister of Emperor Charles (Ep 2100). For Nicolaus Olahus see
   Ep 2339 introduction.
2 Ep 2646; the earlier ones are Epp 2582, 2613.
3 Ie his long-unpaid imperial pension, the resumption of which had been made
   dependent on his return

Jean (II) de Carondelet by Jan Cornelisz Vermeyen
Brooklyn Museum, Brooklyn, New York (Gift of Horace Havemeyer)

At Brussels, 19 July 1532

The reason that I have written you so infrequently in recent times is your own silence.[4] Not that I accuse you of any negligence on that account, but rather that I excuse my own failure to write.

2690 / To Tommaso de Vio, Cardinal Cajetanus   Freiburg, 23 July 1532

First published in the *Epistolae palaeonaeoi*, this letter is the only one between Erasmus and Cardinal Cajetanus to have survived. It answers one from the cardinal that was presumably his reply to the letter from Erasmus mentioned in Ep 2779:12–13. From the same source we learn that Cajetanus showed the present letter to the pope and sent a cordially friendly reply to it (Ep 2779:13–17). Further references to correspondence between Erasmus and Cajetanus are found in Allen Epp 2929:15–19, 2935, and 3100:70–3.

Tommaso de Vio (Ep 839:26n), better known as Cajetanus after his birthplace Gaeta (Caieta in Latin), entered the Dominican order in 1484. Quickly establishing himself as a formidable Thomistic theologian, he taught with distinction at the universities of Pavia and Rome (1487–1508). Rising rapidly to high office in his order and in the church, he became general of the Dominicans in 1508, cardinal in 1517, and bishop of Gaeta in 1518. Although a persistent advocate of ecclesiastical reform, he was also an ardent defender of papal authority against advocates of conciliar supremacy and the supporters of Luther. It was as papal legate to Emperor Maximilian I in 1518 that Cajetanus had his memorable (albeit unsuccessful) encounter with Martin Luther at the Diet of Augsburg. For the rest of his life Cajetanus continued to serve the papacy as adviser and diplomat and to publish important works of scholarship.

Erasmus' earliest recorded statements about Cajetanus, whom he initially judged to be one of those responsible for the destructive harshness of Rome's reaction to Luther, were vituperatively negative; see especially Ep 1188 (c March 1521):24–30. But by the time he wrote Ep 1225 (August 1521), his attitude had changed dramatically as the result of reading Cajetanus' *De divina institutione pontificatus Romani pontificis* (March 1521), which he found entirely admirable in its freedom from personal abuse and its success in throwing light on the subject by means of 'plain arguments' based on properly cited authorities; see Ep 1225:215–21, and cf Ep 1275:85–7. In March 1532 Erasmus had similar praise for the 'learned brevity and the soberness of the discussion' in two short books that Cajetanus had sent him: *De sacrificio missae adversus Luteranos iuxta scripturas*

* * * * *

4 Ep 2055 is Erasmus' most recent surviving letter to Carondelet.

Tommaso de Vio, Cardinal Cajetanus
Biblioteca Ambrosiana, Milan

tractatus, and *De communione, de confessione, de satisfactione, de invocatione sanc-*
torum adversus Luteranos tractatus, both published at Rome in 1531, and both
aimed at refuting positions articulated in the Lutheran Augsburg Confession;
see Ep 2619:11–17 with nn4–5.

ERASMUS OF ROTTERDAM TO TOMMASO CARDINAL CAJETANUS,
GREETINGS

I find that what Augustine wrote is in fact true: there is such a thing as a
good error. For it was an error he made on a journey that saved him, when
through ignorance he took a wrong turn and thus avoided an ambush by   5
the Donatists.[1] So too a mistake of Gumppenberg, who thought that a letter
from you to me was mixed in his packet of letters, opened the way to my
friendship with your most reverend Eminence.[2] But in fact I perceive your
benevolence towards me most of all in that you give me prudent and friendly
advice about how I can both avoid personal suspicions and attacks and also   10
rescue the leisure of my studies in my old age from those who bark and rail
against me.

For the most part, I have already accomplished on my own initiative
what your most reverend Eminence urges me to do;[3] I have noted and corrected many places in which there is clearly a mistake, either mine or the   15
printers'. The moderation you are looking for I have also supplied, in the
judgment of all, by responding to the censures of the Paris theologians, which
were recently issued under the name of the faculty of theology,[4] although in
fact they were the work of one unstable man only, a person hardly acceptable
to his own college because of his behaviour.[5] They are always cackling at me 20
about Augustine, but in fact I have been no less severe in judging my writings than Augustine was in what he called *Retractations,* not a palinode but
a revision of his works,[6] to make sure nothing would be omitted. Although
he sometimes corrects minor points in passing, he defends some things not

* * * * *

2690
1 *Enchiridion ad Laurentinum* 17 (PL 40 239)
2 See Ep 2619:10–11. It would appear that Gumppenberg's letter prompted
  Erasmus to write to Cajetanus the letter mentioned in Ep 2779; see introduction
  above.
3 Ep 2729:16–20 indicates that Cajetanus had urged Erasmus to undertake a
  general revision of his works so as to mollify his critics.
4 For the *Determinatio* of the Paris theologians and the *Declarationes* of Erasmus,
  see Ep 2552 n10.
5 Noël Béda (Ep 2635 n4)
6 See Ep 2660 n9.

without a sense of uncertainty. I would not refuse to do the same in all of my   25
writings, as long as it is clear what places are erroneous or may well cause
some slight scandal because of their resemblance to error. What am I to do
about places misunderstood by critics, or corrupt readings, or passages ma-
levolently twisted to a false meaning, or places where one person is replaced
by another or one period of time by another? And there is an abundance   30
of such places where many yelp at me out of hatred or envy or ambition.
Naturally they pretend they act out of zeal for the church, but nonetheless
they never attacked me more lethally than when I was fighting full force
against the sects that were gaining strength in Germany. And some of them
have such perverse judgment that if I were willing to satisfy their desires, I   35
would have to remove from my writings things that are thought to be excellent by men who are both learned and pious.

　　If I had even a crumb of heretical inclination, I could long ago have
been maddened by such vicious attacks and would have gone over to the
camp of the heretics. As it is, I have never accepted even one of them as a   40
disciple, but if I was able to withdraw someone from their camp, I turned
him over to the church, wishing to have such men not as my own disciples
but as fellow disciples in the church. To many I said nothing; no one outdid
me in moderation. But however that may be, although I had intended on my
own initiative to do what your reverend Prudence urges me to do, I do it all   45
the more willingly because I have the approval of so eminent a man for this
course of action. I will never completely stop up the mouths of my detractors, but only of those who attack me out of a diseased mind, not with good
judgment. I will be quite happy enough if I satisfy good men, but especially
if I satisfy Christ.   50

　　Over and over again I want to assure your most reverend Eminence
that your advice has been most welcome to me, and before long I will show
you that it was not wasted. For I cannot carry it out in time for the fall fair.[7]
But by Easter,[8] with the help of Christ, I will see to it that it is done.[9] I have
also decided to gather together from my writings passages which clearly   55
counter unapproved doctrines as well as the slanders some have directed at
me. Then I will either explain or correct places that have been suspected, so

* * * * *

7 Ie the fall book fair at Frankfurt
8 Ie in time for the spring fair
9 It is not at all clear what Erasmus was thinking of as partial fulfilment of his
　　intent to revise his works as advised by Cajetanus. Suffice it to say that no such
　　general revision ever appeared.

that no person or religious order is satirized by name. I know this will cause some to prepare a triumph and proclaim that Erasmus has been overthrown. But I care more about what contributes to the tranquillity of the church than what serves my reputation.[10] 60

If I am approved by Christ, and by you and those like you who have combined true learning with true piety, that is victory enough for me. I am a nobody, the creature of a day, who is not looking for high offices and benefices, but still it would be very pleasing to me if the supreme pontiff would approve of what I am doing and would give some outward expression of his favour. Rome has already sent us many deceitful books, when the world would expect better ones from this citadel of piety. There is more than enough dissension. Such books are nothing more than seedbeds of discord. Farewell. 65

Given at Freiburg im Breisgau, 23 July 1532 70

2691 / To Adolf Eichholz   Freiburg, 24 July 1532

This letter was published in a collection of extracts from ancient and modern authors in praise of the city of Cologne, printed at the end of *Flora Hermanni Buschii Pasiphili in … urbis Agrippinae Coloniae laudem …* (Cologne: Henricus Mameranus 1550) folio B7 verso. For Adolf Eichholz, who taught canon law at Cologne, see Ep 866 introduction.

ERASMUS ROTERODAMUS TO HIS FRIEND ADOLF DRYOXYLO,[1]
GREETINGS
Your letter was most delightful, my dearest Dryoxylo, as was the map representing all of Cologne. This gift of yours can by no means be called small, since you are sending the very large and wealthy city of Agrippina.[2] I will write more on another occasion. Farewell. 5

Freiburg, on the vigil of St James the Apostle 1532

* * * * *

10 Erasmus had already published a brief *Precatio pro pace ecclesiae* in the spring of 1532 (Ep 2618). His major treatise on the subject, *De sarcienda ecclesiae concordia*, appeared in the summer of 1533 (Ep 2852). Cajetanus, to whom Erasmus likely sent a copy of it (see Allen's introduction to Ep 2935), read it and spoke approvingly of it to Pope Clement VII (Allen Ep 3100:70–7).

2691
1 Erasmus turns Eichholz ('oakwood' in German) into Dryoxylus ('oakwood' in transliterated Greek).
2 Colonia Agrippina was the Latin name for Cologne.

2692 / To Henricus Cornelius Agrippa   Freiburg, 25 July 1532

This letter was first published in the *Agrippae opera* II 1010. Agrippa's reply is Ep 2737. For Henricus Cornelius Agrippa of Nettesheim see Ep 2544 introduction.

ERASMUS TO AGRIPPA
When Polyphemus came back here from Regensburg,[1] I was both weary and engaged in buildng,[2] than which I find nothing more unpleasant, and I am overwhelmed by the labour of my studies. Thus I would rather write to you somewhat belatedly than give you any good reason to complain that you had not received a letter owed to you. We have gone to war against the Turks, with no good prospects at all.[3] They should send there those lusty men with good lungs and loud voices.[4]

Farewell, most learned Cornelius. After the fair,[5] I will write you more eagerly and at greater length.

Freiburg, the feast of St James 1532

2693 / From Nicolaus Olahus   Brussels, 26 July 1532

This letter, Olahus' reply to Epp 2613 and 2646, was first published in Ipolyi page 224. The manuscript is page 234 of the Olahus codex in the Hungarian National Archives at Budapest (Ep 2339 introduction).

RESPONSE TO ERASMUS FROM NICOLAUS OLAHUS, TREASURER OF
SZÉKESFEHÉRVÁR, SECRETARY TO HER MOST SERENE MAJESTY
While I was anxiously awaiting the servant whom you wrote you would send after the Easter just past, so that he could give you detailed information and prepare lodgings to be ready for your arrival,[1] and while in the mean-

* * * * *

2692
1 For Felix Rex, known as Polyphemus, see Ep 2649 n3.
2 Ie the refurbishing of his new house in Freiburg; see Ep 2646 n3.
3 Cf Ep 2654:9–20.
4 Presumably a swipe at those, including a list of popes, who 'clamour for war against the Turks, calling them inhuman monsters, enemies of the church, and a race tainted with every kind of crime and villainy.' See Ep 2285:66–8, and cf Ep 2338 n17.
5 Ie the fall book fair at Frankfurt

2693
1 See Ep 2613:61–3.

time I had no thought of replying to your letter before his arrival, imagining that you would learn my wishes and other things pertaining to your affairs from your servant when he returned rather than from a letter from me, lo and behold! at Ghent there was the physician Gerardus Henricus of Amsterdam with your letter![2] At first I was delighted to see him, thinking he was that servant you had promised to send here. But when I had read your letter and had also spoken with him, both about you and about some dealings he had with me, I recognized that my joy was short-lived. And so, when I could no longer expect the arrival of your man, I did not want to be faulted for remaining silent any longer.

In your letter you write that you are most pleased that I offered my support to Lieven.[3] I will support to the best of my ability not only him (for his learning and character are well known to me) but many others besides whom you recommend. I have actually taken care that in the name of the queen eight gros be paid to him every day for the time being,[4] until some office suitable for him becomes vacant (all the openings in the gift of the queen being now filled) and can be provided for him. The queen has left him to me, to make use of his efforts in managing affairs. I am in daily contact with him, both because he is your protégé and has your recommendation and also because I see nothing in him that is greatly to be shunned.

But alas! listen to what happened. Recently, when we arrived in Ghent after a journey through the cities of Brabant and Flanders in the retinue of the queen, I was by chance afforded hospitality in the house of Antonius Clava, who I learned had been a good friend of yours when he was still alive.'[5] He was survived by a granddaughter,[6] the daughter of his daughter,[7] a virgin of about eighteen, not bad looking, of good character, and (so far as I could see) endowed with more than a few intellectual gifts. Her stepfather is Damiaan van Vissenaken, a physician and a cultivated gentleman.[8] Unbeknownst to

* * * * *

2 Ep 2646; for Gerardus Henricus see Ep 2645 n10.
3 Ie support to Erasmus' former famulus Lieven Algoet (Ep 2278 n2) in his attempt to secure an appointment at the court of Queen Mary: see Ep 2613:3–6.
4 Probably eight groot Flemish and therefore slightly less than the daily wage of an Antwerp master mason/carpenter (9.05d) (CWE 12 691 Table 13)
5 For Clava, who had died in 1529, see Epp 175:13n, 2260:44–53.
6 Catherine Hannot
7 Margareta
8 Damiaan van Vissenaken (d after 1541) was a physician from Tienen who resided at Ghent. In 1541 he published his *Theoricae medicinae* at Antwerp. Apart from this and his marriage to the widow of Antonius Clava, little is known of him.

me, Lieven fell madly in love with her, and she with him. We were there almost three weeks. And in that time I had not been able to learn anything defi-   35
nite about their love, except that one or the other of my servants whispered
something about it in my ear. I passed it over in silence, thinking that if they
were actually in love they themselves would have said something about it to
me. Two days before we were getting ready to return here, Lieven sent Jakob
the Dane,[9] that gadabout herald of your praises, who was also with me there,   40
to ask me to apply to the physician Damiaan for Lieven to have the girl's
hand in marriage. At first I tried to talk Lieven out of it, telling him about the
advantages of marriage and also the disadvantages if it didn't work out, but
finally I was won over by his pleas to at least see what Damiaan might think
of it and I spoke to Damiaan about it. Having consulted with his wife, as I   45
required, Damiaan said that from the time the girl was two or three years old
she had had suitors of no little standing and that now too there were some
rich suitors for her hand in marriage, but that for my sake and in so far as it
was his business to do so, he would hand the girl over to me, for the advantage of Lieven, but only after consulting the paternal and maternal relatives   50
of the girl.

So we came back here, leaving the matter undecided. Vissenaken consulted the girl's relatives at home and then came back to me here about ten
days later. He repeated what he had said before, that he would follow my
wishes and reject suitors who had far better fortunes than Lieven – some-   55
thing he would hardly do for anyone else. I sent him away with Lieven so
that Lieven could take time to think seriously, day and night, about marrying
the girl, find out at Ghent about the dowry and inheritance of the girl, call
together his friends and discuss it with them, and when he had gathered this
information about her dowry, return to me without taking any action, and   60
then we would do whatever was most advantageous and practical for him
(but only after consulting you about the matter), so that an untimely passion
should not bring him to marry a girl without a dowry and make him sorry
for it afterwards. I enjoined him by no means to bind himself there in any
way before he had returned to me and we had written to you about the mat-   65
ter and found out your wishes. But he finally came back and told me, much
to my sorrow, that he had betrothed himself to the girl. When I berated him
and accused him of ignoring my instructions, all he could answer was that
he did indeed remember them but that, either because of an insane passion
(which is in itself powerful magic) or by the incantations of others, he was   70

* * * * *

9 Jakob Jespersen (Ep 2570 introduction)

powerless to do anything but to be formally betrothed to her. I asked about
the dowry. He said that she now has an annual income of about eighteen
ducats a year, and that after the death of her mother she will succeed to part
of the income and the inheritance.[10] 'Good grief,' I said, 'do you think you
can live with a wife on such a pittance per year? And what is this great hope   75
you now entertain of goods to come to you after the death of your mother-
in-law? And in the meantime what are you and your wife going to do? How
will you get clothing and food for her?' Since the whole thing was fixed and
could not be changed, I seemed to be beating the air,[11] but I couldn't stop doing it, partly because I was very excited, partly because I wished him more   80
favourable circumstances.

After that I began to advise him to put off the wedding till somewhat
later so that we could make better and more certain provision for him and
could write to you about it. He said that after the betrothal he had left Ghent
and gone to the dean at Bruges,[12] who had recently become a special friend   85
of mine, and had already invited him and other members of his family to the
wedding on the sixth day of the coming August. When I heard that he had
rushed into the business in this way, without any advice, I said, 'Go ahead,
do whatever you want, carry through the wedding you have entered into.
But I am afraid that one day you will regret what you have done.'   90

Now you know this whole business about Lieven. I am grieved that
he has been so quickly snared in this way. The virgin is born of honourable
parents, as I hear, and she herself seems to be of a modest and praiseworthy
character, a hard worker, not at all accustomed to leisure. But her dowry is
too small to provide for herself and a husband of moderate means. It is possi-   95
ble that, living with me under the sponsorship of the queen, he could before
long have found a virgin with a more ample fortune. Whether his marriage
turns out well or badly, attribute it to his own madness and imprudence; do
not blame it on anyone else.[13]

And now, my most learned and my most dear Erasmus, a few words   100
about your situation. Greatly concerned as I was about your reputation and

* * * * *

10 The Venetian ducat was valued at 80d groot Flemish in 1532, so that at £6 0s 0d
    Catherine Hannot's income was rather less than a year's wage of an Antwerp
    master mason/carpenter (£8 8s 1d) at 9.05d per day and a year of 230 days (CWE
    12 650 Table 3, 691 Table 13).
11 1 Cor 9:26
12 Marcus Laurinus (Ep 651), dean of St Donatian's at Bruges since 1519
13 Erasmus joined Olahus in finding fault with Lieven's marriage; see Epp
    2707:5–6, 2735:17–19, 2759:28–37, 2792:46–57.

your peace, I wrote to you before about your returning here,[14] and out of a
deep desire to give you good advice about your comfort and peace, I urged
you to let me know whether you intend to return, so that I might know how
to approach the queen concerning your status and your future peace of   105
mind. Perhaps out of a lack of confidence in me, you wrote back to me two
indecisive letters;[15] in both of them, listing your reasons and the defects of
your health, you made no clear decision. You seem to want and not to want
to return. Among other reasons you say that you cannot bear the burdens of
the court because of your age. Do you think that I did not consider ahead of   110
time everything about your condition before I sent you my last letter? Pay
no attention to the example of Le Sauvage.[16] If you come back, no one will
force you to undergo the burdens of serving in the court unless you want to
do so of your own free will. Whether you prefer to live here, where the queen
resides, or elsewhere, you will be free to choose where to live (though, in my   115
judgment, here with the queen would be more comfortable for you, for many
reasons) and you will be free here to focus your efforts, as you now do there,
on caring for and increasing the well-being of Christianity through nights
spent in literary studies. Here in your homeland you would have a pension
to live in peace and quiet under the auspices of the queen; you would visit   120
the queen according to your own desires or her own wishes. You would depend on no one but her. But you are afraid that the monks will abuse and revile you.[17] You will never be able to avoid that, wherever you may be, as long
as you draw your breath, especially since you rightfully publish so many
books against false monks. For what mortal can escape the abuse of others,   125
seeing that Christ himself bore so much of it in his flesh, even unto death?

    Therefore, to keep me from seeming to be the only one summoning
you, his Lordship of Palermo is also writing to you.[18] When I could get no
certain response from you, I showed him the letter you sent to me. And so
make up your mind and let us know whether you want to return. Here you   130
will have not only Burgundian wine (access to which keeps you there)[19] but

* * * * *

14 Ep 2607
15 Epp 2613, 2646
16 See Ep 2613:9–15.
17 See Ep 2613:27–33 with nn8–9.
18 Jean (II) de Carondelet, archbishop of Palermo; his letter is Ep 2689.
19 See Ep 2646:7–8 with n5.

all the other wines that you could get there and that in the past have nourished your time of life. Sometimes you will also have Hungarian wine, no
worse or less tasty than Burgundian wine. The queen's ship has brought it
here, and if peace ever comes to my Hungary, it will be brought here every   135
year. If you lose something on the sale of your house there, you will have the
compensation of being with your own people in your native land, besides
other advantages for yourself and for your province; and we who are your
friends will make it up to you with interest.

Write us something definite. I will do everything I can to make you able   140
to judge that I have thoroughly performed the duty of a good friend on your
behalf. For it is not fair that you should be of a divided mind and not open
your mind to us, and it keeps me from being able to urge the queen to do
anything for you. The emperor has not harvested so much of the grain that
he did not leave the queen her own to harvest, enough to support good men.   145

Not only the bishop of Chełmno but I too was more than a little irritated by my Dane for circulating your letter.[20] But that is simply the way he
is, and so he deserves to be pardoned. I employ him in teaching only the rudiments of Greek grammar, very little in other areas. For he was trained from
boyhood in that subject in an elementary school. If you want to employ his   150
efforts in embellishing your name or extending your reputation, write to him
and make use of him as an encomiast, most laudable gentleman that he is. It
was my pleasure to see the physician Gerardus; I took care that the response
he got from the queen was not at all unfavourable.[21] I will proceed to gain the
queen's favour for you, as you request.   155

Forgive me for writing this wordy, incoherent narrative instead of a
real letter, and accept in good part the liberty I take in what I write, since
it springs from a plain and open heart. Unless you outdo me by writing an
even longer letter, I will proceed to write one so long that just to read it will
wear you out.[22] Farewell, and continue to be fond of me.   160

Brussels, 26 July 1532

* * * * *

20 See Ep 2646:14–15 with n7.
21 For Gerardus Henricus see n2 above. For Erasmus' request that Olahus do what
   he could to help Henricus, see Ep 2646:21–4.
22 Erasmus' next letter to Olahus, Ep 2707, is very brief and appears to have been
   written before this letter arrived. Discussion of Erasmus' return to Brabant
   (always fruitless) did not resume until Epp 2759, 2762.

2694 / To Bonifacius Amerbach   [Freiburg], 2 August 1532

This letter (= AK Ep 1667) was first published in the *Vita Erasmi*. The autograph is in the Öffentliche Bibliothek of the University of Basel (MS AN III 15 41).

Greetings. I sent my servant again,[1] so that I may rejoice in the certain knowledge that you have recovered, for I am still anxious and uncertain in my mind. You may send the little letter here enclosed secretly to Hieronymus Froben via your servant,[2] but remind him separately that he alone is to read it, lest this villainous servant of mine find out about it.[3] Farewell.   5
2 August 1532
To Doctor Amerbach

2695 / To Johann Georg Paumgartner   Freiburg, 2 August 1532

This is the preface to Johann Herwagen's edition of Demosthenes (Basel: September 1532). For Erasmus reluctance to write the preface, see Ep 2686:10–24.

DESIDERIUS ERASMUS OF ROTTERDAM SENDS GREETINGS TO THE
DISTINGUISHED YOUNG MAN JOHANN GEORG PAUMGARTNER
Just as in the past those who filled the earth with scurrilous and worthless books out of a desire for paltry gain in the present deserved nothing at all for their learned efforts, so too the favour of all good men is owed to those   5
who devote all their care and industry to calling back for us and honouring the ancient writers who are most approved by the judgment and consensus of many centuries. There is wide agreement among all scholars that among Greek orators Demosthenes holds such a commanding position that you will hardly find anyone you can compare with him. And surely it is a correct   10
precept that we should begin with the best. And for that reason, among the Latins, schoolboys once learned how to read from the most approved of the poets. Horace does not deny this when he makes this prediction about his own poems: 'This also awaits you: that stuttering old age / will occupy you

* * * * *

2694
1 Probably the 'Jacobus' of Ep 2652 n4, who is also the servant referred to again in line 5
2 The letter is not extant.
3 Except for two words, this entire sentence is in Greek.

teaching schoolboys their ABCs in the streets of the booksellers.'[1] For it matters   15
a great deal what liquor saturates the still fresh little clay pots of their minds.

Indeed it was quite practical for the first instruction in the Latin language to begin from select poets because besides their stylistic qualities they
have some elegance and charm of their own, which makes the boys love
their studies as though they were something good to eat, since at that age   20
they enjoy what is sweet rather than what is nourishing. And someone who
understands the poets will have a better understanding of the orators. Among
the Greeks the procedure was different. For the difference between the language of the poets and that of the orators was so great that you would think
they were speaking different languages. Thus students who had learned the   25
rudiments from the poets were at a loss when they went on to read the orators, as if they were suddenly dealing with a foreign language, and though
the students knew what each word meant, they could not understand the
sense of the whole. The reason was the peculiarity of the figures of speech,
tropes, and idioms, in which the lexical meanings do not help very much. On   30
this subject Guillaume Budé has rendered remarkable service to those who
love languages.[2]

But just as Cicero is not immediately suitable for teaching young minds
the language of Rome (for Quintilian thinks that he can fully please only
those who are far advanced),[3] so too I do not think that Demosthenes is very   35
suitable for those who seek skill in the Greek language, because much of his
skill is more concealed than on the surface. For according to the admiring
joke of Demades, he wrote only according to the water and can be understood only by the sober and wakeful.[4] So what Quintilian says about Cicero
can be applied quite well to Demosthenes: he who begins to take great plea-   40
sure in Demosthenes knows that he has made considerable progress in the
art of speaking. Just as no one is fully delighted by a skilful painting unless
he himself has some skill in that art, so too that divine quality which the
most eloquent speakers have always admired in Demosthenes, the vehement
style, will be felt only by those who are trained in the precepts of rhetoric and   45
instructed by a knowledge of history.

* * * * *

2695
1 *Epistles* 1.20.17–18, misquoted; cf 1.20.2.
2 Presumably a reference to Budé's *Commentarii linguae graecae* (1529)
3 10.1.112
4 *Apophthegmata* 6.382 (CWE 38 703). The joke was that while all speakers 'spoke
   according to the water' (ie they were timed by a water clock), Demosthenes
   'wrote according to it as well' (ie he drank only water and missed the inspira-
   tion provided by wine).

And so I will allow the young student to get a taste of Demosthenes, but he should come back to study him seriously when his critical insight is sharp enough to see that truly Attic beauty, that rigorous judgment, those arguments so skilfully adapted, and finally that amazing forcefulness which 50 all admire but hardly anyone can match. At the same time it would be an elegant exercise to do what some of the ancients did with Homer and Virgil, that is, to compare passages to see what one borrowed from the other, and where the Latin equals the Greek or is superior to it, and where imitation is less successful than the original. There is almost no better way to hone the 55 ability to judge.

I will not expend any effort in praising Demosthenes, for to praise him adequately would require the eloquence of Demosthenes himself. In fact there is no need for eloquence to praise him, for everyone agrees in praising him to the heavens. And I will not try to spur you on, my dear Georg, 60 because I perceive that of your own volition you are galloping at a good rate in this splendid racecourse. You will ask how I know about how you are getting on, since I have never seen you. I have seen your best features, you very lucky young man, for Viglius Zuichemus, an artist of the highest level, who by living with you has come to know you very well, has depicted you 65 for me very vividly with his brush. Indeed in your letter to me you yourself have portrayed yourself for me in such a way that I would see no more if you were in my presence.[5] In your letter I cherished that felicitous talent of yours: though you have barely finished your sixteenth year, you write letters that are, first of all, in good Latin and also (which I value more) contain 70 perceptions that are sharp and logically connected. But why should I extol that candid and free-spirited modesty of yours, why should I praise that extraordinary devotion to me which breathes throughout your whole letter?

And here I recognize the true and genuine progeny of that very distinguished gentleman Johann Paumgartner. Long ago I struck up with him a 75 friendship that I certainly number among the foremost good fortunes of my life. For who could be more sincere or loveable? You rightfully insert yourself, my dear Georg, into this bond of friendship. For it is proper and just to inherit such possessions, even when the father is still alive. Moreover, just as you are much more blessed in having such a father than in possessing your 80 father's wealth, so too you are more truly and splendidly wealthy in having the remarkable mental endowments that were partly bestowed on you by the favour and kindness of God, and which you partly developed by your

* * * * *

5 The letter is not extant.

own efforts – more wealthy, I say, than the riches of your ancestors, however ample, could ever have made you. And so accept Demosthenes, who now 85 comes forward like [a serpent] 'that has sloughed off its skin, renewed and resplendent with youth,'[6] as both a token of my devotion to you and as a stimulus for your studies. We owe a great deal to Aldo,[7] who was the first to give us this first among orators; we owe even more to Herwagen, who has contributed to him a good deal both of beauty and utility, at the cost of much 90 expense and vigilance, so that everyone can now rightly exclaim in wonder, 'This is that famous Demosthenes.' And so from now on we will expect from you letters that are semi-Ciceronian and semi-Demosthenesian. Farewell.

Given at Freiburg im Breisgau, 2 August 1532

2696 / To Bonifacius Amerbach   [Freiburg, early August 1532]

This letter (= AK Ep 1668) was first published in the *Vita Erasmi*. The autograph is in the Öffentliche Bibliothek of the University of Basel (MS AN III 15 77). Erasmus appears to be responding to a letter, written from Neuenburg (see Ep 2697:1–4), in which Bonifacius announces his recovery from an illness, evidently the illness brought on by the death of his infant daughter (see Epp 2678:4–15, 2684, 2688:1–24, 2694:1–3). In letters to others of 13 and 16 August (AK Epp 1670:3–4, 1673:13–14) one finds Bonifacius reporting his recent recovery in language similar to that in line 1 here. Bonifacius' reply, Ep 2697, was written before 29 August (see the introduction to that letter). Hence the date assigned to this letter by Allen.

Greetings. I rejoice greatly that you have come back to life. If my Jacobus there has drunkenly blurted out or contrived something that I ought to know about,[1] you can safely write about it via this man. For I have seen that he is trustworthy. Farewell.

To the very renowned Doctor Bonifacius Amerbach. At Neuenburg or 5 Basel

* * * * *

6 Virgil *Aeneid* 2.473
7 Aldo Manuzio, the Venetian printer. The *editio princeps* of Demosthenes was published by the Aldine Press at Venice in 1504.

2696
1 For Jacobus, see Ep 2652 n4.

2697 / From Bonifacius Amerbach   Basel, [early August 1532]

This letter (= AK Ep 1669), Bonifacius' reply to Ep 2696, was first published by
Allen. The manuscript, an autograph with numerous marginal corrections, is in
the Öffentliche Bibliothek of the University of Basel (MS C VIa 73 8). The letter
has to have been written before Ep 2706 (29 August), since a rough draft of the
latter is scrawled upside down in its margins. Allen judged one of the marginal
corrections, that cited in n2, to be important but relegated it to a note. By contrast, Alfred Hartmann, the AK editor, incorporated the same marginal correction and one other, that cited in n1, into the text of the letter itself. We present
Allen's version of the text with the alternative readings given in the notes.

Cordial greetings. I recently undertook a trip to Neuenburg, intending also
to proceed to Freiburg for your sake. But certain business matters frustrated
this plan, as you could have gathered from my letter written there and entrusted to my father-in-law.[1] I have somehow or other come back to life, and
I am all the better for knowing that you are in excellent health. May Christ   5
grant you such strong health for a very long time, worthy as you are of the
years of Methuselah, or rather of immortality.

Your Jacobus spoke of you with complete respect in my presence.[2]
Perhaps my last letter caused to you to suspect him, since I mentioned an
opportunity to send him away quite honourably if he were not suitable as a   10

* * * * *

2697
1 The letter is not extant. Bonifacius' father-in-law was Leonhard Fuchs, burgomaster of Neuenburg am Rhein. For these two sentences in the Allen text
Hartmann substituted the following sentence from the marginal corrections:
'Cordial greetings. I recently set out for Neuenburg with the intention of coming to see you as well, save that I had to change plans counter to my intentions,
as you were able to learn from the letter I sent you.' The deletion of the father-
in-law's name may indicate that Bonifacius arranged for delivery of the letter
in some other way.
2 For this sentence in the Allen text Hartmann substituted the version found in
the margin of the manuscript: 'Your Jacobus contrived nothing in my presence
that you ought to know about.' Although Allen relegated the same sentence
to a note, he pointed out that it more closely matches Erasmus' language in
Ep 2696:1–3 and that it is the proof that this letter is the answer to that one.

servant.[3] But the reason that I wrote about that was Hieronymus,[4] who had told me in confidence that Jacobus was trying to find a place in the house of Wisdom,[5] and that you could do without him, in so far as he understood from your letter to him.[6]

Take care of your health, my dear Erasmus.   15
Hastily, on Saturday, in Basel

2698 / A Tragedy at Basel   [Freiburg, 5–10 August 1532]

Erasmus enclosed copies of this account of a shocking murder-suicide at Basel in letters to a number of friends. Allen was able to identify four of them: Nicolaus Olahus, Piotr Tomicki, Johannes Cochlaeus, and Christoph von Stadion, Only the letter to Olahus (Ep 2707) survives, and Allen based his text of the manuscript on page 332 in the Olahus Collection of the Hungarian National Archives at Budapest (Ep 2339 introduction); cf Ipolyi page 235. For other surviving manuscripts, see Allen's introduction. The version sent to Cochlaeus was printed in his *Commentaria de actis et scriptis Martini Lutheri Saxonis* (Mainz: Franz Behem 1549) 181–2. The earliest printed text, however, was that of Johannes Aventinus in his *Panegyrica oratio ad Carolum Quintum* (Louvain: Servaes Sassenus 1532).

The essential accuracy of Erasmus' account of the tragic events of 4 August 1532 is confirmed in several contemporary chronicles, the most detailed of which available in print is that of Fridolin Ryff (*Basler Chroniken* I 140–2).

A few days ago, on the fourth day of August (that was a Sunday) there happened at Basel something truly tragic and almost comparable with the

* * * * *

3 No such letter is extant.
4 Presumably Froben
5 The *Collegium Sapientiae*, a residence at Freiburg for twelve students who could not otherwise afford a university education. Its statutes were drawn up in 1497, and it began to operate in 1507. See *Statuta Collegii Sapientiae: The Statutes of the Collegium Sapientiae in Freiburg University* ed Josef Hermann Beckmann (Lindau and Konstanz 1957) 8–15. Ep 2735:52–3 indicates that Jacobus, with Erasmus' help, had succeeded in becoming a resident scholar.
6 Not extant

banquet of Thyestes.[1] A respectable and rich citizen, Christoph Baumgartner,[2] suspected that his wife Elisabeth, the daughter of a very rich businessman named Heinrich David,[3] was carrying on a secret affair with a servant named   5 Angelus.[4] This was only jealousy, not supported by any certain evidence. But jealousy was rubbed raw by something that happened. When the servant was away, having been ordered by his master to collect payment from some debtors, the husband went into his room, seeking (I imagine) some evidence to confirm his suspicion. He found some silk shoe straps among   10 the undergarments of the servant. He immediately summoned his wife and asked her whether she recognized the shoe straps. She said yes. 'Where did he get them,' he asked, 'for they are mine.' She confessed that she had given them to him. Then, to worm the truth out of her, the husband pointed his dagger at her belly, promising that nothing bad would happened to her if   15 she told the truth, but threatening her with immediate death if she did not admit it. In order to induce her to confess, he confessed that he himself had committed adultery and that he suspected the same about his wife, but that he only suspected it. At first she denied it, but finally, at the urging of her husband, she herself also confessed, and when she had done so, her husband   20 sent her away.

Terrified, she fled to her sister in a village named Prattelen.[5] Her return to her husband's favour was arranged by relatives and neighbours. The husband appeared to be appeased. The wife came back on 3 August, a Saturday, brought by some relatives and neighbours, whom the husband entertained   25 with a jovial little drinking party. They departed with best wishes, and that night, they say, the husband and wife shared the same bed, so that there seemed to be no trace of ill will.

* * * * *

2698
1 In Greek mythology Atreus, king of Mycenae, took revenge on his brother Thyestes, who had committed adultery with Atreus' wife, by serving him at a banquet the cooked bodies of two of his sons, whose bloody heads, hands, and feet were presented to him at the end of the meal.
2 Baumgartner (d 4 August 1534) was a highly respected cloth merchant who had served in the great council (1519) and been a leader of Basel's military contingent in the First Kappel War (1529). At the time of his death he had several children from a previous marriage, as well as a daughter, four or five years old, called Elisabeth after her mother, Elisabeth David (see following note).
3 Heinrich David (documented 1488–1535) was a highly respected and influential citizen and banker. His daughter Elisabeth (d 4 August 1532) is known only for her role in the tragic drama reported in this letter.
4 Identified in the *Basler Chroniken* IV 98 as 'Engell,' but otherwise unknown
5 In the Liestal, about five miles south of Basel

The next day, which was Sunday, they had lunch together with similar friendliness. Rumour had it that some relatives were also invited to the same 30 luncheon, and when it was finished, he thanked them, asking them to agree to come to dinner, when he would offer them a more elegant repast. But that rumour is unfounded. What is certain is that shortly after lunch he sent away the maidservant to a sermon and his children from a former marriage to buy some pears. Having thus secured privacy, he bolted the door, stabbed 35 his pregnant wife and then his barely four-year-old daughter. When he had done these things, he wrote a letter to the city council, went quickly up to the highest floor of the house, called upon the name of Jesus three times, and then threw himself down, so that he scattered the road with his brains, to use a comic expression for a tragic event.[6] 40

Using one of the shoe straps he had tied to his boot the letter just mentioned, telling what he had done, for what reason, and what he was about to do. He killed a confessed adultress; she deserved the punishment. He killed his daughter, lest someone in the future would throw up to her the wrongdoing of her mother and father. He was his own executioner, to avoid a death 45 by extended torture after being sentenced by the judges. For in fact his body was treated outrageously, the bones broken on a large wheel, then put into a tough leather bag and thrown into the Rhine; what will happen to his soul God only knows. This horrible and sudden crime struck the father-in-law, the wife's father, so hard that he was rendered speechless. The brother of the 50 husband, Jakob Baumgartner, went out of his mind with grief and is now restrained in bonds.[7]

However impious it may be, this example may be of some use in deterring people from adultery, which had already begun to be taken as a joke, even among the evangelicals. 55

2699 / From Stanislaus Thurzo   Kroměříž, 8 August 1532

For Stanislaus Thurzo, bishop of Olomouc in Moravia, see Ep 1242 introduction. First published on pages 105–7 of *De puritate tabernaculi* (Basel: Froben 1536), this is Thurzo's letter of thanks for the dedication to him of the *Enarratio psalmi trigesimi octavi* (Ep 2608).

* * * * *

6 Terence *Adelphi* 3.2.19
7 A cloth merchant like his brother Christoph, Jakob Baumgartner (documented 1511–38) was notorious for his merrymaking and tendency to get involved in brawls and other illicit activities. The tale of his mental breakdown following the tragedy in his brother's family is not repeated in any of the other sources.

STANISLAUS THURZO, BISHOP OF OLOMOUC, SENDS GREETINGS TO
DESIDERIUS ERASMUS OF ROTTERDAM

Now at last, my most upright and sincere friend Erasmus, we see fully realized what Ursinus Velius promised us a while ago and what we had been
most eagerly awaiting.[1] For we have received your delightful letter, together   5
with Psalm 38, which David sang in a truly prophetic spirit, and which you
have so happily tempered with your diligent and thoughtful commentary
that there is no discordant note from the strings of his lyre; and out of the
Christian goodness of your heart you have dedicated it to our name. Be assured that this gesture of your fraternal charity towards us, or more truly   10
this enormous and imperishable product of your benevolence, is certainly
most pleasing to us. You intended it especially as an expression of gratitude
towards Velius, who deserves very well of you, and also as a cause of great
joy for us. In both our names, that is, of Ursinus and me, we offer many
thanks to your Honour. And further, in view of your good will, and in view   15
also of the long-standing respect we have for you, be pleased to accept from
us in return this gilded goblet,[2] a reminder and a genuine token of our gratitude to you. At the same time we will take the greatest delight in your lyre
because it resounds for us with a heavenly and manifestly divine harmony.
Would that we could follow it not only with our ears but with our whole   20
body and soul, seeking the goal to which it strives to draw us! Indeed, in this
age of ours there is no lack of those who write a great deal with elegance and
sophistication. But there is no one (and I say it with no offence to anyone)
who does it with more honesty, learning, faithfulness, ease, and felicity than
Erasmus. This is why we find nothing more delightful than your intellectual   25
labours, why we always have your books and volumes in our hands, why in
fact there is nothing we read with such salutary profit. You have no reason at
all, my remarkable friend Erasmus, to have any doubt about our affection for
you, our loyalty, our complete devotion, however far we may be separated
in distance; here with us everything is safe and sound for you. And there is   30
no impudent tongue that can make us think anything about you except what
is fitting, since we know very well the intention, the faith, the soundness of
everything you undertake to write or to interpret.

* * * * *

2699
1 It was at the suggestion of Caspar Ursinus Velius that Erasmus had dedicated
  the psalm commentary to Thurzo; see Ep 2517 n13.
2 It is listed among Erasmus' gold cups in both inventories of his belongings,
  that of 10 April 1534 and that of 22 June 1536. At Erasmus' death it went to
  Bonifacius Amerbach. See Major 41, 53.

But even while I am writing this, here comes your thoroughly dependable messenger,[3] who terrified us mightily about the Turks, saying that they   35
have made a quick march, first devastating Hungary, then invading Syria,[4]
harrowing that province with sword, fire, and slaughter, reducing much of
it to ashes, as they always do in whatever regions they invade.[5] Thus we are
forced to make an end of this letter and put off what is in our hearts to another time. Unless God views us with favour, we have to fear that the mighty   40
tyrant will come here and punish us badly indeed. But in this respect I want
to be a false prophet. Good wishes for your happiness and safety.
    Given at Kroměříž, 8 August 1532

2700 / To Karel Uutenhove   Freiburg, 9 August 1532

> This letter was first published in the *Epistolae palaeonaeoi*. For Karel Uutenhove,
> see Ep 2001 n7. Having completed his studies in Italy, he was now back in his
> native Ghent in Flanders. Apart from the opening and closing paragraphs, the
> letter consists of a renewed assault on Erasmus' critics among the Observant
> Franciscans.

ERASMUS OF ROTTERDAM TO KAREL UUTENHOVE, AT GHENT,
GREETINGS
I have received your letter,[1] my dearest Karel, querulous as it was, even ac-
cusatory, but I was not at all offended by it because I saw in it your affection

* * * * *

3 The text here, which is perhaps corrupt, refers strangely to a *tibi certissimus ex-
   plorator*, literally 'a to you most dependable explorer / scout / spy.' The important point is that someone showed up with alarming news about the advance
   of the Turks at this time.
4 A mistake for 'Styria,' the Austrian province located on the path of the Turks'
   chosen route of invasion in 1532
5 In April 1532 the Turks under Suleiman I once again embarked on a campaign
   to take Vienna but for some reason turned aside to lay siege to the border town
   of Köszeg (Güns) in Hapsburg-controlled Hungary and became bogged down
   there for three months. Meanwhile, the Hapsburg defenders refused to offer a
   pitched battle, and at the end of August the Turks suspended their campaign
   without having reached Vienna. In June 1533 Ferdinand and Suleiman signed a
   truce that left Ferdinand in control of 'Royal Hungary,' while Ferdinand's rival
   for the kingship of Hungary, John Zápolyai, remained the Ottoman puppet rul-
   ing the rest of Hungary from Buda.

2700
1 Not extant

for me, so intense as to be almost immoderate and therefore jealous. Rest as-   5
sured that nothing has made me forget you or turned my mind against you,
much less angered me. But you cannot be unaware of how I am inundated
by my studies, almost always overwhelmed by bundles of letters. Add to
that domestic chores, for which I am temperamentally unsuited and therefore find them rather hard to bear. The labours grow, my powers decline.   10
Consider also how few go from here to Flanders, and among those how few
there are to whom I can safely entrust anything. I have learned that through
much experience, and you can see what sort of times we live in. And so just
as you take me to task for not writing to you, I could more rightly take you to
task because you say I have a duty to write to you when, things being as they   15
are, there is nothing more to say than 'If you are well, I am well.'² I think it is
enough if you are safe and sound even if I do not bid you be so, and that you
are well even though I do not bid you be so.³

So much for your recriminations: the more freely you speak, the more
pleasant I find it. I had a good laugh at what you write about the seraphic   20
actors,⁴ who have so often struck me down with words and have now buried
me here once more, stricken by a thunderbolt the moment I had the temerity to rage against the sacrosanct Order of Francis.⁵ I have not in fact raged
against anyone, not even the order of charioteers,⁶ so far am I from attacking
the Order of Francis. I think the ones I stigmatize are more odious to Francis   25
himself than are any other mortals. They are outraged, I imagine, because I
took a swipe at Medardus in my *Colloquies*.⁷ Why aren't they outraged at him
instead, since he disgraced their order by shamelessly making a fool of himself in public and still continues to do so? And as if it were not enough to play

* * * * *

2 *Si vales, valeo*, a shortened version of the formulaic Latin greeting *Si vales, bene
   est; ego valeo* frequently found in Cicero's letters but not often imitated in the
   correspondence of Erasmus
3 This sentence consists of word play on *salvere* 'to be safe and sound,' *salvere iu-
   bere* 'to greet someone by bidding him be safe and sound,' *valere* 'to be in good
   health,' and *valere iubeam* 'to greet someone by bidding him be in good health.'
4 Ie his critics among the Franciscans, who were the 'seraphic' order (in contrast
   to the 'cherubic' Dominicans)
5 For the history of Erasmus' recent quarrels with Franciscans and the *Epistola ad
   gracculos* against them, see Ep 2275.
6 We have no idea what 'the order of charioteers' refers to.
7 For Medardus, the Franciscan preacher who had publicly attacked Erasmus
   during the Diet of Augsburg in 1530, see Ep 2640 n3. Erasmus took his revenge
   by publishing (September 1531) a colloquy in which he turned Medardus into
   'Merdardus' (Shitty); see Ep 2408 n7.

the buffoon at Augsburg, he wrote a letter to the court of King Ferdinand, a   30
copy of which, written in his own hand, was sent to me by courtiers of the
king. It contains these words about me: 'I am expecting from your Worship
the little book of Master Doctor Erasmus against Merdardus.'[8] But he hopes
enough who always despairs. In Horace how much more reasonable is the
language of Nomentanus and Balatro than that of this seraphic disciple of   35
Francis the most modest?[9] They think I have angered Francis because I have
censured those who promise heaven to people who are buried in Franciscan
garb.[10] But recently, after midnight, St Francis appeared to me in my sleep,
looking calm and friendly, and he thanked me for criticizing what needed to
be corrected, which he himself had always detested, and he numbered me   40
among the friends of his order. He was not dressed as he is in the pictures
they display. His garb was not of varicoloured wool but of dark wool, just as
it was sheared, undyed, and he did not have a peaked hood but a gathering
of the shirt attached at the back so that it could be pulled up over the head
if it happened to be raining hard, the sort of thing we sometimes see in the   45
clothing of certain Irishmen. And his cincture was not artfully knotted but
was plain and rustic, a piece of rope without knots. And his gown did not
reach all the way to the ground but was a palm's width or more above his
ankles. And he did not have shoes with fancy cutouts; he just went barefoot.
Of the five stigmata that they paint, I saw not a trace. As he went away, he   50
stretched out his right hand and said, 'Fight the good fight. You will soon be
with me.' I do not think much attention should be paid to clothing, as long
as his followers represent their founding father by portraying the virtues in
which he thought the perfection of his order consists. They call the six wings

* * * * *

8 This letter is not extant, and one wonders if it ever existed. In Ep 2408:12 Erasmus
   was informed that Medardus had distorted his name into 'Herr Asinus' (Sir
   Jackass). But nowhere else do we hear of it having been turned into 'Eras mus'
   (you were a mouse or rat). For Erasmus' own distortion of Medardus' name,
   see the preceding note.
9 In Horace's last satire an elaborate banquet given by the gourmet Nasidienus is
   ruined when the canopy collapses. One of those present, Nomenatus, comforts
   him with the words 'What pleasure fortune derives from mocking the enter-
   prises of men,' and another guest, Balatro, chimes in with a few platitudes of
   his own; Satires 2.8.20–41, 60–74.
10 Presumably a reference to the colloquy Exequiae seraphicae 'The Seraphic
   Funeral,' in which Erasmus lampooned the burial of Alberto Pio in the garb of
   a Franciscan (CWE 40 996–1032)

seraphic.[11] The first is absolute obedience; the second, evangelic poverty; the   55
third, immaculate chastity; the fourth, the deepest humility; the fifth, peaceful simplicity; the sixth, seraphic charity. Would that they all bore these in
their hearts as well as on their bosoms! Then they would be embraced as
angels of peace by everyone, not just women but also truly wise men. As it is,
how few of them teach pure evangelical wisdom, and moreover what a flock   60
of them wander around in the courts of princes or the houses of the rich: they
do not teach, and their morals do not leave the houses in which they dwell
any the purer. The wise reader will understand what I do not say here and
what my silence nevertheless speaks. Would that they did not do things that
must be covered over with silence! They display a handwritten letter by a   65
friar Leopold, a friar Bernardine, people whose existence nobody has ever
heard of. And they think that this is quite enough for them to be considered
good men. For a long journey, they demand money, but they take it in a little
piece of cloth, not touching it with their bare hands.[12] What intelligent person
could see such things without laughing?   70

And now some have thought up the idea of persuading rich, uneducated people who are drawing their last breath not only to be buried in a
Franciscan habit, thinking that by giving a gift they participate to the full in
all the good works done by the order, but also to grant in their will to any and
all members of the flock of the Observants the right to drop in at their houses   75
and be received, whether they were invited or not. And first of all, in this way
the heir is deprived of the liberty that rightly belongs to every household,
against the law of nature and civil law. Isn't it a heavy sort of servitude that
someone who has children, young men and women, a wife who is grown
up, a flock of maidservants, should be bound, willy-nilly, to receive into his   80
house people he does not know, Spaniards, Italians, Frenchmen, Englishmen,
Scotsmen, Irishmen, Germans, and Indians, even if there is in the same town
a monastery of the seraphic brotherhood? Don't we see how very carefully
they themselves make sure that there is no way of looking into their monas-
teries from anywhere in the vicinity? What quarrels, what catastrophes they   85
stir up on that account! The pagan who was once promised by a carpenter

* * * * *

11 In the vision during which he received the stigmata, Francis beheld Christ sur-
    rounded by six seraph wings, to each of which Franciscan tradition assigned
    symbolic importance.
12 In literal observance of the rule not to touch money

that for the payment of a talent[13] he would make changes so that no one in the neighbourhood could look into his residence offered him ten talents if he could instead make changes so that whatever he was doing in his house would be visible to all the neighbours.[14]   90

They will say, 'We are only human.' I recognize this, and I do not object to their rejoicing in being called 'seraphic.' But what do they imagine those grovelling householders suffer who are required daily to admit into the intimacy of their homes new guests, unknown to them, unexamined, who like the Cereal Aediles can disseminate to the whole world whatever they   95 hear or see there?[15] At all events, men of good sense ought to have been left to estimate the intentions of others according to their own judgment. They can easily guess that in such a mob not everyone will be of good character, since some would have been banished from their own regions because they did something shameful there. And even if they were all pious, all sober, all   100 chaste, they are still human, carrying around the same flesh as other people. And so I am not surprised that some of them should think that this is a good way to look after their bellies. I am surprised that the satraps of their order should allow them to be troublesome to others and to expose themselves to such great danger. For I will not relate here the stories that are commonly   105 told by those who admit such guests into the intimacy of their homes.

They will say, necessity requires it. But that necessity could be eliminated or alleviated in many ways. First, what need is there for such flocks to wander up and down throughout whole world? Not all of them are doing the work of the gospel, but only, I fear, a very few. And then, it would   110 be more suitable for them to lodge with the brothers or sisters of their own flock. But they don't want to burden their own people. Yet that burden could easily be lightened by the generosity of those into whose home they now intrude, causing much trouble for those who take them in and no little danger to themselves. Here I am not seeking seraphic charity from those who   115 refuse hospitality to the men of their own profession, especially since such guests are content with very little, emulating, as they do, the apostles. How little it costs to share with their dearest brothers a crust of bread and a few

* * * * *

13 In ancient times a talent of silver was a large sum, the equivalent of several man-years of work.
14 See *Apophthegmata* 6.342 (CWE 38 691), where the initial offer is given as five talents.
15 In republican Rome aediles were officials in charge of the maintenance of public buildings and the regulation of public festivals. Cereal Aediles, instituted in 44 BC, were put in charge of public granaries.

beans, together with a cup of cold water? However that may be, it is proper for those professing to be beggars to ask for shelter, and when it is refused, to ask for it from someone else. But to burst in on someone whether he agrees or not is not to take on the role of a guest but to play the master of the house.

Almost forty years ago I knew Friar Dietrich of Münster.[16] He never visited any place except to preach, and he never took bodily food unless he had distributed food for the soul. Sometimes he was invited into the homes of the rich and would stay there ten or eight days, but only if there was an abundant hope of good result. When he was invited elsewhere, he excused himself. Once he went to Bergen-op-Zoom to spend some days there preaching, and he was lodged in the house of Jan van der Meer, a leading citizen.[17] Having been told about the friar's remarkable holiness, the burgomaster[18] of that city invited him to lunch. He politely replied that if he were permitted to live by himself he would preach there for eight days; otherwise, he would immediately go on his way. But what an undemanding guest this holy man was! He chose for himself a little cell at the rear of the house, next to the back door, and he would accept nothing from his wealthy host except bread to eat and cold beer. He refused to have a fire. There, together with his companion, he read, prayed, meditated. He never went out except to church, and he left only through the back door; he was never seen in the main part of the house, where the wife lived together with her children and maidservants. When could such men as this be refused hospitality? Or who could be so poor as to begrudge anything to such a guest? The friars complain that charity has grown cold everywhere. Perhaps the reason is that their own piety has grown cold. Let them accuse the world of not giving them their due, as long as they give the world its due. As it is, it is not surprising that the world should neglect the world. If they sow what they have of the spirit, it is right for them to reap from others the benefits of the flesh. But if they encounter people who are so inhumane as to deny a living, even a very simple one, to those who are fulfilling their duty, they have the example of Paul,[19] who was the most seraphic of the apostles. If anyone gives them such advice, he might perhaps be considered to be their enemy, even though he is making a very great contribution to the welfare of their order.

* * * * *

16 Dietrich Kolde; see Ep 1347 n13.
17 Unidentified
18 Erasmus writes *civitatis Princeps* 'the leading man of the city.'
19 In Acts 18:3 Paul is described as a tentmaker by trade.

But I have already said too much about these matters. I praise you, my dear Karel, for looking for a wife, for it is better to marry than to burn.[20] But take urgent care that you choose a wife not only with your eyes but also with your ears,[21] and that you are especially careful in doing something which, once it is done, cannot be undone. Go on now, scold me because you have received no letters at all. Now, unless I am mistaken, you have a letter much longer than you would like. Recently I was reading through my letters, published under the title of 'blooming,'[22] but actually 'wilted,' and I ran across one or two written to you.[23] That leads me to suspect that not all of those I send are delivered there. Cordial greetings to your kinsman Edingen and to Ammonius, a man of extraordinary piety.[24] Give my best regards to the accomplished Willem de Waele.[25] I would have related here how splendidly his kinsman Karel Sucket is doing at Turin except that I suspect he himself has already written all about it.[26] Farewell.

Given at Freiburg im Breisgau, 9 August 1532

2701 / To Juan Ginés de Sepúlveda   Freiburg, 16 August 1532

This letter, Erasmus' reply to Ep 2637, was first published in *Sepulvedae epistolae* folio A verso. Sepulveda's reply is Ep 2722.

DESIDERIUS ERASMUS OF ROTTERDAM SENDS CORDIAL GREETINGS
TO GINÉS DE SEPÚLVEDA
I received the Paris printing of your book long before the one printed in Rome was delivered.[1] The more I love the learning, intelligence, and eloquence to

* * * * *

20 1 Cor 7:9. At about this time Uutenhove married the niece of Erasmus' old
   friend Willem de Waele (see n25 below).
21 An ironic twist on *Adagia* I i 100, 'Better trust eyes than ears'
22 The *Epistolae floridae*
23 Only one letter to Uutenhove (Ep 2288) was published in the *Epistolae floridae*.
   Another (Ep 2188) had appeared in the *Opus epistolarum*. Epp 2093 and 2209 are
   also addressed to him. It is noticeable that, with the exception of Epp 2288 and
   2799, Erasmus' letters to Uutenhove tend to be rather long and discursive.
24 For Omaar van Edingen see Ep 2060. For his close friend Levinus Ammonius
   see Epp 2016, 2062.
25 Ep 301
26 See Ep 2657:88–90 with n17.

2701
1 The *Antapologia pro Alberto Pio*, see Ep 2637 introduction and n1.

be found in it, the sorrier I am that you put so much effort into such subject   5
matter. I perceive that you have served the interests of certain people, but
your mind should be devoted only to the Muses and to Christ. From the exchange of such books, I do not see what can arise except discord, and there is
more than enough of that in the world already. And so I think it makes better
sense not to reply.   10

I am pleased by what you wrote about the annotations of Zúñiga.[2]
Someone sent me a sample of them.[3] I have been engaged in this business for
a long time. The third edition of the Jerome is coming out at great expense.[4] I
myself have made far more corrections in the Jerome than Zúñiga, though he
caught some that I had missed. You will make me eternally indebted to you,   15
my dear Ginés, if you see to it that the excerpts come to me. I hear that he has
made some notes on the annotations I wrote on the New Testament.

I would also have written to Cardinal Quiñones, but at that moment the
news reached me here by chance that he was about to depart.[5] Whatever you
send to Anton Fugger in Augsburg will be safely delivered to me.[6] Farewell.   20
Freiburg, the day after the Assumption of the Virgin 1532

2702 / To Julius Pflug   Freiburg, 23 August 1532

This letter (= Pollet Ep 73), the response to one now lost, was first published in
the epistolary appendix to Erasmus' *De praeparatione ad mortem* (Basel: Froben
1534) 125. For Julius Pflug, humanist scholar and counsellor to Duke George of
Saxony, see Ep 2395 introduction. His reply to this letter is Ep 2751.

Just as volume x of Allen was about to be printed, the editors were informed
of the existence of a version of this letter that included two sentences missing from their text as well as from all the others previously known to them.
The version in question was published by Johannes Augustinus Egenolf as an

* * * * *

2 See Ep 2637:24–36.
3 'Someone' is unidentified. The sample was clearly not the notes sent to Erasmus
   via Mendoza, the delivery of which was delayed for several months; see Ep
   2705 n2.
4 Ie the Paris edition of Claude Chevallon (Ep 2758). The first two editions were
   those published by Froben in 1516 (Ep 396) and 1524–6 (Ep 1465).
5 From Rome. For Francisco de Quiñones and his connection with Sepúlveda see
   Ep 2637 introduction.
6 Concerning Erasmus' reliance on Anton Fugger and the network of the Fugger
   firm to assist him with the remitting of money and the forwarding of mail, cf
   Ep 2403:16–25.

addendum to his edition of *V.E. Loescheri Literator Celta, seu de excolenda liter-
atura Europea, occidentali et septentrionali consilium et conatus* (Leipzig: Johann
Christian Martin 1726) 104. The Allen editors printed the two sentences, with
commentary, as an addendum to their volume (Allen x xxiii–xxiv), and Gerlo
incorporated them into his translation of the letter (x 114:12–14). For the reasons stated in n8 below, we have rejected Egenolf's text as spurious and have
excluded it from our translation.

TO THE HIGHLY ILLUSTRIOUS GENTLEMAN MASTER DOCTOR JULIUS
PFLUG, COUNCILLOR TO THE MOST SERENE DUKE GEORGE
I always long for your letters, most esteemed Julius, for they give me great
pleasure. But I would never require of you the duty to write, aware as I am
that your kindness could never be remiss in any duty. I was informed con-   5
cerning the decisions of the diet by letters from others.[1] It is well if an offering has been made to Consus,[2] all that is left for us to do is to propitiate

* * * * *

2702
1 For 'concerning the decisions of the diet' Erasmus writes *De synodi decretis*, another example of his use of *synodus* (normally used with reference to ecclesiastical synods or councils) to refer to an imperial diet (cf Epp 2348 n4, 2517 n9).
   He is clearly referring to the Diet of Regensburg (17 April–27 July 1532), news
   of which was apparently included in Pflug's letter. The only one of the 'letters
   from others' about the diet to have survived is Ep 2654.
2 The god of good counsel. This sounds like an allusion to the so-called Religious
   Peace of Nürnberg, which was the outcome of negotiations between representatives of the emperor and the Lutheran estates that took place in Schweinfurt
   and Nürnberg (1 April–24 July) while the diet was meeting in Regensburg.
   Desperately in need of the support of the Lutheran estates for the defence of
   the Empire against the Turks, who in April 1532 renewed the attempt to capture
   Vienna that had failed in 1529, Emperor Charles was now willing to enter into
   a truce with the Lutheran estates that conceded limited recognition of the legal-
   ity of the religious changes they had made. Accordingly, he issued an imperial
   mandate (3 August 1532) that banned all armed hostilities between estates of
   the Empire on grounds of religion, pending the decision of a future council.
   He had, moreover, already given his personal assurance that the prosecution
   of cases in the Imperial Supreme Court (*Reichskammergericht*) against Lutheran
   estates arising from the reform measures they had taken (eg their appropriation
   of ecclesiastical properties) would be brought to a 'standstill' (*Anstand*). Known
   both as the Nürnberg Standstill (*Nürnberger Anstand*) and the Religious Peace
   of Nürnberg, it was essentially a truce between the emperor himself and the
   Lutheran estates. The Catholic majority of the diet, whose approval (certain
   to be denied) had not been sought, were not a party to it and did not consider
   themselves bound by it. But for the Lutherans it was crucial that the emperor
   did not intend to make war on them and that they could safely ignore hostile

Enyalus.[3] I am afraid, however, that the thrice-great one and the triple-crowned one[4] are doing[5] what oarsmen usually do: they look in one direction and propel the ship in the other.[6] But since these matters lie in the lap of the   10
gods, as Homer says,[7] there is nothing left for us except to pray for a happy outcome.[8] When you call my letter a trumpeter of your fame, I do not quite

* * * * *

decisions of the court. That was sufficient to persuade them to take their seats in the diet and vote aid against the Turks. At this point no one could foresee that this temporary truce would subsequently be renewed (1539) and reaffirmed (1541) and remain in force until the outbreak of war between the emperor and the League of Schmalkalden in 1546.

3 Another name for Ares, the Greek god of war, known to the Romans as Mars

4 Greek in the text. 'Triple-crowned' is an obvious reference to the pope, who is paired with the 'thrice-blessed' emperor. The word 'thrice' was a proverbial way of adding emphasis (cf *Adagia* II ix 5), as in the once-common English expression 'thrice (ie greatly) blessed,' and was not construed literally as indicating three of something. In this case, however, 'thrice-great' may have been intended as a reference to Charles V's status as duke of Burgundy (ie ruler of the Netherlands), king of Spain, and Holy Roman emperor.

5 Allen has *faciat*, singular, but the verbs in the rest of the sentence are plural, which matches the dual subject of the sentence. We have therefore corrected *faciat* to *faciant*. The same correction is found in Pollet Ep 73 n3.

6 An expression of Erasmus' continuing scepticism about the peaceful intentions of the emperor and the pope; see Ep 2645 n6.

7 This is a common expression in Homer; see, for example *Iliad* 17.514, *Odyssey* 1.267.

8 It is here that the Egenolf text (see introduction above) includes two sentences found in no other edition of the letter: 'I very much like the little book by your Martin Luther that you enclose, concerning the proper names of the Germans. I will return the favour to those who deserve it.' The reference is clearly to *Aliquot nomina propria Germanorum ad priscam etymologiam restituta* (WA 50 135–59), first published by Nicolaus Schirlentz at Wittenberg in 1537, with no indication of the author. Only the editions published from 1554 onwards attribute authorship to Luther (WA 50 144–6). In the preface to his volume (pages x–xi) Egenolf states that the letter, seemingly in Erasmus' own hand, had come to him from one Johann Elias Heder, to whose sons he had once been tutor. Since neither he nor Heder had been able to find the letter in any of the printed texts available to them, Egenolf himself expresses some doubt concerning its authenticity: 'if it is genuine' (*si germana est*). There are more reasons for doubt than Egenolf knew. First of all, there are good grounds, summarized at considerable length by the WA editor, for questioning Luther's authorship of *Aliquot nomina*. More important is that even if Luther was the author, it is difficult to see how Erasmus could have known that five years before the first known (and unattributed) publication of the work. One would have to assume that there was an edition of 1532 or earlier that named Luther as the author but that disappeared

understand what you mean.⁹ Nor is there any reason, my dear Julius, that
you should thank me on that account. There is a wise saying by Euripides,
I think: when someone had said to him, 'I always sing your praises every-   15
where and to everyone,' he said, 'And I have always given you something
to verify your praises.'¹⁰ He thanked his encomiast by showing himself to be
worthy of the encomium.

Farewell. Given at Freiburg, 23 August 1532

2703 / To Bonifacius Amerbach   [Freiburg], 27 August [1532]

> This letter (= AK Ep 1676) was first published in the *Epistolae familiares*. The
> autograph is in the Öffentliche Bibliothek of the University of Basel (MS AN III
> 15 30). Bonifacius' reply is Ep 2706.

Greetings. Because whatever I do through you usually turns out well, I am
now sending you a letter for Sadoleto.¹ I am sending another copy through
someone else. You can add to it a copy of Basil *On the Holy Spirit*, translated
by me,² and a copy of my new *Clarifications*.³

I send you as a gift a volume containing letters old and new,⁴ the first of   5
which takes issue with you.⁵

The man delivering these items is Joachim of Ghent, a young man
skilled in both languages and in medicine.⁶

* * * * *

without leaving a trace anywhere except in one letter by Erasmus, from which
he chose for no apparent reason to excise any mention of it. That is too much to
be asked to believe. Whatever the origin of Egenolf's text may have been, it is
not part of the authentic record of Erasmus' correspondence.

9 Erasmus' most recent extant letter to Pflug is Ep 2522, published in the *Epistolae
floridae*.

10 Reference not traced; it bears some resemblance to *Apophthegmata* 5.87 (CWE 38
481).

2703

1 Not extant
2 See Ep 2643.
3 Ie the new edition of the *Declarationes* (see Ep 2666 introduction), the title-page
of which bears the date September 1532
4 Ie the *Epistolae palaeonaeoi*, also published in September 1532
5 Ep 2684, the long letter of consolation on the death of Bonifacius' daughter
Ursula
6 Joachim Martens (Ep 2049 introduction)

Farewell. 27 August

He is going to Italy, if you want to write to anyone through him. I think   10
he is going by way of Augsburg.[7]

To the outstanding Master Doctor Bonifacius Amerbach. At Basel

2704 / To Erasmus Schets   Freiburg, 27 August 1532

This letter was first published by Allen on the basis of the autograph in the
British Library (MS Add 38512 folio 71). For Erasmus Schets, the Antwerp
banker who looked after the collection and transmission of the income from
Erasmus' livings in England and the Netherlands, see Ep 1541 introduction.

Cordial greetings. At the last fair[1] I took special care to keep any of my letters
from falling into the hands of the printer Bebel.[2] And yet he got a letter of
mine, I don't know how, and sent it to the archbishop of Canterbury and another to Thomas More, and he did not bring back any response except for one
letter from Canterbury.[3] He is, as everyone says, a marvellous dissimulator.   5

A pot of sugar was given me by the Portuguese ambassador, a disciple
and patron of Resende.[4] As for your thinking about an honorific gift for me,
my dear Schets, if my means corresponded to my mind, it would be fairer if
I offered thanks to you for all the services you have rendered me. I wish that
the Portuguese ambassador had sent Dutch linen instead of sugar.   10

Hieronymus Froben gave me in perfect faith the sum in florins of approved currency and proper weight.[5] Nor should you have any doubts about
placing anything in his hands.

* * * * *

7 He returned to Freiburg on 29 August (Epp 2706:12–15, 2709:1), and then abandoned his trip to Italy, returning instead to Ghent to look after his ailing mother
   (Ep 2799:23–6).

2704
1 Ie the spring book fair at Frankfurt
2 For the Basel printer Johann Bebel and Erasmus' distrust of him, see Epp 2530
   n15, 2761:4–6.
3 None of these letters is extant.
4 For André de Resende, the Portuguese humanist, poet, and admirer of Erasmus
   who in 1531 had joined the entourage of the Portuguese ambassador to Brussels,
   Pedro de Mascarenhas, see Ep 2500 introduction. For a similar gift to Erasmus
   by another Portuguese admirer, see Ep 2511:29–33.
5 See Ep 2625:3–17.

I have sent to England this new and inexperienced Dutch servant of
mine, Quirinus, to get via him reliable information about certain matters.[6]   15
For I suspect there are some people who are trying to alienate some of my
old friends from me.

I have renovated this house in such a way that it seems it will be comfortable for me.[7] All the same, my heart is in Flanders and Brabant. But the
fates stand in the way.[8] I hope that all goes well with you and yours.   20

Freiburg, 26 August 1532

Do not ask for anything from Jan de Hondt. He has transferred the burden of the pension to that thrice-over theologian Pierre Barbier.[9]

Luis de Castro also seems to have asked for something from the bishop
of Rochester.[10] He owes nothing.   25

To that outstanding gentleman Master Erasmus Schets. At Antwerp

2705 / From Iñigo López de Mendoza y Zúñiga   Rome, 28 August 1532

First published as Ep 176 in Förstemann / Günther, the manuscript was in the
Burscher Collection of the University Library at Leipzig (Ep 1254 introduction).
Iñigo López de Mendoza (Ep 2163 n2) was cardinal-bishop of Burgos and a

* * * * *

6 This is the first reference by name in the correspondence to Quirinus Hagius
   (documented 1524?–35), who delivered this letter. He is probably the Quirinus
   Ghysberti of The Hague who matriculated at Louvain in April 1524, and he is
   doubtless the eager young Dutchman who entered Erasmus' service in May
   1532 (Ep 2644:1–3 with n2). As indicated here, Erasmus had sent him to England
   on the first of several missions aimed at expediting the payment of sums owed
   him by patrons and friends there. For some time Quirinus retained his master's
   complete confidence. By 1534, however, Erasmus had become convinced that
   Quirinus had embezzled some money entrusted to him in England, and they
   parted company. Quirinus' subsequent fate is not known, but in the correspondence of Erasmus' last years he appears repeatedly as the 'monster' or 'viper'
   who had betrayed him, severely wounded his feelings, and revealed his secrets
   to those who wished him harm. For more details, see Allen's introduction to
   this letter.
7 For Erasmus' purchase of a new house and the long process of refitting it to his
   satisfaction, see Ep 2646 n3.
8 See Ep 2646:1–13.
9 See Epp 2404 n10, 2527:60–4 with nn7–8. For the complicated business of the
   Courtrai pension, Barbier's role in it, and the development of Erasmus' unjusti-
   fied distrust of him, see CEBR I 94. On the use of 'thrice-over' see Ep 2702 n4.
10 Luis de Castro was Schets' agent in London for the collection of monies owed
   to Erasmus. The bishop of Rochester was Erasmus' patron John Fisher (Ep 229).

diplomat in the service of Charles v. He was currently on a mission in Italy before returning to his diocese in 1533.

IÑIGO, CARDINAL AND BISHOP OF BURGOS, SENDS CORDIAL
GREETINGS TO DESIDERIUS ERASMUS OF ROTTERDAM
We recently sent you a letter, together with some annotations of Zúñiga.[1]
They were forwarded to you from the emperor's court by Valdés, as he indicated in a letter to us.[2] We have not yet learned whether you have received 5
them, and we certainly hope you have, so that we are not left in suspense
and do not feel a scrupulous duty to send them again. We now send the rest
of the annotations to you because (as we told you) there was then too little
time to copy all of them, the reason being that a large batch of them had
come in shortly before and the courier was leaving too soon to permit us to 10
get everything finished. Approximately eighty notes concerning your scholia
on the letters of Jerome were, however, sent earlier, and indeed one hundred
thirty-five on your annotations on the New Testament are being sent now.[3]
But I am very much afraid that in the end you will think they are greater in
number than in substance. Certainly some of them (and you will be the bet- 15
ter judge of all of them) seem to us to be such that the author himself, if he
had lived, would have been ashamed to publish or (in my opinion) to send
them to you. But it seems best to me to send them all to you lest I arrogate
to myself the right to select and reject things in a work by someone else,
or lest you should find us lacking in good faith. But it will be up to you in 20
your candour and honesty to take into consideration the great difference you
yourself make between writing comments for yourself alone within the four
walls of your own chamber, and issuing something in public to be judged
by others. Moreover, if you encounter some harsh words that there was not
enough time to cancel, remember that Zúñiga wanted to suppress the whole 25
thing; and we should not be surprised that a man who was vehement and
forceful by nature could hardly control himself in his writings or even in
conversation, since no one is born without vices, and apart from this failing,

* * * * *

2705
1 For Diego López Zúñiga and his annotations on Erasmus' works, see Ep
   2637:24–36.
2 The letters mentioned are not extant. From Allen Ep 2905:1–10, it appears that
   Alfonso de Valdés, Latin secretary to Charles v (Ep 1807), had forwarded neither Mendoza's letter nor Zúñiga's notes. Mendoza found them among Valdés'
   papers after the latter's death in 1532 and then sent them on to Erasmus.
3 In Ep 2810 Erasmus reports having received, through the good offices of
   Mendoza, all of Zúñiga's notes on Jerome and the New Testament Annotations.

in all other aspects of his life and behaviour he is commended as morally upright and blameless. And his death was not unlike his life, as we have heard   30
from those who were present. All that remains, my dear Erasmus, is that you
should accept my high esteem for you as one of the greatest admirers of you
and your undertakings. Farewell.

Given at Rome, 28 August 1532

To the most learned and renowned Desiderius Erasmus of Rotterdam   35

2706 / From Bonifacius Amerbach   Basel, 29 August 1532

First published by Allen, this letter (= AK Ep 1677) is Bonifacius' answer to
Ep 2703. The unaddressed autograph is in the Öffentliche Bibliothek of the
University of Basel (MS C VIa 73 14). A rough draft of the letter is found in the
margins of the manuscript of Ep 2697.

Cordial greetings. I will see to it that your letter to Sadoleto, together with the
books, will be delivered by a trustworthy messenger, as you have directed
me.[1] Would that everything you do through me might equal in its outcome
my willingness to obey any order or perform any task for your sake. For your
gift I give you my undying gratitude.[2] It is a rare one, to be preferred to the   5
gold of the Tagus or the Pactolus,[3] for by this gift you have consecrated me
to immortality.[4] I am bound to give a gift in return. But what can I give you,
to whom I have long since owed my very soul? Unless you kindly allow my
debt to you to be diminished by my high regard for you[5] and my eagerness
to look up to you and venerate you as my absolute master, I go to my death   10
as the most ungrateful wretch of all; for apart from that nothing I can do is
enough. The reason I write so briefly is the sudden and unexpected departure of Joachim of Ghent;[6] I hoped he would lunch with me (for he agreed to
that yesterday evening when he delivered your letter), but he has changed
his mind and says that he will set out for there as fast as he can, now that he   15

* * * * *

2706
1 The letter is not extant. It and the books were entrusted to an unnamed French
   doctor for delivery to Sadoleto; see Ep 2765:1–5.
2 The gift was a copy of the *Epistola palaeonaeoi.*
3 Rivers (in Spain and Lydia respectively) said to abound in gold-bearing sand;
   see *Adagia* I vi 75.
4 The first letter in the gift volume was Ep 2684.
5 Allen's 'observantia adversus *et* mea' appears to be a typo for 'observantia adversus *te* mea.'
6 See Ep 2703 n6.

has acquired a travelling companion. Farewell, my incomparable patron, my sweet shining light.[7]

> Basel, in haste, the day after the feast of St Augustine 1532
> Basilius sends you cordial greetings.[8]
> Cordially yours, Bonifacius Amerbach   20

2707 / To Nicolaus Olahus   Freiburg, 29 August 1532

> This letter was first published in Ipolyi page 235. The manuscript is page 331 of the Olahus codex in the Hungarian National Archives at Budapest (Ep 2339 introduction). Although Erasmus seems not yet to have received Ep 2693, the news of Lieven Algoet's marriage had already reached him (see lines 2–3 below). For Olahus, see Ep 2646 introduction.

ERASMUS OF ROTTERDAM TO NICOLAUS OLAHUS, TREASURER
OF SZÉKESFEHÉRVÁR, SECRETARY AND COUNSELLOR TO HER MOST
SERENE MAJESTY

Most distinguished sir, I wrote a while ago to you and to my servant Lieven;[1] I am glad you are fond of him and have taken him under your wing. I have   5
heard that he has married, happily I hope.[2] I beg you to continue to help and advise him. I am sending this servant of mine, Quirinus, to England.[3] When he gets back you can safely send a letter by him if you want me to know something. Please let me know if there is any way in which I can be of service to her serene Majesty or to you. Give my greetings to Lieven. Farewell.   10

> Freiburg, 29 August 1532

I have sent you *The Tragedy at Basel*, faithfully described,[4] in case you want to know about it. It was a horrible and gruesome crime, but one to be remembered.

* * * * *

7 Horace *Odes* 1.1.2
8 Basilius Amerbach, Bonifacius' older brother

2707
1 The letter to Olahus is Ep 2646; that to Lieven Algoet is lost.
2 This indicates that Ep 2693, in which Olahus discusses in detail his efforts to dissuade Lieven from his foolish decision to marry for love rather than money, had not yet reached Erasmus.
3 Quirinus Hagius; see Ep 2704 n6.
4 Ep 2698

2708 / From Pietro Bembo   Padua, 29 August 1532

This is Bembo's answer to Ep 2681. It was first published in Bembo's *Epistolarum familiarum libri* VI (Venice: Scottus 1552) 321–2.

PIETRO BEMBO SENDS CORDIAL GREETINGS TO ERASMUS
OF ROTTERDAM
I was already fond of Viglius, for I had come to know him both in person, when he came to see me on a few occasions and I perceived his marvellous temperament and the charm and elegance of his speech,[1] and from the testi-   5
mony of Georg von Logau (whom I see often)[2] that he is (by Hercules!) genial and highly regarded. Now, however, your recommendation of him in your letter makes him much dearer to me and adds a great deal to my previous good will towards him. I wanted him to know that, and I put myself completely at his disposal, so that if I could be of assistance to him in any way,   10
he had every right to make use of my help. But I am also very grateful to you because, seeing that you are fond of me and that I have the greatest affection for you, you are taking care and making an effort to see that we have friends and associates in common.
      Concerning Rodolphus Agricola, you write that you think I know   15
about him;[3] indeed, I regard his writings with more approval than I give to any writer living in our time. If Viglius turns out to be such a writer, he will have won the highest prize. He is indeed running the race, but I will follow your advice and never cease to spur him on to win the highest praise.
      Farewell. 29 August 1532. At Padua   20

2709 / To Bonifacius Amerbach   [Freiburg, early September 1532]

This letter (= AK Ep 1679) was first published in the *Epistolae familiares*. The autograph is in the Öffentliche Bibliothek of the University of Basel (MS AN III 15 85). The approximate date is indicated by the reference (line 1) to Joachim Martens, who had left Basel on 29 August 1532 (Ep 2706:12–15).

* * * * *

2708
1 See Ep 2657:72–87.
2 See Ep 2568 n4.
3 See Ep 2681:16–17 with n10.

Greetings. Joachim the physician has given me hope that you will come.[1] We have gone from one thing to another other,[2] from apophthegms to adages.[3] If by chance in your wanderings in the fertile fields of the jurists you come across anything you think might be of use to us, I beg you to share it with your usual kindness. Farewell.   5

To Master Bonifacius Amerbach

2710 / To Bonifacius Amerbach

This letter has been redated to 'after 19 October 1532' and appears below as Ep 2730A.

2711 / To William V, duke of Cleves   Freiburg, 1532

This is the preface to two new books (7 and 8) of apophthegms added to the second edition of the *Apophthegmata* (Basel: Froben 1532). For the first edition, see Ep 2431 introduction. The book has no month-date, but this letter and Ep 2720 indicate that it was probably finished in time for the autumn book fair.

A translation of this letter by Betty I. Knott and Elaine Fantham has already appeared in CWE 38 763–4. We have adopted some apt turns of phrase from that version and have made free use of the material in the notes to it.

TO THE MOST ILLUSTRIOUS CROWN PRINCE WILLIAM, DUKE OF
CLEVES, JÜLICH, AND BERG, COUNT OF MARK AND RAVENSBERG,
ETC ERASMUS OF ROTTERDAM SENDS GREETINGS
Among the ancients, most illustrious prince, not only the Greeks but also the
Romans, the speakers and the advocates in the law courts were limited by   5
the amount of water poured into the water clocks, so that their superfluous
verbiage would not bore the judges and also impair their own cases and even
block the way of others who wished to speak. But it was not so for philosophical discourses: they were to last as long as the hearers could cheerfully take
them in, especially if the speeches contributed either to liberal learning or to 10
a good and blessed way of life. For this reason Plato very aptly admonished

* * * * *

2709
1 For Joachim Martens see Ep 2703 n6.
2 Literally 'from the lime-kiln to the charcoal-burner's fire' (*Adagia* II iv 96)
3 The second edition of the *Apophthegmata* was finished (see Epp 2711, 2720:8–9), and the new edition of the *Adagia* (Ep 2773), published in March 1533, was in preparation.

Antisthenes, who was speaking at great length, with these words: 'You don't seem to realize,' he said, 'that the length of the speech is determined not by the speaker but by the listener.'[1] Likewise, when Carneades was holding forth too vociferously, he was admonished by the director of the gymnasium to moderate his voice. But when Carneades asked the director to tell him how loudly he should speak, he received this apposite reply: 'The answer that you seek from me you will get more properly from your audience.'[2]

Now we see that some people measure a banquet not with water clocks but with sand clocks.[3] I admit that this would be a convenient, even necessary, measure to instil some degree of restraint at least in those who don't know enough to get up from table until they are stuffed like leeches to the point of crawling out, ready to burst. But it would not be appropriate (I think) for someone who wants to extend genial hospitality to refined and elegant guests. Rather he should seek to measure the amount of his provision according to the appetite of his guests. For my part, in the writing of this book I took on the role of the host, furnishing the number of courses to match the acts of a comedy,[4] and adding a desert course that is not at all meagre.[5] I think I have played my part in such a way that I can be taken to be, if not a Lucullus,[6] then certainly an elegant and sophisticated host. In so doing I was afraid that the champions of restraint would blame me more for extravagance than for meanness. But as soon as the work was published, it was received with such enthusiasm that a second edition was immediately demanded from the printer, whether it was because of the genius of the work or (as I think more likely) your own genius,[7] most distinguished prince, which I trust will be most fortunate not only for your realm but also for scholarly pursuits. And so, having revised and enlarged six books, I have added two more, which

* * * * *

2711
1 *Apophthegmata* 7.168 (CWE 38 808)
2 *Apophthegmata* 7.217 (CWE 38 819–20)
3 Sand clocks (ie hourglasses) measured only an hour, while water clocks were used to time speeches that went on for much longer than that.
4 According to Horace *Ars poetica* 189–90, the prescribed number of acts for a comedy was five.
5 The first edition of the *Apophthegmata* (1531) contained six books, ie five 'main courses' and a 'dessert.' For Erasmus' use of the metaphor of a book as a meal, see CWE 37 220 (final paragraph of book 2) with n1.
6 Lucius Licinius Lucullus (c 116–57 BC) was a Roman general and consul proverbial for his wealth and luxurious banquets.
7 Young prince William was the dedicatee of the first edition of the *Apophthegmata* as well as of the expanded second edition.

(not to depart from the metaphor of a banquet) you may call the dessert, the after-dinner fruit, or (if you will) the *epidorpismata* 'things coming after dinner.'[8] Farewell.

40

2712 / From Ennio Filonardi   Lucerne, 2 September 1532

This letter, the reply to one not extant, was first published as Ep 104 in Enthoven. The manuscript is in the Rehdiger Collection of the University Library at Wrocław (MS Rehd 254 147).

For Ennio Filonardi, bishop of Veroli, see Ep 1282 introduction. He and Erasmus had exchanged friendly letters in 1522–5, during Filonardi's years as papal legate to the Swiss cantons. This letter marks the resumption of their correspondence after Filonardi's return as papal diplomat to Switzerland, where he resided at Lucerne (1532–3).

Most excellent and very reverend master, worthy of my respect as a brother.[1]

I have received the letter of your most reverend Excellency, which pleased me very much, as always. But since I had to weigh carefully certain matters in it that I was reluctant to commit to a letter and am now hindered by a variety of duties, I defer answering it to another time.[2]

5

I was happy to see Master Henricus,[3] a perfect gentleman, whom I had previously known extremely well, and whom I saw and embraced all the more gladly because, apart from what we have mentioned, we fell into conversation about matters at Glarus,[4] how by his authority and that of his

* * * * *

8 For the word ἐπιδορπίσματα, see Athenaeus *Deipnosophistae* (*Doctors at Dinner*) 640A, 664F. Erasmus here uses two newly invented Latin equivalents of it: *postcoenium* (a direct translation of the Greek, here rendered as 'dessert'), and *pomenta*, which appears to come from *pomum* 'fruit.'

2712
1 This formula is repeated in line 19, but in line 17 Veroli refers to himself as Erasmus' 'son.' In Ep 2738:1 he addresses Erasmus as 'most respected father.'
2 Perhaps a reference to the matters discussed in Ep 2738
3 Glareanus (Ep 2664 n2)
4 Glarus, capital city of canton Glarus, was the birthplace of Glareanus (Heinrich Loriti). The religious conflict in Switzerland, which came to a formal end with the second Peace of Kappel in November 1531 (Ep 2564 n8), had left the city and canton of Glarus divided in religion, with both officially tolerated. Filonardi clearly hoped that Glareanus, who was known for his efforts to strengthen the Catholic party in the Confederation, would do his best to remedy that 'insanity.'

fellows that commonwealth might be able to return to sanity. If your very   10
reverend Worship would deign to encourage him in that holy work, your
Worship knows that he would be doing a work acceptable to God and pleas-.
ing to the supreme pontiff. Your Worship should expect to hear very shortly
what I think about other matters.⁵ In the meantime, I sincerely offer and commend myself to him, wishing him a long and very prosperous life.   15

     Lucerne, 2 September 1532
     Your very reverend Worship's son, E, bishop of Veroli
     To the excellent and reverend Master Erasmus of Rotterdam, to be
esteemed as my brother

2713 / To Piotr Tomicki   Freiburg, 2 September 1532

> This letter was first published as Ep 27 in Miaskowski 320–1, using manuscript
> copies in the Raczynski Library at Poznań (MS 310 folio 8) and the Czartoryski
> Museum at Cracow (MS CN 48 49). Allen judged the Poznań manuscript to be
> the better of the two. For Piotr Tomicki see Epp 1919, 1953.

ERASMUS OF ROTTERDAM TO PIOTR TOMICKI, BISHOP OF CRACOW,
VICE-CHANCELLOR OF THE KINGDOM OF POLAND
Cordial greetings. I am most grateful, as I ought to be, for the affection that
you constantly maintain, most renowned sir, towards Erasmus. That is what
you expressed in your last letter,¹ though I have long been most assured of   5
this without any letter. I only wish that I had something here at home with
which I could respond, not only out of mutual love but also out of duty.
     The emperor and the German princes, on the authority of the pope,
are weaving a web here; I don't know how it will end up. Those crusading
expeditions have often come out badly for us. And if this war is being under-   10
taken against the whole dominion of the Turks in the name of all Christians,
it should have been undertaken with the consent of all the Christian kings.
They say that this was not done.² But if this this fierce contention is over

* * * * *

5 See n2 above.

2713
1 The most recent surviving letter from Tomicki is Ep 2521.
2 Ie France and England were not involved; see Ep 2654 nn7–8.

the Helen of Hungary,³ why is the pope getting mixed up in it? He has two
legates with the emperor: Girolamo Aleandro, the archbishop of Brindisi,   15
a powerful man, and a certain Cardinal de' Medici, nephew of Clement, a
handsome, hardy, and valiant man.⁴ When the halcyons appear, there is hope
of calm.⁵ When such birds as these fly out,⁶ we should expect something different. The outfitting of the soldiers proceeds slowly; the money is being collected energetically; few think the omens of this war are good. I hope that the   20
omens are mistaken.

At present, the sects here are growing calm.⁷ It is uncertain what they
hope for or fear. Would that the other side were so calm that we could all
return to Christian concord. This could easily happen if the princes and the
people would shake off the world and look to Christ with sincere hearts. So   25
far that attitude, even among the priests and the monks, is more to be hoped
for than perceived. The Lord will inspire in everyone a pious and a pure
mind whenever it pleases him and we deserve it.

If you want to know what your humble client is doing, I am still building in my very own house, not without many troubles and with no small cost   30
to my health.⁸ But I intend to quit, not because I have finished everything I
wanted but because I am tired and my purse is completely exhausted. If your
Highness is in good health, it gives me cause to rejoice, most distinguished
sir, to whom I owe esteem on many grounds.

Given at Freiburg, 2 September in the year of our Lord 1532   35

* * * * *

3 Ie as in the case of the personal struggle of Menelaus and Paris over Helen of
  Troy, a contention in which others should not become involved; see *Adagia* I
  iii 69, III viii 75. Here the reference is to the personal rivalry of Ferdinand of
  Austria and John Zápolyai over the control of Hungary.
4 Ippolito de' Medici (1511–35), illegitimate son of Giuliano de' Medici, duke of
  Nemours, and nephew of both Leo x and Clement vii, was created cardinal in
  1529 at the age of 18. In July 1532 he was named legate to the emperor's court,
  which he joined at Regensburg on 12 August, and there addressed himself
  to the task of raising troops for the war against the Turks that was then in
  prospect.
5 In classical myth a seabird, called halcyon in Greek, was said to nest on the
  open sea during periods of calm, known as 'halcyon days,' a term that became
  proverbial for periods of tranquillity and quiet; see *Adagia* II vi 52.
6 Ie the two legates
7 Probably a reference to the conclusion of the Religious Peace of Nürnberg
  (Ep 2702 n2)
8 See Ep 2646 n3.

2714 / From Christoph Eschenfelder   Boppard, 2 September 1532

First published as Ep 177 in Förstemann / Günther, the autograph of this letter
was in the Burscher Collection of the University Library at Leipzig (Ep 1254
introduction). For Christoph Eschenfelder, customs officer at Boppard (on the
Rhine in the ecclesiastical principality of Trier) and keen admirer of Erasmus,
see Epp 867:50–60, 879.

Cordial greetings. I offer you my undying gratitude and will do so as long as
I live, most learned Erasmus, very dear to my heart, who, in the midst of so
many great projects have deigned to honour me with your most entertaining
letter.[1] I would like you to be assured 'how deeply I have fixed you in the
intimate recesses of my heart.'[2] Your Polyphemus (and mine also) has given   5
me great pleasure by restoring to you the not yet obliterated memory of me.[3]
Moreover, when I read your clever and delightful thoughts about him, a
certain wonderful pleasure crept into my mind. You asked about my two
younger sons; this is how it stands. For my older son Balthasar, who has been
a secretary to the archbishop of Trier for some years now, I arranged a mar-   10
riage to a certain talented and wealthy young lady, sprung from an honourable and ancient family. Gabriel (for that is the name of the other one), who is
less strong in body than in mind, has already entered holy orders.[4] My wife,[5]
who shares my love for you, always venerates the name of her Erasmus of
Rotterdam and sends her cordial greetings. And so if 'God ever brings you   15
to our shores'[6] (which we certainly hope will happen) we will receive you
with great joy and will entertain you splendidly. May Christ the Best and
Greatest keep you safe and sound for as long as possible, to the glory of his
most holy name.
    From Boppard, 2 September 1532   20
    Your most devoted servant Christolf Eschenfelder, prefect of the town
and the customs house at Boppard

* * * * *

2714
1 Not extant
2 Persius 5.27
3 For Polyphemus (Felix Rex) see Ep 2649 n3.
4 Nothing else is known of these sons except that Gabriel received a BA at
   Heidelberg in 1528.
5 Name unknown
6 Cf Virgil *Aeneid* 3.338.

To the most learned gentleman Master Erasmus of Rotterdam, high
priest of true virtue, at Freiburg im Breisgau, teacher and most venerable
friend

25

2715 / From Georg Witzel   Frankfurt, 8 September 1532

This letter (= Ep 178 in Förstemann / Günther) was first published by Witzel
himself in *Epistolarum ... libri quatuor Georgii Wicelii* (Leipzig: N. Wolrab 1537)
folio Ee verso. The autograph, which was in the Burscher Collection of the
University Library at Leipzig (Ep 1254 introduction), contained variants of a
sort to suggest that Witzel polished the letter before printing it. Erasmus sent no
reply to this letter, and when Witzel wrote again (Ep 2786), that letter too went
unanswered. Erasmus' excuse was that he was too busy and that he lacked
Witzel's proper address; see Allen Ep 2918:6–7.

Born in Vacha (Thuringia) Georg Witzel (1501–73) studied at Erfurt and became a priest at Vacha, but when he married (1523), he lost that position and
moved to Eisenach, where he became an assistant to the Lutheran preacher.
With the help of Luther and others, he was appointed to a parish in Niemegk,
north of Wittenberg. In 1530 he was briefly suspected of antitrinitarian views
and, though absolved of blame, he resigned his post and returned to Vacha in
1531. By this time Luther and the Reformation had lost their appeal for him,
largely because of their rejection of the importance of good works in achieving
salvation, and he had become an irenic Catholic who never ceased to dream
of a Catholic church reformed along humanist lines and reunited with those
who had abandoned it because of its abuses. In 1533 he was appointed Catholic
preacher at Eisleben, where he remained until 1538, when he was summoned
to the court of Duke George of Saxony to help with preparations for a religious
colloquy aimed at finding the basis for a restoration of ecclesiastical unity in the
Empire. In 1540, following the death in1539 of Duke George and the Lutheran
reformation of Albertine Saxony that followed, Witzel moved to Berlin, where
Elector Joachim II of Brandenburg appointed him to the commission that was
to draw up a church order for his principality. Disappointed when the elector threw his support behind the Lutherans on the commission, Witzel departed in search of suitable employment elsewhere, ending up in 1541 at Fulda,
where the abbot of the imperial monastery (an ecclesiastical principality with
a seat in the imperial diet) appointed him a councillor. From his base in Fulda,
Witzel also served as a consultant on religious matters to Charles V and King
Ferdinand, who made him a councillor. (Witzel would later continue to serve
in the same capacity under Emperor Maximilian II.) Driven from Fulda in 1552
by the troops of Elector Maurice of Saxony, who had raised a rebellion that
chased Charles V out of the Empire, Witzel took up residence at Mainz, where

he spent the last twenty years of his life, devoting himself mostly to writing
and to advising the princes who consulted him. A prolific author, Witzel's literary activity culminated in his *Via regia* (finished by 1564 but not printed until
1600), in which he took the Augsburg Confession (Ep 2333 n8) as the basis of a
'royal middle way' between the extremes of Catholicism and Protestantism, a
solution that had long since been firmly rejected by both sides for reasons that
Witzel never really understood.

To Desiderius Erasmus of Rotterdam, cordial greetings. Hail, man of God!
Someone who is about to paint a famous hero hesitates thoughtfully and
anxiously, scratches his head, bites his fingernails, and does not readily set
his hand to the panel, doubtless in order to work out the proposed portrait
with appropriate majesty – something he would hardly do if he were paint-   5
ing a plebeian; that is almost what is happening to me now, Erasmus, as I set
out to write to you. It is not a difficult matter to deal with a Satyr, a Silenus, or
a Pan; but it is very important how you treat a Jove, a Mars, or a Neptune. It
is by no means easy for me to express how high in fact is my esteem for you.
Because of your great modesty you might find it hard to bear, and someone   10
else might take it to be mere flattery, if I were to call you the sun, as it were,
and the phoenix of the Christian world. But when I consider how many valuable contributions you have made to the world, I cannot but think that you
are worthy of such lofty titles. No honour has ever been granted to any mortal that is not fully due to you because of the labours and the incomparable   15
vigils by which (not without arousing envy) pious and well-wrought writings have been imparted to us. Your contribution to humanity exceeds that
of Socrates, Solon, Numa,[1] Cicero, the seven sages of Greece,[2] together with
the whole multitude of philosophers. No theologian after the Apostles has
bestowed on Christianity more than you, whether you list the ancients or   20
the moderns, not even those who are noblest owing to the celebrity of their
many books, such as those four Doctors of the church, two of whom you have

* * * * *

2715
1 Pompilius Numa, legendary second king of Rome (seventh–eighth century BC),
  who was credited with having created much of the framework of Roman public
  religion
2 A group of seven sixth-century BC philosophers, statesmen, and lawgivers renowned in ancient Greece for their practical wisdom expressed in aphorisms.
  The list usually included Solon of Athens, Chilon of Sparta, Thales of Miletus,
  Bias of Priene, Cleobolus of Lindos, Pittacus of Mytilene, and Periander of
  Corinth.

Georg Witzel
Kupferstichkabinett Dresden

surpassed in renown by restoring theirs.[3] In brief, no one has contributed as much as you alone have done. Leave aside the Herculeses, the Scipios, the Maccabees, the Charleses; take away the Plinys, Gelliuses, Quintilians, Vallas,   25
Ermolaos, Rodolphuses,[4] all the way even to the Budés and Reuchlins. None of these surpass you (even if Envy herself should be the judge) in labour or bravery or fame for deeds well done or excellence or dignity or faith or doctrine. In the end, if anyone should dare to deny this, he would be judged to be completely out of his mind.   30

Why, you say, is such splendid praise spoken to your face? I know, noble sir, that you do not acknowledge it. That is the very reason I need to lavish praise on you among your own followers as well as others. But may God punish me if I am writing insincerely! I do this, encouraged partly by my love for you, which has hitherto been the motivation for my unceasing   35
defence of your reputation against scoundrels, and partly by the state of the commonwealth. It is above all on this account that I thought I should write to you as someone who takes on himself the promotion of the public good with the greatest solicitude. You see the condition of the church, you see how her enemy Satan attacks her. Even before she was oppressed by the perfidy of the   40
sects, she was not like herself. She is even less so now, and so little has she been rendered more pure that she can sometimes seem to be even less pure, not without great dishonour to religion. For tell me, by Christ the immortal, what has been made better anywhere, what more holy, or more praisewor-thy? Indeed, nowadays even the deficiencies and depravities of the church   45
are beginning to be defended, so far are we from having any hope left of see-ing change for the better. I have not been able to decide whether wretched men do this out of hatred of the sects or blindness or ignorance. You cannot be unaware of this, since you have constantly struggled with them, and with some success. I am continually amazed, but more deeply grieved, that there   50
are Christians who would prefer that Christianity be polluted rather than pure and more acceptable to themselves than to Christ. We are constrained to call these people 'theologians,' and even 'the sole possessors of wisdom,'[5] to defer to their judgment in everything, to listen only to them, and all but

* * * * *

3 The four Doctors of the church were St Augustine, St Jerome, Pope Gregory I, and St Ambrose. Witzel is probably referring to the Froben editions of Jerome (1516) and Augustine (1529), though Froben also published Erasmus' edition of the works of Ambrose (1527).
4 Ermolao Barbaro (Ep 126:150n) and Rodolphus Agricola (Ep 2681 n10)
5 Witzel uses a coinage from Greek, *monosophos* 'sole sages.'

prostrate ourselves in adoration at their feet. O what a miserable, not to say   55
utterly deplorable, condition of religion!

But perhaps it will be more fitting to lament this elsewhere. It seems to
me that you, Erasmus, should be urged not to cease doing what you are doing. Fight with both hands, resist with both feet[6] the schemes of the schismatics as well as those of the sophists.[7] Fight for orthodoxy, hold out for the old   60
theology![8] You are attacked from both sides, I know: fight back on both sides,
strike on both sides, triumph on both sides! Seize the appropriate common
ground between both and defend what you have taken. The sects are drag-
ging down the church; but the barbarous schools[9] inflict as much damage,
though in a different way. The former overthrow everything; the latter defile   65
what they conserve. The former thrust in their own ideas; the latter refuse
to abandon theirs. The former want the world to dance to their music, so do
the latter. Neither side keeps to the right road; both are driven by ambition
and lust for power. The heretics do not want anything in the church to be retained; the Sorbonnists do not want anything to be removed. No one can be a   70
more suitable Palaemon than you,[10] God-sent as you are, no one a more righ-
teous areopagite,[11] no one a more incorruptible Amphyction than you.[12] Our
sole refuge, in so far as it lies in mankind, is in you. You have knowledge of
both sides. For there is no one living in Europe who understands matters of
the faith more rightly than you (Begone, Envy!) or keeps guard over the faith   75
more vigilantly or judges it more severely or is able to do these things better than you. If no one confronts the sects, we are lost. If the schools are not
reined in, there will be no restoration of the church. The mass of Christians,
miserably confused, waver now one way, now another in their thinking.
The evils in the church were the original reason that people went over to   80
the sects, who (it was thought) would manage things in a more Christian

* * * * *

6 'With both hands' and 'with both feet' both mean 'with all one's might.' See
   Adagia I ix 16, III i 34.
7 'Sophists' was the common pejorative for scholastic theologians.
8 Ie the theology of the church Fathers and the pre-scholastic theologians
9 Ie the faculties of theology, homes of the 'schoolmen' (scholastic theologians)
10 In Virgil's third *Eclogue* (55–9, 108–11), Palaemon, asked to judge a poetry com-
   petition between Menalcas and Damoetas, declares that he cannot choose between them, which may explain why Witrzel thinks of him in this context.
11 Ie member of the Areopagus, the highest court at Athens
12 Mythical founder of amphyctionies, leagues of Greek states connected with
   temples and the maintenance of their cults. The most important of them, like
   the one amphyctiony of Delphi, could punish those who committed offences
   against the sanctuary and even declare sacred war against an offending state.

fashion. But now, wherever the plague of the sects has broken out, people are
beginning to understand and they hesitate at the crossroads, not knowing
what they should believe or do next. They dislike the sects for many reasons;
but for many reasons they think it difficult to return to the church. They are   85
horrified by so many superstitions, so many ceremonies (or rather the abuse
of ceremonies) further by so many unreformed bishoprics, and finally, by
the exceedingly shameful scandals of the clergy. They know that being men
they err, but they do not know where to go or how to go back. For after all
this, they will not easily have faith in any prophet who has just appeared,   90
for we Germans are Epimetheuses.[13] All the more reason for you, with God's
help, to take up the task of offering assistance in these afflictions and providing some remedy (as indeed you already do). Carry through your full
labours to the end, turn away the anger of God by your most holy prayers.
Fight to the finish in disputations with the enemies of the church,[14] and also   95
with your mindless babblers.[15] With frequent exhortations goad monarchs
into taking heed of the most important matters; redouble that Socratic 'Take
heed.'[16] Help with advice, offer plans, beseech, entreat, sweat, in order that
the church be rendered more worthy of her Christ, in so far as that is possible. For now her religion and her conduct are such that the pious among   100
her members are very much ashamed in front of the infidels.

Unhappy me, whose soul is constantly tortured by the foul stains in
this house and temple of God the Greatest and Best. Those who do not fear
to contend with you in defence of such stains increase my torment. But I
am tortured even more by the impiety of the schism, to which I myself, just   105
a few years ago, clung to for dear life.[17] Above all, in your words and your
urgent letters, fire up those you can reach so that they will not merely think
about an ecumenical council but will actually call one while there is still time.
For this remedy can put an end to discord more quickly than the venom of
abuse that now seethes everywhere. How many souls are irretrievably lost in   110

* * * * *

13 The name of Epimetheus, brother of Prometheus, was proverbial for someone
who acts hastily, without due reflection, and becomes wise only after making
costly mistakes. Prometheus, by contrast, was known for acting only after careful consideration and thus avoiding calamity; see *Adagia* I i 31.
14 *Antecclesiasticos*, ie the reformers
15 *Mataeologos*, Greek for people who say inane things, ie Erasmus' Catholic critics
16 Plato *Crito* 46B–50A, where Socrates argues that when considering arguments
one should heed only those that seem true on reflection and not abandon the
truth simply because it would be convenient or safer to do so
17 Literally 'held fast with my teeth'; see *Adagia* I iv 22.

these dissensions! What an unspeakable disaster for religion! What a delight for the devil! What guffaws from the Jews! What applause from the Turks! The guilt for this unspeakable evil will fall upon your heads, you pillars of society, because you could have made things better for the spouse of Christ but did not. But it is foolish to bewail her lot to you since you do so yourself 115 everywhere and abundantly. May the Lord long keep you for the benefit of the apostolic church. Farewell.

At Frankfurt.[18] On the Nativity of Mary in the year 1532

Georg Witzel, disciple and servant

To the incomparable D. Erasmus of Rotterdam, his teacher and master, 120 always to be honoured and loved. At Freiburg im Breisgau

2716 / From Viglius Zuichemus   Padua, 8 September 1532

This letter, Viglius' answer to Ep 2682, was first published as Ep 33 in VZE.

Nothing, my most learned Erasmus, could be closer than the comparison you made.[1] There is a perfect resemblance between the sect of Franciscans and those who have made the imitation of Ciceronian style their *summum bonum*. The only thing lacking to them is some garb to distinguish them from the general run of scholars. In attitudes and behaviour they match so perfectly 5 that no religious profession could tie them together more closely. Indeed I began to understand this more fully when through some pretence of reconciliation I stopped opposing their tiresome superstition in literary matters clearly and openly. But not even now will I allow Logau or anyone else of the same stripe[2] to make much of their own skill by their reckless attack on 10 someone whom I cherish and love.[3] For I have never pretended either to play

* * * * *

18 Witzel's wanderings at this time included visits to Fulda, Würzburg, Frankfurt am Main, and Mainz. See Gustav Lebrecht Schmidt *Georg Witzel, ein Altkatholik des XVI. Jahrhunderts* (Vienna 1876) 70–1.

2716

1 Betweeen Ciceronians and Franciscans; see Ep 2682:7–10.

2 Literally 'of the same flour' (*Adagia* III v 44)

3 Concerning Logau (Ep 2568 n4) cf Allen Ep 2961:158–61 (22 August 1534): 'There is someone called Georg von Logau of Świdnica who considers himself a poet and a Ciceronian. He has made a thoroughly insipid attack on my *Ciceronianus*. The book has not yet been published, but for some time it has been passing rapidly from hand to hand in Rome and has now reached the hands of the pope.' In Allen Ep 3005:20–5 (18 March 1535) Erasmus writes that

their game or to look the other way or to betray those under whose standard
I have enlisted my name once and for all, and from whose banner no one will
ever make me withdraw. But it is truer than truth[4] that they have adopted this
plan of praising Cicero to the skies for no other reason than to eradicate the   15
fame of Erasmus, for they cannot bear that his fame has risen to such heights.
And they have not been able to think of any more convenient pretext to cover
their malicious envy and to keep unwary aspirants to good letters from admiring and reading you. For what is the reason that they never praise the
man they are always talking about without some criticism of your writings?   20
But in doing so they simply magnify their reputation among true judges of
literary worth; what they maliciously snipe at in the presence of others they
like to read in their cubicles, and they profit from your books. And so their
dishonesty is all the more contemptible because it is joined with ingratitude.

Recently some writer, whoever he might be, was so blatantly shame-   25
less as to turn the truth upside down by daring to publish a notorious book,
swarming with slanders and lies.[5] He accuses you of wanting to obscure the
brightness of Cicero so that only your books will be read. In fact, their only
reason for lifting up Cicero to the Capitol of Latin literature is to throw down
from there the Terminus of Erasmus.[6] But Erasmus' symbol has not usurped   30
a place there and held it by bad faith,[7] but rather has vindicated its station
by a completely just entitlement, granted by learned men and established by

* * * * *

the book, still unprinted, has been sent to him in manuscript from Rome. Now,
however, he attributes authorship not to Logau himself but rather to someone
from Wrocław whom he had suborned.

4 *Adagia* IV ix 2
5 Julius Caesar Scaliger's *Oratio*; see Ep 2564 n2.
6 The Capital (or Capitolium), a citadel on one of the smallest of the hills in
  Rome, accessible from the Forum, was known primarily as the site of the great
  temple devoted to Jupiter, Juno, and Minerva. Erasmus had taken as his symbol
  the Roman god Terminus (see especially Ep 2018), of whom it was said that (in
  Erasmus' words) he 'was the only one who refused to yield to Jupiter, because
  when the birds of augury allowed the deconsecration of all shrines they had
  made an exception for the shrine of Terminus. Livy reports ... that "when after
  the due observance of the auguries the Capitoline was divested of its gods ...
  Terminus refused to be removed"' (Ep 2018:51–7).
7 The motto on the image of Terminus that Erasmus used was *Cedo nulli* 'I yield
  to no one'; see illustration in CWE 14 242. Despite his repeated explanation that
  the words were those of Terminus himself and indicate that everything and everyone inevitably comes to a terminus, Erasmus' critics liked to read the motto
  as an arrogant boast by Erasmus himself; see, for example, Ep 2424:141–4.

undying written monuments. Yes indeed, that writer made a fine and auspicious introduction to his comedy, giving it a fictitious title.[8] Who could be so
impudent, who could dare to attack someone openly with such bare-faced   35
lies and slanderous insults, and yet remain anonymous? 'Erasmus has not
read Aristotle.'[9] And he would like us to think he has, a man who seeks fame
through slander and mendacious insults, whereas the characteristic method
of the Peripatetics consists in seeking the truth. Oh yes indeed, this is a sharp
and Ciceronian orator! Give him the rod of the censors! Let him be the mas- 40
ter to direct our studies! He is the signpost for learned men! From him let us
learn eloquence! Yes, this consists in criticizing the reputation of your adversary, making yourself notorious among men of good will, and (as one says)
spitting in the basin.[10] For what else is he doing by making obviously false
accusations and reckless incriminations than relieving his victim of the task 45
of refutation and exoneration in such a way that he could not have been of
more help to his victim's cause and done more injury to his own reputation
than by attacking him in this way?

No one here, however, has seen the book yet, as far as I have been able
to determine. But if the rest of it corresponds to the headings you have briefly 50
noted,[11] there is not much reason we should want to see it. Nobody here
gave any indication of knowing anything about it until Eppendorf wrote to
Logau.[12] For I didn't say anything about it, so as to ferret out something to
tell you, and to keep those who envy your renown from having a new source
of pleasure. For they were as glad to hear a new enemy had arisen against   55
you as Logau was to tell them about it. But when Logau also told me about
it, I said, 'What surprises me is that Giulio hid it from us here.'[13] He denied
that Camillo was the author. 'But you often said to me that he was preparing
something or other against Erasmus. And the book was published in France;
Camillo just came from there and is trying to make a reputation for learning 60
there.' At this point Logau himself began to have some doubts. But when we
had talked some more about the matter, we agreed to go together to greet
Camillo, who had just come here from Venice. But when we had for some

* * * * *

8 Accepting Erasmus' claim that 'Julius Caesar Scaliger,' the author named in the
  title, was a pseudonym for someone else
9 Cf Ep 2682:36–8.
10 'As one says' should indicate a proverb, but this is not in the *Adagia*.
11 See Ep 2682:23–38.
12 Nothing is known of such a letter from Erasmus' old enemy Heinrich Eppendorf
  (Ep 1934 introduction) to Georg von Logau (n3 above).
13 Giulio Camillo (Ep 2632 n17)

time contemplated the Theatre,[14] which was not yet completely constructed, he recited to us a poem he had addressed to Bembo, the subject of which was   65 that magnificent work.[15] Finally Logau introduced the book, giving its title and subject matter. Camillo listened attentively but responded with not even a grunt.[16] I said, 'I think it must have been suborned by Béda,[17] or that some hireling of Pio wanted to get revenge for his master.'[18] When he said nothing to this either, Logau said, 'There are some who think you are the author,   70 and that they have been deceived by an assumed name.' But he changed the subject and left us both still completely in doubt, since he neither admitted nor denied, but to me he seemed to be somewhat doubtful or fearful about some hastily gathered papers.

Then too, Camillo was a frequent visitor at the house of Asulano in   75 Venice.[19] Camillo said that Frederico had found an account book in which his father had entered large sums paid to you. I only wish that he himself had imitated the thrift of his father, for that would have benefitted his studies in some way or other. As it is, he loses everything in illegal games of dice. Now he claims he will live frugally again and refurbish the press.[20] Lazzaro   80 has offered him his assistance.[21] For Egnazio has detested his behaviour for some time now,[22] but he provides lodging to the son of Aldo and tutors him.[23] Egnazio greatly ridicules Giulio's theatre; the latter is not unaware of it and the former does not conceal it, relying on his great authority with the patricians of Venice and also speaking freely because of his age, so that he does   85 not even spare the leaders of the Ciceronian sect. But it is clear to me that this

* * * * *

14 Ep 2632 n20
15 The poem was subsequently published by Janus in his *Delitiae italorum poetarum, huius superiorisque aevi illustrium* I (Frankfurt: Jonas Rosa 1608) 551–4.
16 *Adagia* I viii 3
17 See Ep 2736 n3.
18 Ie revenge for Erasmus' scathing final polemic against Alberto Pio, published after the latter's death; see Ep 2486:35–8 with n10.
19 Ie the home of Frederico Torresani (d 1561), son of the publisher Andrea Torresani of Asola (Ep 2594 n4), who had died in 1528.
20 In 1523 Frederico had been exiled from Venice for four years and fined heavily for cheating at cards. After his return to Venice, he took some small part in the publishing enterprise directed by his older brother, Gianfrancesco, and died a relatively wealthy man.
21 Lazzaro Bonamico (Ep 2657 n18)
22 Giambattista Egnazio (Ep 2657 n3)
23 Apparently Paolo Manuzio (1512–74), third and ablest son of the great Venetian publisher Aldo Manuzio (Ep 207 introduction)

Giulio Camillo has written something against you.[24] For you know how it is
with this sort of person. If they write something, they take great pleasure in
reciting it for their fellow initiates, among whom they hear 'beautiful!' 'well
done!' 'right on!' But they think the ignorant multitude is unworthy of touch-   90
ing those divine lucubrations with their unwashed hands. And Giulio wants
his writing to be read only by kings; for he is building that elaborate theatre
just to please Francis alone.[25] But the Frenchman who brought your first letter here[26] says that this book is not the work of one man, but was thrown
together by a conspiracy of adherents of Béda and Budé, who gathered all   95
their malicious slanders into one volume. He says it has been two years since
he learned that some people were planning such a project, but he didn't want
to name any of them, afraid that I would pass on their names. If I find out
anything for certain, I will not keep it from you.

I am extremely grateful to you for opening the path to my acquain-   100
tance with Bembo by your recommendation. Before that I had no one except
Logau to bring me to his attention, and I want to be as little indebted to him
as possible. Relying on your recommendation, when Bembo had kindly offered me his friendship and assistance, I began to ask him about some Greek
books on civil law that once belonged to Cardinal Bessarion and are said to   105
be kept in the library of St Mark's, of which Bembo is the prefect.[27] And he
gave me some hope, at least, of learning what is there on that subject and
perhaps of examining it,[28] for I do not dare hope to gain access and make use
of them. But I have learned from your letters to him and to others how much
you continue to love and lavish your praises on your Viglius.[29] Even though   110
I hardly deserve them, I cannot help congratulating myself for having such
a great commender of my efforts. And for my past labours I am happy and
quite content to have no more reward than that. But in the future I will try
harder and harder to be able to justify at least some part of your praises. For
I am afraid it would be futile for me to aspire to the renown of Rodolphus.[30]   115
But his example lends me the strength to believe that the talents I derive from
my native land will be no hindrance to my studies.

* * * * *

24 See Ep 2657 n12.
25 Ie King Francis I; see Ep 2657 n11.
26 Pierre Mondoré; see Ep 2604:3–4 with n2. The letter he carried is not extant.
27 For Cardinal Bessarion and his library, see Ep 2340 n3.
28 For the realization of these hopes, see Ep 2791:58–62 with nn22–3.
29 The letter to Bembo is Ep 2681.
30 See Ep 2681:16–18 with nn10–11.

Certainly I have not sacrificed to the god who ties our native talents to the ground and does not allow them to achieve any honour in literary pursuits. And to avoid this very thing I have been an exile from my own coun- 120
try for thirteen years, though I am still within that age to which the praetor assigns full restitution.[31] For that reason I have preserved good health and have so far never been afflicted with any disease, so that I have no fear at all of being short-lived, although I would not be the least bit averse to dying with that epitaph from Virgil: 'This is all the fates will show of him; they will 125
not let him live any further.'[32] These lines your love bestows on me, though I do not deserve them. I also know from a letter of Zasius how generously you have praised me to him; and indeed he himself has deigned to make me his successor even while he is alive.[33] But I have already told you how I feel about that. And now I am replying at greater length to Zasius and expressing 130
my hearty thanks.[34] I am glad you have written to Crisostomo.[35] My acquaintance with him (reinforced by your letter) has been of great use to me. He has a complete life of Cyprian written by Pontius. He also has some books by St Ambrose against the Arians, which he has promised he would send if you wish it.[36]   135

* * * * *

31 A roundabout, learnedly legal way of saying that he was not yet twenty-five, the age at which, according to Roman law, a man ceased to be a minor. Up to that point the law protected him against economic exploitation, and a magistrate (*praetor*) could award him the full restitution of property taken from him fraudulently (*Digest* iv.4.1). Cf Ep 2632:48–9. Viglius would turn twenty-five on 17 October 1532.
32 *Aeneid* 6.869–70
33 In Ep 2418:15–22 Erasmus had recommended Viglius to Zasius as his successor. Zasius' letter offering the position to Viglius is Ep 31 in vze (4 July 1532).
34 vze Ep 32 (7 September 1532)
35 See Ep 2682:64–5. Born at Bergamo, Giovanni Crisostomo Zanchi (c 1490–1566) was a member of the order of the canons regular of St John Lateran. In 1529 he was sent by his order to Padua, and then in 1533 to Ravenna. In 1540 he became the prior of the convent of Santo Spirito at Bergamo, and in 1559 the general of his order.
36 Pontius (d c 258), deacon of the churches of Carthage and friend of Cyprian, wrote the book referred to here, the *Acta martyrii Cypriani*. On 17 April 1533 Viglius reported to Erasmus that Zanchi had lent him both the Cyprian and the *Sermones contra Arianos* of (pseudo-) Ambrose, both of which he promised to copy and send (Ep 2791:54–7; cf Ep 2767:58–60, Allen Epp 2829:28–9, 2885:18–27). Viglius sent a copy of the Ambrose, but Erasmus made no use of it. As for the *Acta martyrii*, Viglius, learning that Erasmus had already given a manuscript of it to Hieronymus Froben, did not send it. See Ep 2885.

You have given a twofold joy to Johan Georg Paumgartner, a young man worthy of your love: you have deemed him worthy of your letter and you have made him dearer to his father by praising his progress in his stud-ies.[37] Believe me, you will hardly find any other mind that has been better educated, and he has remarkable talents, which his father's care and dil- 140
igence, combined with the faithful instruction of his tutor, are striving to guide to a fruitful maturity. They are all most thankful to me because by my sponsorship I have helped him gain what he wishes from you. And I in turn am most grateful to you because you not only love me but also because, by your kindness to me, you promote the benevolence of others towards me. I 145
beg you to continue to do this. For there are many who want to favour me because of you.

When I consider your age and your constant preoccupation with cor-respondence, how many write to you, how many letters you are obliged to answer, I can hardly forgive myself for writing at such length.[38] But I also 150
have two lodgers who interrupt me every day; I would have satisfied their demands long ago if I had not been afraid that if I annoyed you too often, I would eventually lose your good will. But you would forgive me all the more readily if you knew who they are, how close they are to me and how fond I am of them, and how devoted they are to your name. The father of one 155
of them is Pieter van Griboval, the treasurer of Flanders, who is commonly known as the receiver general. The young man is, moreover, not only noble and rich but also a good and learned student.[39] He writes poetry that is el-egant and fluent and also so full of wise insights that I admire his precocious

* * * * *

37 The letter to Johann Georg is Ep 2683; that to his father is not extant.
38 On Erasmus' difficulties dealing with the volume of his correspondence, cf Epp 2295:1–4 with n2, 2451:11–13, 2800:7, and Allen Ep 2846:8–10.
39 The father, Pieter van Griboval (d 1554) inherited estates in the part of Flanders that is now in northern France. His career as a treasury official culminated in his appointment as head of the treasury of Flanders (1524–43) with the title *Quaestor Flandriae*. From 1530 until his death he was also an alderman, and four times one of the four burgomasters, at Bruges. He also bore the titles of council-lor and chamberlain to Charles v. Pieter's son, Florens van Griboval (1512–62), matriculated at Louvain in 1527, then at Orléans in 1529, before joining Viglius at Bourges as a law student under Andrea Alciati. At some point before the composition of the present letter, Florens had followed Viglius to Padua and moved in with him. His studies completed, he returned to Bruges, where he was mayor in 1539–40. In 1540 he was appointed to the council of Flanders, and in 1543 he was made councillor and master of requests of the grand council of Mechelen, a position he held until his death.

wisdom. At Louvain his teachers were Pieter de Vriendt and Goclenius.[40] In   160
Orléans he resided with Bérault,[41] and at Bourges he attended the lectures of
Alciati.[42] Since he has always been very fond of me, he also followed me here
to Italy. He often looked for an occasion when he could get me to recommend
him to you, and recently in our conversation I complained about how badly
men famous for their learning are treated in our times. Among other things,   165
I mentioned how unjustly treasury officials and other high officers in Lower
Germany[43] deny you your imperial pension. He immediately said, 'How I
wish that my father and I might win the glory of gaining the gratitude of
Erasmus by serving him in this matter.' I praise his intention and his words,
and, since he has wanted to write to you for such a long time, I encouraged   170
him to embrace this opportunity. And so, if you think he can accomplish his
intention, write to the young man with your advice and help in doing so.
His father is not only in a position of high authority but is also very kind and
loves this son, since he has only one other,[44] who is younger, so that he places
his hope mostly in this one.[45]   175

The other lodger,[46] whose letter to you is, as you see, enclosed,[47] has
lived with me for four years now, and you have seen him. For it is he who

* * * * *

40 Pieter de Vriendt (Ep 1173 n2); Conradus Goclenius (Ep 1209 introduction)
41 Nicolas Bérault (Ep 925 introduction)
42 Andrea Alciati (Ep 1250 introduction) taught law at Bourges 1529–33.
43 Ie the Netherlands; see Ep 1998 n6.
44 Unidentified
45 Thus encouraged, Erasmus wrote to the influential father, but soon concluded
   that he was in no position to be of any help with his pension; see Epp 2767:9–10,
   2793:4–5, 2799:9–11; Allen Epp 2810:41–8, 2829:1–5.
46 Johann Georg Hörmann (1513–62), the eldest son of Georg Hörmann (1491–
   1552), friend and relative by marriage of Anton Fugger (Ep 2145 introduction)
   as well as a prominent member of the Fugger firm (chiefly as manager of its
   mines in the entire region of the Alps). Eager to provide the best possible education for his sons, he engaged Viglius to accompany Johann Georg (and three
   other youths from Augsburg patrician families) first to France and then to Italy
   as his tutor; cf Ep 2594 n17. Johann Georg, who cared more for wine and
   women than for learning, did not prove to be a promising student. He stayed
   in Italy under Viglius' care until 1533. In 1539, after having spent a brief time
   (1535–6) working at the imperial law court in Speyer and returning once more
   to Italy (1536), Johann Georg settled down in Augsburg, married, and spent
   the rest of his life as an employee of the Fugger head office, though never in as
   important a position as that of his father.
47 Not extant

came with Glareanus and me to visit you.[48] He is the son of Anton Fugger's
first cousin; he has been raised and educated at Fugger's expense because of
the father's merits and the young man's talents. For many years his father   180
has been in charge of the Fugger accounts and is closely connected to Anton,
who makes use of his advice and experience in administering his fortune.
His father is very rich in his own right. He is a generous Maecenas of learned
men,[49] and is fluent in the Latin language, in which he always writes to me.
Also he has often and strenuously urged me to recommend his son to you.   185
He would have wanted Anton to do this except that he thought it more fitting that I should do so, since I had always directed his studies in such a
way as to make him worthy to be distinguished by the honour of receiving a
letter from you. And he has made satisfactory progress in civil law, in which
I am his instructor. In the field of literature he has not laid a fully adequate   190
foundation. At the same time, I have tried as best I could to remedy his deficiencies in that regard, and I have made him familiar with the best authors,
hoping that, though he may not be the equal of Cascellius Aulus,[50] he will
have some proficiency. Therefore, my incomparable patron, grant Anton his
desire, comply with the wishes of his father Georg Hörmann, answer the   195
prayers of your friend Viglius, so that this young man may be urged on in his
studies by a letter from you.[51] You know that it is my duty – one I fulfil with
the greatest alacrity – to spread the fame of Erasmus. Among whom should
I prefer to do this but among those in whom I have high hopes and in whom
I see remarkable talent? Even in their old age they will sometimes be able to   200
bring back the memory of Erasmus and defend him against those who are
accustomed to wrestling with ghosts.[52]

If Alciati is willing to earn a salary of a thousand ducats, he will come
here next winter. For that is the amount granted him by the prefects of the

* * * * *

48 In the autumn of 1531. For Henricus Glareanus, who is not mentioned in other
   accounts of the visit in question, see Ep 440 introduction.
49 The name of Maecenas, confidant of Emperor Augustus and the patron of Virgil
   and Horace, became (and remains) the byword for a generous and enlightened
   patron of the arts.
50 Roman knight, one of the most eminent lawyers of his day and a man of great
   wit and learning; see Horace *Ars poetica* 371–2.
51 Erasmus appears to have complied with this request, a gesture much appreci-
   ated by the young man's father, who urged his son to reply. After some considerable delay, he did so in Epp 3074 (to which Erasmus replied in a letter now
   lost) and 3117.
52 Said of those who heap blame on the dead (*Adagia* I ii 53)

faculty.[53] The physicians are very upset about Manardo taking over the posi- 205
tion of Matteo Corti,[54] but Corti won't accept a lower salary. I hope that next
year we will have a large and well-known faculty.[55] Sinapius will write back
to you when he finds out anything certain about Manardo.[56] He is a very
upright young man and has just about the highest rank among the medical
students. He asked me to give you his best wishes. I take great pleasure in 210
the company of Ephorinus.[57] In character he is very like Rupilius,[58] yielding
to none of us in his devotion to Erasmus. Farewell.

Padua, 8 September 1532

2717 / From Jan Boner   Padua, 9 September 1532

This letter (= Ep 179 in Förstemann / Günther) was first published as Ep 28
in Miaskowski. The manuscript, probably autograph, was in the Burscher
Collection of the University Library at Leipzig (Ep 1254 introduction). For Jan
Boner, see Ep 2658.

Greetings. Certainly Philip, the king of Macedonia, did not derive as much
pleasure from his triumphs as I did from your letter.[1] I had been distraught
because of the death of my most beloved mother (God rest her soul),[2] but
your letter was a comfort to me. It refreshed and enlivened my spirits when
I was quite numbed and downcast with grief.   5

* * * * *

53 Viglius uses the word *gymnasium*, which could refer to a variety of educational
   institutions. We know from Ep 2594:26–34 that Andrea Alciati wanted to return
   to Italy from France, where he had been teaching civil law at Bourges, and that
   efforts were under way to attract him to Padua, presumably to teach at what
   we would call the 'school,' 'college,' or 'faculty' of law but was known locally
   as the *universitas juristarum* (as distinct from the *universitas artistarum*, which
   included medicine, and the *universitas theologorum*). In the end, Alciati went to
   Pavia.
54 For Giovanni Manardo, see Ep 1587 n52; for Matteo Corti, see Ep 2594 n11.
55 Once again the word *gymnasium*; see n53 above.
56 Johannes Sinapius (Ep 2461 introduction) was at this time studying medicine
   with Manardo at Ferarra.
57 See Ep 2657 n2.
58 See Ep 2682 n21.

2717
1 Not extant
2 Zofia Bethmann, who had died on 5 May 1532

When you write, most distinguished sir, that there is no good reason for us to give thanks to you,[3] you write with more modesty than truth. For certainly you have been so generous in your benefits and services to us that I am for the moment at a loss how to repay you, but nevertheless I will do so one day, as best I can, when age and circumstances will allow. I give you   10
endless thanks for your kind advice, given as from a father to his son; it will always spur me on to acquiring virtue and good morals.

Lastly, I beg you not to be concerned about the Terence.[4] Recently I received a letter from my father in which he mentions the Terence, particularly that it has not arrived and is unknown to him, but that he wants to act in such   15
a way that you will see that your generous and friendly attitude towards his sons will not lack the gratitude of their father. For now, farewell and forgive the brevity of my letter. I postponed writing partly out of shame, partly out of fear. I bid you farewell, time and time again, and please keep me, together with Anselmus,[5] in your favour.   20

Padua, 9 September 1532

Your most devoted Jan Boner

To Desiderius Erasmus of Rotterdam, the most learned man the world has ever known, father and teacher, worthy of the greatest respect. At Freiburg im Breisgau   25

2718 / From Stanisław Aichler   Padua, 9 September 1532

This letter was first published as Ep 29 in Miaskowski. The autograph is in the Rehdiger Collection of the University Library at Wrocław (ms Rehd 254 74). For Stanisław Aichler see Ep 2545 introduction.

Cordial greetings. You should not be at all surprised, dear Erasmus, most learned of all men, that I have not written you before now. By Hercules! I could not do so because I have recently been afflicted with an illness. It was

* * * * *

3 Boner's 'us' includes his companion and fellow student Stanisław Aichler and their tutor Anselmus Ephorinus. In 1531 the three had stayed with Erasmus at Freiburg for five months before proceeding to Italy. They had been in Padua since May or June 1532. See Ep 2539 introduction.
4 Ie the edition of the comedies of Terence dedicated to Jan Boner and his brother Stanisław (Ep 2584). The presentation copy of it sent to the boys' father, Seweryn Boner, had not yet arrived, and indeed would not arrive until 1535; see Epp 2533, 2539 introductions.
5 Ephorinus; see n3 above.

too grievous and severe for me to be able to compose a short letter to you in
a fitting manner. That indeed made me more than a little sad and sorrowful   5
– especially when I noticed that my master and teacher,[1] and also Jan, were
writing to you[2] – thinking to myself: 'Alas, am I the only one who has to be
deprived of good luck, including this one gift of fortune that is more valuable
than all the money in the world?' But now that I have completely recovered
(thanks be to heaven), I could not put off writing to you. Although modesty   10
and shame forbade it, the ardent love I bear towards you conquered both
and did not allow me to be silent any longer. When we lived with you,[3] my
affection made me recognize that your inborn kindness, the generosity with
which you always treated everyone without distinction, is too great for you
to be scornful or take offence at my forwardness, my crudeness, or even at   15
my obviously illiterate letter.

You should know that we are living just as we like, and also are making
undisturbed progress in our studies, enthusiastically embracing the Muses
of Italy, and also that we love and cherish you as our very kind host, indeed
as our parent and teacher, always remembering the hospitality, the kindness,   20
the love with which you once treated us. And so I beg for only one thing from
you: that you deign to grant forgiveness for my silence, and do not ascribe
to negligence or forgetfulness that I let Jan anticipate me in writing to you.
In sum, do not let this fault keep you from loving me as you always have.
It would not have happened except for the hindrance of my unfortunate ill-   25
ness. Certainly I had to bear what I could not avoid. I beg you, over and over
again, accept this letter of mine with equanimity. If there is anything in it that
offends your most cultivated ear, forgive the mediocrity of my small talent,
which still labours under a deficiency of style. May Christ the Greatest and
Best keep you healthy and unharmed until you are as old as Macrobius.[4]   30

At Padua, 9 September, in the year of our salvation 1532
Your most devoted Stanisław Aichler
To Desiderius Erasmus of Rotterdam, most learned of all those upon
whom the sun has looked, to be cherished in every way as my parent and
teacher   35

* * * * *

2718
1 Anselmus Ephorinus (Ep 2657 n2)
2 Jan Boner. His letter, Ep 2658:1–3, suggests that Ephorinus had written at the
   same time, though that letter is lost.
3 For nearly five months, April–August 1531
4 'Macrobius,' which makes no sense in this context, appears to be a mistake for
   'Nestor.' Aichler's first letter to Erasmus concluded with 'Be in good health for
   as many years as Nestor,' ie to a great age (Ep 2545:16; cf Adagia I vi 66).

2719 / From Pierre Du Chastel   [Freiburg], 17 September 1532

This letter was first published as Ep 180 in Förstemann / Günther. The autograph was in the Burscher Collection of the University Library at Leipzig
(Ep 1254 introduction). Erasmus' reply is Ep 2720. For Pierre Du Chastel, who
had lived with Erasmus at Basel for several months in 1527, see Ep 2213 introduction. On 8 June 1532 he matriculated at the University of Freiburg and was
for several months once again in personal contact with Erasmus.

Cordial greetings. I remember, most respected master, that when I was a
little boy, I heard your *Colloquies* and suddenly said, 'Oh that I might some
day hear speaking to me in person this man who, though absent from me,
teaches me to speak so correctly. My ears and mind would then be filled with
that living voice which when merely portrayed by the pen made me love   5
him beyond all measure.' Even then some benevolent spirit bade me be of
good courage, suggesting that though what I asked for was indeed difficult,
it could nonetheless be achieved over time; so confident did that spirit make
me of your kindness, which though doubtless exceedingly generous towards
everyone, seemed to outdo itself in my case, completely undeserving as I am.   10
For through your kindness you not only conversed with me – which I know
I would never have dared even to hope for – but you sent me a short letter,
written in your own hand.[1] But these two gifts did not seem sufficient for
your generosity: you joined to them a third, to bind me even more closely
to you, namely a very elegant little book.[2] For all of these, I will not say how   15
much I am indebted to you for your spontaneous benevolence; I do not intend now to try to express in words or to match it in deeds but rather to
acknowledge it in spirit. I only wish you could one day have proof of it: you
would perceive how truly Pierre Du Chastel has loved Erasmus throughout
his whole life. There is no need for words: pluck my strings to see how I   20
sound if ever something occurs that might require some use of my music.[3]
Maybe I am a bit bold in writing this. But I would rather err in that regard
than fail in testifying in this way to my idea of your authority. Consider also

* * * * *

2719
1 The earliest extant letter of Erasmus to Du Chastel is Ep 2213 (7 September
  1529).
2 The *Apophthegmata*; see Ep 2720:50–1.
3 In this sentence Du Chastel employs strikingly odd language that resists literal
  translation. Imagining himself as a musical instrument, he says '*pulsa quid tin-
  niam* ... [should you ever have need of my] *sonus*,' which means roughly 'strike
  me [as one would the strings of a lyre] to see how I tinkle ... [should you ever

that I want this letter to be a sort of promissory note for service that I owe
you, which I will pay to you as best I can, as long as I live. May God Greatest   25
and Best long keep you safe for the sake of good letters. Farewell.

Given at our upper room on 17 October 1532[4]

Your servant, Pierre Du Chastel

To Master Erasmus, the cynosure of all eyes

2720 / To Pierre Du Chastel   Freiburg, 24 September [1532]

This letter, Erasmus' reply to Ep 2719, was first published in the epistolary appendix to Erasmus' *De praeparatione ad mortem* (Basel: Froben 1534) 126. The
assigned year-date is confirmed by that of the letter to which this is the answer as well as by the references to the recently completed and published
Apophthegmata (lines 8–9 with n3).

DESIDERIUS ERASMUS OF ROTTERDAM TO THE MOST HONOURABLE
YOUNG MAN MASTER PIERRE DU CHASTEL, GREETINGS

If you were surprised, my dear Pierre, that I did not thank you immediately
for your choice gifts and your even more choice letter,[1] I was weighed down
at that time by a double burden. I had an excruciating head cold and to-   5
gether with that a new burden of labours that in itself would have required
a vigorous and healthy mind. For I had to give birth to the *Adagia* yet once
more.[2] And that labour greeted me when I was already exhausted by the
rhapsody of the *Apophthegmata*.[3] That is the kind of breathing space allotted

* * * * *

have need of my] sound.' In other words, he is offering himself as a willing
instrument in Erasmus' hands. Cf Ep 2720:64–7, where Erasmus echoes this
strained metaphor.

4 The 'our' may well indicate that Du Chastel shared quarters with his friend
Claudius Albericus; see Ep 2720:40.

2720

1 The gifts were the partridges mentioned in lines 43–4 below; there is no mention of them in Du Chastel's letter (Ep 2719).

2 Ie the new, expanded edition of 1533, completed at about this time; see Ep 2726
introduction.

3 The expanded version of 1532; see Ep 2711. Erasmus plays on the root meaning
of *rhapsodia*, ie 'a sewing together of pieces' to create something larger. Usually
used in connection with an epic poem, it is here used tongue-in-cheek to describe Erasmus' cobbling together of the collection of apophthegms.

to Erasmus! These are the things I must put up with now that I have con-   10
signed myself to work this field.

     And so, my dear Du Chastel, now that my health has begun to improve
and the burden of my labours is somewhat lightened, I reread with pleasure
the letter that you wished to be a pledge, as it were, of your lasting faith and
good will towards me, not only because it gave me a mirror image, so to   15
speak, of that rare and I might say almost predestined devotion you have
to me but also because it is adorned with Greek phrases showing that you
have embraced the study of both literatures. In this regard you seem to me
to be remarkably fortunate in that God has instilled in you this love in your
flourishing years so that you find more pleasure wandering in the pastures   20
of the Muses than making bad use of good time in banquets and gambling.
My work called *Colloquies* might have seemed to be born inauspiciously and
under an evil presiding spirit if it had not gained your favour,[4] as you write,
and that of many others like you. For since the Fates, according to the proverb, do not allow even Jupiter to please everyone,[5] it is no small comfort to   25
have gained the approval of at least some honourable men. But I only wish
that the subject matter were such that what appealed to schoolboys, as you
write, would deserve to be continuously approved. For there will come a
time when even you, perhaps, will say, 'My age is not the same, nor my
outlook.'[6] I do not know what you saw in the *Colloquies*; perhaps your af-   30
fection deceived your eyes, since it often happens, as that Sicilian says, that
'what is not beautiful seems to be so.'[7]

     There is no reason why you should thank me or congratulate yourself
because of our meeting: you did not see Erasmus but the shadow of Erasmus.
For what is an old man except the dream of a shadow?[8] But if, my most ac-   35
complished young man, your love for me is so great that you take pleasure in
speaking even with a shadow, be assured that this pleasure is yours in abundance, whenever it is convenient for you. But if ever you can take off this
splendid (if not tragic) mask that Fortune has placed upon you, and if you

* * * * *

4 The *Colloquies* were among the works most intensely disliked by Erasmus' con-
    servative critics. In May 1526, for example, the Paris faculty of theology formal-
    ly censured seventy passages in them. For the censures and Erasmus' responses
    to them, see CWE 82 269–326.
5 *Adagia* II vii 55
6 Horace *Epistles* 1.1.4
7 Theocritus 6.18–19, cited in Greek
8 Pindar *Pythian* 8.95–6, cited in Greek

can come, accompanied only by Claudius Albericus as your Achates,[9] to tear   40
apart a chicken in friendly company, or even if you drop in uninvited (the
way Nasica used to visit Ennius),[10] it would be fine, now and again, to grow
young once more in such company. I thank you for sending the partridges
once more, and I am much obliged to you for your devotion to me. But in the
future I would not want you to be impelled by the same solicitude for me, be-   45
cause this poor old body is almost as dry as the skin sloughed off by a snake.
It will hardly tolerate eating such fowl. And so at that time I thought up this
couplet in return for your gift: 'You send me choice edibles, Pierre, but I have
no appetite. If you want to send what would please me more, send hunger.'

I am surprised you think that the *Apophthegms* in eight complete books   50
should be called a 'little book' unless I am to think you meant this as friendly
or affectionate rather than pejorative. For we also use diminutives for things
we are fond of, such as *uxorcula, filiola, corculum, solatiolum* [sweet wife, dear
daughter, dear heart, a bit of comfort]. I only wish that that this 'little book'
would give students as much pleasure and utility as it has cost me in sweat.   55
Some people think it is easy to write apophthegms or adages, but to write
books and chiliads is difficult.[11] Here is a couplet I wrote about that: 'It is
quite easy, I admit, for anyone to write proverbs, but it is quite difficult to
write thousands of them.'[12]

All that remains, most distinguished young man, is to beseech Christ in   60
his goodness and power that I may always deserve your good will towards
me. As for you, may you passionately love more and more the liberal studies

* * * * *

9 Claudius Albericus of Toul matriculated at Freiburg on 28 June 1532. He was a
   cleric and claimed to be an MA. Nothing more is known of him. Achates was the
   inseparable friend of Aeneas in Virgil's *Aeneid*; his name was proverbial for an
   intimate companion.
10 Cicero *De oratore* 2.275–6. Scipio Nasica, arriving at the house of the poet Ennius,
   heard Ennius telling his maid to say that he was not in. When in turn Ennius
   went to the house of Nasica and asked the servant if he was home, Nasica
   himself shouted from an inner room that he was not. Ennius replied, 'What, do
   I not know your voice?' to which Nasica responded, 'You're worse: I believed
   your maid, but you refuse to believe me when I tell you myself.' Cf the colloquy
   Diluculum 'Early to Rise' CWE 40 917:9–15.
11 By the time he published the second edition of the *Adages* in 1508, their
   number had increased from 800 to over 3000, and the volume was entitled
   Adagiorum chiliades 'Thousands of adages.' Thereafter Erasmus frequently said
   'my *Chiliads*' when referring to the *Adages*.
12 A somewhat different version of this couplet appears among Erasmus' poems
   in CWE 85 176–7 no 91.

and philosophy that teach you to live well, and thus gather in your youth
provisions for your old age. As for your asking me to pluck your strings to
test how you sound, what need is there for such a test,[13] since you have al-   65
ready of your own accord made it clear that in your heart everything is pure
gold? Once again you now have a letter that is not only written by my own
hand but also poured forth extemporaneously and hence written badly. But
even this may be pleasing to you, as lovers tend to love even the moles of
their loved ones.[14] But I will come to an end. Farewell.   70
    Freiburg, 24 September

2721 / From Ambrosius Pelargus   [Freiburg, c September–October 1532]

> This letter was first published in the *Bellaria* (folio H5). The approximate date
> of the letter and the four that follow it in this latest exchange between Pelargus
> and Erasmus can be assigned by reference to Ep 2728:44–51, which repeats the
> story of the quarrel with Marius found in lines 13–17 below, and to the date of
> the publication of the *Epistolae palaeonaeoi* (see n1 below). The order in which
> the letters occur in the *Bellaria* is clearly chronological. That Pelargus' letters
> were written from Freiburg is indicated by Erasmus invitation to Pelargus to
> come discuss the matter over dinner (Ep 2722:22). For Pelargus, the Dominican
> who, like Erasmus, left Basel after the victory of the Reformation there and
> moved to Freiburg, see Ep 2666 introduction.

AMBROSIUS PELARGUS TO ERASMUS OF ROTTERDAM, GREETINGS
I had certainly hoped that our affection for each other and our mutual good
will would turn out to be ever greater and more vigorous. But since you have
removed the sinews of our friendship, I fear that it will soon be obliterated.
And so I have reason to remonstrate with you, in particular for violating   5
our friendship. 'What, then, is the matter?' you will ask. It is this. I go to the
shop of the bookseller. I inquire how the *Flowery Letters* of Erasmus, which
had recently been published, are faring.[1] My companion at the time was the

* * * * *

13 See Ep 2719 n3.
14 Horace *Sermones* 1.3.38–50

2721
1 The letter (Ep 2211) concerning which Pelargus complains in the following lines
  was first published in the *Epistolae floridae*, which appeared in September 1531.
  It was reprinted in the *Epistola palaeonaeoi* of September 1532. Pelargus may
  have misidentified the volume seen in the bookseller's shop. In his answer to

Dominican Hieronimus Barba,[2] a man lacking in neither learning nor piety;
he looked at a single copy which was put out for sale, as usual, picked it up,   10
turned through the pages, and then came by chance to the place where you
attribute to Augustinus Marius and Ambrosius Pelargus all the tumult that
had arisen in Basel. This is what you say in your letter to More: 'There was
some hope of a return to moderation. But two monks, one a preacher in the
cathedral, the other a preacher in his own order, the Dominicans, stirred up   15
a great agitation against me. It is true they have decamped, but others are
affected by the same disease.'[3] Come now, my good man, is this a sign of
friendship, to dishonour with lies someone who does not deserve it, who
indeed deserves the gratitude of the Christian commonwealth?

Since my primary concern was that no civil discord should arise at   20
Basel, since I had devoted all my energies as far as I could to making the
members of the same body cohere in mutual charity and not fall away from
the unity of the faith into heretical factions, and finally, since I struggled to
persuade all sides to adhere to peace and harmony, how can you have the
effrontery to make me the instigator of the tumult? I bravely opposed (if I   25
may say so) that stubborn heretic Oecolampadius, who had to be refuted all
the more sternly because once he had adhered tenaciously to an opinion he
stubbornly defended it even in the face of the truth. And I had good reason
to do so. I saw there was danger that his pestilential teaching would be the
ruin of that famous city and of himself as well. And that I was not far from   30
the truth, the result clearly shows; many say that I was not a false prophet.
And while I was doing these things (indeed there was nothing I did not do),
while I resisted the teachings of the heretics with both feet (as they say),[4]
when at the risk of my own life I built a wall in front of the house of the Lord,
while I engaged in hand-to-hand combat with the enemy, both in public and   35
in private, while I admonished the errant in both speech and writings, do I
seem to be a revolutionary? I knew how much you were disturbed by the
words of the prince of Carpi, which you write are full of slander because

* * * * *

this letter, Erasmus clearly understands Pelargus to be referring to the *Epistolae
palaeonaeoi*, pointing out that the letter was 'one of the old ones' (ie one of the
palaeoi), not one of 'the new ones' (*naeoi*), and saying that Pelargus should have
made his complaint earlier so that the letter could be altered or omitted; see Ep
2722:16–18.
2 Otherwise unknown
3 Ep 2211:66–9. The two monks were Pelargus, the Dominican, and Augustinus
   Marius (Ep 2321), the cathedral preacher.
4 Literally 'with my whole foot,' ie 'with all my might; see *Adagia* III i 34.

he says you were the source of all this sedition and rebellion.[5] And do you
think I am so stupid as not to be angered by your words? With what truth,   40
with what honesty you spattered this stain on me, let others judge. Certainly
there are many, both among the leading citizens and among the canons, who
have given me thanks for my efforts, indeed have recompensed me for them.
Therefore, my dear Erasmus, I wonder how you got such an idea. In this matter, my conscience is truly my witness. Certainly I would bear my lot with   45
equanimity, I would accept this slander with indifference, if it were not so
difficult not to vindicate a damaged reputation, and if there were not also a
danger that your words might cause me trouble, especially among those who
will give them some weight and importance.
    Farewell.   50

2722 / To Ambrosius Pelargus   [Freiburg, c September–October 1532]

This letter, Erasmus' reply to Ep 2721, was first published in the *Bellaria* (folio
H6). Pelargus' reply is Ep 2723. On the date, see Ep 2721 introduction.

DESIDERIUS ERASMUS OF ROTTERDAM TO MASTER AMBROSIUS
PELARGUS, GREETINGS
I wonder what you mean. Friends often praised to me a certain man preach-
ing learned sermons among the Dominicans. But I did not think it was you.
For I knew your name. But whoever it was, what does he have to complain   5
about? Being the instigator of tumult does not make a man blameworthy.
Thus Christ's teaching and miracles were the occasion of many evils, and
Paul's candour often caused tumults. I frequently advised Marius to abstain from shouting at the opposing side.[1] That was what the canons would
also have preferred. First of all, I said nothing against you because I did not   10
think you were the preacher, and if you had been, my words were certainly
not directed at you. You will say that it was fitting to shout freely against
the sects. Therefore a good freedom was the occasion of an evil uprising?
There is no harm in that. I would like to hear how I violated the law of
friendship. Farewell.   15

* * * * *

5 See Ep 2486 n10.

2722
1 For Marius, see Ep 2721 n3.

I have found the passage. If it offended you, why did you not say something about it before? For it is among the old letters, where I corrected many
other things; some letters I suppressed completely.[2] Above all, no one is named
there. I never knew until now that you preach among the Dominicans. And
no one is blamed there, except that you provoked the other side by shouting   20
rather freely. Once again, farewell.

If you want to talk about it at dinner, so be it.

2723 / From Ambrosius Pelargus   [Freiburg, c September–October 1532]

This letter, Pelargus' answer to Ep 2722, was first published in the *Bellaria* (folio
H6 verso). On the date, see Ep 2721 introduction.

AMBROSIUS PELARGUS TO ERASMUS OF ROTTERDAM, GREETINGS
Your servant delivered your letter to me today, just as I was about to go
to lunch, adding to it these excuses of yours, as you instructed him to do,
unless I am mistaken. He said there was a certain Dominican preacher at
Basel named Jesus,[1] whom Erasmus criticized. But I will not allow you to   5
make a fool of me with such trifles.[2] I am well aware of the man you mean.
There was no 'Jesus' in Basel when the tumult occurred. At this point you
have to decide whether you want to number that Jesus (whom I know quite
well) among those who still remain and have to pay the price, or whether
he was the very same one who you say fled with Marius.[3] In fact, since both   10
statements are false, it is sufficiently clear that you wanted to play a trick on
me with this clever dissimulation. For it cannot be unknown to you that no
one else among the Dominicans was preaching at that time except Pelargus
alone, and that I caused trouble, by both my writings and my sermons, to
the supporters of Oecolampadius, as you were well aware. But how can it   15
be possible for you to say that I was not being singled out, when I was the
chief target of your letter? In your letter to the prince of Carpi you say that
he whose well-meant words are twisted to create a different meaning is not

* * * * *

2 See Ep 2721 n1.

2723
1 Unidentified
2 Literally 'smear my face with such trifles.' See Ep 2659 n6.
3 Ie Pelargus; see Ep 2721 n3.

responsible for this misrepresentation,[4] and even I do not deny that. How, then, can I be said to have provided the occasion for tumult – indeed of hav-   20 ing stirred up tumult – since I did not depart by a finger's breadth from the duty of a preacher?

How much more proper, therefore, it would have been for you to place the blame for stirring up discord on our adversaries, namely the heretics and schismatics. But since you now prefer to place the blame on the orthodox,   25 consider whether there is danger that you may seem to be more on the side of the heretics than on that of the orthodox. It is of little consolation that your letter mentions no name, since it is certainly clear to all of our supporters whom you are attacking. If there is any scholar who has read your *Old Letters* carefully,[5] I have read and reread them, but I find no such letter in   30 your *Farrago of Letters*.[6] Certainly the assigned date of the letter, that is, the year 1529, clearly shows that it is not among the older collection – those, that is, that were printed long before this one was published. But in the end I sniff out the reason you make up such nonsense. Farewell.

2724 / To Ambrosius Pelargus   [Freiburg, c September–October 1532]

This letter, first published in the *Bellaria* (folio H7 verso), is in sequence to Ep 2723 but does not respond to it. On the date, see Ep 2721 introduction.

TO MASTER AMBROSIUS PELARGIUS FROM ERASMUS OF ROTTERDAM, GREETINGS

I beg you, most learned Ambrosius, to return to me the works of St Augustine that I lent to you.[1] For now it sometimes happens that I need them. I have

* * * * *

4 The reference is to Ep 1634:78–86 (1526), which was published with the *Responsio ad epistolam Pii* (1529).
5 This is evidently a reference to the *Epistolae palaeonaeoi* (Letters Old and New), which in Ep 2721 Pelargus had confused with the *Epistolae floridae*; see Ep 2721 n1.
6 Pelargus' references to the published collections of Erasmus' letters (cf preceding note) are consistently confused and inaccurate. Here he can scarcely be referring to the *Farrago nova epistolarum* of 1519, which obviously could not have included a letter describing events that took place nearly a decade later. Perhaps he was thinking of the *Opus epistolarum* of 1529, but that too was published too soon to include a letter written in September of that year.

2724
1 Ie the Froben edition of 1529 (Ep 2157)

annotated many places in them and this new index is remarkably useless.[2] 5
I can't find anything using it. I would have asked for it back two months
ago, but I put it off because I suspected that it would be of some use to you
because of your disputations.[3] Now that they are successfully finished, I recall the volumes for my own use, with no great inconvenience to you. The
Augustine printed at Paris does not cost much.[4] Farewell. 10

2725 / From Ambrosius Pelargus   [Freiburg, c September–October 1532]

This letter, Pelargus' answer to Ep 2724, was first published in the *Bellaria* (folio
H7 verso). On the date, see Ep 2721 introduction.

AMBROSIUS PELARGUS TO ERASMUS OF ROTTERDAM,
CORDIAL GREETINGS
In the letter in which you ask me to return the Augustine, which I thought
had long ago become mine, I detect a faint odor of some stubborn resentment
stuck in your gullet. Actually I hear that the reason you are irritated is that 5
I cast down or undervalued some of your writings. Certainly I do not deny
that when I first read the letter in which you accuse me I was so angry that I
almost decided never again to set eye on any of your writings. And perhaps
at that time I gave some outward sign of my feelings in a word or two, as
they say.[1] But one who says that he has almost reached the point of decid- 10
ing not to read your works has certainly not yet decided to do so. And one
who has made up his mind not to read the works of some author or another
does not necessarily have a low opinion of his works. At that time I had not
decided on anything and I considered your lucubrations to be magnificent,
even though I do not find all of them so pleasing as to think I should give 15
all of them my complete approbation. What servant, what disciple of yours
had the effrontery to say that I had a low opinion of even the slightest of
your writings? But even if something like that had slipped out, as often happens with those who have an irascible temperament, I did not think that you,

* * * * *

2 Would this perhaps be the index in the Chevallon Augustine (see n4 below)?
3 Probably academic disputations that were part of qualifying for his degree at
  the university.
4 The edition published by Claude Chevallon in 1531; see CWE 15 220 (Ep 2157
  introduction).

2725
1 Literally 'in three words' (*Adagia* IV iv 84)

with your self-restraint, would conceive such anger as I perceive you did   20
because of some remark that issued from an impetuous spirit. But come now,
Erasmus, I appeal here to your good judgment – consider which complaint is
more justified, which of us has the right to be angry with the other. Certainly
I was grievously offended by you, and that happened first. Nevertheless, as
far as I am concerned, I would wish that whatever bitterness and hostility   25
may still stubbornly linger in either of our minds be obliterated and wiped
away. That is what is required by the circumstances and the reputation of the
both of us. Baer,[2] out of his kindness and his good will towards each of us, is
deeply grieved that there was ever any reason for quarrelling. But he wants
us to calm down, and he says he will see to it that the slightest trace of our   30
disagreement will disappear and that we will be the best of friends. For my
part, I am glad to comply with his wishes, but only on the condition that in
one of your published letters you make honourable mention of my name,
and both mend and restore my reputation. For my part, I am extremely sorry
that I poured out my bitter feelings. I beg you, in Christ's name, to forgive me   35
if I have sinned in this regard. I will leave nothing to be desired on my part
in restoring and furthering concord.

Farewell.

Sometime this afternoon, if that is convenient, I will meet you. There is
something that it is important for you to know but that it would be best to   40
keep for private conversation. Once more, farewell.

2726 / To Charles Blount   Freiburg, 1 October 1532

In the seventh edition of the *Adagia* (September 1528) Erasmus had included
a new preface (Ep 2023), addressed to Charles Blount, fifth Baron Mountjoy
and eldest son of William Blount, the fourth baron and dedicatee of the earlier
editions of the *Adagia*. The present letter was inserted into the eighth edition
(March 1533) immediately before the 488 newly added adages; see Ep 2773
introduction. Blount's letter of thanks is Ep 2830.

A translation of this letter by John N. Grant and Betty Knott has already
appeared in CWE 36 317–19. We have made free use of the information in their
notes for the annotation of this new translation.

* * * * *

2 Ludwig Baer, who in 1529 had moved with the Basel cathedral chapter to
   Freiburg (Ep 2225 introduction)

TO THE RENOWNED YOUNG MAN CHARLES BLOUNT DESIDERIUS
ERASMUS OF ROTTERDAM SENDS GREETINGS

Your father, most distinguished young man, was happy to share with you the
dedication of the last edition of the whole work.[1] Far from being offended,
he was actually delighted that this was like a spur provided for your talent, 5
although on your own you were already running at no sluggish pace in the
fields of the Muses. He is a prudent and pious man, who considered that it
was a splendid gain to have you as a companion and competitor in this kind
of association, which through sharing brings profit rather than loss. Far from
thinking he is disadvantaged in any way, he considers his own happiness 10
marvellously redoubled if he sees those virtues in which he himself excels
reproduced in his son. Therefore it seemed proper to dedicate to your name
this addition to the work, which is large enough to constitute a real volume
in itself, so that you may run the faster and he rejoice the more. Indeed, out
of his special affection for you and his own modesty, he enjoys your gains 15
more than his own; or rather, he considers his son's flourishing good fortune
more as his own than what he had accomplished himself, for the goods of
the soul know no old age. Go on then, my fine young fellow, keep the same
resolve. Press on in what you have begun. Continue day after day, both augmenting the joy of the best of fathers and increasing your own happiness in 20
every way. You will accomplish this if you model your efforts on the pattern
of your family by combining true piety with liberal learning and if you allow
neither the renown of your descent, nor the kindness of fortune, nor life at
court, nor love of your wife, nor care for your children to distract your mind
from engagement with the study of literature. 25

If at this point someone should object that the limits of the human
mind and the lack of time make such a large enterprise impossible, I ask
you to consider what a great part of life others waste in cards and dice, and
to think with how much less expense, with how much more pleasure, and
lastly with how much more profit, this time could be spent in reading good 30
authors. And so, my dear Charles, model yourself on your father, only with
this exception: from dinner to night time until he goes to bed he is usually
muttering over his books, so much so that I often wonder that he can do this
without harm to his health.

I wrote this in sorrow and grief, my mind totally devastated, because I 35
learned from good sources that William Warham, archbishop of Canterbury,

* * * * *

2726
1 In the edition 1528, Ep 2023 (to Charles) was inserted at the end of the introductory sheets, probably as an afterthought, to fill a blank page.

that unmatched, heroic soul, had exchanged life for death,[2] or, to speak more truly, had left this life that is a shadow[3] to enter into true and immortal life. I deplore my own fate, not his. He was truly my sheet anchor.[4] We had made a vow to die together;[5] he had promised a common grave, and I had no doubt that, even though he was fourteen years older, he would outlive me. To be sure, neither age nor disease took him from us, but an unhappy accident,[6] disastrous not only to him but also to learning, to religion, to the kingdom, to the church – so great was his holiness, his wisdom in counsel, his kindness to everyone. Now that heavenly soul, in return for the good seed which he sowed here, reaps a rich harvest with Christ.[7] And at the same time I am held back here half-alive, still owing the debt from the vow I had made, which (if my forecast is not erroneous) I will soon pay. It could have seemed to be just a pact of friendship, but truth cries out that it was a serious compact, because my mind is so completely downcast by his death that it cannot be uplifted by any distractions. Instead, even time, which is supposed to cure even the most grievous sorrows,[8] merely makes this wound more and more painful. What more can I say? I feel that I am being called. I will be glad to die here together with that incomparable and irrevocable patron of mine, provided I am allowed, by the mercy of Christ, to live there together with him. He was a bright star of the church; now he has gone to heaven as an even brighter star. Would that I could join my sun as a tiny star!

This commemoration was given not only as a solace to my grief, but also because I thought it would be good for you to revive the memory of this prelate who was easily the most praiseworthy of all, so that you might more studiously pattern your studies and your life after two models, your father and your father's friend. Farewell.

Given at Freiburg im Breisgau, 1 October 1532

* * * * *

2 Warham, Erasmus' friend and patron, died in August 1532.
3 Cf Ps 144 (Vulgate 143):4, 1 Chron 29:15, Job 8:9.
4 Ie anchor of last resort; see *Adagia* I i 24.
5 'To die together' is cited in Greek: συναποθνῃσκόντων. It is the title of a play by Dilphius, a writer of Greek comedies, to which Terence refers in the prologue to his *Adelphi*. It may refer to lovers who agree to die together.
6 All evidence indicates that Warham died of natural causes while visiting his nephew.
7 Cf *Adagia* I viii 78: 'As you have sown, so also shall you reap.'
8 A commonplace in letters of consolation; see *De conscribendis epistolis* CWE 25 164, and cf *Adagia* II v 5.

William Warham, archbishop of Canterbury, by Hans Holbein the Younger
Musée du Louvre, Paris/Clichés des Musées Nationaux

2727 / From Germain de Brie   Paris, 1 October 1532

This letter was first published on page 10 of *Divi Ioannis Chrysostomi in epis-tolam divi Pauli ad Romanos Homiliae octo priores*, translated by Germain de Brie (Basel: Froben and Episcopius, March 1533). For Germain de Brie, French humanist with a particular interest in the works of St John Chrysostom, see Ep 2021 introduction.

GERMAIN DE BRIE TO ERASMUS OF ROTTERDAM

When I got back to Paris following various journeys of our king, in a number of which I had to take part because of some private business of my own, Philippus Montanus was conveniently at hand for me. I was at any event planning to visit him or at least have him come over to see me, since I was   5 eager to find out from him everything about you.[1] For there is no one from whom we learn more precisely or more fully about your affairs. When he told me he had heard that your friend Froben was eager to have those sermons of Chrysostom that I had translated into Latin, I complained to him forcefully about the thoroughly corrupt codex you had sent to me,[2] saying that (if I had   10 any concern for my reputation) I could hardly venture to publish what I had translated and that I was waiting for another codex from Rome that would help me to fill in the gaps I left where your codex is undoubtedly so corrupt or deficient that we would need not just an Aristarchus but the author Chrysostom himself to restore them.[3] While I was complaining about this, he   15 announced to me that the very same work of Chrysostom, printed in Greek at Verona,[4] was being sold here at last. When I had indicated that I very much wanted access to it, lo and behold, your Montanus immediately brought me the work itself. Without any delay, I looked up some of the places that I had found to be corrupt in your codex, some of which I had marked with an   20 asterisk and some with an obelisk, and which were so numerous that I had almost begun to despair of translating the work. Since most of these places were correct and complete in the Verona edition, I immediately began to feel sorry for myself because of the work and the labours I had expended trying to correct them, fretting and torturing my mind for this whole year. But I   25

* * * * *

2727
1 For Montanus, see Ep 2065 introduction.
2 Cf Ep 2379 n6.
3 Aristarchus was a famous textual critic (especially of Homer) who lived at Alexandria in the second century BC.
4 The edition by Gian Matteo Giberti; see Ep 2340 n2.

also convinced Montanus that not only your codex but also the copy from
Verona was corrupt, so that I will have to wait for a more accurate copy. To
that end, I hope (as I told you) that the library in Rome will be a help to me.
This was promised to me in a letter from Cardinal Agostino Trivulzio, a man
who (as you are aware) must be numbered among the principal ornaments   30
of our age.[5] Otherwise not even you, if I truly know you (although you also
favour very much the interests of Froben) would encourage me to hasten
our edition, which would be so full of the faults and errors of the codices,
especially since we are surrounded by so many envious and wicked men, so
many malignant and perverse minds, so many sharp and virulent tongues.   35

I implore you, most excellent Erasmus, do you not see how many malevolent whispers, how much hissing from poisonous vipers, how many le-
thal bites from asps await those who write and publish for no other reason
than to promote literary studies to the best of their abilities, if they should
happen to doze off a bit and almost fall from their chariot, as they say?[6] Tell   40
me, in all honesty, how many readers today are looking for something to
approve of and praise rather than to pick apart and revile? Such today is the
perversity (to use no stronger word) of so many that whatever could win
the approval of learned and virtuous men is attacked by these Zoiluses with
the pronouncements of a Hipponax.[7] For their nature is such that when it   45
would be more suitable to imitate bees (an old saying that my Greek teacher
Janus Lascaris often used to cite),[8] which by nature fly about gathering flowers in gardens or meadows, they, however, hunting everywhere for something to carp at, resolve to imitate flies, which, very hungry and noisome,
are always ready to suck sores. A certain unusually learned friend of ours   50
compares such men (if they can be called that and not beasts instead) to the
soldiers rebuked by Memnon who, when he was waging war for Darius
against Alexander, found them impudently hurling witty barbs against
Alexander. He is said to have struck them with a spear, saying, 'I feed you
to fight Alexander hand to hand, not to hurl insults at him from afar.'[9] Such   55
people, the very ones I am talking about, are such brawlers that they only

* * * * *

5 See Ep 2405 n1.
6 Said of someone 'who forgets what he set out to do and adopts another plan.'
   See *Adagia* II iii 22.
7 Zoilus was a stupid critic of Homer; see *Adagia* II v 8. Hipponax was notable for
   inventing a bitter, satiric kind of iambic verse; see *Adagia* II ii 56.
8 For Lascaris see Ep 2027 n14.
9 Cf *Apophthegmata* 5.32 (CWE 38 466), which gives a somewhat more concise version of Memnon's statement.

know how to insult but do not dare stand up to an enemy; they are the same
ones who, to quote my beloved Chrysostom, take more pleasure in defaming than others do in praising.[10] I say nothing here about that modern clique
of ours that never ceases to amaze me, for they pursue pleasures day and   60
night to such an extent that they have no other goal and thus have no notion
of how to speak, but if they happen to hear someone else being praised for
intelligence they are overwhelmed by a fit of envy and cannot bear to hear
it. These fine fellows wonder how it is possible that someone among them
who is praised for his knowledge of Latin or Greek or for some other intel-   65
lectual achievement should have earned his current reputation, completely
unaware that eloquence and learning are achieved by work and practice just
as somnolence and inertia produce ignorance and faltering speech.

And so, although I have translated almost all of this collection of sermons (I intended to give Montanus evidence of what I have done by showing   70
him all my pages), nevertheless, before I allow this edition to be published
I will wait to see if I can still get a more correct copy from some place of
other. Sparta is my portion,[11] and I want to adorn it in every way, both for
his honour and my own. Believe me, Erasmus, best of friends, this work of
Chrysostom is so outstanding and excellent, so learned and elegant, so rare   75
and perfect, so Christian and even divine that I believe that man will be truly
blessed to whom it will have been given, by a magic wand, as it were, to publish this work in the Latin tongue, worthily and faultlessly, even if it takes ten
years. I have always liked that saying of Socrates in Plato: it is surely better to
do a few things well than many things badly.[12] Even though I do not require   80
ten years to finish the translation, I will bring it to fruition in a fitting and
appropriate way.

In the meantime, until I issue the whole edition, I am publishing, with
your encouragement and sponsorship, the first eight sermons, a quarter of
the whole work, both in Chrysostom's Greek and in my translation, in order   85
to give the reader a specimen, a taste as it were, of my work. It will be up to
you to defend my lucubrations from the sniping of detractors and backbiters,
if there should be any. Farewell, and continue in your affection for me.

At Paris, 1 October 1532

* * * * *

10 Allen could not identify this quotation, and neither could we, not even with the
   help of a computer search of databases.
11 See *Adagia* II v 1: 'Sparta is your portion; do your best for her.'
12 Cited in Greek from Plato *Theaetetus* 187E

2728 / To Johann Koler   [Freiburg], 5 October 1532

This letter was first published in the *Vita Erasmi*, evidently on the basis of an
often inaccurate copy of the original. Allen based his text on the autograph
('written rapidly ... [and] sometimes difficult to read'), which he found in the
Humanistenbriefe collection of the Town Library at Zofingen in Canton Aargau
(MS P 14 I 9). The address sheet is missing, but Allen accepted the validity of
the address indicated in the *Vita*, pointing out the connection of this letter to
Ep 2814, addressed to Koler. For information on the complicated history of the
manuscript, see Allen's introduction to this letter.

Cordial greetings. I have thus far not been able to discover, in letters either
from you or from anyone else, whether that packet containing letters to
Johann Paumgartner, to his son, to Anton Fugger, to Anselmus, to Viglius,[1]
and to some others has been delivered.[2] Nowadays there is great treachery
in such matters.   5
      Recently a seventy-year-old monk at Basel married a nun and not long
afterwards made her his servant.
      A while ago, at a certain city in the duchy of Jülich (named Soest, I
think, on a par with Strasbourg),[3] Lambertus Campester – a man who, after
persuading a printer that the work would sell, published at Paris an edition   10
of my *Colloquies* as if it were corrected by me, adding a preface under my
name and mixing in throughout the work amazing insertions in which I corrected myself,[4] all of them full of a clownish stupidity. When he had finished
that he fled to Lyon, where he pretended to be a good friend of Erasmus and
found a patron, from whom he soon stole three hundred crowns; then he   15
fled, and in his flight he was captured in the company of some young ladies,

* * * * *

2728
1 Johann Paumgartner (Ep 2603), Johann Georg Paumgartner (Ep 2683), Anton
   Fugger (Ep 2145), Anselmus Ephorinus (Ep 2539), Viglius Zuichemus (Ep 2657)
2 This is probably a reference to the packet of letters sent in July 1532, of which
   only Epp 2681 to Pietro Bembo, 2682 to Viglius, and 2683 to Johann Georg
   Paumgartner are extant.
3 The Westphalian city of Soest (Erasmus spells it Zoest), having won its independence from the archbishop of Cologne in the mid-fifteenth century, was aligned
   with the duke of Jülich-Cleves. It was by no means the equal of Strasbourg in
   size, wealth, or importance. Erasmus perhaps means that like Strasbourg, Soest
   had gone over to the Reformation (1531–2). Cf n6 below.
4 For the German Dominican Lambertus Campester and his unauthorized edition
   of the *Colloquies*, see Ep 1341A:307–412 with nn72, 85, 86; and cf Ep 1581:464–72
   with n59.

and he would have been fastened to a cross except that the holy cowl of
Dominic saved him.⁵ This Campester, I say, having perpetrated many other
outrageous crimes, threw off his cowl in Soest and taught 'the gospel' – that
is, pure sedition. He is an Anabaptist. The duke requested that the city expel   20
him but they answered that they could not do without 'their preacher.'⁶ And
this plague creeps on from day to day. They have almost reached the point of
bursting into England and establishing their tyranny there.⁷

In Basel, as a replacement for Oecolampadius, they have chosen Myconius, a senseless man, once the insipid head of a grammar school.⁸ I wonder   25
what the city council hopes for or has in mind. As for me, I see nothing but a
disastrous outcome. They are creating open anarchy, where the wicked can
do whatever they like.

The princes will finally be forced to adopt extreme remedies. You know,
I suppose, that my friend More has obtained from his most generous mon-   30
arch release from the greatly burdensome office of chancellor. The Lutherans
boast that he has been rightly deposed and has been replaced by a certain
nobleman who immediately released some forty evangelicals from prison, to
which they had been consigned by More.⁹ They have their couriers, through

* * * * *

5 Cf Epp 1655:13–18, 1686:58–63, 1697:94–6.
6 The Dominican preacher to whom Erasmus is referring cannot possibly have
  been Lambertus Campester, who in 1538 was in France, in Riom as canon of
  Saint-Amable's, where he composed an oration in praise of Francis I, reas-
  serting his hatred of Luther and his enthusiasm for France. It was indeed a
  Dominican whose preaching inaugurated the Reformation in Soest, but his
  name was Thomas Borchwede. There was, however, another preacher in Soest
  named Johann van Kampen (Campius or Campanus in Latin) whose arrest
  (21 December 1531) for trying to preach despite a ban imposed by the city council led to a popular tumult in support of the Reformation, the end result of which
  was the victory of the Reformation and the issuance of an evangelical church
  order on 16 April 1532. Johann van Kampen would seem to be the Fleming
  otherwise known as Johannes Campanus (Ep 2643 n9), who, after being driv-
  en out of Saxony in 1530 because of his antitrinitarian views, found refuge in
  Jülich-Cleves and was before long denounced as an Anabaptist (cf lines 20–1).
  At all events, Erasmus seems somehow to have misunderstood 'Campanus' as
  'Campester' and to have drawn the unwarranted conclusions recorded here. Cf
  Ep 2780:57–76 and Allen Ep 2825:14–15. For the events in Soest in 1531–2, see
  Werner Freitag *Die Reformation in Westfalen: Regionale Vielfalt, Bekenntniskonflikt
  und Koexistenz* (Münster 2016) 97–9, 106.
7 Cf Ep 2659:97–112.
8 For Osvaldus Myconius see Ep 2605 n3.
9 See Ep 2750:1–6.

whom they search out everything. I was hoping that those who were taught   35
by the disaster at Lucerne would return to a more tolerable condition.[10] But
they are planning harsher policies than before. At Basel they have revised
their constitutions. They say they will not force anyone, but if anyone receives the Eucharist elsewhere, he is fined a pound; the second time, two
pounds; the third time, four pounds; the fourth time, exile. And this is 'not   40
to force.'[11]

What has happened to Nachtgall I do not know,[12] but recently at a banquet among the Carthusians he said that Erasmus was a ne'er-do-well and
that all who read his books are turned into ne'er-do-wells. I think he must
have been instigated by Pelargus,[13] a Dominican to whom I had granted   45
many good turns, but who, when I had some inkling of his character and
stopped giving, became soured and tried to accuse me of having injured him
because a letter to More in my *Flowery Letters* contained these words: 'Two
monks stirred up this uproar among us, one of whom was preaching at the
cathedral and the other among the Dominicans. To be sure, they decamped,   50
but others are affected by the same disease, etc.'[14] When everyone discouraged him from accusing me, he humbly asked me to have mercy on him, and
I did so.

If you are seeking sugar from Frankfurt, I have already provided myself with some. But it is of the sort that is normally sent to Germany.   55

Do not be concerned about a servant, unless there happens to be a
suitable one at hand. For I have a reliable Frenchman,[15] and another one
who is also reliable, whom I have sent to England and who will return in
November.[16] But neither knows German very well.

* * * * *

10 The reference is clearly to the Second Kappel War, which ended in the disastrous defeat of Zhrich's poorly prepared forces on 11 October 1531. Lucerne
   was one of the leading participants on the Catholic side, but the decisive battle
   took place near Kappel. Cf Ep 2564 n8.
11 See Ep 2519 introduction.
12 Ottmar Nachtgall (Ep 2166 n3)
13 For Pelargus see Ep 2721. If it was indeed Pelargus who egged Nachtgall on
   to speak ill of Erasmus, then the latter must have been in Freiburg again in
   September–October.
14 Cf Ep 2721:14–17.
15 Gilbert Cousin (Ep 2381 n1)
16 Quirinus Hagius (Ep 2704 n6); on his errand to England see also Ep 2741 n2.

When Polyphemus left there,[17] he did not want anyone to know   60
where he was going.[18] But he went straight to Luther and Melanchthon, and
weighed down with letters of recommendation, he went to John, the duke
of Saxony, pretending to be the servant and close friend of Erasmus. He was
treated splendidly for some months. Finally, when he left, the Duke gave
him a fine horse and forty gold pieces. From there to Cologne. There, with   65
Tielmannus,[19] a very good friend of mine, he drank away several months.
Then he came here, to be the steward of my house. I got rid of him by sending him to Regensburg.[20] There he drank away six weeks and extorted a lot
of money. Coming back from Regensburg, he stopped by at Augsburg to visit
the bishop.[21] There he extorted a horse and a crown.[22] He had decided to   70
stay in my house with his lame horse. The horse I excluded; him I received
for some ten days and then sent away, not very happy to go. He wanted to
go to England. I persuaded him not to. Then to Poland. So he went back to
Cologne, which he left with no thanks from his host Tielmannus, who says
many foul rumours were circulating about him. He went to Frankfurt with   75
a letter from me, intending to go to Poland. But I had taken care that a letter
was sent to the factor. When Polyphemus saw this, he went back to Hessen
and asked for a recommendation from the chancellor of the duke, who was
a close friend of mine.[23] Things have come to extremes with this rascal, and I
have no doubt that he will soon come to a miserable end.   80

I have no doubt that Konrad Heresbach was with you and I sent a brief
letter through him.[24] The man through whom I promised to write at greater
length changed his plans and went back to Flanders – a learned young man

* * * * *

17 Augsburg
18 For the recent movements of Erasmus' wayward servant Felix Rex, known as
    Polyphemus, see Ep 2649 n3 and the lines that follow.
19 Tielmannus Gravius (Ep 2103)
20 Ie to the imperial diet
21 Christoph von Stadion (Ep 2029)
22 Most likely a French écu au soleil (also called 'crown' or 'sun crown'), which
    was officially valued in 1532 at 76d groot Flemish and therefore equivalent to
    about eight days' wages of an Antwerp master mason/carpenter at 9.05d per
    day (CWE 12 650 Table 3, 691 Table 13)
23 Johann Feige (1482–1543), since 1519 chancellor to Landgrave (not Duke) Philip
    of Hessen. Despite Erasmus' claim here of close friendship with Feige, there is
    no evidence of direct relations between them.
24 Heresbach (Ep 1316) had visited Erasmus in September 1532 to consult him about
    the new church order for Cleves; *Jülich-Bergische Kirchenpolitik am Ausgange des
    Mittelalters und in der Reformationszeit* 1: *Urkunden und Akten 1400–1553*, ed Otto

and devoted to me, but infected, I am afraid, with the disease of the sects.[25]
These people see to it that literary studies rise or fall depending on the sect. 85
At Basel, of course, they are reopening the university.[26]

Gumppenberg seems to me to be a diligent and straightforward man.[27]
I suspect that the business Cardinal Cajetanus wrote me about was to get me
to explain a few things in my writings.[28] I replied that I am doing that and
that if anyone showed me some real errors I would not fail to do the duty of a 90
Christian.[29] There is a certain remarkable deviser of misdeeds who is striving
to destroy Erasmus, and yet he pretends to be my very best friend.[30] And if I
send someone to Gumppenberg, what then? If he communicated any secrets
to you, I can know about that through you. It is not a matter of any great importance. Pious partisans are seeking revenge. Sepúlveda confessed to me in 95
one of his letters that they had compelled him to add to his book some things
more harsh than he wished.[31] Let them plot all they want, they will not make
me join the sects. I have written freely; I am not sure that this messenger is
reliable. Farewell.

5 October 1532   100
Very truly yours, Erasmus of Rotterdam
To the very distinguished gentleman Master John Koler, provost of
Chur

* * * * *

R. Redlich (Bonn 1907) 255 n1. Epp 2736:15–16, 2753:1 indicate that Heresbach
went to Italy at about this time. The letter he carried is not extant.

25 Joachim Martens, who in September 1532 visited Erasmus in Freiburg and
Bonifacius Amerbach in Basel, expecting to continue on to Italy, only to change
his mind and return to his ailing mother in Ghent; see Epp 2703:7–8, 2706:12–15,
2709:1, 2799:23–6.

26 Following the adoption of the Reformation in 1529, the Basel city council officially closed the university to prevent the faculty and students from abscond-
ing with the regalia and establishing a 'university in exile' at Freiburg. Lectures
continued unofficially and irregularly until the official reopening of the university in September 1532. See Rudolph Thommen *Geschichte der Universität Basel,*
1532–1632 (Basel 1889) 1–13. (Thanks go to Amy Nelson Burnett for supplying
this information.)

27 Ambrosius von Gumppenberg (Ep 2619 introduction)

28 See Ep 2690:6–8 with n2.

29 See Ep 2690:8–37.

30 Presumably Girolamo Aleandro; see Epp 2638–9, 2679–80, and cf Ep 2738:13–17.

31 See Ep 2637:15–20.

2729 / From Juan Ginés de Sepúlveda   Rome, 15 October 1532

This letter, Sepúlveda's reply to Ep 2701, was first published in the *Sepulvedae epistolae* folio A3 verso.

JUAN GINÉS DE SEPÚLVEDA SENDS GREETINGS TO MASTER
ERASMUS OF ROTTERDAM

I received at Rome on 14 October your letter dated at Freiburg on 16 August, so I was not surprised that my book reached you so late. In your letter you write that you think it would be more prudent not to answer it, so as to avoid any quarrel between us, and in this opinion you display remarkable kindness and wisdom, since you do not want my leisure time to be taken away from more profitable pursuits and to be wasted in troublesome arguments, which would serve no useful purpose anyway. And I cannot say how acceptable and pleasant I find this straightforward expression of your intention. For what could be more burdensome and troublesome to me than to be pushed to the point (very much against my will) of being forced to enter into a dispute with Erasmus, whom I look up to as the bright light of our age? In fact, I was certain of such equanimity not only because of your well-known prudence – which assured you that I have acted out of no other motive than my duty – but also because of the letter that you recently wrote to Tommaso Cardinal Cajetanus,[1] saying that of your own accord, but also strengthened by his authority, you are especially concerned about revising all your books so as to satisfy the cavils of even your most exacting critics without any controversy.

Although, as I see, you need no encouragement to press forward, nevertheless, because of my good will and respect for you, I also beg you insistently and implore you with all the supplication I can muster to do so; by this single act (believe me) you will silence your detractors and you will win extraordinary praise from all good men and – what will be most in accord with your piety – in your strength you will support the weaknesses of those less strong according to the precept of Paul.[2]

As for the annotations of Zúñiga, I imagine that all those extracted and sent by the order of Cardinal Iñigo Mendoza are in your hands. When he arrived at Rome, Cardinal Quiñones gave him that commentary, retaining

* * * * *

2729
1 Ep 2690
2 Rom 15:1

a copy for himself, together with some other Latin books bequeathed to Mendoza by Zúñiga.[3] And Mendoza, that excellent prelate, who is also very fond of you, enlisted my labour, which I mostly willingly granted him in order to comply with your wishes.

Farewell, my Erasmus, and know that I am your most eager supporter, 35 and that if there is anything I can provide for you by my effort, endeavour, and diligence, there is nothing I would not strive to do for your sake.

Rome, 15 October in the year after Christ's birth 1532

2730 / From Bonifacius Amerbach [Basel], 19 October 1532

The manuscript of this letter (= AK Ep 1683) is a much corrected autograph rough draft in the Öffentliche Bibliothek of the University of Basel (MS C VIA 73 25). Accompanying it are notes with adages drawn from the works of jurists as well as from classical authors, evidently intended as suggestions for inclusion in the *Adagia*. In Ep 2709 Erasmus had asked Bonifacius to send him any adages he could find in the writings of jurists.

When I look over the adages I marked from a hasty reading, and also the commentaries of Alciati,[1] and compare them with your *Chiliads*,[2] I find that most of them are already taken care of there. The rest I send under the rule that they stand or fall as you see fit.[3] For whether they should be entered into the list of the adages, or if there is something that is not found among yours, 5 I cannot say for certain. In fact, after skimming through the index with a light touch (as they say)[4] I found that none of them occurred.[5] About these please decide for yourself just as you wish, and please take this delay in good part.

* * * * *

3 See Epp 2637:23–36, 2705.

2730
1 For Andrea Alciati see Ep 1250 introduction. His 'commentaries' were *D. Andreae Alciati iurecons. clarissimi de verborum significatione libri quatuor. Eiusdem in trac- tatum eius argumenti veterum iureconsultore commentaria* (Lyon: Gryphius 1530). The final page of the index includes a list of 'Proverbia iureconsultii peculiaria.'
2 See Ep 2720 n11.
3 The list is on folios 26–7 of the Basel manuscript; see AK Ep 1683 n2.
4 *Adagia* I iv 27
5 Allen found the following variant of this sentence in the margin of the let- ter: 'When I searched the latest index of the penultimate edition they did not appear.'

For when I got home, I had to go away again, and there was no messenger at
hand, certainly not one to whom I could safely entrust a letter. I do not want   10
you to ignore that Alciati, at the beginning of book 4 of his commentaries on
the meaning of things and words, has also gathered some things that have
not been sufficiently attended to, not only from the *Pandects* but also from the
interpreters of the law.[6] If you want to get a notion of them, you will find that
Zasius has them.[7]   15
    The day after the feast of St Luke 1532

2730A / To Bonifacius Amerbach   [Freiburg, after 19 October 1532]

This letter (= AK Ep 1684) was first published in the *Epistolae familiares*. The
autograph is in the Öffentliche Bibliothek of the University of Basel (MS AN
III 15 85). In both the *Epistolae familiares* and the Basel manuscript collection, it
follows immediately after Ep 2709, and that is where Allen left it, as Ep 2710,
reasoning that it was the answer to a letter, not extant, in which Bonifacius had
responded to the request in Ep 2709 for contributions to the new edition of the
Adagia. As the AK editor Alfred Hartmann has pointed out, however, the supposed proverb about a sleeping dog (line 2) appears on the list that Bonifacius
attached to Ep 2730 (cf n3 of that letter). This letter, therefore, has to be seen as
the response to Ep 2730 and redated to 'after 19 October 1532.'

Greetings. Many thanks. If anything new turns up, let me know. Who told
you that 'a dog sleeping on the same roof-tile' is a proverb? You were led
astray by 'they say.'[1] Many of them had eluded me. Many I had already published. Farewell.
    Erasmus of Rotterdam (if perhaps you do not recognize the handwriting)   5
    To the very renowned gentleman Master Bonifacius Amerbach

* * * * *

6 *Pandects* is another name for the *Digest*, the compendium of Roman law compiled in the sixth century at the order of Emperor Justinian. For the recommended attention to Alciati, see *Adagia* IV ix 36, where Erasmus cites Alciati's
  De verborum significatione (n1 above) as the source of an adage that first appeared in the edition of 1533 (CWE 36 442–3 with nn2, 3).
7 Udalricus Zasius, famed jurist and professor of law at Freiburg

2730A
1 Bonifacius identified as his source Aristotle *Magna moralia* 2.10 1208a; see AK Ep
  1684 n1.

2731 / To Johann Kleberger   Freiburg, 20 October 1532

This letter was first published in the *Epistolae universae* page 1116. For Johann Kleberger, a native Nürnberger who had settled as a banker in Lyon, see Ep 1977 n28.

ERASMUS OF ROTTERDAM TO JOHANN KLEBERGER, GREETINGS

Man most dear to my heart, there was no serious matter for me to write to you about, but since highly reliable men through whom I can write to you have offered themselves, and since I suspected you would be there on business,[1] I could not pass up the opportunity to send you greetings in a letter, however   5 brief, to let you know that the miserable Erasmus, whom you visited twice in Basel when he was only half-alive,[2] is still breathing (I wouldn't go so far as to say living) and still remembers your kindness. But as long as I know that you are in good health and that things are going well for you, I will have good reason to rejoice. If there is something you want me to know, you can   10 safely tell it to those who will deliver this letter. The pope triumphs together with his cardinals.[3] But I would offer them more congratulations if this triumph were shared with the whole church.

Farewell. At Freiburg im Breisgau, 20 October 1532

2732 / From Philippus Melanchthon   [Wittenberg], 25 October 1532

This letter (= MBW Ep 1287) was first published in *Epistolae selectiores aliquot Philippi Melanchthonis* ed Kaspar Peucer (Wittenberg: Johannes Crato 1565) 37–9.

PHILIPPUS MELANCHTHON TO ERASMUS OF ROTTERDAM

Since I have found a reliable, trustworthy courier, I could hardly refrain from sending you a letter, especially since you very kindly invited me to fulfil

* * * * *

2731
1 Probably not Lyon, where he resided, but somewhere on his business travels; perhaps the autumn fair in Frankfurt
2 See Ep 1977:63–4.
3 Reference unclear

Johann Kleberger by Albrecht Dürer
Kunsthistorisches Museum, Vienna

this sort of obligation some months ago.[1] For two whole years, while I was
engaged in disputes and altercations, which are completely foreign to my   5
character, there was nothing that I found quite as soothing as your delightful letters.[2] For that reason I would like you to be assured that this friendly
duty of yours was not only most agreeable but also delightful; for just as I
have great esteem for the good will of any man who is a lover of wisdom, so
I have no love or trust in vulgar associations with the uncultured.[3] I would   10
write to you about other things, partly about what is going on now, partly
on what is impending, if my deliberations were of any use to the commonwealth. But since neither side is at all inclined towards moderation, my advice is rejected. But I implore you as strongly as I can to use your authority
to promote peace whenever the occasion arises and to exhort those in power   15
not to fragment the churches any further by civil war. For what would be the
result of civil war except universal destruction? And I have no doubt that
those whose hopes are excessive and who for that reason thrust firebrands
into that gentle temperament of the emperor in order to incite him to wage
war are quite deceived. So far as these disputes are concerned, I hope that   20
my advice is understood and approved by those who are prudent. I have
cut short many controversies and now I am endeavouring in good faith to
clarify some matters that are necessary to piety. I am also trying to treat suit-
ably the basic principles of ecclesiastical government. Whatever happens,
my judgment and wishes will be attested in my commentary on Romans,   25
which is now published.[4] As for you, if you can give any energy to the totter-

* * * * *

2732
1 In a letter no longer extant
2 For the two years in question only four letters from Erasmus to Melanchthon,
  sent to Augsburg in 1530 during the imperial diet of that year, survive: Epp
  2343, 2358, 2363, 2365. Saddled with the role of chief spokesmen for the
  Wittenberg theologians and for the Saxon government in the quest for a religious settlement, at Augsburg and later, that would prevent civil war in the
  Empire, Melanchthon had to contend not only with the refusal of the Catholics
  to make even the most minimal concessions (marriage of the clergy, communion in both kinds, and the suspension of private masses) but also with the
  harsh criticism of those (particularly in Nürnberg) who felt that Saxony was
  prepared to yield too much (recognition of the jurisdiction of the bishops).
3 The clause 'for just ... uncultured' is in Greek, not intended to be read by all.
4 *Commentarii in epistolam Pauli ad Romanos, recens scripti* (Wittenberg: Josef
  Klug, [October] 1532); see MBW Ep 1287. For Melanchthon (as for Luther)
  the Epistle to the Romans, with its (to them) clear teaching of justification
  by faith alone, was the indispensable key to the correct understanding of all
  Scripture. It followed that any religious settlement had to be based on the careful,

ing commonwealth, do what he says happens in good poems:[5] in this last act of your life, as it were, let the whole world perceive your wisdom above all.

A certain young man, Dietrich Reiffenstein, descended from a family greatly devoted to you, has arrived in Freiburg. He had a young uncle, a very   30 fine man, who was with you a good while in Louvain.[6] Hence I beg you, both because of the favour of his ancestors towards you and because of my recommendation, to consent to welcome him. While he was with us his behaviour was most suitable, and I hope that, strengthened by your teachings, he will not be unworthy of your company.   35

Farewell. 25 October 1532

2733 / To Jean Lambelin   Freiburg, 26 October 1532

This letter was first published by A. Castan in the *Revue Historique* 1 (1876) 125. The manuscript, a contemporary copy made c 25 November 1532, is in the Bibliothèque municipale at Besançon (MS BB 14 folio 450).

Jean Lambelin (d 1538) of Jussey in the Franche-Comté, was secretary of the town council of Besançon, which he represented at the Diet of Worms in 1521. After he returned home, he began to advocate Lutheran reforms in a town already riven by antagonism between the town on the one side and the archbishop and chapter on the other. In 1537, after being charged with heresy, embezzlement, and abuse of his authority, he was tortured and then beheaded in the market square. Following the exchange of letters documented here, Erasmus and Lambelin kept in touch, largely through Lambelin's kinsman Etienne Desprez; see Allen Ep 3115:67–71.

Cordial greetings. A while ago I asked you to extend my gratitude to the magnificent and most illustrious city council for their heart-felt kindness to

* * * * *

fair-minded examination and sound interpretation of that book. See MBW Ep 767 (Melanchthon to Hermann von Neuenahr, March/April 1529), which served as the preface to Melanchthon's *Dispositio orationis in epistola Pauli ad Romanos* (Haguenau: Johannes Setzer 1529).
5 Ie Horace; cf *Ars poetica* 126–7: 'If you dare to create a new character, let it be maintained at the end as it was when it made its entrance, and remain consistent.'
6 For the uncle, Johann Reiffenstein, see Ep 1982 introduction. The nephew, Dietrich Reiffenstein, has not been identified. He may be the Theodericus Reyffenstein of Königstein who matriculated at Wittenberg in 1525.

me and their most gratifying letter,[1] which I am sure you have already done.
I have bought a house here and renovated it at considerable expense, beyond
my slender resources; I was constrained by necessity to do so.[2] But I have 5
not yet given up my intention to move there. This time of my life requires
nothing so much as rest and quiet. But to make sure the city council knows
I have not considered this matter lightly, I am sending two letters from the
emperor, one to the city council, the other to the clergy, both of which I ask
you to deliver, if you will.[3] I have sent this third messenger in the hope that 10
he will bring back at least one barrel of old wine;[4] in that matter I beg you to
help him with your advice and your authority. He has been given ample payment for it. I beg you, my dear Lambelin, to be so kind as to add this favour
to the ones you have granted to me in the past. Best wishes to you and all
your dear ones. 15

Freiburg, 26 October 1532
Erasmus of Rotterdam, in my own hand

2734 / To Gerrit van Assendelft   Freiburg, 29 October 1532

This letter was first published in the epistolary appendix to Erasmus' *De praepa-*
ratione ad mortem (Basel: Froben 1534) page 130. For Gerrit van Assendelft,
known to Erasmus as an influential admirer, see Ep 2645 n9. Assendelft's response to this letter, in which Erasmus praises his nobility and generosity (see
lines 32–44) and offers whatever service he might require from his devoted
follower (lines 45–8), was to help arrange for a handsome cash gift on behalf of
the Estates of Holland; see Ep 2819.

* * * * *

2733
1 No other letter of Erasmus to Lambelin, and no letter of the city council of
  Besançon to Erasmus is extant. In their letter, the city fathers had evidently
  encouraged Erasmus in his stated desire (Ep 2514) to move to their city. In a
  letter of 5 February 1533 Erasmus reports that he had received two letters of
  invitation from the council (Ep 2761:29–30).
2 See Epp 2462 introduction, 2506, 2517.
3 The letter to the city council is Ep 2553; that to the clergy is not extant.
4 The messenger is unidentified; possibly Gilbert Cousin (Ep 2381 n1). On
  Erasmus' preference for wine from Burgundy, see Ep 2646 n5.

DESIDERIUS ERASMUS OF ROTTERDAM TO THE RENOWNED
GENTLEMAN MASTER GERRIT VAN ASSENDELFT,
KNIGHT OF THE GOLDEN FLEECE AND PRESIDENT
OF THE COUNCIL OF THE HAGUE, GREETINGS

In his letters, most renowned sir, my servant Talesius prods me from time to   5
time to write to you,[1] at least to let you know that I am aware of and grateful
for your notable favour towards me, and indeed I am most grateful for it, as I
should be. But even if someone does not know how consumed I am by excessive labours in this state of health and at this age, which demands freedom
and release from duties, perhaps he will expect from me a little more civility   10
in this regard. On the other hand, someone who is aware of what saddlebags
I bear on my back will be surprised that I would write to anyone at all unless
driven by some dire necessity. A certain sense of shame has also prevented
me from writing, because I am afraid that, having no subject matter, I might
seem to be a man of lowly estate writing to a powerful personage not so   15
much to express gratitude for a favour as to seek one.

There was never any age of the world with such faultless morals that
those striving after some outstanding goal were not impeded by envy, barked
at by dogs, chattered at by jackdaws and magpies. But I do not think there
was ever an age that gave more rein to slander and ingratitude. Therefore, in   20
my opinion, those who bestow kindness and favour on highly gifted people,
protect them with their authority, honour them with their testimonies, or
encourage them with applause and praise are no less deserving than those
who by their own study and industry strive to deserve well of the learned
community and the commonwealth. If I had made any such contribution, I   25
would thank you in my own name because by your kind vote of approval
you spur on my studies and show yourself a soldier in the front lines protect-
ing me with your shield against the barking of malevolent curs. As it is, since
I find nothing in myself deserving of such favour, I am certainly ashamed in
my own mind, but I think myself all the more obliged to you the less I am   30
worthy of being raised to this level of honour.

Therefore I thank you, extraordinary man that you are, not so much
personally as publicly, in the name of intellectual pursuits and piety. In fact,
when you favour me because of the virtues you believe I have you are really
bestowing that honour on the virtues themselves, which all who are truly   35

* * * * *

2734
1 No letters of Quirinus Talesius (Ep 1966) to Erasmus are extant.

noble rightly honour. Therefore noble, generous Assendelft, you are worthy of being loved by all those everywhere who cultivate liberal studies and true piety, especially since there is every reason to believe that those who admire learning and religion in others are not lacking in those qualities themselves. You certainly, as I hear, are an ornament to Holland no less for your extraor- 40 dinary mental endowments than for the insignia of your ancestors. For the ornaments of your high birth you owe largely to your ancestors or to fortune, but those others are your own. I confess that I owe a great deal to your gen- erosity and I am most happy to acknowledge it. Would that I could deserv- edly congratulate myself on your opinion of me as well. In me you have an 45 assured supporter, you have a follower devoted to you, so that if you wish to ask my services in any matter I want you to know that, though all else be lacking, my will, ready and eager to serve, will not be lacking.

I wanted to take up other matters with you, but my labours call me away. Apart from other matters, two works are being printed at one and the 50 same time: at Basel the *Adagia* expanded by some hundreds,[2] and at Paris my Jerome, revised for the fourth time with almost unimaginable labours.[3] My very best wishes to you and to your dear ones.

Given at Freiburg im Breisgau, 29 October 1532

2735 / To Quirinus Talesius   Freiburg, 31 October 1532

> This letter was first published in the *Vita Erasmi*. It is Erasmus' reply to one, not
> extant, in which Talesius, Erasmus' former servant-pupil (Ep 1966) informed
> him of his marriage to a widow named Haasje Dircksdochter.

ERASMUS OF ROTTERDAM TO THE VERY LEARNED GENTLEMAN
QUIRINUS TALESIUS, PENSIONARY OF THE FAMOUS CITY
OF HAARLEM
Cordial greetings. I am wonderfully happy, my dear Quirinus, that you have been lucky enough to find a wife after your own desire. You seem to me all 5 the happier in this respect because, according to the epigrammatical poet, you are what you wish to be.[1] I pray that just as you have found Juno to be

* * * * *

2 See Epp 2726, 2773.
3 See Ep 2758.

2735
1 Martial 10.47.12

propitious, so too you may gain the favour of Ilithyia.[2] You should not be sorry that you have married a widow. That is the preference of those who choose a wife to take care of a household rather than for pleasure. And those who want horses for their own use choose tamed rather than untamed ones. And if she bore children to her former husband you are freed from the fear of the great misfortune of having married a woman who is sterile. More often used to say to me that if he were to marry a hundred wives, none of them would be a virgin. He is now married to an aging woman who is too full of life; if she had passed away, he could have married a woman of wealth and standing.[3] There is this disadvantage, that you can never be a bishop unless you first become single.[4] My servant Lieven has found a wife, but because he neglected the warnings of his friends, not happily.[5] It was something done more impetuously than wisely.[6]

Our friend Hilarius left Lyon with his wife but it is not clear where they went.[7] Some say to Italy. It doesn't matter: wherever he is, he will be Hilarius. I am most grateful for your wife's little gift;[8] I will gladly return the favour if I get the chance. You wrote at night, against the protests of your wife. At this point I could hardly keep from laughing. Mountjoy, against the protests of all the servants, used to come to bed at midnight. That at least smacked of servitude, but she justly demands her rights. As for your still sighing after France out of a love for studies, when you have pricked your cohabitant sufficiently that her belly swells up, you can easily persuade the city council to let you

* * * * *

2 Juno was the Roman goddess of marriage. Ilithyia was the Greek goddess of childbirth.
3 More's wife, his second, was Lady Alice (maiden name unknown), the widow of a prosperous London merchant.
4 Erasmus uses the word *monachus* 'monk,' but evidently in the meaning that it had in ancient Greek, ie 'alone,' 'single.' This sounds like a reference to the rule of the eastern churches that priests can be married but that bishops must be single. That, however, seems a bit far-fetched in this context.
5 For Lieven Algoet's marriage, of which Erasmus strongly disapproved, see Ep 2693:26–99.
6 Erasmus puns on the words *calide* 'heatedly,' 'impetuously' and *callide* 'wisely,' 'expertly.'
7 Hilarius Bertholf (Ep 1712) was evidently in Lyon at the end of November 1532; see Ep 2743:19–20. He had in fact settled there on Erasmus' advice; cf Ep 2581:14–20. There is no evidence that he had gone elsewhere.
8 The nature of this gift is unknown. In 1534 she sent him a gift of linen; see Allen Ep 2913:34.

spend some months in Orléans.[9] But if the council has some business there, 30
you will take care of your studies and that matter at the same time.

I am now occupied in the very noisome workhouse of the *Adagia*,
which is being printed once more.[10] I have enlarged the *Apophthegmata* by
two books.[11] I have also enlarged my *Clarifications*.[12] They are once again
demanding the *Colloquies*, a work that brings vehement odium to me but 35
big profits to the printers.[13] The Jerome is being printed at Paris, revised by
me at the cost of almost incredible sleepless vigils.[14] And so there was no
time to write more carefully to those to whom you wanted me to write. I am
also somewhat afraid of being branded as an opportunist, but you will wash
away that stigma, just as you brought it upon me.[15] 40

You know, I think, that Lee has been made the archbishop of York.[16]
And that More, after much pleading, has received permission from the king
to resign the chancellorship.[17] Perhaps he was afraid of falling into disfavour because of the divorce, which he always opposed.[18] The archbishop of
Canterbury came to his end in the month of August;[19] with him truly per- 45
ished my sheet anchor.[20] Aleandro, who has been honoured with two mi-
tres (of both Brindisi and Oria),[21] is the apostolic legate to the emperor. My

* * * * *

9 The reference is to the city council of Haarlem, where Talesius was pensionary
(chief legal officer, secretary of the council, and the city's principal representa-
tive at meetings of the provincial estates). Orléans was a leading centre of legal
studies.
10 The edition of March 1533; see Epp 2726, 2773. See also Epp 2709, 2730, 2730A,
2742.
11 See Ep 2711 introduction.
12 Ie the second edition of the *Declarationes*, done with the help of Ambrosius
Pelargus; see Ep 2666 introduction.
13 The final edition of the *Colloquia* would be that of March 1533 (Basel: Froben
and Episcopius).
14 The Chevallon edition of the *Hieronymi opera* (Paris 1533); see Ep 2758.
15 The word translated as 'opportunist' is *captator*, which could also mean a legacy
hunter. Without the text of Quirinus' letter, it is impossible to say what this
refers to. Nor can we know to whom Quirinus wanted Erasmus to write.
16 Edward Lee (Ep 765) became archbishop of York on 10 December 1531.
17 Thomas More resigned as lord chancellor on 16 May 1532.
18 More was indeed opposed to the divorce, but the occasion of his resignation
was the 'Submission of the Clergy' on 15 May 1532; see Ep 2659 n2.
19 William Warham died on 23 August 1532.
20 Ie anchor of last resort; see *Adagia* i i 24, and cf Ep 2726:35–57.
21 Aleandro was in fact bishop of the single see known as 'Brindisi and Oria.' Oria
became an independent see in 1596.

friends decrease; my enemies increase. I wrote to those you wanted me to. Please excuse my presumption; I will excuse the rest. I wish happiness to you together with your sweet wife, your parents, and your sisters.   50

Given at Freiburg, 31 October 1532

My Gilbert sends his greetings.[22] For I pushed Jacobus into the Sapientiae.[23] Together with a new maidservant he had produced a wonderful comedy here. If he had been able to keep house with her any longer, he would have emptied the storage jars, the chests, and in the end the whole   55 house.[24] Margarete has returned: thievish, rapacious, bibulous, mendacious, loquacious.[25]

2736 / To Viglius Zuichemus   Freiburg, 5 November 1532

This letter was first published in LB III/2 1754 *Appendix epistolarum* no 369. For Viglius see Ep 2657 introduction. His reply to this letter is Ep 2767. Both letters were carried by the Basel printer Johann Bebel; see AK Epp 1689:1–2, 1719:1–3.

ERASMUS OF ROTTERDAM SENDS GREETINGS TO THE MOST WIDELY LEARNED FRISIAN VIGLIUS ZUICHEMUS

My most learned friend Viglius, I must be Laconic.[1] Scaliger's book is so mad that Orestes could not write more insanities.[2] I could readily believe that Béda

* * * * *

22 Erasmus' famulus Gilbert Cousin (Ep 2381 n1)
23 For Erasmus' rogue of a servant Jacobus, see Ep 2652 n4. For the *Collegium Sapientiae* at Freiburg and Jacobus' desire to gain admission to it, see Ep 2697:8–14 with n5.
24 Cf Ep 2745:15–17. The accounts of this incident in Allen Epp 2868:40–7, 2897:25–31 make no mention of Jacobus.
25 Erasmus had replaced his indispensable but intolerable housekeeper Margarete Büsslin, who had been with him since at least 1522, with a younger woman, who turned out to be a thief. So Margarete was welcomed back and there were no more attempts to replace her. The full force of Erasmus' description of Margarete – *furax, rapax, bibax, mendax, loquax* – cannot be duplicated in translation.

2736
1 Ie practice Spartan brevity (*Adagia* II x 49)
2 For having killed his mother Clytaemnestra to avenge the death of his father Agamemnon, Orestes was hounded by the furies and driven mad. 'Scaliger's book' was the *Oratio pro Cicerone contra Erasmum* of Julius Caesar Scaliger; see Ep 2564 n2.

added some poison, for that is what he does in everything written against me 5
printed in Paris.[3] And it could be that Camillo contributed something.[4] But
I know who the author is as well as I know that I am alive.[5] I could respond
like for like, but the affair has ended up in complete madness. The actors
are suborned: who the authors are they conceal royally.[6] I still have not been
able to guess why these Budé lovers are so angry at me.[7] The people who 10
are forming this faction of Ciceronians do not realize what a plague they are
releasing on the scholarly community; for what would happen if everything
that does not conform to the phrasing of Cicero is be rejected? I have not yet
read through Scaliger's book. Johannes the Dane has attacked him in a poem.
I would prefer that he be quiet.[8] I think Konrad Heresbach is already here, 15
or certainly was here.[9] There was no time to write more at present. Farewell,
and continue to be fond of me.

Given at Freiburg, 5 November 1532

2737 / From Henricus Cornelius Agrippa   Bonn, 13 November 1532

This letter, first published in the *Agrippae Opera* II 1015, is Agrippa's answer
to Ep 2692. It failed to reach Erasmus until some time after 9 December 1532
(Ep 2748). For the circumstances of its composition see Ep 2739 introduction.

* * * * *

3 It was indeed Noël Béda who helped Scaliger find a publisher for the book; see
  Ep 2564 n2.
4 Learning that Giulio Camillo (Ep 2632 n17) had written a work criticizing his
  Ciceronianus, Erasmus initially jumped to the conclusion that the work in question was Scaliger's *Oratio*. By this time he knew better, but still suspected that
  Camillo had contributed something to it; See Ep 2632:157–60 with n18.
5 Erasmus still believed that 'Julius Caesar Scaliger' was a pseudonym for
  Girolamo Aleandro; see Epp 2564 n2, 2565 n12.
6 Clearly a reference to the publication under royal licence of Scaliger's allegedly
  pseudonymous and multi-authored *Oratio* (see preceding note). For the royal
  licence see Ep 2577 introduction.
7 Erasmus' *Ciceronianus* had caused great offence in France because of an unfortunate jest at the expense of the great humanist Guillaume Budé; see Ep 1948
  introduction.
8 'Johannes' is a mistake for 'Jacobus,' and the reference is to the Danish poet
  and scholar Jakob Jespersen (Ep 2570). For Erasmus' annoyance at Jespersen's
  epigrams against Scaliger, see Ep 2792:58–63.
9 See Ep 2728 n24.

AGRIPPA TO ERASMUS

From your letter, Erasmus, my most splendid friend, which Polyphemus delivered to me before the fair, I gathered that you were so overcome by physical exhaustion, the exertion of your studies, and the troubles of house renovation that you could not send me a longer letter at that time, but you 5 promised that after the fair you would be happy to write a more lively and lengthy letter. And so, since I was expecting a letter from you, I did not want to bother you before now. But now that I have by chance this opportunity of using a courier,[1] I have decided to break my silence once more, not because I want to complain but to let you know that I have not received any letter 10 from you, so that, if by chance you had written to me and the letter had gone astray, you would not have good reason to attribute my failure to respond to laziness or ingratitude. And so when you write me a letter, address it to Tielmannus Gravius in Cologne.[2] The letters I write to you I will send to Froben or Cratander at Basel.[3] In this way I hope that neither one of us will 15 be disappointed.

But I also want you to know about my war with the theosophists at Louvain.[4] Thus far I have been attacked in various ambushes within my camp and I have defended myself by sallying forth lightly armed into the skirmishes. But now that the battle has grown more intense, I have opened 20 the gates and stormed out mail-clad to fight in open battle.[5] They will not lack for reserve troops from Cologne and Paris.[6] I do not know whether I will get protective troops – except that I am confident that my case cannot be refuted by contrary arguments, cannot be blotted by falsehood, cannot suffer any injury from a lack of advocates or from corrupt judges. Defended in this 25 way, I do not hesitate to expose myself to danger alone, but if I win the battle, the glory is no less yours than mine, since I fight vigorously no less with your weapons and missiles than with mine, and for that reason I rush forth all the

* * * * *

2737
1 One of the couriers of Lorenzo Cardinal Campeggi; see Ep 2739:11–12.
2 Ep 2103
3 Hieronymus Froben, head of the Froben press; Andreas Cratander, bookseller and printer at Basel. Both travelled often to the Frankfurt book fair.
4 Ie the Louvain theologians, to describe whom Agrippa coined the word *theosophistas* ('sophist' being the common derogatory term for scholastic theologians). They had condemned Agrippa's *De incertitudine et vanitate scientiarum atque artium declamatio* (1530) as scandalous, impious, and heretical.
5 Agrippa had written an *Apologia contra theologistas Lovanienses* that he was currently attempting to get published; cf Ep 2739 n2.
6 Ie the theologians of Cologne and Paris

more boldly into the field, and you will soon see me as a new soldier joining
the fray with undaunted freedom. Then you will laugh, I know; others will   30
be amazed. The sophists will snap their middle finger at me,[7] but at the same
time I will either conquer them or escape from them. Farewell and take it for
the best.

From Bonn, 13 November 1532

2738 / From Ennio Filonardi   Lucerne, 13 November 1532

> This letter was first published as Ep 181 in Förstemann / Günther. The manu-
> script, in a secretary's hand but with the opening salutation and the signature
> in Filonardi's hand, was in the Burscher Collection of the University Library
> at Leipzig (Ep 1254 introduction). For Ennio Filonardi, bishop of Veroli, see
> Ep 2712 introduction.

Reverend master and most respected father. If I have in fact put off fulfilling
the promise I made to your reverend Lordship, namely that I would make an
effort to get the Holy Father to suppress your assailants at Paris, and if your
Reverence has thus far received no reply about these matters, you should not
be surprised; indeed you should rest assured that I was and will be as de-   5
voted to your honour as I am to my own. But recently my nephew, who deals
with my affairs,[1] went back to the city and managed to get a response to the
letter that I had written to the Holy Father against the man who is harrass-
ing you at Paris with his calumnies.[2] His Holiness responds by writing that
he has warned this detractor to cease attacking you, that he did this out of   10
benevolence towards you, and that it is his intention to treat you most kindly
whenever there is an occasion to commend your virtues as they deserve.[3]

* * * * *

7 The text says simply *crepabunt medium* ('they will snap their middle'), which
   seems to be a somewhat garbled reference to the adage *Medium ostendere digi-*
   tum 'To show the middle finger,' ie to show supreme contempt; see *Adagia* II iv
   68. One wonders what sound the snap of one finger would make.

2738
1 The nephew could have been either Antonio Filonardi (d 1569), to whom
   Filonardi ceded the see of Veroli in 1538, or Ennio Filonardi (d 1565), who in
   1549 succeeded his uncle as bishop of Montefeltro.
2 Noël Béda?
3 We know of no other evidence of this correspondence.

As for what you wrote about Aleandro, I have given some thought to passing it on to someone active at Rome, if you should think it appropriate, so that, when the occasion arises, he could broach the subject with the 15 supreme pontiff or one of the very reverend Lordships among the cardinals. But I didn't want to do anything without consulting you. And so please write to tell me what you want me to do in this matter. I will not neglect any duty of a friend that could be to your advantage. And if there is anything within my power that you would like to have done for you, it would give me the 20 greatest pleasure to be able to please you, since in such matters as these there is no one there whom I want to oblige and favour more than you. I heartily commend and offer myself to your reverend Lordship and also to the reverend Doctor L. Baer, our common friend.[4]

Lucerne, 13 November 1532   25
To your reverend Excellence
P. S. From the enclosed letters your reverend Lordship will understand that my nephew did not neglect to execute what I had commissioned him to do, that is, faithfully to deliver your letter. He finally found the addressee and obtained a response, which I send to you tied together with this letter.[5] 30
Your very obedient servant, Ennio, bishop of Veroli
To the reverend Master Erasmus of Rotterdam, as an honourable brother

2739 / From Henricus Cornelius Agrippa   Bonn, [22] November 1532

This letter was first published in the *Agrippae opera* page 1016, where the date given is 12 November 1532. Since Agrippa says in lines 10–11 that he had already written to Erasmus on 13 November (Ep 2737), the day-date of this letter has to be corrected. Allen adopted the date given by John Jortin in *The Life of Erasmus* (London 1758/60) 2 vols II 469.

AGRIPPA TO ERASMUS
I am ashamed, my most cherished friend Erasmus, to interrupt your activities with so many poorly written letters, which have nothing to say beyond greetings and farewell, but since your young servant came through here

* * * * *

4 For Ludwig Baer see Ep 2638 n12.
5 The letter is not extant, and the identity of the addressee is unknown.

giving me your greetings,[1] I could be accused of the most flagrant ingrati-   5
tude if I did not write. Reverence for your name, which does not allow me to
be silent, has constrained my sterile pen, even though it has nothing more to
relate than that if there is anything I can do that you think would be of advantage to you, make use of my efforts. For you will discover that the mind
of your Agrippa is neither slow nor weary. On the thirteenth of this month I   10
sent a letter to your Excellency by means of the courier of the most reverend
Cardinal Campeggi, which the Basel printer Cratander was supposed to deliver to you. From it you will understand the sort of warfare I am engaged in
with the theologians.[2] With best wishes for your happiness.

From Bonn, [22] November 1532   15

2740 / From Bonifacius Amerbach   [Basel], 26 November [1532]

This letter (= AK Ep 1693) was first published by Allen. The manuscript, an autograph rough draft, is in the Öffentliche Bibliothek of the University of Basel
(MS C VIa 73 28). Allen assigned the year-date on the basis of the references to
the readiness of Anselmus Ephorinus to procure medicines.

Cordial greetings. Last April, most renowned Erasmus, you sent here a sheet
with a prescription from which Ephorinus had a powder made up for you

* * * * *

2739
1 Allen does not identify the 'young servant' (servulus). Gerlo identifies him
  as Quirinus Hagius, who in November 1532 was on his way home via the
  Netherlands from a journey to England on Erasmus' behalf. But if, as seems
  beyond doubt, Quirinus was in Mons on 24 November and had arrived there
  via Ghent (see Ep 2741 n2), it is impossible for him to have been in Bonn on 22
  November. Nor does it seem possible that he could have visited Bonn on a journey from Mons back to Freiburg that commenced no earlier than 26 November
  (the date of Ep 2741, which he carried) and ended no later than 3 December (see
  Ep 2747 introduction and n1). On the other hand, we have no information that
  anyone else in Erasmus' service was travelling at this time.
2 At some point Agrippa had sent his *Apologia contra theologistas Lovanienses* to
  Cratander, instructing him to print it. On 13 November 1532 he wrote letters to
  both Erasmus (Ep 2737) and Cratander (*Agrippae opera* II 1015), telling the latter
  to send Erasmus a copy of the book. The messenger found his way neither to
  Cratander nor to Erasmus (Epp 2748:4–6, 2790:11–13), nor did Cratander print
  the book (Ep 2790:9–11).

by a pharmacist.[1] I have been importuned time after time by his host, an old
man not unknown to you,[2] to use my influence with you to get from you a
copy of that prescription. For he claims that taking that powder, which the   5
generosity of Ephorinus made available to him, has done him so much good
that he expects it will add many years to his life. I beg you to be so kind as to
humour him by sending him a copy, if it is not too much trouble.

At the present time nothing occurs to me that I should write except that
you permit me to remind you of my devotion and esteem for you. But I think   10
there is no need to repeat what you have long since believed. In a word, you
know that I am yours with all my heart and that there is nothing I am not
prepared to do for your sake. Take care of your health, I beseech you, if you
want us to stay well, for (as he says)[3] life is pleasant as long as you survive
and joyless if you do not.   15

My wife sends undying thanks for the sweetmeats, and as soon as she
returns home she promises to take care not to seem that she has been ungrateful to you. Recently one of the pharmacists brought here a vial of chebulic myrobalan.[4] If you still like it – unless I am mistaken, in recent years you
sent Karl to Venice to get some[5] – please let me know. The same pharmacist   20
brought a container of citric preserves (for that it what they call it).[6] Farewell.

Yesterday I received a letter from Alciati saying he has recovered and
wishes to send you his most heartfelt regards.[7]

The day after the feast of St Catherine[8]

2741 / From Nicolaus Olahus   Mons, 26 November 1532

This letter was first published in Ipolyi page 288. The manuscript is page 265
of the Olahus codex in the Hungarian National Archives at Budapest (Ep 2339

* * * * *

2740
1 For Anselmus Ephorinus see Ep 2539 introduction. For his readiness to procure
   and supply medicines, see Epp 2554:44–6, 2559:34–7.
2 The Basel organist Johann Gross; see Ep 2539 n6.
3 Horace *Epodes* 1.5–6
4 *Terminalis cherbula*, an herbal concoction valued for the treatment of (among
   other things) constipation and stomach disorders
5 In 1525 Karl Harst, Erasmus' secretary and courier, had brought *myrobalanos* to
   Erasmus from Venice; see Allen Ep 1674:11 (in CWE Ep 1674:15 *myrobylanos* is
   translated as 'preserved fruit').
6 Bonifacius deleted this entire sentence from the draft. It is not included in the
   AK text.
7 AK Ep 1687:31–5
8 25 November is the feast day of St Catherine of Alexandria.

introduction). For Nicolaus Olahus, secretary to Mary of Hungary, regent of the Netherlands, see Ep 2646 introduction.

TO ERASMUS OF ROTTERDAM

I was so upset by my residence in Binche, for many reasons but especially because of the inconvenience of my accommodations and the drunkenness (or rather, the insanity) of my host, that I hardly expected to be freed of that trouble and to move here to Mons, a very pleasant town filled with refined 5 inhabitants. I arrived here three day ago; I do not think I need tell you about the joy of the populace or the enthusiasm of the children, the young people, and the mothers with their families,[1] since your servant Quirinus,[2] who came to see the queen to manage some business of yours, has returned and could have told you all about it. And so, my dear Erasmus, do not think that I have 10 forgotten your affairs. Moreover, Quirinus himself saw – indeed all of your friends here saw – that we have left nothing undone to promote your affairs to the best of our abilities, in so far as either their importance or the business of the queen seemed to allow.[3] Therefore, have no doubts about us. To what Quirinus has now told you (which I think you will find not at all disagree- 15 able) we will soon add many more details, once we have understood that you have received favourably the reply sent to you now.

Farewell. Mons in Hainaut, 26 November 1532

2742 / To Bonifacius Amerbach   Freiburg, 29 November 1532

This letter (= AK Ep 1695) was first published in the *Epistolae familiares*. The autograph is in the Öffentliche Bibliothek of the University of Basel (MS AN III 15 42).

* * * * *

2741
1 On the occasion of the 'grand entry' of Queen Mary of Hungary, regent of the Netherlands, on 24 November 1532
2 Quirinus Hagius (Ep 2704 n6), whom Erasmus had dispatched (c end of August 1532) on a mission to England. He appears to have been in Brussels in September (Ep 2759:38–9), and on 5 October Erasmus was expecting him back sometime in November (Ep 2728:57–9). He was on his way home when on 11 November he visited Levinus Ammonius in the charterhouse at Koningdal near Ghent (Allen Ep 2817:179–83). This letter indicates that he witnessed the grand entry of the queen at Mons on 24 November. He had carried Ep 2707 to Olahus, and he carried the present letter back to Erasmus.
3 Olahus writes *principis occupacio* 'business of the prince,' but in context he can only mean Queen Mary.

Cordial greetings. In a recent letter I admonished Grynaeus about a certain passage in Plato,[1] but I excused him because he had followed the Aldine edition.[2] He didn't reply about that, but he sent a supercilious and acidic letter,[3] in which he reproaches me with his decade.[4] How could he be so easily offended if he had an open-minded attitude towards me? Time after time 5 I have followed your advice and put aside my suspicions. From now on I think it better to leave him to his own devices. If I am not entirely mistaken, there is lurking beneath his mask of probity the personality of a thoroughgoing braggart. I sent him the sheet in which you point out some items useful for the *Adagia*.[5] You should get it back from him. He writes just as if I could 10 not complete my work without the assistance of others.

Farewell, my dearest Bonifacius. The vigil of St Andrew 1532

You recognize the hand.

To the renowned gentleman Master Bonifacius Amerbach, doctor of laws. At Basel 15

2743 / From François Rabelais Lyon, 30 November 1532

The autograph of this letter (= Ep 182 in Förstemann / Günther), address sheet missing, was in the Burscher Collection of the University Library at Leipzig (Ep 1254 introduction). The manuscript in the Zentralbibliothek at Zürich (MS F 46 569), once thought to be the autograph, is evidently a contemporary copy. The text was first published in *Clarorum virorum epistolae centum ineditae* ed Johannes Brant (Amsterdam: Sebastian Petsold 1702) 280–1, with the heading *Bernardo Salignaco* 'to Bernard Salignac.' (Salignac was a mathematician from Bordeaux, several works by whom on arithmetic and algebra were published in the period 1574–93 at Geneva, Frankfurt, and Heidelberg.) The seemingly obvious identification of Erasmus as the real addressee was finally established (using the

* * * * *

2742
1 The letter is not extant. For Simon Grynaeus see Ep 2659 n5.
2 Rather than the new Froben edition (Ep 2432)
3 Not extant
4 Ie the 'decade or decade and a half of proverbs' that Grynaeus had sent to Erasmus, not knowing 'whether they are to be found among yours.' See Ep 2433:39–41.
5 Sent with Ep 2730

François Rabelais
Musée de Versailles/Clichés des Musées Nationaux

supposed autograph at Zürich) by Theodore Ziesing *Érasme ou Salignac? Étude sur la lettre de François Rabelais* (Paris: Alcan 1887). The text is liberally sprinkled with words and phrases in Greek.

Fond greetings in Christ Jesus our Saviour

Georges d'Armagnac, the illustrious Bishop of Rodez,[1] recently sent me Flavius Josephus' *Jewish History, Concerning the Conquest*,[2] and asked me, in the name of our old friendship, that if I ever obtained a reliable courier who was going there, to see to it that it be delivered to you at the earliest opportunity.[3] I gladly seized this occasion to show you, my most benign father, how very respectful and devoted I am to you by some obliging gesture. I called you a father. I could also call you a mother to me if, by your indulgence, I might be permitted do so. For we see every day that pregnant women nourish and protect a fetus that they have never seen from the hazards of the outside air; you too had this very same experience because, even though you did not know what I look like and had never heard my name, you nevertheless brought me up, you nourished me at the chaste breasts of your divine teaching so that if I did not attribute to you alone whatever I am and whatever I am worth, I would be the most ungrateful of all men who now exist or ever will exist in years to come. Hail, then, I say again, hail most loving father, father and glory of your native land, proponent and defender of learning, invincible champion of truth.

Recently I learned from Hilarius Bertholf, with whom I am on the most familiar terms here,[4] that you are putting together something against the slanders of Girolamo Aleandro, who you suspect has been writing against you under the guise of a certain factitious Scaliger.[5] I will not allow you to be uncertain any more or to be so misinformed. For this Scaliger is from Verona, from that family of the exiled Scaligers, himself an exile; he is now in fact a practising physician in Agen, a man well known to me, but by heaven, not well thought of. Moreover, that man is, to put it succinctly, a devil, not unskilled in matters of medicine, but completely godless in other respects, like no one else anywhere. I have not yet had a chance to see his book, and in all

* * * * *

2743
1 See Ep 2569 introduction
2 Ie *The Jewish War*, which concludes with the conquest of Jerusalem by the emperor Titus in AD 70
3 For the sequence of events that led d'Armagnac to entrust the manuscript of Josephus to Rabelais for delivery to Erasmus, see Ep 2569 introduction.
4 See Ep 2735 n7.
5 See Ep 2564 n2.

these months no copy has reached us here, and thus I think that in Paris it
was suppressed by those who wish you well. Farewell, and may your good   30
fortune continue.

Lyon, 30 November 1532

Yours as much as his own, François Rabelais, physician

2744 / From Bonifacius Amerbach   Basel, 2 December 1532

First published by Allen, this letter (= AK Ep 1696) is Bonifacius' reply to Ep
2742. The manuscript, a much rewritten autograph rough draft with two versions of the second paragraph, is in the Öffentliche Bibliothek of the University
of Basel (MS C VIa 73 15). Erasmus' reply is Ep 2747.

Recently I sent you a letter,[1] which I think Zasius,[2] to whom I entrusted it for
delivery, has faithfully delivered to you. What I said then was no more than
this: at the special request of Anselmus' host, I wrote to get a copy of the
recipe of the powder that you took pains to get made up here last April; and
I also wrote that our friend Alciati wanted to send his best regards, and he   5
solemnly and at length entreated me faithfully to do this for him. I can hardly
say how much I rejoice that he has recovered his health, partly because he
is outstanding for his integrity and also because, if anyone is outstanding in
proclaiming your praises, then he certainly is. Finally, I wrote that chebulic
myrobalan has arrived here, and if you would like to have any, I asked you   10
to let me know in time, and I implore you earnestly to do so by the very first
messenger, because the pharmacist's stock will not last much longer.

What is this that I hear about Grynaeus?[3] I cannot imagine what spirit
possesses him when he writes; otherwise he is calm, and when I am with
him and hear his living voice, he is outstanding in his praise and enthusi-   15
asm for you. If the poet told the truth, as he most certainly did when he said
that the advice of a companion is a good thing,[4] then there is no one who
would consider an admonition from Erasmus as anything but the greatest
of favours. But since these are his feelings now, it would be best, according
to the proverb, to know the character of a friend, not hate it,[5] and to leave   20

* * * * *

2744
1 See Ep 2740, of which this paragraph is a summary.
2 Udalricus Zasius, famed jurist and professor of law at Freiburg
3 See Ep 2742.
4 Homer *Iliad* 11.793
5 See *Adagia* II v 96.

him to his own devices. Undoubtedly he will one day come to his senses,
abandon this aberration, feel grateful for such friendly advice, and thank you
abundantly for it. Erasmus' abilities and pre-eminence as a writer would be
acknowledged by our age, however ungrateful it may be, if it were not that
by nature we praise what we hear more than what we see, and we react with   25
the envy felt now, not with the veneration felt in the past.[6] But posterity will
proclaim this with full voice. Does Erasmus need help from someone else in
completing his work on the *Adages*? Water to the sea.[7] I think you have no
doubt about my devotion to you. Easier to separate *consortium* from *coniu-*
gium than Bonifacius from Erasmus.[8] Farewell.   30

2 December 1532

2745 / To Daniel Stiebar   Freiburg, 7 December 1532

This letter was first published by Allen. The autograph is in the Bibliothèque
Royale at Brussels (ms Bibl. Royale 6916). For Daniel Stiebar, canon at Würzburg
and an important figure in the administration of the diocese, see Ep 2069
introduction.

After the letter you sent me at the conclusion of the Diet of Regensburg,[1] I
have received nothing from you. I wrote once to Joachim, as you requested;[2]
I do not know whether you have received it. But because I am uncertain

* * * * *

6 The words 'by nature ... in the past' occur again in AK Ep 2113:47–9, where
   Bonifacius identifies as his source the Roman historian Velleius Paterculus
   (2.92, quoted from memory and not quite accurately).
7 See *Adagia* I vii 57, where Erasmus gives 'carrying water to the sea' as the equivalent of 'carrying wood to the forest,' ie supplying someone with things that he
   already has in abundance.
8 *Consortium* is legal Latin for the fellowship and marital intercourse that marriage partners owe one another. *Coniugium* is marriage. The AK text has *conca-*
   vum a convexo ('the concave from the convex'). Neither phrase is in the *Adagia*.

2745
1 The letter is not extant. The diet officially concluded on 26 July 1532. Stiebar
   had attended as a member of the delegation of the ecclesiastical principality of
   Würzburg.
2 Probably Joachim Camerarius (Ep 1501), Stiebar's lifelong friend and corre-
   spondent. The letter is not extant.

about your location, since you are taking part in a lively play,[3] I didn't want
to expend useless effort. But when a distinguished young man mentioned 5
casually that he was sending one of his people there,[4] I did not think that I
should bear the blame of sending him away empty-handed, even though at
that time I was more constrained by tasks than I have ever been.

I had a good laugh about the Spanish trick of the one who stole your
purse and left you unarmed.[5] At Paris something similar happened to the 10
Pole Zebrzydowski, who once boarded with us.[6] He was looking at some
play or other in a thick crowd, wearing a garment to which he had attached
some silver buttons, hollow but gold-plated. Someone cut off all except one.
At that point there was a serious quarrel with Marcin Słap.[7]

In fact, I had at home some people who were certainly not born in Spain 15
but who would have quickly brought about great privation in my house if I
had not detected their trickery.[8] To them nothing was sealed or locked up.[9]

If you want to know how things are with me, they go the way of
Mandraboulus.[10]

From day to day this little body is threatened with ruin. My enemies are 20
raised on high; my friends diminish. The archbishop of Canterbury, who was
my sheet anchor,[11] has given up the ghost.[12] Lee has been made the archbishop of York.[13] More has laid down the burden of the chancellorship, the office

* * * * *

3 Erasmus once again uses the term *fabula motoria* to describe life at court, forever
  on the move; cf Ep 2643 n3. Stiebar was frequently away on diplomatic missions on behalf of the bishop.
4 To Würzburg
5 Nothing is known of this incident.
6 Stiebar's time as a guest of Erasmus at Basel (1527–8) had overlapped with
  that of Andrzej Zebrzydowski (1528), and both departed for Paris in September
  1528; see Epp 1826, 2036, 2069 introductions.
7 Słap was Zebrzydowski's companion on the journey from Poland, and stayed
  with him at both Basel and Paris; see Ep 2351 introduction.
8 Erasmus uses the Greek word σπανία 'privation,' punning on *Hispania* 'Spain.'
  For the same pun, using (instead of *Hispania*) Σπανία, the word for Spain used
  by Paul at Rom 15:24, see Ep 2473 n4.
9 This is clearly a reference to Jacobus and the new housekeeper; see Ep 2735:52–6
  with nn23–4.
10 A certain Madraboulos found a treasure, from which each year he gave a smaller offering to the gods. So when something goes in Madraboulos' fashion, it
  gets worse day by day. See *Adagia* I ii 58.
11 See Ep 2735 n20.
12 See Ep 2735 n19.
13 See Ep 2735 n16.

next in rank to that of the king.[14] Indeed I love the king more for granting More's plea by taking off that packsaddle and imposing it on another than for bestowing that high office on him in the first place. I will write at greater length when I have learned under what skies you are living. Farewell, my dear Stiebar, among my bright friends the brightest.

The day after the feast of St Nicolas 1532

Erasmus of Rotterdam, in my own hand

To the distinguished gentleman Master Daniel Stiebar. At Würzburg

2746 / From Jan (II) Łaski   Cracow, 7 December 1532

This letter was first published by Allen. The manuscript, a contemporary copy, was in the same ill-fated folio volume as that of Ep 1954. On Jan (II) Łaski, canon of Cracow, provost of Gniezno, royal secretary, prominent Erasmian, and (in the end) Calvinist reformer, see Epp 1593 n18, 1821 introduction.

Greetings. My dearest friend Erasmus, your letter has thoroughly restored my spirits.[1] Although I had no doubts about your good will towards me, I was surprised all the same because, even though I wrote to you from the congress at Poznań two years ago,[2] and then once more from here last year, you did not reply to me for such a long time, unless perhaps you wanted to take vengeance because of my previous neglect, and to torment me in turn by making me wait so long for a letter from you, or perhaps you still thought it better to avoid association with me because of the odium attached to my name, as I hear, serious indeed as it may be but not at all deserved. For my part, my dear Erasmus, so far am I from having diminished in any way my long-standing love and respect for you that I almost perish from the desire to be with you, and I would not choose to be anywhere more gladly than where you are. And indeed I would already be there if it were permitted by his most serene Majesty King Ferdinand, without whose letter of free passage (as they

* * * * *

14 See Ep 2735 n17.

2746
1 There are no surviving letters between Erasmus and Łaski between this one and Ep 2033 (27 August 1528).
2 A special congress in October 1530 at which a years' armistice was concluded between Ferdinand of Austria and John Zápolyai, the rival kings of Hungary; cf n4 below.

say)[3] it would not be safe at all for me to travel there, for your sake as much   15
as mine. And since I was not able to procure one, I am forced to make other
plans for myself.

My brother involved me in these tumults, but in such a way that I did
nothing at all at that time that did not promote concord.[4] Now he continues
as he has begun.[5] As for me, when I saw that things were becoming more   20
violent every day and there seemed to be no hope of peace, I came here to
court, lest I seem to scorn the favour of my prince, although, as you know, I
am by no means a courtier, so that I do not know how to sew on a fox's skin,[6]
and would certainly not have the least desire to do so even I did. Still, I have
some friends whose company I enjoy: Leopolitanus,[7] a man who in addi-   25
tion to being learned is also upright and widely regarded as almost saintly;
our friends Justus and Antonin,[8] Strozzi of Florence, a young man learned in
Latin and Greek, also modest and entirely devoted to you.[9] This is how we

* * * * *

3 *Litterae commendatus*, diplomatic Latin for what is now called a passport or a
  letter of safe conduct
4 Jan's elder brother Hieronim (Ep 1242 n5), was a Polish diplomat. Although
  Poland remained officially neutral in the conflict between Ferdinand of Austria
  and John Zápolyai for control of Hungary that broke out in 1526, Hieronim committed himself to Zápolyai, undertook diplomatic missions on his behalf, and
  was instrumental in winning him the support of the Turkish sultan. Together
  with his brother Jan, he represented Zápolyai at the Poznań congress referred
  to in note 2 above.
5 Hieronim continued in the service of John Zápolyai, though increasingly dis-
  contented by what he thought was inadequate reward for his services. In 1534
  his involvement in a failed coup against Zápolyai led to his imprisonment at
  Buda. Released in 1535, he entered the service of King Ferdinand.
6 Ie to behave with the necessary guile and deceit. The alternative (not contemplated here) is to sew on a lion's skin and achieve things by force. See *Adagia* III
  v 81.
7 Johannes Leopolitanus (Jan Leopolita) of Lvov, canon and preacher at the chapter of St Florian at Cracow, avid reader of Erasmus' books; cf Ep 1916 n15.
8 See Ep1393 introduction (Justus Ludovicus Decius) and Ep1602 introduction
  (Jan Antonin).
9 Ciriaco Strozzi of Florence (1504–65) taught Greek and Greek philosophy at
  Florence, Bologna (1536–43), and then for twenty years at Pisa. His principal contribution to scholarship was a two-volume supplement to Aristotle's
  Politics, written in Greek and translated into Latin (Florence: Giunta 1562). As a
  young man he had visited Poland, matriculating at the Jagellonian University
  of Cracow in 1532, lecturing for two semesters (on a subject unrecorded), and
  publishing an edition of Aristotle's *Topics* (Cracow: Hieronym Wietor, May
  1533). Concerning this sojourn in Poland, which Allen could not document and

live, my dear Erasmus, since we cannot live as we would wish. And on your part, remember me and be assured that I both am and will always be truly yours, however things turn out. For the time being, farewell. 30

Cracow, the day after the feast of St Nicolas, 1532

2747 / To Bonifacius Amerbach [Freiburg, 9 December 1532]

This letter (= AK Ep 1698) was first published in the *Epistolae familiares*. The autograph is in the Öffentliche Bibliothek of the University of Basel (MS AN III 15 90). The date is determined by the close connection to Epp 2740, 2742, and 2744. Ep 2740 (26 November) had not yet reached Erasmus when Bonifacius wrote Ep 2742 (29 November). He then wrote Ep 2744 (2 December) in which he summarized the content of Ep 2740. From the present letter it appears that Ep 2744 reached Erasmus on Tuesday, 3 December, while the letter entrusted to Zasius (Ep 2740) did not arrive until the evening of 4 December. By this time, however, Trübelmann (see n2), who could have carried Erasmus' answer, had already left Freiburg. So Erasmus wrote this letter to Bonifacius on the following Monday, 9 December.

Cordial greetings. Things have gone awry. My young man[1] came back here on Tuesday evening, shortly after Trübelmann had already left.[2] On the evening of the next day Zasius sent your letter.[3] Hence I could not reply. In important matters I want to comply with the wishes of that excellent man.[4] But I wanted a little box of the powder to be made according to this prescription 5 for me as well.[5] I will send the money as soon as possible.

Farewell. Monday morning

To Master Bonifacius Amerbach

* * * * *

CEBR does not mention, see Henryk Barycz *Historja Uniwersytetu Jagiellońskiego w epoce humanizmu* (Cracow: Nakładem Uniwersytetu Jagiellońskiego 1935) 63–4. (Reference kindly provided by Jacqueline Glomski.)

2747
1 Presumably Quirinus Hagius (Ep 2704 n6)
2 Georg Trübelmann, who regularly carried letters back and forth between Basel and Freiburg; see Ep 2554 n1.
3 Ep 2740
4 Ie Ephorinus' host, the organist Johann Gross, who wanted the medicinal powder; see Ep 2740:3–5 with n2.
5 Reading *ut ad hoc exemplar* (AK) for Allen's *ut hoc exemplar*

2748 / To Henricus Cornelius Agrippa   Freiburg, 9 December 1532

First published in the *Agrippae opera* II 1017, this is Erasmus' answer to Ep 2739.
Ep 2737 had not yet reached him. Agrippa's reply is Ep 2790.

ERASMUS TO AGRIPPA
Cordial greetings. Until now, learned sir, I have not responded to your letter,
thinking it better to send nothing than to send a negligent reply. So far I have
been waiting for some free time, but thus far have not had any. I do not know
which courier you are talking about.[1] Nor did Cratander deliver to me your   5
letter with your narrative of a theological history.[2] But in future, if you want
something delivered reliably, have it sent to Hieronymus Froben. I am sorry
about your business with the wasps.[3] Disentangle yourself as best you can.
Few have derived any benefit from fighting with them. Christ willing, I will
write more when the swallows first appear. In the meantime, be assured that   10
Erasmus is among the number of those who wish Agrippa well. Farewell.
        Freiburg, 9 December 1532

2749 / To Bonifacius Amerbach   [Freiburg], 27 December 1532

This letter (= AK Ep 1699) was first published in the *Epistolae familiares*. The
autograph is in the Öffentliche Bibliothek of the University of Basel (MS AN III
15 43).

Cordial greetings. The wicked, according to the proverb, need only to find
an occasion.[1] But you take every occasion to do something good. Your generosity of spirit has long been clearly evident, with or without the tiniest gift
as a reward. The matter requires no haste.[2] You could have handed it over

* * * * *

2748
1 The courier of Cardinal Campeggi; see Ep 2739:11–12.
2 Ie his controversy with the Louvain theologians, first mentioned in the still un-
    delivered Ep 2737:17–32 but referred to again in Ep 2739:13–14.
3 Ie the Louvain theologians

2749
1 *Adagia* II i 68
2 'The matter' appears to be that of the medicinal powder, the prescription for
    which had been given to Erasmus by Anselmus Ephorinus (Ep 2740:1–3 with
    n1). On behalf of the man who had been Ephorinus' host in Basel (see n5 below)
    Bonifacius asked Erasmus to provide a copy of the prescription. In complying

to Hieronymus.[3] To the boy who brought this I have given three batzen.[4] To   5
Anselm's host I send the very best wishes.[5]

    Farewell. 27 December 1532

    To Master Bonifacius Amerbach. At Basel

2750 / To Johannes Fabri   [Freiburg, late 1532]

This letter was first published in the epistolary appendix to Erasmus' *De praeparatione ad mortem* (Basel: Froben and Episcopius 1534) 93–102. The surviving
manuscript, an autograph rough draft, is in the Royal Library at Copenhagen
(MS G K S 95 Fol folio 162). Allen assigned the approximate date on the basis
that Erasmus included with this letter a copy of Thomas More's letter of 14
June 1532 (Ep 2659), which had been delayed for some time in delivery; see
lines 13–14 below. For Johannes Fabri, bishop of Vienna since 1530, see Ep 2097
introduction.

    The letter is an encomium of Thomas More composed in response to the
news of his resignation as lord chancellor of England. A shorter version of it is
found in Ep 2780:21–54.

TO THE REVEREND LORD JOHANNES FABRI, BISHOP OF VIENNA,
ERASMUS OF ROTTERDAM SENDS GREETINGS

How swiftly the rumour has made its way there that the most renowned gentleman Thomas More has been formally removed from the office of chancellor and replaced in that position by another noble,[1] who immediately   5
released those whom More had thrown into chains because of their

* * * * *

with the request, Erasmus asked that some of the medicinal powder be prepared for him as well (Ep 2747:4–6). This passage indicates that he was in no
   hurry for it.
3 Ie to Hieronymus Froben, the Basel publisher, via whom letters and packages
   were often delivered to Erasmus.
4 On batzen, see Ep 2477 n4. Three batzen were equivalent to just under 12d
   groot Flemish, a third more than a day's wage of an Antwerp master mason/
   carpenter (CWE 12 650 Table 3, 691 Table 13).
5 During his recent sojourn in Basel, Ephorinus had stayed in the home of Johann
   Gross, organist at the cathedral; see Epp 2539 n6, 2740 n2.

2750
1 Cf Ep 2728:29–31. More resigned as lord chancellor on 16 May 1532 and was
   succeeded by Sir Thomas Audley.

contentious teachings.² Homer raises up Ossa,³ as Virgil does Fama,⁴ each
covered with plumes and feathers to indicate that nothing is swifter. But any
winged speed seems to me slow and sluggish compared to the speed with
which this rumour was suddenly spread far and wide. It flashes faster than   10
lightning to all parts of the world. But though this story flew persistently
from mouth to mouth, and though I had not yet received any letter from
Britain (for the letter of Thomas More which I am now sending to you was
held up for several months in Saxony),⁵ nevertheless I was absolutely certain that the rumour so bruited about was utterly false. For I knew the very   15
kind nature of the king, with what loyalty he cherishes his friends once he
has welcomed their friendship, how reluctantly he removes anyone from his
favour, even if he discovers some human fault in them. Then again, I knew
the incorruptible character of Thomas More and his skill in managing matters large and small, and his unfailing and extraordinary prudence in keep-   20
ing a sharp eye out for details. Indeed I think the king more clearly revealed
his benevolent attitude towards More by freeing him from a prestigious but
also burdensome and perilous office than by bestowing such a great honour
upon him. For when the king imposed the packsaddles of this office on More
against his will, the king was a lover of his country, he was consulting the   25
interests of himself and his realm; when he took the office away from one
who asked for discharge, he showed himself to be a lover of More. In the
first case he earned the praise and applause of everyone for his patriotism
and prudence by bestowing a very difficult position on one who was better
suited than anyone else in the kingdom to undertake such a great task. In this   30
case, he gained extraordinary praise for his kindness by granting something
to the prayers of his friend, even somewhat against his own judgment and
the consideration of the public interest, in compliance with his friend's desire
for the kind of retirement that Cassidorus once obtained from his prince.⁶ I
do not doubt that More had excellent reasons to ask the king for retirement.   35

* * * * *

2 Cf Epp 2728:31–4, 2780:28–31.
3 Ossa, the personification of rumour, a voice that comes from Zeus (*Odyssey*
  1.282)
4 Fama, Roman goddess of rumour (*Aeneid* 4.173–88)
5 Ep 2659
6 Cassiodorus (c 490–c 585) held high offices in the Ostrogothic kingdom in Italy
  until about the middle of his life, when he retired and established a monastery
  important for initiating the tradition of monastic learning and the preservation
  of manuscripts.

Otherwise he would never have been so audacious as to ask to be relieved so soon, or the king so accommodating as to pay attention to any mere pretexts.

He was not unaware that the condition of the whole kingdom depends in large part on the uprightness, learning, and prudence of the chancellor. For in this case 'chancellor' is not equivalent to 'secretary,' as it is in some countries. It is a dignity second only to that of the king. In procession he carries in his right hand a golden mace surmounted by an imperial crown of gold; in his left hand is a book. The first signifies the highest power under the king; the other, his learning in the law. For he is the highest judge in the whole kingdom of Britain, and for the king and the royal council he is the right eye, so to speak, and the right hand. A king of such great wisdom would never have assigned this arduous task to anyone who had not been thoroughly proven. Hardly anyone else but the king could have had such a profound knowledge or high regard for his rare and almost divine mental endowments. In fact, even the cardinal of York, a man who was not stupid (whatever his lot may have been), once it was clear to him that he had no hope of returning to his former dignity, asserted that no one in the island was equal to that task except More.[7] (Nor did he give this vote out of favour or benevolence. The cardinal, while he lived, was hardly fair to More; he feared him more than he loved him.) And the people were of the same opinion. And so, just as he undertook the office with such public rejoicing as no one before him had ever received, so too he resigned from it to the great sorrow of all men of wisdom and virtue. When he resigned he had earned the highest praise of all: that no one before him had exercised the duties of that office with more skill or equity. And you know how full of complaints the common people are against those who hold the highest positions, especially in the first years of their holding office. And I could easily give proof of this if I produced the letters of the highest-ranking men heartily congratulating the king, the kingdom, themselves, even me (who was elated) when he received this honour, and letters from the same men grieving that the commonwealth had lost such a judge, such a counsellor, to use a word from Homer.[8]

I have no doubt that the king has chosen an outstanding gentleman as More's replacement;[9] nevertheless, he is quite unknown to me. But as far

* * * * *

7 The cardinal of York was Thomas Wolsey (Ep 284), More's predecessor as chancellor. On his view of More as his successor, cf Chambers 238–9.
8 *Boulephoros* (literally 'counsel-bearing'), an epithet frequently applied to princes and leaders in the *Iliad*
9 See n1 above.

as high birth is concerned, Thomas More, who is of a philosophical cast of
mind, has never laid claim to it or vaunted it. He was born in London, the   70
most illustrious city of the realm; to be born and brought up there constitutes
some degree of nobility among the English. And then his father was not at
all obscure:[10] he was a doctor of British law, a status of the highest dignity
among the English, from which a large part of the nobility of that island is
said to derive.[11] In that status the son so succeeded the father that he over-   75
shadowed a parent who was himself famous for all sorts of honours – though
no one more truly lends lustre to his forebears than someone who obscures
them in this manner.

I say nothing now about the dignified titles bestowed on each of them,
gained not through ambition or bribery but freely granted by the judgment   80
of the king – unless perhaps we think that true nobility is achieved by deeds
of war executed vigorously time and time again and that no honour at all is
due to outstanding services performed for the commonwealth in peacetime
with wisdom rather than arms. As for military pursuits, the more prosperous
the state, the less it has need of them. But the activity of men who excel in   85
learning, wisdom, or jurisprudence is necessary to kings and kingdoms in
times of war and of peace. We hear Holy Scripture saying: 'Through me kings
rule.'[12] That is not the voice of warfare but of wisdom, which prefers that no
war be started, or, if it cannot be avoided, that it do the least possible damage
to the commonwealth. For it is more fortunate to flee from war than to wage   90
it courageously. But peace cannot be long-lasting, or if it is, it corrupts mankind, unless it is governed by the counsels of prudent men. Did Torquatus
become famous because he snatched the neck chain from an enemy Gaul,
and will he not be renowned because for many years he served his country
as a fair judge and faithful counsellor?[13] The ancient emperors were of quite a   95
different opinion: they paid the highest honour to their assessors, who were
renowned for their knowledge of the law.[14] In fact, if grammarians, dialecti-

* * * * *

10 John (I) More, d 1530, was sergeant-at-law (1503), judge of Common Pleas
   (1518), and judge of King's Bench (by 1523).
11 The title 'doctor of British law' (cf Ep 2780:37–8) appears to be Erasmus' in-
   vention. In More's day English universities did not teach law; one studied for
   several years at one of the Inns of Court (in More's case Lincoln's Inn), received
   a licence, and was called to the bar.
12 Prov 8.15
13 Livy 7.10 and Aulus Gellius 9.13.8
14 Assessors were lawyers whose job it was to provide legal advice to Roman
   magistrates with jurisdiction in civil and military cases.

cians, and professors of law gave evidence of their learning and uprightness for twenty years, the emperors bestowed on them the same insignia of rank as were worn by vice-regents. And the rank of vice-regents equalled that of counts and dukes. This is testified by the Codex, book 12, 'De professoribus.'[15] Today, however, those to whom not birth but the prince accords (I would not object if they should say 'sells') insignia are not recognized as nobles. But if it is by the authority of the prince that honour is bestowed on those who deserve well of the commonwealth, then in my judgment nobility is twofold, since to virtue, the source of all true nobility, the authority of the prince is added. If ancient ancestry is demanded, it is still more magnificent to have earned nobility than to have inherited it from one's ancestors.

But I know that this sort of praise was of very little importance to More; he preferred to leave to his heirs the love of piety rather than the honour of insignia. Moreover, whether what they bandy about concerning prisons is true, I do not know. But this much is certain: a man who was so mild by temperament was not harsh to anyone who, after being warned, was willing to come to his senses and avoid the contagion of the sects. Do they demand that the highest judge of such a great kingdom should have no prisons? He detests seditious teachings, by which the world is now miserably shaken. He does not try to hide this or wish to keep it secret; he is so committed to piety that if he is the least bit inclined to one side or the other, he seems to be more favourable to superstition than to impiety. One proof of his extraordinary clemency is that under his chancellorship no one was put to death for condemned beliefs,[16] whereas in both parts of Germany and in France a great many were executed. When one has the right to put someone to death, is it not a merciful hatred of the wicked if one seeks to remedy vices but saves the lives of the offenders? Are they not asking that the vicegerent of the king favour seditious innovation against the judgment of the king and the bishops? Let us imagine that he was not entirely horrified by these new doctrines (which is far from the truth): either he would have had to resign from the office he had assumed or conceal his preference.

Finally, to say nothing about the conflicts concerning doctrine, who is not aware of how many light-headed and seditious criminals would be quite

* * * * *

15 See *Codex Iustiniani* book 12 title 15.
16 In fact, six heretics were executed during More's term as chancellor, three with his personal involvement. See Richard Rex 'Thomas More and the heretics, statesman or fanatic?' in *The Cambridge Companion to Thomas More* ed George M. Logan (Cambridge 2011) 93–115, here 105–8.

ready to cloak their licentious criminality under this pretext if their increasing temerity were not checked by severe governmental measures? And are they outraged because the highest judge in England does what town councils in cities taken over by religious innovators are sometimes constrained to do? And if this had not been done, the pseudo-evangelists would long since have broken into the storerooms and chests of the rich, and anyone who possessed anything would be a papist! And such is the audacity, such is the unrestrained wickedness of many of them, that the very authors and defenders of the new doctrines themselves take up their sharpened pens against the plunderers. And they want the supreme judge of England to look the other way when such dregs, with impunity, flood into a kingdom where wealth and talent and religion flourish. It may also be true that, in honour of the new chancellor, some prisoners, whether non-violent or guilty of lesser offences, were released, as is usually done to gain the favour of the crowd when the king makes his first entrance. I think the same thing was done when More took up his office. So what are these judicial Triptolemi doing by sowing such stories?[17] Are they trying to persuade us that in England protection is being provided for sects and the promoters of sects? But letters to me from serious-minded men make it quite clear that the king is somewhat less lenient to new doctrines than bishops and priests. There is no pious man who does not want the practices of the church corrected, but no prudent man thinks that general confusion is acceptable.

When I heard that Thomas More had been raised to the highest dignity, I wrote that I publicly congratulated the king and the kingdom, but privately I by no means congratulated him, because I thought I knew his temperament pretty well from much association with him. But now I congratulate him from the bottom of my heart because, with the highest favour from his prince and with the most honourable testimony of the whole country, he has managed in good time to extricate himself from the labyrinth of public duties – something not granted to either Scipio Africanus or Pompey the Great or Cicero. Octavius Augustus wanted to lay down the burden of the Empire but was not allowed to. Now, while still unimpaired by age, Thomas More has acquired in a dignified way the sort of life to which he was inclined from his adolescence: to be with his family (for he is affectionate towards his family if anyone ever was) and to have free time for his salutary studies

* * * * *

17 Triptolemus, who was taught the arts of agriculture and grain production by Demeter, travelled the world teaching these arts to all mankind. He was also seen as a lawgiver and became a judge in the underworld.

and his religious devotions. On the banks of the Thames, not far from the
city of London, he has built a country house, neither shabby nor ostentatious
enough to provoke envy, but comfortable. There he lives in the bosom of
his family, with his wife, his son and daughter-in-law, his three daughters,
and the same number of sons-in-law, together with eleven grand-children.   170
Christ willing, 'he has seen the sons of his sons and will see those born of
them.'[18] Since they are all at a flourishing age, they will probably produce
numerous progeny. Indeed he himself could also still be the father of many
children, except that his wife because of her age has long since ceased to bear
children. He married her when she was a widow, and she has borne him   175
no children. The children he has come from a former young wife, whom he
lost when she was still a girl, together with some children. His present wife,
though she is infertile and of an advanced age, he loves and cherishes as if
she were a girl of fifteen. No one loves his children more, and he makes no
difference between an older woman and a young girl. His character is so   180
engaging, or to put it better, such is his piety and prudence that if he encoun-
ters something that cannot be corrected, he accepts it as fondly as if nothing
happier could have fallen to his lot. You would say that his home is another
Platonic Academy. But I insult his household by comparing it to the Platonic
Academy. For in that Academy they disputed about numbers and geometric   185
figures and sometimes about moral virtues, but this home you could more
properly call a school and gymnasium of the Christian religion.[19] Every girl
or boy there is occupied in the liberal disciplines and wholesome reading, although the first and special concern is piety. No quarrel, no aggressive word
is heard; you see no one unoccupied. But he maintains this extraordinary   190
discipline in the family not by arrogance or strife but by friendliness and
good will. They are all busy, but cheerfulness and sober good fun are present.

In the village church he has built a tomb to be shared by him and his
family,[20] to which he has transferred the bones of his former wife – to such
an extent does he find any separation unacceptable. On the wall is a plaque   195
testifying to his fortune and his mode of life, which my servant has copied
word for word. You will receive a copy with this letter. I see that I have been
too wordy, but it is a pleasure to talk to a friend about a friend. All good
people are delighted that you act as a true bishop by regularly preaching to
the people. I hope that your example motivates many to do likewise.   200

* * * * *

18 Cf Virgil *Aeneid* 3.98.
19 *Gymnasium* = a secondary school or academy
20 The village church at Chelsea, where More's manor house was located

What you write about the affairs of King Ferdinand I found most gratifying. I have good reason to hope that from these beginnings the fortunes of
this best and holiest prince will one day correspond to his virtues. Farewell.

2751 / From Julius Pflug   Zeitz, 4 January 1533

This letter (= Ep 77 in Pollet), which is Pflug's answer to Ep 2702, was first published in *Epistolae P. Mosellani [et al.] … ad Iulium Pflugium* ed Christian Gottfried
Müllet (Leipzig: Ioannes Ambrosius Barthius, 1802) 140–1. The manuscript, apparently autograph, is in the Universitäts- und Forschungsbibliothek Erfurt/
Gotha (MS Chart A 385 folio 104).

Cordial greetings. When I received your last letter I was most pleased, first of
all because it was from you, then because it demonstrated that the evil which
has oppressed our nation for so long is diminishing there. Although matters
here have come to the point that things are going exceptionally well for us, if
that plague does not get any worse, I nevertheless do not so much envy you   5
as rejoice that some part of our nation is faring even a little bit better.[1] If it
were completely remedied, that blessing would undoubtedly be shared with
us; for the very nature of our affiliation would bring that about for us. Hence
I desire all the more that, if anyone is capable of providing a beneficial, that
is to say not bitter, remedy, he should undertake to cure it at this moment.   10
Since such a favourable opportunity of treating the malady has presented
itself, there is nothing more to seek. You can easily understand what I mean.[2]
I do not prescribe anything, however. For I see what these times require, but
I don't see what I ought to ask for. Wherever I turn, I see for what reason

* * * * *

2751
1 This passage is puzzling. 'There' (*istic* = there where you are) can only mean
  Freiburg. 'The evil' / 'that plague' referred to is presumably the religious conflict
  in the Empire and the consequent threat of civil war. The meaning here could
  conceivably be that, thanks to the Peace of Nürnberg (see following note) the
  danger of a war that would engulf Freiburg had receded. But Erasmus does not
  say that in Ep 2702. Instead, while hoping for the best, he expresses pointed
  skepticism about the peaceful intentions of both the pope and the emperor
  (Ep 2702:6–12). Moreover, as many letters in this volume attest, he had not
  abandoned his plans to resettle in a safer place.
2 Presumably a reference to the recently concluded Religious Peace of Nürnberg
  (Ep 2702 n2) and the renewed hope for a peaceful settlement of the religious
  question via negotiation. Pflug would be a leading participant in such efforts
  on the Catholic side.

all good men owe you an immense debt of gratitude. As for that passage of   15
Euripides that you apply to me,[3] it is such that if I were to put it into practice,
I would immediately take leave of my office. As for your splendid opinions
about me, which describe me not as I am but as I should be, I only wish I
could succeed in living up to them at some future time. But I will put an end
to this letter, especially since I have nothing more to write, and I would not   20
want to distract you with an insignificant letter from the activities in which
you never cease to be so honourably engaged.

    Farewell. Zeitz, 4 January 1533
    Julius Pflug
    To the highly renowned and learned gentleman Desiderius Erasmus of   25
Rotterdam, a friend to be especially respected

2752 / To Bonifacius Amerbach   [Freiburg], 5 January [1533]

This letter was first published in the *Epistolae familiares*. The autograph is in the
Öffentliche Bibliothek of the University of Basel (MS AN III 15 24). The year-date
is assigned on the basis of the reference to the adage 'A story for Alcinous,' the
second version of which first appeared in the edition of the *Adagia* published
by Froben in March 1533.

Cordial greetings. If you have come upon anything about the story of Alcinous,
please let me know by this messenger. Or if there is anything else you would
like me to know. For I have separated this proverb from the others.[1]

    Best wishes to you and to all those who are dear to you. The vigil of the
Epiphany   5
    Yours, Erasmus of Rotterdam
    To the highly renowned gentleman Master Bonifacius Amerbach. At
Basel

* * * * *

3 See Ep 2702 n10.

2752
1 The adage *Apologus Alcinoi* 'A Story for Alcinous' (a phrase 'applied to rambling
   narratives and old wives' tales') first appeared as *Adagia* II iv 32, attributed to
   Homer's *Odyssey* 9–10. Having found a different explanation of the source of
   the adage in book 3 of Aristotle's *Rhetoric*, Erasmus published a second version
   of it in *Adagia* v i 82, though reserving judgment concerning the validity of the
   alternative explanation, which he doubted (cf Ep 2754:4–5). Aristotle's *Poetics* 16
   shows that Erasmus' original attribution was correct; see CWE 36 589–90 with n2.

2753 / From Viglius Zuichemus Padua, 14 January 1533

This letter was first published as Ep 36 in VZE.

TO ERASMUS OF ROTTERDAM

After the letter that you sent to me via Heresbach,[1] my most learned friend
Erasmus, I have not received any from you, even though I sent you several
bundles and wrote you concerning matters about which I hoped you would
be willing to respond. Hence I fear my letters were not properly handled or 5
were not delivered to you. I would very much like to know what happened,
so that I can either tell you the same things once again or be able to retrieve
the neglected letters from those to whose care I had entrusted them. The issue at that time was something I wanted Amerbach to know, and in fact the
courier willingly agreed to take the letter to you; but he made it clear that 10
he was not prepared to go as far as Basel, so I had to ask for your help and
write you a quick (and hence unpolished) letter.[2] Amerbach wanted to know
from me whether the presses at Venice were producing an edition of Cicero,[3]
which I have still not been able to find out for certain, but I hardly think so.[4]
He also asked for emendations of some works of Cicero, which he would 15
need later; it is very difficult to get them here, like snatching Hercules' club
from him.[5] But I have a few on the epistles to Atticus that seem to me to be
of some importance, and I would be most willing to send them.[6] I have in
my personal possession a manuscript copy of the *Institutes* translated into
Greek,[7] and I also wrote Amerbach about printing it.[8] Earlier I did not dare 20
inform you that I had undertaken a public professorship here, since its term

* * * * *

2753
1 Not extant. Konrad Heresbach could not have carried Ep 2682, which had already been answered before his departure for Italy (Ep 2728 n24), or Ep 2736,
which was carried by Johann Bebel.
2 The letter from Viglius to Amerbach was AK Ep 1704 (15 January 1533), which
(according to AK) Erasmus sent on to Bonifacius at Basel with Ep 2770. For the
matter dealt with in the letter, see the lines that follow.
3 Johann Herwagen was planning an edition of Cicero at Basel; see Epp 2765 n5,
2766A:5–7.
4 Cf AK Ep 1704:6–16.
5 *Adagia* IV i 95
6 These were corrections given him by Giovanni Crisostomo Zanchi (Ep 2716
n35); see AK Ep 1704:17–19, 1719:11–16.
7 See Ep 2791 n22.
8 See AK Epp 1704:21–5, 1719:39–42.

is limited to a year, just as the rule and jurisdiction of our praetors once was.[9]
Still I have been moderately successful in it, and so far I have somehow
managed to hold out against the ambition and envy of an Italian colleague
(whom we call a competitor).   25

Sucket, who was the only companion of my studies and a close friend
since we were boys, recently died an early death at Turin.[10] For me no blow
could have been more grievous than his death. I had premonitions for a long
time, and I tried in many letters to call him away from there, but without success. I wrote you about the departure of Logau;[11] he is expected to come back   30
here.[12] We heard the news that he has become the tutor of the son of some
count and will come back with a full purse.

The emperor is still at Bologna with the pope.[13] Recently legates from
the French king arrived there: Cardinal François de Tournon and another
bishop (of Tarbes, I think).[14] What they are planning is not widely known. But   35
they say that after the marriage there between his daughter and Alessandro,
duke of Florence,[15] he will withdraw to Milan.[16] The time is too short to tell
you more. I hope that you will take that in good part and will write something to me in turn, since I am very eager to receive your letters.

Farewell. Padua, 14 January 1533   40

* * * * *

9 Roman praetors, two in number and chosen annually, were magistrates responsible for (among other things) the administration of law.
10 For Karel Sucket and his early death at Turin (3 November 1532), see Ep 2657
   n17.
11 In a letter no longer extant. For Georg von Logau see Ep 2716 n3.
12 He had not returned by April 1532; see Ep 2791. By June he had returned but
   had already gone on to Rome; see Allen Epp 2829:26–7, 2854:99–103.
13 On his journey from Germany back to Spain, Charles met with Pope Clement
   at Bologna in December 1532. Charles did not leave Bologna until 28 February
   1533; cf Ep 2767:38–58.
14 François de Tournon (Ep 1319 introduction), bishop of Bourges and royal diplomat, had been created cardinal in 1530. The bishop of Tarbes was Gabriel de
   Gramont (d 1534), who had been created cardinal at the same time as François
   de Toulon. Also an able diplomat, he was French envoy at the papal court 1529–
   30, and 1532–3.
15 The marriage of Margaret (1522–86), natural daughter of Charles v, to Alessandro
   de' Medici (1510–37) took place in June 1536, only six months before the death of
   Alessandro. Margaret would in due course earn her place in history as Margaret
   of Parma, regent of the Netherlands for her half-brother Philip ii (1559–67).
16 He went from Bologna to Genoa, where he set sail for Spain on 9 April. By 11
   May he was in Barcelona; see Ep 2593 n11.

2754 / To Bonifacius Amerbach   [Freiburg], 15 January [1533]

This letter (= AK Ep 1703) was first published in the *Episolae familiares*. The autograph is in the Öffentliche Bibliothek of the University of Basel (MS AN III 1525). The year-date is supplied by the connection to Ep 2752.

Cordial greetings. The matter of the boy is of no importance and there was no need to mention any loss. He did not ask for anything. What was given was freely given by my command, and it was rightly given.[1]

I was guessing about the 'story for Alcinous'; it is not safe to take what I said as true.[2] I am grateful for your friendly words of consolation about a 5 friend,[3] but you are ministering to a corpse.[4] The death of the archbishop is a pretext; there are other things that are weighing on your spirit.[5] I am thinking about revising my will. If the one whom I previously made my trustee does not recoil from this burden,[6] there will be no change.[7] I will handle the matter in such a way that there will be much less trouble and more convenience. I 10 will completely abandon any plan to have my books printed after my death.[8] And so what the heir thinks about it I would like to know through you.

* * * * *

2754
1 In Ep 2749 Erasmus says that he had given three batzen to the boy who delivered the letter. In a letter no longer extant, Bonifacius must have apologized for
   the boy's supposedly bad conduct in asking Erasmus for money.
2 Erasmus himself was not persuaded of the accuracy of the alternative explanation of the adage 'A story for Alcinous' supplied in his second version of it; see
   Ep 2752 n1.
3 Evidently (see the following sentence) a letter of consolation on the death of
   William Warham, archbishop of Canterbury, who had died on 22 August 1532
4 Cf *Adagia* III iii 30.
5 Possibly the death of Amerbach's infant daughter Ursula on 20 June 1532
6 The 'heir or trustee' of the first will was Bonifacius himself; see CWE 12 540:6–7,
   550:135–6 (text of Erasmus' first will, 22 January 1527). Erasmus does not name
   him here (see also line 12 below), lest an unauthorized reader of the letter discover whom he had named as his heir.
7 On 26 November 1533 Erasmus made and signed a new will in his home at
   Freiburg, but no copy of it survives; see AK Ep 1775 n1 (citing the certificate of
   the notary). He made his final will in Basel, on 12 February 1536; see Allen XI
   362, CWE 12 538–9.
8 For this plan, carefully outlined in his first will, see CWE 12 542:36–547:110. The
   final will of 1536 (Allen XI 362–5) makes no provision for the publication of
   Erasmus' works. But Bonifacius and Beatus Rhenanus (who had been named
   as one of the executors of the first will) nonetheless decided to give effect to the

Best wishes to you and all your loved ones. 15 January.
Erasmus of Rotterdam
To Master Doctor Amerbach   15

2755 / From Bonifacius Amerbach   [Basel, c 22 January 1533]

This letter (= AK Ep 1711) was first published by Allen. The manuscript, which
bears no date, is an autograph rough draft in the Öffentliche Bibliothek of the
University of Basel (MS C VIa 73 103 verso). It includes three previous attempts
to write the letter, none of which Allen judged to be of any importance. The
month-date is based on Ep 2756, which is clearly an answer to this letter. As
for the year-date, the reference to a planned visit or migration from Freiburg to
Basel at first suggests 1535, but in January of that year Erasmus was confined
to his bed by an illness that had begun at Christmas 1534 (Allen Ep 3000:21–3).
In 1534 he was also ill throughout January (Allen Epp 2898:1–7, 2899:3–7). The
year 1532 is excluded by the content of Epp 2597–8, and 1531 by that of Ep 2420.
This process of exclusion leaves 1533, which is consistent with Erasmus' statement in Ep 2770:1–6 that he had enjoyed good health during the entire winter
until the last days of February. It is also supported by a letter of 10 February 1533
(VZE Ep 38) in which Viglius Zuichemus states that he has heard that Erasmus
intends to return to Basel. It seems likely that the entire business had its origin
in Erasmus' contemplation at this time of making a new will (Ep 2754:7–8). In
1531 he had proposed to visit Neuenburg for that purpose (see Ep 2490:11–12
and cf lines 4–6 below).

Cordial greetings. Hieronymus[1] announced today that you would be arriving here in a few days – my best wishes that all goes well! I would like you
to tell me the time of your departure, so that either I can come there, or if you
do not find that agreeable, I can at least tell my father-in-law about your arrival.[2] Indeed I will make sure to be present also myself at Neuenburg on the   5

* * * * *

intention expressed in the earlier document; cf BRE Ep 300 (Beatus to Bonifacius,
20 August 1536). The result was the Froben nine-volume edition of the *Opera
omnia* (1540).

2755
1 Presumably Hieronymus Froben
2 Bonifacius' father-in-law, Leonhard Fuchs, was the burgomaster of Neuenburg
  am Rhein, where Erasmus would have boarded ship for the journey up the
  Rhine to Basel.

appointed day (for he does not know Latin), but only if you will not allow me to come to Freiburg in order to accompany you, which I would be happy to do if I knew that was agreeable to you.

I think you have received my last letter,[3] which I wrote very hastily because the courier had said he was leaving at dawn. I would have told   10 Anselmus' host about the twenty gold pieces already sent to his kinsman Hieronymus Veldt[4] so that they would be delivered to you, unless by chance Hieronymus interfered with that plan by letting it be known that the money was sent yesterday and would be repaid to him by a merchant here. Farewell.

2756 / To Bonifacius Amerbach   [Freiburg], 25 January [1533]

This letter (= AK Ep 1712) was first published in the *Epistolae familiares*. The autograph is in the Öffentliche Bibliothek of the University of Basel (MS AN III 15 65). For the assigned year-date see Ep 2755 introduction.

Cordial greetings. There was no need to spread the word about my arrival, which is quite uncertain, and you know that in matters of this sort I am accustomed to make haste slowly. I received your letter,[1] which I enjoyed very much. I am deeply grateful to him whose fondness for me is so firm and sincere.[2]   5
Farewell. 25 January
Your Erasmus
To Master Bonifacius Amerbach

* * * * *   .

3 Not extant, but mentioned again in Ep 2756:3
4 The name in the manuscript is difficult to decipher. Allen hesitantly made it 'Hieronymus,' while Alfred Hartmann (AK Ep 1711) made it 'Florianus.' It is not clear whether he was a kinsman of Anselmus Ephorinus or of 'Anselmus' host,' Johann Gross (see Ep 2740 nn1–2). Nothing else is known of the transaction described here in such cryptic language.

2756
1 Not extant; first mentioned in Ep 2755:9
2 Possibly Leonhard Fuchs (Ep 2755 n2) or perhaps Bonifacius himself (referred to in the third person as in Ep 2754:7, 12)

2757 / To Jean de Pins   Freiburg, 30 January 1533

This letter, Erasmus' reply to Ep 2665, was first printed by Preserved Smith in Appendix II of *Erasmus: A Study of His Life, Ideals and Place in History* (New York 1923; repr New York 1962) 450. The surviving manuscript is a seventeenth-century copy in the Bibliothèque Municipale at Nîmes (MS 215 folio 170).

TO THE VERY REVEREND MASTER JEAN DE PINS, BISHOP OF RIEUX, ERASMUS OF ROTTERDAM
I laughed at the tragic tumults of those people, which had a comic ending, etc.[1]

The Josephus is already in the hands of Froben.[2] In that respect I am   5
most grateful for your kindness, well known to me for a long time. I will take care that the codex gets back to you undamaged. For Froben has not yet decided to print the Greek text but rather to emend the Latin translation by comparing it with the Greek. Actually he had hoped to get all of Josephus, but your codex contains only *The History of the Jewish War*, etc.   10

Farewell.

Freiburg, 30 January 1533

2758 / To the Reader   Freiburg, [c end of January] 1533

This is the preface to the third edition of the *Opera omnia* of St Jerome. The autograph rough draft, which Allen also consulted, is in the Royal Library at Copenhagen (MS G K S 95 Fol folio 190).

The first two editions of Erasmus' Jerome (1516, 1524–6) had been published by Froben. The third edition was undertaken at the instigation of the Paris publisher Claude Chevallon, who in 1531 had published a revised version of Erasmus' edition of St Augustine; see CWE 15 220 (introduction to Ep 2157). Chevallon revised the Froben edition on the basis of manuscripts available to him in France, and Erasmus cooperated by revising his annotations in the first four volumes (the letters) and adding this new general introduction.

* * * * *

2757
1 See Ep 2665:1–30.
2 Ie the manuscript of Josephus' *History of the Jewish War* that De Pins had lent to Froben at Erasmus' request. For the history of the quest for the manuscript, see Ep 2569 introduction. Froben's Latin edition of the works of Josephus was published in 1534.

On 15 March 1533, Erasmus sent to Andreas Silvius at Paris a second copy
of the preface, fearing that the copy originally sent had not reached him (Ep
2779:3–5). This puts the date of the preface at some point between 1 January
and 15 March 1533. Ep 2757 shows that Erasmus dispatched letters to France on
or about 30 January. No other letters to France between that date and 15 March
are extant. There is thus good reason to place the first dispatch of this letter at
'c end of January.'

The greater part of the letter (lines 35–78) is a moving tribute to the recently
deceased archbishop of Canterbury, William Warham, to whom the Froben
Jerome had been dedicated (Ep 396).

DESIDERIUS ERASMUS OF ROTTERDAM SENDS GREETINGS
TO THE PIOUS READER
Although from my early boyhood I admired the writings of Jerome, not so
much from judgment as from a certain hidden natural feeling, and this admiration increased as I grew in years and in learning (such as it is), nevertheless,   5
when I undertook the task of both correcting and annotating his letters, I had
not fully perceived the manifold riches amassed from every arcane source of
languages, disciplines, and literatures. For what is there in any kind of books,
whether large or small, whether sacred or profane, that he does not have
available like ready cash?[1] I therefore confess that I was at fault in more than   10
one way when I undertook such a difficult task without either sufficient learning or appropriate care. For when I first came to Basel, I had not even thought
of translating the New Testament; I had only written some brief notes, and I
had decided that I was content with that. I brought to Jerome almost nothing
more than good intentions. Here Johann Froben of happy memory availed   15
himself of my readiness, or rather my rashness, and set many presses to work
on both undertakings, even though this little bodily frame of mine could
measure up to only a quarter of the labours.[2] And at that time I was preparing them not for learned men but for a pious but uneducated audience,
among whom I found a Jerome so riddled with errors that it could not even   20

* * * * *

2758
1 *Adagia* IV iii 82
2 This account of the origins of the New Testament and of the first edition of
  Jerome gives the seriously misleading impression that both projects had their
  origins in Basel at the behest of Johann Froben during Erasmus' first sojourn
  in that city (1514–16). His Latin translation of the New Testament was actually
  done in the period 1505–9; see Allen II 182 (Ep 384 introduction). The edition of
  Jerome was begun no later than 1500, and Erasmus was at work on it again in
  1511–12; see Ep 396 introduction.

be read; more than once this carelessness filled me with shame and regret. All that was left was to take refuge in the proverb which says that second thoughts are better[3] and to correct previous defects by later carefulness, and that is what I did, over and over again.[4] So when I heard that the volumes of the letters were being reprinted at Paris, I revised some of my previous notes   25 as time allowed,[5] and I sent them out for the use of the learned community, not content until I had demonstrated my good faith and industry to the fair and candid reader.[6] But as for the ungrateful and the unfair critics who simply ignore much that is well said and only gnaw away at any careless slips, or (what is even worse) don't even read what I wrote but close their eyes and   30 stop their ears, loudly condemning what they don't even know, for them all I can hope for is that they will be given a better frame of mind by divine intervention: for the gods are all powerful. But in the meantime it is not so much royal as it is Christian to be called bad when you do good.[7]

While this edition was being prepared, that incomparable hero William   35 Warham, archbishop of Canterbury and primate of all England, left the earth and migrated into the heavenly fellowship.[8] He was a man adorned with every virtue and honour, whether you consider his graciousness towards the lowly, even in his lofty station, or his unaffected sobriety of life in the midst of such great wealth, or his unceasing tranquillity amidst the turmoil of such   40 pressing affairs (which seems to be the mark of a godly mind), or his sincere devotion to piety and religion, which he both taught and exemplified with the greatest intensity but without the least haughtiness. No one ever saw him unoccupied. And who would not willingly have forgiven such a man if occasionally, wearied as he was with external affairs, he should have sought men-   45 tal relaxation with jokes and games? In the place of hunting, hawking, dice, card-playing, jesters, or other vulgar pastimes he chose fruitful reading or

* * * * *

3 *Adagia* i iii 38
4 In the first Froben editions of Jerome, 1516 and 1524–6. For the history of the
   three editions of Jerome, see CWE 61 xiii–xxx.
5 Erasmus' principal contributions to the edition of Jerome had been the revision
   and annotation of the letters (four volumes in the first edition) and his identification of the spurious works attribute to Jerome.
6 On the labour involved in this revision see Ep 2776:55–7.
7 As Erasmus notes in his explanation of it, the adage 'The gods are all powerful' (*Adagia* iv vi 11) suits 'monarchs who are quick to do whatever they fancy, whether it is right or wrong.'
8 Warham died on 22 August 1532. For an earlier memorial to him, see Ep
   2726:35–62.

conversation with a learned man. Why should I say anything about his kindness to everyone, but especially to scholars? About myself I will say nothing,
since I did not receive a great deal from him, and that was thrust upon me   50
rather than bestowed, though I reckon as received whatever he offered, and
he frequently and sincerely offered me a share in all his fortune. But his generosity towards others was unstinted, as is clear from something he said a little before his death. When his servants told him that there were hardly thirty
gold minted coins left in the treasury, he said with great satisfaction: 'That is   55
fine. I have always wanted to die in those circumstances. That is enough travel provision for someone who is about to depart hence.' That is a sentiment
worthy of an eminent bishop! Out of such a great fortune he spent very little
on himself. His table was splendid, in accord with the custom of the district
and with the dignity of such a great prelate. But in the midst of delicacies he   60
himself preferred common fare, and even very little of that. His dinner was
as sparing as could be. On very rare occasions he merely tasted rather than
drank wine, content with very thin ale, which the common people call beer.
He was equally frugal in his dress: he did not wear garments made entirely
of silk except when he said mass. He was also very sparing in his attire, so   65
much so that at the meeting of the emperor Charles and the king of England
that occurred at Calais about eleven years ago (if I am not mistaken),[9] when
an edict of the cardinal of York[10] required that not only bishops but also men
of even lower rank dress in very costly fine linen and damask, he alone of
all of them scorned the edict of the cardinal and did not change so much as   70
a thread of his clothing. What could be more incorruptible than that soul?
And now that happy spirit, once the shining light of the church, has added
a bright star to the heavenly Jerusalem. Frequently he would cry out among
his friends: 'How I would like to see and embrace just once more my dear
Erasmus before I depart. I would never let him be parted from me.' The wish   75
was mutual, but neither of us obtained what he hoped for. May Christ in his
mercy grant that we soon embrace one another there where there will be no
separation and no one will begrudge him to me or me to him.

Farewell, whoever you may be who reads this.

Freiburg im Breisgau. In the year of our Lord 1533   80

* * * * *

9 The meeting between Charles v and Henry viii took place in July 1520.
10 Thomas Wolsey, the lord chancellor (Ep 284)

2759 / From Nicolaus Olahus   Brussels, 31 January 1533

This letter was first published in Ipolyi page 276. The manuscript is page 333 of the Olahus codex in the Hungarian National Archives at Budapest (Ep 2339 introduction). For Nicolaus Olahus, secretary to Mary of Hungary, regent of the Netherlands, see Ep 2646 introduction.

NICOLAUS OLAHUS, TREASURER OF SZÉKESFEHÉRVÁR,
TO ERASMUS OF ROTTERDAM, GREETINGS

Last July, my dear Erasmus, I sent you a somewhat lengthy letter about your affairs in which I set out what seemed best to me and to his excellency of Palermo, who also sent you his letter together with mine.[1] We cannot quite 5 imagine why we have not received a reply from you for such a long time. We are afraid that, through the negligence of the master of the letter carriers, the letter was not delivered to you; if that is so, may the gods punish him![2] The gist of our letters was that if you want to return home you should signify your intention to us more clearly. He and I will see to it as best we can that 10 here in your native land you will have a standing with the queen that you will not regret. And so, whether you have received our letters or not, let us know what you wish, so that our action in your favour will not be wanting. His Excellency of Palermo, whose company I often enjoy, has often asked me if I have had any reply from you. We have attributed your complete silence to 15 the master of the letter carriers. Therefore, at your convenience, let us know what you think. But the reason I am asking you about this matter is that the vicar of the said Excellency of Palermo, who is at Besançon, came here some days ago and said he had heard for certain that you had received letters from the emperor and King Ferdinand to the citizens of Besançon to the effect that 20 they should admit you to that city, to which you intend to move.[3] If this is so,

* * * * *

2759
1 The bishop of Palermo was Jean (II) de Carondelet, since 1531 president of the privy council of the Netherlands. Olahus' letter is Ep 2693, and that of Carondelet is Ep 2689.
2 It seems more likely that Ep 2693 (26 July 1532) took several months to reach Erasmus, and that Ep 2762 (7 February 1533) was his answer to it.
3 The idea of settling in Besançon had been in Erasmus' mind for some time. In 1529, having decided to leave Basel, he considered it for a time before eventually deciding to settle in Freiburg instead (Epp 2112:5–14, 2514:3–6). Then and since, the easy availability at Besançon of his favourite Burgundian wine was a major factor (cf Epp 2761:29–31, 2778). A serious obstacle to the plan, however, was tension between the city council and the canons of the cathedral, which

what are you doing but failing ever to revisit your native land and the friends you have here? Why this sudden change? Maybe your desire for Burgundian wine has torn you from us. As you could have learned from my previous letter, you could have had both Burgundian and Hungarian wine from the 25 stores of the queen to nourish your advancing years.[4] And so write me to let me know how things stand.

Concerning the marriage of Lieven and his precipitate action, undertaken totally against my advice, I have no doubt you have learned everything from his letter and another one of mine, which I think has been 30 delivered to you by now.[5] If he had obeyed my advice and commands, we would soon have found for him a virgin of ample means and a good dowry. Now he is being asked by some secretary of the emperor to become his scribe. Because of the more liberal income, I would not discourage him from taking this position if I did not see how unchristian and even dangerous it 35 would be for a husband to desert his young wife, who is already pregnant, for a year or two, as I see these fellow countrymen of yours are accustomed to doing. In the month of September your servant Quirinus,[6] whom you sent to England, took a side trip to me with your very brief letter.[7] He was hurrying to England, as you had ordered him to do, and I enjoined him to come visit 40 me on his return trip from there. The queen was away from Brussels for three months' time, during which we traversed all of Hainaut. For this reason I

* * * * *

in 1529–30 made Erasmus' welcome there uncertain and moving there consequently inadvisable (see Epp 2112:10–14, 2410:48–50). In July 1531 he again raised the subject with the city council (Ep 2524), and Emperor Charles wrote a letter to the council (Ep 2553) urging them to accommodate Erasmus' wishes (no letter from King Ferdinand survives). But in 1533 the tension between council and canons still persisted: the council wanted Erasmus to come, but the canons were opposed (see Epp 2761:29–31, 2792:34–6). The hostility of the canons appears to have had its origin in an incident during Erasmus' visit to Besançon in 1524 in which he was thought to have responded irreverently to a prayer invoking the 'blessed womb of the Virgin Mary' (see Epp 1679:100–15, 1956:26–38). Letters written in 1535–6 show Erasmus still considering the relative advantages of Besançon and Brabant as alternatives to Basel or Freiburg, with Besançon enjoying the advantage of geographical proximity and the availability of good wine, but with his poor health standing in the way of his moving anywhere (see Allen Epp 3025:18–20, 3049:83, 3063:3–4, 3104:53–4, 3130:23–5).
4 Ep 2693:130–6
5 See Ep 2693:26–99 (from Olahus); the letter of Lieven Algoet is not extant.
6 Quirinus Hagius (Ep 2704 n6)
7 Ep 2707

think he did not make a side trip to me, but went straight back to you.[8] And so if I made some mistake in not writing to you, attribute it to the fact that I was still waiting for Quirinus.   45

Farewell. And whether you return or whether you remain in a place that is more suitable to your present condition and your age, remember me and know that I am completely devoted to you.

At Brussels, on the last day of January 1533

2760 / To Theobald Fettich   Freiburg, 1 February 1533

> This is the preface to the *Geographia* of Ptolemy (Basel: Froben 1533), the *editio princeps* of the Greek text. The autograph rough draft of the preface is in the Royal Library at Copenhagen (MS G K S 95 Fol folio 188). There is no indication in the volume that Erasmus had any role in the editing. The dedicatee, Theobald Fettich (Ep 1767), physician to Wolfgang von Affenstein (Ep 1774), had supplied a copy of the Greek manuscript in the library at Ladenburg, which was under the stewardship of Affenstein.

DESIDERIUS ERASMUS OF ROTTERDAM SENDS GREETINGS
TO THE OUTSTANDING GENTLEMAN AND SKILLED PHYSICIAN
THEOBALD FETTICH

So that you may understand, most accomplished sir, that the wise men of old were not off the mark when they said that good deeds come back to their   5 doers,[1] your Ptolemy comes back to you, and I have no doubt that because of your gentle temperament you will cherish it all the more and consider it all the more yours because you hold it in common with all those who pursue good letters. The gold-plated blessings of Fortune decrease by sharing; true

* * * * *

8 Olahus has evidently forgotten that Quirinus, on his way home from England, visited him at Mons, the capital of the province of Hainaut, in November 1532 (Ep 2741:6–17).

2760

1 Greek in the text. Erasmus refers here to the myth of the charitable reciprocity of the three Graces, symbolized in their throwing a ball one to another, which is expressed in the word παλιμβόλους, literally 'throwing back.' In the usual interpretation, as in Seneca *De beneficiis* 1.3.2–4, one bestows a benefit, another receives it, and a third returns it. So here Fettich supplied a copy of the manuscript to Froben, and in return received the dedication of the book via Erasmus. This same idea is expressed in *Adagia* 1 i 34, *Gratia gratiam parit* 'One favour begets another.'

blessings, the more you spread them abroad, the better and the more illus- 10
trious they become. You gave the printer access to this Greek volume at no
charge. You could not have sold it, believe me, more favourably if Hercules
owed you his tenths,[2] or if you had Mercury on your side.[3] As it is, how many
thousands of students will celebrate the name of Theobald, how many will
be overwhelmed by the generosity of Theobald, how many will give thanks 15
for the munificence of Theobald? What reward could a noble mind prefer to
this recompense?

I am often surprised to learn that such an ancient author (who flourished under Trajan and Antoninus Pius, as is quite clear both from chapter
5, book 7 of *The Great Construction* and from book 1, chapter 2 of the same 20
work),[4] one, moreover, who treated geography (a subject than which there
is hardly any more pleasant or more necessary among the mathematical sci-
ences) in such a way that he eclipsed all his predecessors and lit the way for
his followers, found no one for so many centuries to present him worthily
to Latin readers. There is no point in mentioning how he was handled by 25
his two translators,[5] since it speaks for itself and was also set forth in an appropriate volume by the highly learned Johannes Regiomontanus.[6] Recently
Willibald Pirckheimer, a man worthy of undying memory, happily undertook
a marvellous work that I wish he could have completed. But death deprived

* * * * *

2 Wealthy men often dedicated a tenth of their goods to Hercules in the expecta-
  tion that he would reward them with great riches; see *Adagia* 1 i 73 and IV x 93.
3 In antiquity those about to throw dice (or embark on a new venture) would
  ask Mercury for good luck, and profit earned unexpectedly was called a gift of
  Mercury; see *Adagia* IV vii 2 and 4.
4 Trajan was emperor AD 98–117, Antoninus Pius AD 138–61. Ptolemy's dates are
  c AD 100–c 175. His best known work was *The Great Construction of Astronomy*
  (commonly referred to as the *Almagest,* after the title of its ninth-century Arabic
  translation) in thirteen books. The citations given here by Erasmus do not
  match the numberings in the edition of the *Almagest* that we have seen. Suffice
  it to say that the work has been firmly dated to the reign of Antoninus Pius
  (c AD 150) and that it contains numerous references to both Antoninus Pius and
  Trajan. See *Ptolemy's Almagest* trans and ed G.J. Toomer (London 1984) 1.
5 The first translator was Jacopo Angeli, whose version was published at Rome
  in 1478; see Ep 2606 nn13–14. The second translator was probably the Nürnberg
  mathematician Johann Werner (1468–1522) who in 1514 published at Nürnberg
  (J. Stuchs) a Latin translation (with commentary) of the first book of Ptolemy's
  treatise.
6 Johannes Regiomontanus' notes on the errors in Angeli's translation of the
  Geographia (see preceding note) were appended to Willibald Pirckheimer's
  translation of the work (1525); see Ep 2606 n13.

him of finishing and us of enjoying this fruit.[7] But now, through the efforts of   30
the Froben workshop, Ptolemy comes forth speaking his own language. For
though he was from Alexandria, at that time Egypt for the most part spoke
Greek, in which it is apparent that he was fluent, although language that
treats subjects like this requires more accuracy, soundness, and clarity than
splendour or abundance. Certainly I do not deny that much praise is owed   35
to Willibald, but those who know Greek and who read Ptolemy in Greek will
admit that there is considerable difference between a pond, however pure,
and the spring itself.

Certainly many writers, both Latin and Greek, have written books that
consist of geography combined with chorography. Among these none was   40
more diligent or copious than Strabo.[8] But Ptolemy was the first of all to lay
out the underlying plan, having devised the measurement of the latitudes of
the world from pole to pole and the longitude from east to west; he also made
the comparison of the habitable parts of the earth with the heavens so that it
is not easy for anyone to go astray, as the saying goes, throughout the whole   45
sky.[9] I only wish we had the correct numbers as they were noted down by
Ptolemy, especially in book 8. But I hope that someone who has the talent, the
learning, and the leisure necessary for the task will survey this territory also.
But there is one feature that cannot be attributed to the copyists: a surprising
discrepancy in the degrees. Ptolemy in book 1, chapter 7, and again in book   50
7, chapter 5, writes that each degree of the great circles of the heavens corresponds to 500 stadia on the earth.[10] But Eratosthenes, whom Pliny, Strabo,
and many of the ancients seem to follow, says 700.[11] How this came about I
still cannot discover. It is hardly credible that such great men would differ in
measuring a single degree by 200 stadia. And it is not much more likely that   55

* * * * *

7 Pirckheimer published a Latin translation of the *Geographia* (see preceding
   note), but did not live to publish an edition of the Greek original.
8 Strabo (64 or 63 BC to c AD 24) of Pontus, Greek geographer whose *Geographia* in
   17 books is the most important source for ancient geography
9 Ie to go entirely astray; see *Adagia* I i 49.
10 There was no agreement among the ancients concerning the length of the unit
   of measure known as a stadium (or 'stade'). Ptolemy used the so-called Attic
   stadium, which measured approximately 185 meters or 606 feet.
11 Eratosthenes of Cyrene (c 285–194 BC), whose works on mathematical and
   descriptive geography are known primarily via citations of them in Strabo
   (n8 above). He estimated the circumference of the earth at 252,000 stadia, hence
   700 Attic stadia for each degree. Ptolemy shared the estimate often attributed to
   the Stoic polymath Posidonius (c 135–c 51 BC), ie 180,000 stadia, which amounted to 500 Attic stadia for each degree.

Ptolemy accused all the ancients of such an extraordinary error, especially since he also does not argue against it anywhere else, as he was often careful to do – for example, when he refuted so many points in Marinus.[12] But if, perhaps, Ptolemy had a different measurement for the stadium than his predecessors, it was of no little importance for him to inform his reader about that. But whatever the discrepancy is, I leave it to the learned to sort it out.[13]

Those who are in charge of young people seeking a liberal education would do well to stimulate them in every way to study geography and to undertake this immediately after they have acquired a taste of grammar, just as the ancients did. Thanks to the great labours of many scholars, this discipline does not demand much labour or much time. It used to require more effort when it was not certain whether the heavens have a spherical shape, when there were those who claimed that the orb of the earth floats in the ocean as a ball floats in water, with only the top part sticking out and the rest covered by water; and those who wrote about the subject also erred in many other points. But now that other writers, but especially Ptolemy, have held out a thread that enables anyone to extricate himself from these labyrinths, the road is open to reach the summit of this subject quickly and effortlessly. Those who fail to do so will necessarily be bewildered when they read good authors. But as for me, most learned sir, I offer you the deepest gratitude, as is fitting, not only for myself and for the printer but also on behalf of all scholars, who are duty-bound, in return for this extraordinary benefit, to pray for all happiness and prosperity for you and yours. Farewell.

At Freiburg im Breisgau, 1 February in the year after the birth of Christ 1533

80

2761 / To [Erasmus Schets]   Freiburg, 5 February 1533

This letter was first published by Allen on the basis of the autograph in the British Library (MS Add 38512 folio 74). The address sheet is missing, but there is no doubt that the letter was written to Schets (for whom see Ep 2704 introduction).

* * * * *

12 Marinus of Tyre (fl c AD 120) is known only via the citations of him by Ptolemy in the *Geographia*.
13 On this matter of stadia and the circumference of the earth in Ptolemy, see J. Lennart Berggren and Alexander Jones *Ptolemy's* Geography, *an Annotated Translation of the Theoretical Chapters* (Princeton 2000) 21–2.

Cordial greetings. If this letter reaches you in time, I would prefer that you still keep the little money you have, provided this will not cause you any trouble.

Be especially careful that no letters of mine come into the hands of Bebel or Grynaeus.[1] For at the spring fair just past, Bebel somehow or other got his hands on letters of mine, one of which he finally delivered to Thomas More.[2] Letters to the archbishop and to the bishop of Lincoln concerning serious matters were held back.[3] Hieronymus asserts that he did not hand over anything to Bebel.[4] Whether he got them from you or hunted them down in England, I do not know.

Here we have no reliable news about the emperor except that the pope arrived in Bologna with a majestic retinue and received him on the next day in the church of San Petronio for the kissing of the feet.[5] From here he went to the palace. But he has a large troop of soldiers with him. And in Burgundy one troop is said to be still moving in the fields from place to place.

I do not know anything about whether there is to be a council,[6] and if there is, I don't see that it would be of much use. The evangelicals have

* * * * *

2761

1 Erasmus often sent letters to England via Schets, who had an agent in London. In the spring and summer of 1531 Johann Bebel, the Basel printer (Ep 2644 n4), and Simon Grynaeus, professor of Greek at Basel (Epp 2487 n9, 2659 n5), had travelled together to England, entrusted by Erasmus with the delivery of letters and the collection of sums of money owed to him. For reasons that are not clear, Erasmus concluded that they had short-changed him. Both men managed to clear themselves of the charges, but Erasmus remained permanently suspicious of Bebel and was much given to disparaging remarks about him as well as charges of malfeasance. See Epp 2530 n15, 2552 n4, 2763:9–11.

2 None of these letters is extant.

3 William Warham, archbishop of Canterbury, and John Longland, bishop of Lincoln

4 Hieronymus Froben, who often carried letters of Erasmus to the spring and fall book fairs for forwarding

5 Erasmus had received a report of the meeting at Bologna from Viglius Zuichemus (Ep 2753:33–7) but the mention of the church of San Petronio, the patron saint of Bologna, shows that Erasmus is relying on the report of another informant.

6 Ie a general council, much demanded in Germany and elsewhere, but feared and dreaded by the pope; see Ep 2654 n11.

already gathered in some places concerning the restitution.[7] Such matters are the prelude to greater evils. I pray that it will come to a happy ending.

The bishop of Canterbury did not bequeath anything to me.[8] This was caused by the scheme of somebody who usually acts as the intermediary between me and the bishop.[9] He is an evangelical to the point of insanity, and he is a clandestine enemy of mine because I dared to answer Luther. Through him what was owed to me from my pension is being transferred to others.[10] Many who hide under the title of evangelical are actually pagans. May God give all of us a good conscience!

I have already spent more than eight hundred golden florins on my house,[11] and yet I have my mind set on leaving this place. But I don't know where to go. The city council of Besançon has already twice sent me letters inviting me to go there.[12] And recently they even sent me as a gift two barrels of Burgundian wine. I would prefer to go to my native land, but there is much against it.[13] Farewell.

Freiburg, 5 February 1533
Your friend, Erasmus

* * * * *

7 Presumably a reference to Protestant resistance to the demand of the Catholics in Germany that churches and other ecclesiastical properties appropriated by Protestant governments be restored to them. To this end, Catholic estates had launched a large number of suits in the Imperial Supreme Court (*Reichskammergericht*). The principal concession made by the emperor to the Protestants in the Religious Peace of Nürnberg (Ep 2702 n2) had been to suspend the prosecution of those cases pending a religious settlement. This pleased the Protestant estates and secured their support for defence against the Turks, but it did not please the Catholic estates, who were not a party to the peace and did not feel bound by it. They continued to file cases before the Supreme Court, and the Protestant estates continued to offer concerted resistance, usually through the agency of the League of Schmalkalden. Erasmus could have heard reports of any number of meetings at which the matter was discussed.
8 He means 'archbishop' of Canterbury
9 This particular person has not been identified. For Erasmus suspicion of the hostility to him of people in Warham's entourage, see Ep 2776:31–9.
10 For Erasmus' fear of the loss of the income from his English livings following the death of Warham, see Epp 2776:28–39, 2783:6–9. Warham's successor, Thomas Cranmer, in fact maintained the payment of Erasmus' pensions, and in June 1533 made one of the payments out of his own pocket; see Allen Ep 2815:13–18.
11 See Ep 2530 n1.
12 See Epp 2759 n3, 2778, 2785:4–6, and cf Ep 2733:3 with n1.
13 On the reasons for this reluctance to return to Brabant see Epp 2646:1–13, 2762, 2792:3–45, 64–73.

2762 / To Nicolaus Olahus   Freiburg, 7 February 1533

This letter was first published in Ipolyi page 277. The manuscript is page 341
of the Olahus codex in the Hungarian National Archives at Budapest (Ep 2339
introduction). For Nicolaus Olahus, secretary to Mary of Hungary, regent of
the Netherlands, see Ep 2646 introduction. Olahus' answer is Ep 2785.

ERASMUS OF ROTTERDAM SENDS GREETINGS TO SECRETARY
NICOLAUS OLAHUS
I beg that you read this letter alone and do not give the letter carrier anything
confidential except in a sealed letter, so that the Dane will not know anything
about these matters.[1]   5
 There are many reasons for me to leave Germany, even if it should become peaceful. But there are many reasons that keep me from going there.
The principal one, my dear Olahus, is the condition of my body, broken by
age and by labours, so that I can barely stay alive even when I am shut up at
home. My poor body, more porous than a sieve, cannot bear even summer   10
weather. If the court should want to call me away from this quiet, it would
most certainly be the death of me, I know it for certain. If I can do something
useful while staying at home, I would be very willing to do it. I have the very
highest regard for the reverend Excellency of Palermo, but he is a smooth
talker.[2] And if I know enough about the character of that court, once I ar-   15
rived there nothing would be paid me. What I would like most of all for you
to arrange is that a letter written either by the chancellor or in the name of
the queen,[3] recalling me, should be sent here, so that I would have a proper
reason to change my country, without seeming to do so because of some
personal antipathy.[4] And then I would like to have a suitable sum for travel 20
expenses sent to me. I am currently owed ten years of my pension, or even

* * * * *

2762
1 The Dane was Jakob Jespersen; for him and for Erasmus' reasons for distrusting
  him, see Ep 2570 introduction.
2 In July 1532 Jean (II) de Carondelet, bishop of Palermo and president of the privy
  council of the Netherlands, had also written to Erasmus (Ep 2689) concerning his prospective return to the Netherlands. Cf Epp 2784 (from Carondelet),
  2785:86.
3 The imperial chancellor for German and Netherlandish affairs was Nicolas
  Perrenot de Granvelle (d 1550). For more on his role in the discussion of
  Erasmus' return to the Netherlands, see Epp 2784–5.
4 The letter of invitation would come from Carondelet (Ep 2784).

more than that.⁵ It would be no great matter for them to send the pension for
one year. But if you think the treasury officials should not be called upon,
a gift could be sent in the queen's name. When I was asked for a book on
widowhood, I received six letters making the same request; when everything   25
had been supplied, Henckel lost interest.⁶ My move will cost a great deal,
both because of the furnishings and because of my fragile health. But above
all I would want it to be honorific. If a letter cannot be sent by this messenger from Freiburg, send it via Erasmus Schets to Hieronymus Froben at the
spring fair.⁷ Send the gift of the queen (if there is one) by the same messenger.   30
But whatever happens, let me know in time so that I will be able to make my
plans. My mind longs for my native land. I beg you, keep my return from
becoming common knowledge so that my journey may be safe. People employ all manner of tricks. I beg you earnestly to engage in this matter with the
same straightforward honesty that is manifest in your letter.⁸   35

It is rumoured that my servant Lieven has married.⁹ If it is true, I pray
that it may be happy and prosperous. For I have no doubt that he has sought

* * * * *

5 In January 1516 Erasmus had been appointed councillor to Prince Charles, the
   future Charles v, at an annual salary of 200 florins; see Ep 370:18n. Payment of
   this imperial pension, slow and infrequent at best, had ceased altogether when
   Erasmus left Louvain to settle in Basel, and the regent Margaret of Austria
   made its resumption dependent on Erasmus' return to the Netherlands; see Ep
   1380 introduction.
6 For *De vidua christiana*, written in 1529 at the request of Johann Henckel and
   dedicated to Mary of Hungary, who in 1531 would become regent of the
   Netherlands, see Ep 2100 introduction. Henckel (Ep 2783) did not really 'lose
   interest'; he lost his job. Regarded by Charles v as too sympathetic to the
   Lutherans, Henckel was dismissed from Mary's service as court preacher and
   confessor in 1531, when she moved to the Netherlands to become queen regent.
7 Ie the book fair at Frankfurt
8 It is not clear what letter is referred to here. Epp 2693 and 2759 may not yet
   have reached Erasmus (see following note). In an earlier letter (Ep 2607) Olahus
   had argued the case for Erasmus' return to Brabant, but Erasmus had already
   replied to it. At all events, if there was another letter, now lost, it repeated arguments already made before.
9 It is not at all clear why Erasmus speaks here having heard only a rumour of
   the marriage of Lieven Algoet. In Epp 2693 and 2759 Olahus had discussed in
   detail his efforts to prevent the unsuitable match. It may be, as Allen suggests,
   that those two letters had not yet reached Erasmus. In Ep 2707:5–6 Erasmus
   writes, as here, of having heard rumours of the marriage. In Ep 2735:18–20, on
   the other hand, Erasmus is clearly much better informed, reporting that Lieven

out someone worthy of him. If he had persevered in his studies, he would by now have attained some eminence.

I have no time to write more. The letter carrier is pressing. I have not reread it – please forgive me.

Freiburg, 7 February 1533

2763 / To Erasmus Schets   Freiburg, 7 February 1533

> This letter was first published by Allen on the basis of the autograph in the British Library (MS Add 38512 folio 76). It appears to have been written hastily two days after the dispatch of Ep 2761, in order to forward a letter to Thomas More (lines 7–8) that is not extant (Ep 2211 is the last of Erasmus' surviving letters to More).

Cordial greetings. I was not angry because the money was not sent, but I was afraid that something untoward had happened to you. In fact I would like you to keep that money in your possession until I write you to do otherwise.

Johannes de Molendino writes that you said I had come to terms with Barbier.[1] In fact Barbier openly makes fun of me and that Molendino character is conniving with him.[2] They are both Frenchmen and both are theologians.[3]

I ask that you arrange for this letter to be reliably delivered to Thomas More as soon as you can.

I have warned you, and I warn you again, take care that no letter of mine that I am sending to England fall into the hand of Bebel. He is an extraordinary schemer.[4]

Farewell. Freiburg, 7 February 1533

Your friend, Erasmus of Rotterdam

* * * * *

had married 'not happily,' but impetuously and against the advice of friends. So whether or not Olahus' letters had arrived, there is no evident reason why Erasmus should feign ignorance here.

2763
1 Molendino's letter is not extant.
2 Erasmus had come to believe that Johannes de Molendino (Ep 371 introduction) was complicit in Pierre Barbier's alleged plot to deprive him of the income from his living at Courtrai; see Ep 2781:9–14.
3 They were both French-speaking Flemings; cf Epp 2781:12–13, 2799:27–31.
4 Cf Ep 2761 n1.

As for that Benedictine who has enough time on his hands to write two letters to me,[5] I cannot see any better advice for him but to adapt himself   15 to his circumstances and not stir up enmity against himself for my sake. To change your habit nowadays makes you into a Lutheran; nevertheless, the pope would easily grant permission if the young man has been drawn into the net[6] and has enough to live on. Certainly it is not my part to call down hatred on my head as if I were calling someone forth.[7] The best thing he can do   20 is to adapt to necessity. If he cannot do that, let him find others to conduct his business. If he wants to go to Rome himself, he can obtain his wish for eight ducats, or else through some legate.[8] I If were to respond to him, it would stir up a new tragedy both for himself and for me. Once more, farewell.

To the most distinguished gentleman Master Erasmus Schets, mer-   25 chant. At Antwerp

2764 / From Bonifacius Amerbach

> This letter has been redated to c 20 February 1533 and appears as Ep 2766A below.

2765 / From Bonifacius Amerbach   Basel, 13 February 1533

> This letter (= AK Ep 1715) was first published by Allen. The autograph is in the Öffentliche Bibliothek of the University of Basel (MS C VIa 73 206). Erasmus' reply is Ep 2768.

Cordial greetings, most renowned Erasmus. A few months ago a French physician who was about to send a messenger from here to Avignon asked me whether I wanted to send anything there.[1] I entrusted to him your letter to

* * * * *

5 The letters are not extant, and the Benedictine has not been identified. In Ep 2793:12–14 Erasmus says that he has written to him and calls him a 'good young man.'
6 Ie if he is now in a position from which there is no escape
7 Ie calling on someone to leave the convent
8 'It' is presumably permission leave the order. Eight ducats were equivalent to £2 8s 0d groot Flemish, that is, about 70 days' or just under a third of a year's wages of an Antwerp master mason/carpenter (CWE 12 650 Table 3, 691 Table 13).

2765
1 The physician has been identified by Alfred Hartmann as Balthasar Noguerius, colleague of Bonifacius at the University of Basel; see AK Ep 1675 n1.

Sadoleto together with some books that were to be sent at that time according to your instructions.[2] The messenger finally came back, bringing nothing 5
except a copy of a letter from Sadoleto to you. How this happened you will
hear from the man himself. For even though I advised him against it, he
was determined to set out, saying repeatedly that this was a chance to see
Erasmus. There is no reason, my dear Erasmus, for you to pay him anything.[3]
For Sadoleto was more than generous and paid him two crowns[4] on his 10
own for delivering the books, although the books had not been the reason
he had gone there.

In preparing his edition of Cicero, Herwagen wants to know through
my intercession what you think is the most suitable way to divide up such an
outstanding body of work into volumes and print them in a fitting manner. 15
Moreover, he begs you, if you have any notes on it, to share them with him.[5]
I agreed to his request all the more willingly because I was not unaware that
you were born to help and advance students and the works they study, and
that you are especially devoted to such an outstanding author. Please be so
kind, I earnestly beg you, as not to begrudge us a word or two giving us your 20
opinion. Farewell, my most renowned Erasmus.

Basel, the vigil of St Valentine's day, 1533
Cordially yours, Bonifacius Amerbach

2766 / From Haio Cammingha   Leeuwarden, 15 February [1533]

This letter was first published by Allen. The manuscript, possibly autograph, is
in the Archives de la ville de Strasbourg (MS Epist eccl v no 20). The year-date
cannot be earlier than 1532: Cammingha did not deliver Ep 2262 (31 January
1530) until 'almost two years later,' after his return to Friesland from Italy

* * * * *

2 In a letter to Sadoleto of c end of August 1532 (AK Ep 1678) Bonifacius says that,
  following Erasmus' instructions, he is forwarding a letter from Erasmus (not
  extant), together with copies of the *Declarationes* and the translation of Basil's
  De Spiritu Sancto (cf Ep 2706:1–2).
3 The courier, too, was a Frenchman; see Epp 2766A:1–4, 2768:12–20, 2769:1–17.
4 Most likely the French écu de soleil, which was officially valued at 76d groot
  Flemish. Two crowns were therefore equivalent to 12s 8d groot Flemish or sev-
  enteen days' wages of an Antwerp master mason/carpenter at 9.05d per day
  (CWE 12 650 Table 3, 691 Table 13).
5 For Erasmus' response to this request, see Ep 2768:4–11. Herwagen's edition of
  Cicero was published at Basel in 1534. He had been unsuccessful in repeated
  attempts to secure from Erasmus a preface for the edition; see Epp 2775:1–5,
  2788:14–15.

and Louvain; see Ep 2624 (16 March 1532):92–4. Had the letter been written in 1532, Haio would hardly have omitted any mention of his travels and recent homecoming.

For Haio Cammingha of Friesland, who had been a paying guest in Erasmus' household (1529–30) but had departed owing Erasmus money that he was slow to pay back, see Ep 2073. This outlandishly effusive letter is one of Haio's unsuccessful attempts to appease Erasmus. Erasmus evidently wrote no reply, for Haio's last extant letter to him (Ep 2866, dated 2 September 1533) indicates that his only news of Erasmus had come via third parties.

HAIO CAMMINGHA TO THE MOST NOTABLE GENTLEMAN
MASTER DESIDERIUS ERASMUS OF ROTTERDAM, HIS PATRON
AND VENERABLE FATHER, CORDIAL GREETINGS

Cordial greetings. Recently a letter carrier returning to us from Louvain brought me greetings in the words of Goclenius[1] and reported that a cer- 5
tain letter of yours to me had been held up among the couriers. Good lord, what a comfort it was to me to have the memory of an old friend renewed! For that reason, when I declared time and time again how happy I was, the memory of you also caused me to revere your kindness over and over again, since, even after so many and such long intervals, my absence had not yet 10
caused you to forget me. And so at that moment, sustained by that joy, I fed and nourished myself with the thought that the great Erasmus, in the full splendour of his circumstances and the brilliance of his fortune, had not let the memory of his servant Haio fade so far from his thoughts as to preclude greeting him with some little word or two, so to speak. 15

I was flattered and charmed by this idea until another messenger arrived with the sad news that the letter had not been sent to me but to someone else and that Master Erasmus' attitude towards me was not favourable or benevolent but quite the opposite, hostile and alienated. As I kept turning this over in my mind, with many a sigh, continually lamenting my fate and 20
fortune, my mind was struck with such great sadness that I was very close to despair. At the same time I cannot divine who designed this plot to undermine my innocence, striving to turn away your benevolence towards me and

* * * * *

2766
1 Conradus Goclenius (Ep 1209 introduction), professor Latin at the Collegium Trilingue in Louvain

to put in its place a more than Vatinian hatred.² For my part, O teacher and
ever venerable father, just as nothing could have had a higher priority with   25
me than the inviolability of our friendship, so too I never did offend against
the kindness with which you welcomed me on many occasions most loving-
ly, as is your wont. And if I could match your innumerable services and your
extraordinary kindness and benevolence towards me, you would certainly
never say that your Haio had ever failed in his devotion to you. Therefore,   30
this is all I ask of you: that nothing be decided against me without the case
being heard, and that in your kindness you would no more impeach my innocence because of some unfavourable suspicion than you would think it
proper to follow heedlessly some baseless and empty rumours. I never gave
priority or greater importance to anything than to our mutual friendship and   35
I wanted it to be fastened tightly by a kind of everlasting glue, but it has been
weakened by the trickery of I know not whom. Then too, I would have discussed my plans and the reasons for everything at greater length, so that it
would be more apparent that I intended nothing against our mutual friendship, if it were not that in several previous letters I had exculpated myself   40
concerning the occasions and events of my journeys and the late payment
of the money with which you in your kindness assisted me in my poverty.³
     But if I have not yet been restored to your kindness on that account and
on that of those fatal and execrable Ulyssean wanderings (how I wish I had
avoided them as if they were the Sirens rather than crashing so miserably   45
upon the fearsome crags of your anger, with the loss of our friendship),⁴ I
turn from your anger to your immense mercy and supreme clemency, begging and imploring, by the goodness and greatness of God, that in your kindness you be willing to forgive my human weakness and allow your mind to
become oblivious of all my failings, especially since that trip was accidentally   50
and unexpectedly offered to me after I left you and was not willingly sought
by me. Actually I put myself in the hands of some men whom I encountered
as I left and who may have seemed friendly but were really kidnappers; they
completely undermined my intentions and got me to make a different trip in
their company.   55

* * * * *

2 Publius Vatinius was a corrupt and scheming politician so detested by the
  Roman people that his name became proverbial for someone cordially hated;
  see *Adagia* ii ii 94 and Catullus 14.3.
3 For Haio's debt to Erasmus, see Epp 2325 n1, 2364:10–14, 2403:35–41 and 69–71,
  2413:24–8, 2573:66–7, 2587:47–52, 2593:37–41.
4 For Erasmus' disapproval of Haio's journey to Italy in 1530, see Ep 2587:49–52.

Therefore, since, as Hannibal says in Livy, 'it is easier to condemn what is past than to correct it,'[5] I beg you again and again to grant me forgiveness for a fault I confess to. But if, after this, you perceive something in me that you judge to be less than pleasing, feel free to admonish me. For in the end that will make me all the more certain that Cammingha's teacher is looking   60
after him, if he shows him good example and inspires virtues in him. For just as I have always wanted you to approve of me no less than you love me, so too (by Hercules!) I am plunged into deep grief when I notice that others who are not as inclined to be as fond of you as I am are in possession of the love which your kindness was once disposed to bestow on me, not because   65
I envy them their happiness but because I am tormented by a pain which only you can relieve, and which consumes me when I realize I can no longer attain to the level of my former friendship with you. For what else can that Vatinian line mean which I remember some spiteful person, envious of our love, cunningly wrote on the door of the room which you kindly assigned   70
to me in your house at Freiburg: 'All love is vanquished by the succeeding lover,' etc[6] as if a change of place has to mean a change of friendship, and as if it were not more fitting that friends who are apart should be more helpful to one another in times of grave trouble than that those who are together when all is well and peaceful should adulate one another. But certainly, so   75
far as I am concerned, I would not refuse to suffer the most grievous and bitter punishment if I should ever fail in the faith I owe to you, my patron, whether present or absent. Therefore I want that clever artificer, slanderous in this inscription and scornful of his absent friend, to become silent. For in my opinion he gives a quite different and better judgment who said that   80
suppositions about an absent person should be nothing but favourable – a judgment that seems more in accordance with nature and that I find more upright and commendable.[7]

In fact, when I myself am in Friesland I seem to be living right there with you in Freiburg, for those sweet and honeyed words of yours are with   85
me day and night, so much so that there is never a time when I do not feel as if I am in your sacred presence and seem to enjoy within myself that

* * * * *

5 Livy 30.30.7; cf 36.29.9.
6 Ovid *Remedium amoris* 462. Cammingha's citation is not exact. The line is 'Vatinian' in that it expresses intense hatred; cf n2 above.
7 Reference unidentified

consummate eloquence which flows as if from a holy and gushing fountain. Would that it could be granted to me to live there forever, as I never cease to hope will happen. But in the meantime, in my many and manifold thoughts I 90 can enjoy for myself this one consolation: that no one can come after me who has stronger feelings of benevolence towards you than I, and no friendship of kings or princes can surpass your friendship.

Therefore I wish that you be convinced that nothing is more important to me than gratitude, of which, as I hope, I will acquit myself very soon by 95 my promises and my endeavours. But from you, on the other hand, I pray you and beg most earnestly, in the name of our shared affection, that you let me know about your health, for I am no less concerned about your good health than I am about my own. I hear that your Benevolence is going to move elsewhere, but it is uncertain where.[8] If, however, the grandeur of our 100 country is sufficient to extend to you a reception equal to that of other regions, I would be extremely ready and willing (so help me God!) to grant you free of charge the use and enjoyment of my house (where Doctor Haio now lives) and of my garden for as long as you want to reside there.[9] I only hope against hope that you would accept this plan and that it would suit your pur- 105 poses. For because of the huge debt I owe you and your exceptional kindness to me, I confess that there is nothing I do not owe you – something I trumpet forth to everyone, as indeed I should, and proclaim it like a herald to all and sundry. Thus I want everyone to believe that there is nothing so arduous that Haio is not bound to undertake and execute most willingly, to the utmost of 110 his power, for his patron Desiderius Erasmus. And in the meantime, may God preserve your Excellency and keep him safe for us and for the Christian commonwealth, together with all who are most dear to him, for as long as possible. Please forgive my stammering.

From Leeuwarden, 15 February 115

Yours willy-nilly, Haio Cammingha of Friesland, friend and most obedient slave

2766A / From Bonifacius Amerbach   [Basel, c 20 February 1533]

This letter (= AK Ep 1716) was first published by Allen. The autograph rough draft is in the Öffentliche Bibliothek of the University of Basel (MS C VIa 54 230). Allen, who saw the letter as an earlier version of Ep 2765, assigned the date 'c 13

* * * * *

8 For Erasmus' indecision about where to move, Brabant or Besançon (or neither), see Ep 2759.
9 This offer is repeated in Allen Ep 2866:39–41.

February 1533' and published it as Ep 2764. But the numerous references in the
past tense to Ep 2765, the content of which is summarized here, indicate clearly
that this is the later of the two documents. For that reason the AK editor, Alfred
Hartmann, redated the letter to 'c 20 February 1533,' and (like Gerlo) we have
renumbered the letter accordingly. Erasmus' answer to both letters is Ep 2768.
(For another example of Bonifacius summarizing the content of one letter in a
later letter, see Epp 2740, 2744.)

Cordial greetings. When a certain Frenchman recently set out to go there, not
wishing to entrust to me the copy of Sadoleto's letter to you, I warned you
not to pay him anything – and I think that is what you did, for he did not
come back to us.[1]

   I added further that Herwagen now has in hand some volumes of   5
Cicero and wants to know what you think would be the most convenient
way to divide the volumes and print them according to their importance. I
could be induced to do this all the more easily because I was not unaware
of the very high value you placed on this extraordinary author and on such
studies. But since you have not yet replied, and that same Herwagen, who is   10
clearly a great admirer of yours, has plucked my ear,[2] I earnestly beg you, if
it is not too much trouble, not to refuse to send us a word or two giving your
opinion. Farewell.

2767 / From Viglius Zuichemus   Padua, 22 February 1533

This is Viglius' reply to Ep 2736. It was first published in Van Heussen 113.
Allen also consulted two manuscript copies in the Royal Library at Brussels (MS
II 1040¹ folio 55 and MS 6919 page 112).

When I returned from Bologna on 8 February,[1] my most learned friend
Erasmus, I received the letter you sent on 5 November,[2] which I had looked

* * * * *

2766A
1 Cf Epp 2765:1–12, 2768:12–20, 2769:1–17.
2 '"To pluck by the ear" was used by the Ancients in the sense of "to remind"'
  (*Adagia* I vii 40).

2767
1 Allen cites a letter to Konrad Heresbach (MS II 1040¹ folio 54 in the Royal Library
  at Brussels) in which Viglius relates his visit to Bologna, where he witnessed the
  gathering of the dignitaries for the meeting of the emperor and the pope (cf
  Ep 2753 n13).
2 Ep 2736

forward to for a long time and therefore rejoiced when my wish was ful-
filled; and I was also greatly pleased that you received that bundle of letters in which I had included the letter of Bembo and those of many others. 5
Many thanks for the letters you wrote to those two young favourites of mine,
whom I had recommended to you;[3] they will also send their thanks.[4] When I
wrote this they were both in Venice, and therefore I beg you to forgive their
tardiness. Florens is an enthusiastic adherent of your cause, and I hope he
will be able to get something done.[5] The new president at Mechelen, Briaerde 10
by name,[6] is related to him and is himself the son-in-law of Micault,[7] who, as
you know, is a financial magnate there, and I think Queen Mary will be more
favourable to you than Margaret was.[8] Whatever happens, it will do no harm
to have tried.

I have already told you what came of your recommendation of me to 15
Bembo,[9] but I am afraid that your letter to me in the *Palaeonaeoi* may have
somewhat offended that father and patron of the Ciceronians,[10] though I
have not yet seen any sign of it. And there is no reason why I should prefer
his benevolence or that of anyone else to your splendid services to me, by
which you strive to recommend me to men of learning. But here I am always 20
pursuing something greater, by which I can assist and advance the pursuits
that we have in common, so that I cannot afford to neglect anyone who can
be of great help in accomplishing that. And so this profession in Italy which,
as you know, is mostly advanced by the currying of favour, requires not only
that I retain but also that I acquire friends here. And I am forced to play the 25
fool here for several months. Then I intend to say goodbye to Italy, which my
friends also urge me to do. Among them I have one in particular who offers
me support, namely Matthias Held, who holds the office of chancellor at the

* * * * *

3 Doubtless the letters, no longer extant, to Florens van Griboval and Johann
  Georg Hörmann that Viglius had asked Erasmus to write; see Ep 2716:150–97.
4 No letters from either survive.
5 Florens van Griboval, who had volunteered to urge his influential father to
  secure the restoration of Erasmus' imperial pension; see Ep 2716 n39, and cf Ep
  2791:39–41.
6 Lambert de Briaerde, president of the grand council of Mechelen; see Ep
  2571 n4.
7 Jean Micault, until 1531 receiver-general of the Netherlands; see Ep 2571 nn5, 8
8 Ie with respect to the payment of his imperial pension
9 See Ep 2716:100–17.
10 Ep 2604

imperial court.[11] And recently he gave me good reason to hope for a splendid appointment in the imperial chamber;[12] and he can fulfil that hope if he   30
actually makes the effort to match the favour he shows me.[13] He is extremely
learned and has a high opinion of our learning and all our scholars and of
you who are the patron of both, which you will discover if the occasion pres-
ents itself. And have no doubt that, if you should happen to want something
at that court, you will easily obtain it with his help. For he has great influ-   35
ence, and he wants the very best for Erasmus, and he also thought more of
me because he understood that this would not be at all displeasing to you.

I cannot tell you very much with any certainty about the meeting
at Bologna. For everything between the pope and the emperor is enacted
and carried out in private and secret conversations. But there is a persis-   40
tent rumour that they have concluded a treaty among the Italian princes.[14]
When I was at Bologna, three dukes were there, those of Milan, Savoy, and
Florence,[15] the latter chosen to be the son-in-law of the emperor to gratify the
pope.[16] There was also a great crowd of cardinals there, two of whom had

* * * * *

11 Nothing is known of the early life of Matthias Held (d 1563) of Arlon in
   Luxembourg. In 1527 he became an assessor at the *Reichskammergericht* in
   Speyer, and in 1530 he joined the court of Charles v, becoming vice-chancellor
   in 1531. Always a vehement opponent of the reformers, he never approved of
   the strategic concessions to the Protestants undertaken by the imperial court in
   the 1530s. This led to his fall from favour and his dismissal from the office of
   vice-chancellor in 1541. For the rest of his life he lived in retirement at Cologne.
   There is no record of any personal contact with Erasmus, but Held was a steadfast friend of Viglius.
12 Ie in the *Reichskammergericht*
13 In 1535 Held bestowed on Viglius the office of assessor at the *Reichskammergericht*.
14 From mid-December 1532 until early March 1533, Clement vii and Charles v
   held a conference in Bologna at which they conducted difficult negotiations on
   a variety of subjects; see Pastor 10 213–23. On 24 February 1533 the pope and
   the emperor signed a secret treaty in which they made promises to cooperate
   in the holding of a church council, to collaborate in defence against the Turks,
   to maintain the existing state of things in Italy, and to try the English divorce
   case in Rome. Three days later Clement vii, Charles v, and the dukes of Milan,
   Mantua, and Ferrara, with the cities of Siena, Lucca, and Genoa, agreed on the
   contributions they would make in the event of any attack on Italy. See Pastor
   10 218–19.
15 Cf Pastor 10 216, who reports that the dukes of Milan, Mantua, and Florence
   arrived in the emperor's suite.
16 See Ep 2753 n15.

recently arrived from France;[17] the common gossip was that they had some 45
proud and wicked design. I was also present when, at a public session of the
cardinals presided over by the pope, an embassy was heard from the king of
Ethiopia, whom they call Prester John. It announced his new reverence and
devotion to the Holy See. It requested from the Holy See that he be received
in obedience as a son and king of the Roman church, and many other things I 50
do not want to enumerate.[18] Nor is there any need to do so, since most people
think this was a device of the pope to claim greater veneration for himself
among the others. And a suitable time was chosen for this play-acting, for a
little before that the cardinal of Trent had been led into the public assembly
in a solemn procession,[19] accompanied by a large German retinue, who they 55
think can still be taken in by such trickery and sleight of hand. The emperor
is getting ready to leave for Spain and is said to be expected by the empress
at Barcelona.[20] Now you know the story of the court. I informed you recently
about the *Life of Cyprian* and the books of Ambrose that Crisostomo has in his
possession,[21] and from your silence I pretty well understand what you think. 60
Farewell, my incomparable patron.

Padua, 22 February 1533

2768 / To Bonifacius Amerbach   [Freiburg, c end of February 1533]

This letter (= AK Ep 1720) was first published in the *Epistolae familiares*. The autograph is in the Öffentliche Bibliothek of the University of Basel (MS AN III 15
44). The year-date is indicated by the close connection to Epp 2765 and 2766A,
to both of which this is Erasmus' reply. The month-date is indicated by the final
sentence of the letter.

Cordial greetings. I congratulate Cicero, who will come to light under your
auspices. But be careful to avoid not being able to extricate yourself from that
wearisome treadmill, once you have involved yourself in it.

* * * * *

17 See Ep 2753:34–7.
18 On 29 January 1533 at Bologna, Pope Clement VII received in open consistory
   a delegation from David, King of Ethiopia, 'commonly called Prester John.'
   The delegation brought letters, gifts, and solemn professions of obedience to
   the pope. See Pastor 10 367 with n3.
19 The cardinal of Trent was Bernhard von Cles (Ep 2651).
20 Empress Isabella. Charles had embarked at Genoa on 9 April 1533 and on
   11 May was in Barcelona; see Ep 2753 n16.
21 See Ep 2716:132–5.

There is no difficulty about the division: the first is theory;[1] the second, the works themselves, that is the orations; the third, the letters; the fourth,   5 philosophy.

In the edition of Cratander I saw some additions from Budé's citations and from my own.[2] Aldus made many mistakes. I pointed out one in particular in the saying 'a saddle for the ox.'[3] In the adages that I have now added to the *Chiliads* I have cited many passages from Cicero.[4] If anything perchance   10 occurs to me I will let you know.

When I asked that Frenchman of yours (a very unreliable fellow) how much he had been given by Sadoleto,[5] he said he had received four *capita*, that is, one crown,[6] but to Quirinus he had said two.[7] The Frenchman showed me the copy of Sadoleto's letter. He said that the letter itself had been taken   15 from him by someone who had captured and tortured him merely because it was suspected that he was a Lutheran. But he had nevertheless been released at the request of Farel.[8] When I had sniffed out his character, I gave him a drink and eight plappards.[9] What a waste! you say. No, it was well spent to get rid of such a charlatan so cheaply. The world is full of such vagabonds.[10]   20

This weather is hard on me. Take care to keep you and yours in good health. For March is at hand.[11]

* * * * *

2768
1 Ie the works on rhetoric
2 The 1528 edition of Andreas Cratander, published at Basel
3 *Adagia* II ix 84 (the correction of Aldus' mistake is found at CWE 34 122–3)
4 In the new edition of the *Adagiorum chiliades* (March 1533) that was currently being printed; see Ep 2735 n10, and on the title see Ep 2720 n11.
5 Cf Epp 2765:1–12, 2766A:1–4, 2769:1–17.
6 The crown was probably a French écu au soleil, which was officially valued at 76d groot Flemish and therefore equivalent to about eight days' wages of an Antwerp master mason/carpenter at 9.05d per day (CWE 12 650 Table 3, 691 Table 13). The term *capita* is unknown to us.
7 Quirinus Hagius (Ep 2704 n6)
8 Guillaume Farel (Ep 1341A n305) had settled at Geneva in 1532.
9 The plappard was a Swiss coin valued at twenty-five to the Rhenish florin (Gerlo 10:208 n5). Eight plappards were therefore equivalent to 19d groot Flemish or just over two days' wages of an Antwerp master mason/carpenter at 9.05d per day (CWE 12 650 Table 3, 691 Table 13). Cf Ep 1543 n2.
10 Literally 'planets' or 'wandering stars' (*planetae*)
11 March 1533 appears to have been an unusually cold and blustery month at Freiburg. Erasmus repeatedly refers to this, blaming it for his bout of poor health; see Epp 2770:1–6, 2776:62–5, 2780:79–80, 2782:6–10, 2783:16–23, 2788:1–6, and Allen Epp 2818:1–14, 2827:3–6, 2858:1–6.

Erasmus of Rotterdam, in his own hand

To Master Bonifacius Amerbach, the most learned gentleman to be
found anywhere. At Basel   25

2769 / From Bonifacius Amerbach   [Basel, February 1533]

> First published by Allen, this letter (AK Ep 1721) is Bonifacius' answer to Ep
> 2768. The autograph, with the end torn away leaving only the last words of
> three lines still showing, is in the Öffentliche Bibliothek of the University of
> Basel (MS C VIa 54 230 verso). The words in square brackets are Allen's filling-in
> of the gaps in the text.

Cordial greetings. I already advised you before, most renowned Erasmus,
not to pay anything to that money-grubbing Frenchman, to whom Sadoleto
had already paid two crowns for the books delivered to him, to say nothing
of myself.[1] But as I learn from your letter,[2] you too wanted to pour something
into the leaky barrel – a sign of your extraordinary generosity. Otherwise,   5
when you had received the copy of the letter,[3] he should rightly have been
dismissed with a thrashing. You will say, 'What do you have to do with such
people?' Nothing, indeed. A French physician living here had let it be known
a few months ago that he was sending a messenger to Avignon. When he
asked whether I had anything to send there, I entrusted to him a letter and   10
some books, not knowing whom he had hired until afterwards, when the
vagabond returned here. Though he had been paid two crowns by Sadoleto,
I saw at our first meeting that he was not satisfied and hoped for more. I had
pledged in good faith that I would send there the copy of the letter brought to
me. But I am telling a tale to deaf ears. I thought I should yield to the wishes   15
of someone who said that this was an opportunity to see Erasmus and that I
should humour him.

I am most [grateful] to you for [so kindly telling me] how the works
of Cicero [should be arranged].[4] But that you should congratulate him [for

* * * * *

2769
1 On the story told here, cf Epp 2765:1–12, 2766A:1–4 with n1, 2768:12–20.
2 Ep 2768
3 Ie the copy of the letter from Sadoleto (Ep 2766A:2)
4 Ep 2768:4–6

coming to light under our auspices][5] is nothing more than [to speak], as the   20
Greeks say, 'in a broad sense.'[6]

2770 / To Bonifacius Amerbach   [Freiburg], 28 February 1533

This letter (= AK Ep 1752) was first published in the *Epistolae familiares*. The
autograph is in the Öffentliche Bibliothek of the University of Basel (MS AN III
15 45).

Greetings. Although I was in reasonably good health all winter, March has
sent forth its advance forces and afflicted my left foot with such sharp and
constant pain that I can neither sleep nor eat.[1] I have experienced this ailment
once or twice before, but it went away after three days and didn't extend
above the foot. But now it has seized my whole lower leg.[2] I have summoned   5
the physician, but these days he was never at home.[3]

Viglius has written something to me about Cicero, but no doubt he has
written the same to you.[4] He is a most unaffected young man.

Anselmus writes a great deal,[5] though he doesn't know what it means
to write. He calls you 'brother,' this pedagogue, just as if he were a bishop or   10
a cardinal.

He fills all his letters with promises, as if I were sitting here waiting for
Polish gifts. To remind someone of what has been given is a kind of reproach,

* * * * *

5 Ep 2768:1–2
6 Ie to say something a bit more than can be proved; see *Adagia* IV vii 75 (quoting
   Digest 22.3.28).

2770
1 See Ep 2768 n11.
2 The text reads *tibiam in feriorem*, which means nothing. Allen corrected it to *in
   fervore* (in fever). Like Gerlo, we follow the sensible AK correction to *inferiorem*
   (lower).
3 This bout of ill health continued throughout the spring and summer of 1533;
   see Ep 2768 n11.
4 At the same time that he wrote Ep 2753:10–18 to Erasmus, Viglius wrote AK Ep
   1704:6–20 to Bonifacius. Both address the possibility of a new edition of Cicero
   at Venice.
5 Although several letters of Anselmus Ephorinus (Ep 2539 introduction) to
   Bonifacius from this period are extant (Basel MS G II 16 281, 285, 288–9), all
   letters from him to Erasmus between February 1532 and August 1535 are lost.

but to make promises so often is to make reproaches for what has not been
given.[6] But more of this another time.   15

 Farewell. The day before the first of March

 Erasmus of Rotterdam

 To the eminent gentleman Master Bonifacius Amerbach. At Basel

2771 / To Jan of Heemstede   Freiburg, 28 February 1533

This is the preface to *Pia brevis ac dilucida in omnes Psalmos explanatio sanctissimi
viri D. Haymonis* (Freiburg: Johann Faber Emmeus 1533). There is little reliable
biographical information about Haymo (or Haimo, d 853), the monk at Fulda
and abbot at Heresfeld who in 840 became bishop of Halberstadt. In his youth
he had been a friend of Rabanus Maurus (780–856) and his fellow student at
Tours of Alcuin of York. Rabanus' *De rerum natura* was dedicated to Haymo.
Most of the works formerly attributed to Haymo on the authority of the biogra-
phy by Johannes Trithemius (1462–1516), abbot of Sponheim, are now deemed
to have been written by others. The psalm commentary under discussion here
is an anonymous work of the twelfth century. See Gerhard Baader 'Haimo'
Neue Deutsche Biographie 7 (1966) 522–3.

 There is nothing to indicate whether Erasmus undertook to publish this
work on his own initiative or merely provided an introduction at the request of
someone else, perhaps the dedicatee or the publisher. What is clear, however,
is that he seized the opportunity to describe monasticism as it should be and
to castigate the vices of those who had brought the name monk into disrepute.

 For Jan of Heemstede, Carthusian of Louvain, see Ep 1646 introduction.

DESIDERIUS ERASMUS OF ROTTERDAM TO JAN OF HEEMSTEDE,
A GENTLEMAN OF EXTRAORDINARY PIETY, CARTHUSIAN
AT LOUVAIN, CORDIAL GREETINGS

Athough I am not unaware, dearest brother, that you have people to talk to
who enliven your solitude and do not allow that silence to be mute, I am 5
pleased to provide you with another interlocutor who speaks more piously
than eloquently, although I do not see how one can deny that what is spoken
piously is spoken eloquently. This is the monk Haymo, abbot and bishop,
briefly explaining the psalms of David with wonderful simplicity and clarity. For some centuries, it was the aim of learned monks to make summaries 10
of what the ancients had written (with more subtlety when they wrote for

* * * * *

6 Seneca *De beneficiis* 2.15.2 and 2.11.1

learned readers or more diffusely for a broader audience) and to make the compendiums brief and clear, so that they could be easily understood by those who were busy or were very not very literate. Leading figures in this group are Anselm, Bede, Claudius,[1] and this man whom you will now wel-   15
come into your midst, Haymo. The industry of these writers was of no little use to the church, especially if we consider both the times and the places in which they lived. It is fitting that those who, rejecting all delays, hasten to that heavenly life should be as unhindered as possible and not weighed down by unnecessary baggage. Hence it is all the more surprising that some people   20
who profess apostolic simplicity in their discipline and way of life embrace teachings that are far from simple but rather incredibly thorny with superflu-ous subtleties and Averroist dogmas,[2] and, in addition, novel fantasies.

When there were monks like those,[3] the name of monk enjoyed the fa-vour and respect of everyone. Now the bad behaviour of some is the reason   25
why good ones too suffer the vexation of general dislike. Aristippus, when he was greatly pleased by a certain perfume, said 'A curse on those horrible perverts who have discredited such a fine thing.'[4] It would not be inappro-priate to address such an angry indictment at those who through their vices have brought the name of monk into such disgrace, when in fact none should   30
be more praiseworthy. For who would not love men who are truly dead to the world and have dedicated themselves completely to God? Such is their life, such their speech that everyone goes away a better person after seeing them or speaking with them. No one should fear any harm from them: not fraud, since they consider money to be rubbish, and what they do have they   35
distribute to the poor; nor vengeance, since according to the teaching of the gospel they pray for those who persecute them, bestow love on those who

* * * * *

2771
1 Claudius of Turin (fl 810–27), bishop of Turin from 817 until his death
2 Averroes (Ibn Rushd, 1126–98) of Cordoba is best known for his commentaries on Aristotle, which, translated into Latin, exercised great influence on Christian scholars and theologians in the thirteenth century. Among the theologians, however, his views quickly became controversial because of his denial of the universal providence of God as well as of free will and personal immortality. Also controversial was the attachment of his Christian followers to the doctrine known as that of 'the double truth,' ie the idea that things not true accord-ing to Catholic doctrine can still be true according to philosophy. After 1277 Averroism could no longer be taught at the University of Paris, though there was a revival of its influence in the fourteenth century. It survived in Italy, espe-cially at Padua, into the Renaissance.
3 Ie monks like Anselm, Bede, Claudius, and Haymo
4 *Apophthegmata* 3.135 (CWE 37 262)

hate them, repay injuries with good deeds;[5] nor is there any danger to one's chastity from those who are uncorrupted in mind and body, who in their self-effacement do not take precedence over anyone or envy anyone or look 40 down on anyone, but the more they approach the pinnacle of perfection, the more they consider themselves the lowest of all and, though they are in fact the gems and blossoms of the church, call themselves the dregs. The faults of others they mitigate or interpret favourably; of their own they are severe critics. They generously make much of the good deeds of others; they modestly 45 diminish their own. They do not flatter anyone. They do not lavish shameless praise on someone to his face; they do not disparage anyone behind his back. You hear nothing from their mouths that is not in their hearts: words of charity, words of consolation, words of friendly admonition and gratitude. Their friendliness is not feigned but proceeds from a good conscience. In sum, they 50 present us with an image, as it were, of that heavenly city, and in a way they bring before us the choirs of angels, either because they continually sing the praises of God, or because, transformed into spirits, they have no commerce with affections of the flesh, or because they live in perfect harmony, or because, like the angels, they are like intermediaries between mankind 55 and God, and they present the prayers of the people to him and obtain many benefits from him by their constant prayers, not for themselves alone but for the community as a whole.

Furthermore, what if the gift of prophecy is added to these virtues, so that they teach the people gratuitously, purely, honestly, whether by preach- 60 ing or by writing books or by both? What if by fasts, vigils, and works they crucify their flesh and make up, in so far as that is permitted, for what is lacking to the sufferings of Christ,[6] and in some fashion immolate themselves for the salvation of the people? And can you, O layman, bear ill will towards those who watch and pray for you while you snore loudly in your 65 drunken stupor? those who make vigil and fast for you while you provoke God's wrath with your gambling, whoring, and other sins? those who speak to God on your behalf while you spread among men slanders against them? Who would not venerate such men as demigods, would not love them as if given by God for the common good, even if he himself is a depraved sinner? 70 For even their enemies are carried away with admiration, and those who do not deserve well of anyone revere with a kind of natural instinct those who do good to the bad as well as the good. Therefore how perverse it is for some

* * * * *

5 Matt 5:44
6 Cf Col 1:24.

people to scorn anyone just because he is a monk. The word 'monk' denotes
the very highest reaches of heroic virtue, which earns good will and favour   75
from the good and extracts it from the bad. But if they are displeased only by
the word, let them use the word 'simple' or 'solitary' if they want.[7] But their
solitude is to be judged not by the number of those living together but by
their isolation from evil passions; otherwise even the Carthusians are not
solitary.[8] Wherever we find such solitude there is the closest fellowship. He is   80
happy to be alone who is not corrupted by living with someone wicked and
whose mind is free of the tumults of passions that conflict with one another
but yet do not agree with God. In this way a man can be a monk in the courts
of princes and in city governments and in the midst of the affairs of men.
What perversity of mind it is to hate a monk for the very reason that he is   85
a monk! You claim you are a Christian and you shun those who are most
like Christ!

   At this point I know there are those who immediately chant the refrain
that there are many monks far removed from this portrait. We will never approve of any mode of living if because of the bad we also hate the good. And   90
so what is left for us? What else but to love them, to interpret ambiguous
matters in the best light, to overlook small faults, to seek to improve serious
ones rather than to aggravate them, and also to venerate the order itself and
its rule of life? But if monks were to devote themselves with all their heart to
what constitutes true religion and conform themselves to the civility of or-   95
dinary men, the former good opinion of the world would easily be restored,
the mouths of slanderers would easily be stopped. And so the result would
be that their lives will be pleasing not only to God and agreeable to men, but
also happy and cheerful here in this world. No one lives more calmly and
agreeably than those who are truly monks; none more miserably than those   100
who are not monks in their hearts. To the one the monastery is paradise; to
the other, a treadmill. But everyone has the power, to a great extent, of chang-
ing a treadmill into a paradise.

   I return to Haymo, who plucks the harp of David and inspires your
angelic assembly to become spiritual choirs so that you may sing hymns and   105
canticles to God in your hearts.[9] No one should despise the simplicity of his

* * * * *

7 The root meaning of 'monk' (*monachus*) is 'one who lives alone.'
8 The Carthusians were a strictly contemplative order, the members of which
   took a vow of silence, lived in their own cells, and saw their brethren only
   during the recitation of the office, at mass, and during meals on feast days.
9 Eph 5:19, Col 3:16

language but rather should embrace the piety of his sentiments. I give this warning especially because I suspect that many are as I once was, full of loathing for anything that lacks the condiments and ornaments of the rhetoricians. For when I was a child in Christ my tastes were those of a child, but I hope 110 that now I have altogether put away the things of a child.[10] If this friendly office of mine deserves any gratitude from you, I beg you to commend this sinner to Christ sometimes in your prayers. The copy was furnished by the venerable monastery of canons regular called, in the vernacular, Marbach in Alsace – from what was left after the ill-fated uprising of the peasants.[11] May 115 the Lord requite their evil with good. Farewell.

Freiburg im Breisgau, 28 February in the year 1533 after the birth of Christ

2772 / To Thomas Boleyn   Freiburg, [c March] 1533

> This is the preface to the *Explanatio symboli apostolorum sive catechismus* (Basel: Froben, March 1533). A catechetical exposition of the Apostles' Creed (with some thoughts about the Ten Commandments and the Lord's Prayer thrown in at the end), the *Explanatio* is a expansion of ideas first adumbrated briefly in the colloquy *Inquisitio de fide* 'An Inquiry Concerning the Faith' (1524). On first publication, the catechism was received enthusiastically, Erasmus noting with satisfaction that it sold out in three hours at the Frankfurt book fair. But despite eight printings in the next two years and almost immediate translation into English, it never achieved the diffusion or influence of the catechisms of Luther, the Jesuit Petrus Canisius, and others, doubtless because it did not appeal to ardent partisans in the religious controversies of the day. Meanwhile Luther, in his *Epistola de Erasmo Roterodamo* (March 1534), cited the *Explanatio* extensively in his attempt to demonstrate that Erasmus had no religion at all. Erasmus responded with his *Purgatio adversus epistolam non sobriam Martini Lutheri* (April 1534), the final instalment in the public controversy between him and Luther. See CWE 70 xx–xxii; CWE 78 396, 400.
>
> For Thomas Boleyn, see Ep 2232 introduction. His response to this dedication is Ep 2824.
>
> A translation of this letter by Louis A. Perraud has already appeared in CWE 70 235. This new translation is by Charles Fantazzi.

* * * * *

10 1 Cor 13:11
11 Founded c 1090, the monastery of the canons regular of St Augustine at Marbach, southwest of Colmar in Alsace, was damaged during the Peasants' Revolt of 1524–5.

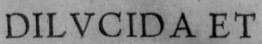

DILVCIDA ET

PIA EXPLANATIO SYMBOLI QVOD APO
ſtolorum dicitur, decalogi preceptorum, & domini‑
cæ precationis, per DES. ERASMVM
ROT. opus nunc primum, &
conditum & æditum.

FRO BEN.

BASILEAE EX OFFICINA FROBENIANA
ANNO M. D. XXXIII
Cum gratia & priuilegio Cæſareo ad ſex annos.

Explanatio symboli apostolorum sive catechismus title-page
(Basel: Froben, March 1533)
Austrian National Library

ERASMUS OF ROTTERDAM TO THE MOST RENOWNED THOMAS
OF ROCHFORD, EARL OF ORMOND AND OF WILTSHIRE, GREETING

Illustrious earl, I saw that a charge of impropriety would be laid against me
by some people if I wrote something on the Apostles' Creed in the wake of so
many distinguished Doctors of the church, of whom Cyprian was the first of   5
the Latin Fathers to treat this theme in such a way that no one so far has been
able to equal him.[1] On the other hand, I would seem guilty of impropriety
in my own eyes if I did not comply with your wishes, especially when you
ask for something so pious with such pious intention, and above all since
you have so kindly regarded that earlier work of mine, in which I explained   10
Psalm 22, which was more an act of homage than a duty.[2] Nor is it a secret to
me that you, who do not need me as a teacher, ask for this little work of mine
for others who are less well educated. Accordingly, I have treated the subject
in such a way as to accommodate the entire discourse to the comprehension
of more simple minds. I do not at all see what praise I shall gain from my   15
endeavour, unless perhaps it is that some points are explained more simply
and more fully. Indeed, I have no regard for praise, but wish that the recruits
in the Christian army may derive as much benefit from it as you, renowned
sir, in your notable piety desire and as I with my modest talent have been
able to impart. Meanwhile, we must pray God that in his goodness he supply   20
what is wanting in my strength; may he who inspired you with this devout
sentiment deign to crown it with happy success, not only in this enterprise,
but also in everything that you undertake in your zeal for piety.

    At Freiburg im Breisgau, in the year of our Lord 1533

                                                                                 25

2773 / To All Men of Letters   [Freiburg, c March 1533]

> This is the preface to the new, eighth edition of the *Adagia* (Basel: Froben, March
> 1533), which included 488 new adages (see Ep 2726 introduction). Much of the
> preface is devoted to Erasmus' consistent but inaccurate denial that the un-
> named Polidoro Virgilio's *Proverbiorum libellus* (1498) had been published be-
> fore his *Adagia collectanea* (1500). For a summary of the complicated history of
> the dispute over priority see CEBR III 398–9.

        * * * * *

2772
1 The commentary on the Apostle's Creed attributed to Cyprian (d 258) was in
  fact the work of Rufinus of Aquilea (c 345–410).
2 The commentary on Psalm 22 that Erasmus wrote at Boleyn's request in 1530;
  see Ep 2232.

DESIDERIUS ERASMUS OF ROTTERDAM TO ALL MEN OF LETTERS,
CORDIAL GREETINGS

If, according to the old proverb, 'in all matters a proper limit is best,'[1] then it
is right to apply a proper limit to the collection of proverbs; for in excellent
things also, if there is less abundance, there is surely a proper limit.[2] And so   5
for many reasons I had decided from now on to take a holiday from this sort
of pursuit: either because the nature of the subject has no bounds, so that it
is pointless for anyone to pursue it in an effort to omit nothing at all (especially as ancient authors formerly unknown come to light); or because this
business requires such an expenditure of effort that I would imagine a reader   10
would be more likely to be wearied with the abundance and cry out 'Oh,
that's enough!'[3] than that he would desire any increase; or because my age
and mind, surely no longer the same, recoiling from this kind of literature,
are carried away towards things in which it is not unbecoming or useless
to spend one's time;[4] or because I thought that the flowers and gems with   15
which learned writers were accustomed to adorn their works would have
more charm if one gathered them for oneself from authors who are not readily available to everyone instead of taking them from worn out collections of
this sort. Nevertheless, this consideration did not prevent many serious and
learned men among the Greeks from writing collections of proverbs.   20

I was also won over by the argument from utility, since I saw that this
labour would contribute a great deal both to correcting errors in the texts
of ancient authors and also to removing rough spots that have often held
up those who are only moderately literate. Likewise, to tell the truth, I have
added this substantial final flourish more in compliance with the demands   25
of the printers than from my own initiative. For the Pyladean friendship
that once existed with that best of men, Johann Froben, and is now shared
with Hieronymus Froben, a son very much like his father,[5] together with the

* * * * *

2773
1 See *Adagia* I vi 96, which cites many versions of the idea 'nothing to excess.'
  The one quoted here is attributed to Hesiod *Works and Days* 674 (though in CWE
  32 64 *modus* is translated as 'due time' rather than 'proper limit').
2 Although the language here (*si minus satietas, certe modus quidam*) is difficult, the
  intended meaning is the commonplace thought that too much of a good thing
  is to be avoided through the observance of reasonable limits.
3 Martial 4.91
4 Cf Horace *Epistles* 1.1.1–13.
5 The name of Pylades, friend and inseparable companion of Orestes, was proverbial for intimate and unshakable friendship. For the phrase 'Pyladean
  friendship' see Cicero *De finibus* 2.26.84.

marvellous industry that each of them displayed in furthering the best kind of learning, has such an effect on me that when at times I wanted to deny them 30 certain things, and perhaps should have done so, I simply could not do it.

I hope, however, that this part of the work will bring students as much utility as it brought me little pleasure. But then, even if there were no such justifications, it seemed rather discourteous and ungenerous to leave nothing to be done by other scholars girt and ready to undertake the same sub- 35 ject matter, for with their vigorous spirit or youthful energy or more copious reading they can bring a richer harvest to such studies. I am so far from being inclined to stand in the way of their efforts that I would be utterly delighted if someone should throw my work into the shade. But I would only like the reader to remember a caution I mentioned long ago, not to be 40 surprised if some things occur in this work that were written at different times. This comes about because of the frequent editions and new supplements.[6] For I issued the first foretaste of this subject matter in Paris, printed by Johannes Phillipi, of the German nation, who had his workshop under the sign of the Trinity in the rue Saint-Marcel, in the year 1500. The printer 45 did not give the month, but the preface by Fausto Andrelini has 15 June of the same year. Somewhat later Josse Bade duplicated this edition; and then Matthias Schürer did the same at Strasbourg. After these I published the work, by then augmented to the size of a large volume, at Venice, with the printer Aldo Manuzio, in the year 1508. At Basel Johannes Froben, with- 50 out my knowledge, duplicated the Aldine edition; he reprinted it more than seven times, never without some additions.

However, because this literary genre consists in the labour of choosing excerpts from here and there, not much praise was awarded to the first among the Latins to gather proverbs, except that some credit is earned by 55 skilful display of discernment and critical acumen. If someone brings forward an edition earlier than the one I have shown to be the first, I would be quite willing to praise him as the first to whom it occurred to undertake this not illiberal task before it did to any others. And indeed it is surprising that so many renowned Greek writers expertly treated this genre, whereas 60 among the Latins, even among the flock of grammarians, there was no one who undertook a similar enterprise, even though, in my opinion, just as many flowers of this sort blossomed in the gardens of the Latins as in those of the Greeks. But I do not know how admiration and partiality towards the Greeks seemingly caused the Latins to neglect their own writers. In any 65

* * * * *

6 See the introductions to Epp 126, 211, 269, 1204, 1659, 2022–3.

event, I do not see why Virgil should be considered inferior to Homer or Hesiod, or Seneca, whoever he was,[7] to Euripides, or Plautus and Horace to Aristophanes – for Cicero, as far as this is concerned, is far superior to Demosthenes. Therefore whoever was the first to embark on this enterprise among the Latins undertook a task that was neither illiberal nor unreward- 70 ing. Two years had already passed after I had given a first sample of this un- dertaking at Paris when, while I was living at Louvain, I became aware of a small book professing to contain adages,[8] perhaps from Jérôme de Busleyden, who had recently returned from Italy. In it I found about seventy proverbs, collected from Latin commentaries, particularly that of Filippo Beroaldo.[9] I 75 compared the year and the day: the year was the same but my edition was three months earlier.[10] And it was sufficiently clear that neither of us knew of the other's work but that the same idea had occurred to both of us. And so, if it is of any importance which of us was the first to try to do it, each of us was the first if 'the first' means someone who was not following anyone 80 else (I am speaking only about the Latins). But if someone is said to have en- riched proverbs if he published more of them, then I clearly enriched them, since in my very first edition I gave more than eight hundred, the greater part of which I drew from the Greek fragments of Diogenianus.[11] But after I had published so many *Chiliads*,[12] it required little effort for anyone to make 85 an addition to his collection, which he could claim to have drawn from good authors, and he would not be lying. For I drew all the *Chiliads* from all of the best authors, carefully naming (as was proper) each author and what I had drawn from each of them, so carefully in fact that I did not defraud

* * * * *

7 Ie whoever the author was of the collection of 149 proverbs attributed to Seneca the Younger that had long circulated under the title *Proverbia Senecae*. Erasmus, who included the collection in his editions of Seneca (1515, 1529), attributed them to Publilius Syrus, the first-century BC author of mimes and aphorisms, 'and others.'

8 Polidoro Virgilio's *Proverbiorum libellus*, first published at Venice by C. de Pensis in April 1498

9 Ie the commentary on *The Golden Ass* of Apuleius (1500)

10 It seems that Erasmus had seen only the third edition of Virgilio's collection (cf preceding note), published on 6 November 1500, almost four months after Erasmus' *Adagia collectanea*; see Ep 126:112–13n.

11 Diogenianus of Heraclea in Pontus, a Greek grammarian of the second century, whose collection of proverbs was first printed in Παροιμίαι Ἑλληνικαί: *Adagia sive Proverbia graecorum ex Zenobio seu Zenodoto, Diogeniano & Suidae collectaneis* ed Andreas Schott, sj (Antwerp: Plantiniana 1612).

12 See Ep 2720 n11.

Apostolius of his due share of praise.[13] So far I was from wanting to deck   90
myself out in the feathers of others.

I would have thought it improper to mention such matters, except that
I saw a serious effort being made by some to pretend that they were the first
to introduce this genre, and by others to make it appear that they have not
borrowed from my *Chiliads* but have acted on their own initiative and tal-   95
ent. But if they collect what they publish from the ancient authors, in whom
there is a huge quantity of proverbs that I have passed over, why is it that
they omit those and gather so many that I have presented and so few that I
have not touched upon? Why do they so rarely cite authors I have not cited?
And if they put out some trifling novelty, do they think they are hiding their   100
thefts by attaching new handles to old jars?[14] If they haven't read my work,
how can they dare to proclaim that they have nothing in common with me?
If they have read my work and think they can conceal it, they should have
done so with care and ingenuity, so that no one would detect their fraud.
As for me, though I appear to be so well versed in good authors that I have   105
no great need to steal from modern collections, nevertheless there is no elementary schoolmaster today, however insignificant, whom I would not be
willing to read if he published a book professing to offer adages, as it is said
that there is no book so bad that you cannot pluck something good out of it.
To refuse to read authors who treat the same subject that you do is shameful   110
arrogance; to pretend not to have read them when you have is even more
shameful ambition; to deny having received any benefit from them is the
most shameful ingratitude.

I have said such things more for their sake than mine. As far as my
opinion is concerned, I want everyone to be perfectly free to print and reprint   115
proverbs, whether they prefer old ones or new ones. If they do this less felicitously than I, they will not harm my reputation, but rather their inferior purple patches make my purple all the more brilliant; if it is more successful, then
I will congratulate our studies in common and myself as well as them. And
I have no doubt that in our times there will be many young people who can   120
outrun me in this race; the palm is available to all, let him grasp it who can.

* * * * *

13 Michael Apostolius (c 1420–post 1474, known as Apostolius Paroemiographus
     (Apostolius the Proverb-writer). His *Paroemiae* (a collection of 2027 proverbs)
     was published by Johann Herwagen at Basel in 1538. Erasmus, who had bor-
     rowed extensively from him, mentions him by name three times in the *Adagia*
     (iii iii 42, 66; iii iv 77), the first two times with derogatory comments on his
     character.
14 Cf *Adagia* i iv 66.

But I have said more about this than I had intended. There is one point on which perhaps I need the reader's indulgence: since this work was published over such long intervals, I think I have not always avoided repetitions. Farewell, gentle reader, whoever you are.   125

2774 / To Johann (II) Paumgartner   Freiburg, 1 March 1533

This is the preface to *Aliquot homiliae divi Joannis Chrysostomi* (Basel: Froben, March 1533), Erasmus' translation of eight sermons by St John Chrysostom. For Johann Paumgartner, the wealthy Augsburg merchant and patron of learning who had sought contact with Erasmus via Udalricus Zasius, see Ep 2603 introduction. Paumgartner reacted to this dedication with the gift of a gold goblet (Ep 2809).

TO THE MOST DISTINGUISHED GENTLEMAN JOHANN
PAUMGARTNER DESIDERIUS ERASMUS SENDS GREETINGS
The Peripetetics[1] assign to the register of the happy those who by their own efforts have added the goods of the mind to those of fortune; they divide happiness in two, ascribing half to chance and half to man. But I consider   5
you, most distinguished sir, to be much more happy in that the one giver of good things (to use the words of Hesiod)[2] has lavished upon you a mind that enables you to understand that those goods which the philosophers call external are not the gifts of fortune but of God, given as the instruments not of pleasures and pride but of virtue and duties. For whoever is endowed with a   10
truly Christian mind possesses them more as a steward than as a master; he acknowledges that what he has is borrowed and that the lender will demand a reckoning of what has been received and spent down to the last penny. And so ordinary people often speak falsely when they say about wealthy people 'he has riches.' For to have riches is a matter of philosophy and therefore   15
pertains to the few.
        Once, when Aristippus was blamed because he had relations with Thais, as one among many, he replied that there was a great difference in his case, because the others were possessed by Thais but he had possessed Thais.[3] But no one can have riches if he does not have a philosophic mind,   20
which knows both how much should be attributed to this kind of goods and

* * * * *

2774
1 Ie the school of philosophy founded by Aristotle
2 *Theogony* 46
3 *Apophthegmata* 3.132 (CWE 37 261), where one finds 'Lais' rather than 'Thais'

how they should be used. Thus you owe more to the goodness of God for giving you a mind superior to all riches than for lavishing on you an abundance of material possessions. It is more honourable to despise such wealth than to possess it, and he despises it who does not serve it but compels it to serve pious purposes. For what are such goods to those who do not know how to use them? No more than a cithara ornamented with gems and gold to someone who knows nothing about music. No more than a measuring rule, a pair of compasses, an axe, or a hatchet to someone who knows nothing about the art of carpentry. I would hardly dare to add something that I nevertheless believe to be true: it is a higher degree of philosophy to maintain temperance in the midst of lavish wealth than to endure poverty with a generous spirit. Thus I rank Plato, who, seated at Sicilian banquets, touched almost nothing more than beans, higher than Diogenes, who, if he couldn't get anything more delicate, would placate his growling stomach with raw vegetables.

And so good sir, truly dear to me as you are, you act wisely by applying yourself to good writings and to philosophy, which enables you to use riches well when you have them and not to be tormented if by some chance they should be snatched from you, as long as you keep those goods that are the only ones that make one happy. For you see how absurd it is to have a house resplendent everywhere with tapestries, marble, paintings, gold, jewels, and various ornamentation, but to have a heart adorned with no studies, no virtues. And so, just as you do not consider yourself rich because of an abundance of external goods if your soul is not enriched with true blessings, so too you do not think you will have rich children unless they succeed you as inheritors of better possessions. And for that reason your primary concern for them is that they be instructed from their earliest years in the most noble studies, but especially the pursuit of piety.

Would that many others would imitate this splendid example, which you and Anton Fugger, two extraordinary men, have introduced into that city, for then that city, which is rightly called *Augusta Vindelicorum* because of its many ornaments, would correspond more and more to its name by claiming splendour and majesty for its true blessings.[4] Indeed, I especially wish that those individual parents who have the resources would see to it that their children should be educated in liberal studies; and if their restricted circumstances prevent them from doing this, that they make them master some sedentary skill. I think the same should be done in cases where it is not the money

* * * * *

4 In the Latin name of Augsburg, *Augusta* means 'venerable,' 'splendid,' 'majestic' [city], while *Vindelicorum* means 'of the Vindelici' (an ancient Celtic people of Switzerland and South Germany).

that is lacking but that Minerva refuses her graces to the children.[5] If this were done, surely our Germany would have fewer vagabonds, idlers, robbers, and soldiers for hire. As it is, through the carelessness of the parents, many reach   60
the age of twenty completely illiterate and have no skill to protect them from idleness, the fountain of all vices, or poverty, the mistress of many evils.

But because of our mutual good will, I had intended for quite a while (with Udalricus Zasius spurring the galloping steed, as they say)[6] to send you something from my studies which would not only motivate you to reach   65
your goal but also help you to get there. But until now nothing had come up which could be thought worthy of Paumgartner or Erasmus' devotion to him. But lest I seem reluctant in fulfilling my duty, I send you as a pledge some homilies of Chrysostom, never before translated or printed. And I am not at all concerned that someone might throw that Greek insult at me, that send-   70
ing Chrysostom the theologian to a layman is like putting a party-frock on the cat.[7] For these are discussions that saintly man presented to an ordinary, mixed audience, not about theological mysteries, but about controlling pas-sions, like the speeches we read that Socrates addressed to anyone at all in the midst of the crowd. For this part of philosophy belongs to everyone. Indeed,   75
his way of speaking is itself completely suited to the ears of ordinary people.

There is hope that what happened to me in translating will happen to many others in the course of reading. For I felt within me the soothing of certain passions, as if they were obliterated by a magic charm, as Chrysostom brought before my eyes how extraordinary the mental restraint of those an-   80
cient personages was. I noted also how wrong it is to read the histories of the Old Testament in almost the same spirit as we read Livy or Sallust. For in the sacred stories an immensely greater and richer philosophy lies hidden. Chrysostom so unveils it, so explains its details, and so fixes it in our minds with such marvellous accuracy that no one would have thought such spiri-   85
tual delights lie hidden under the cloak of the story. And so if you devote some hours to such discussions during these forty days of Lent, I am confi-dent that you will not do so without profiting spiritually.

I was about to add some other homilies, but I discovered that most of them were either spurious or contaminated by spurious passages. How of-   90
ten, alas, are we forced to deplore such foolhardiness when we turn the pages

* * * * *

5 Minerva, goddess of wisdom, presided over 'the arts and the talents' (*Adagia* I i 37).
6 *Adagia* I ii 47
7 Ie giving something to someone who does not know how to use it; see *Adagia* I ii 72.

of ancient authors! The codex was beautifully written, magnificently illumi-
nated with colors and golden letters. But the very first homily, which begins
multo tempore silui [I was silent for a long time], had nothing of Chrysostom.
I translated it only to provide evidence that my frequent complaints are not   95
groundless. The author took his subject matter from history. This is a common
trick. But after that it all falls apart. From tumults he comes to those among
whom everything was calm. And suddenly, as if he had forgotten himself, he
bursts out into tragic exclamations: everything in human affairs is in turmoil;
nothing is trustworthy, nothing genuine. From this stage he suddenly leaps   100
down to riches and greed, as the fountainhead of such evils. And here the
commonplace denunciation of greed and the praise of poverty is dragged
in. Then he puts Job on display, to show that the highest philosophy for the
rich is to expect poverty in the midst of wealth. In sum, you would think the
words just poured out at random, the sheets filled up with the confusion of   105
words, and that nothing springs from the heart. The greed of booksellers
has played this sacrilegious game with all the most popular authors, both
Greek and Latin. And, shame to say, the heedlessness of Christians towards
the holy Doctors of the church was far greater than that of pagans towards
secular books. I sing this tune so often to encourage scholars to search for less   110
corrupt copies and to exert themselves with all their might to correct the
corrupt copies we have. I will not think that this book is of little importance
if I learn that it has been of some profit to your pious studies. Farewell.

At Freiburg im Breisgau. 1 March in the year 1533 after the birth of
Christ   115

2775 / To Bonifacius Amerbach   [Freiburg], 8 March [1533]

This letter (= AK Ep 1724) was first published in the *Epistolae familiares*. The
autograph is in the Öffentliche Bibliothek of the University of Basel (MS AN
III 15 46). The year-date is indicated by the connection with Epp 2765, 2788
and by the reference in lines 5–6 to the *Homiliae Chrysostomi* (Ep 2774) and the
Explanatio symboli (Ep 2772).

Herwagen has already written to me twice, as if I had taken the whole of
Cicero upon myself.[1] And he confers on me the honour of writing the only
preface to that author. I thought that you had undertaken this task. As for me,

* * * * *

2775
1 The letters are not extant. For Johann Herwagen and his projected edition of
  Cicero, see Ep 2765 n5.

I have decided to take a vacation from this sort of work in the coming summer. If you find someone who is going to see Sadoleto, send him the *Homilies* 5
I translated and the *Creed*.[2]

Farewell. 8 March

To the renowned Doctor, Master Bonifacius Amerbach

2776 / To Piotr Tomicki   Freiburg, 10 March 1533

The earliest and best source for this letter was a tiny book (eight pages) with
a long title: *Ad Serenissimum et Illustrissimum Principem dominum Sigismundum
Augustum Poloniae Regem iuniorem, Lasari Bonamici Epistola. Item Epistola Erasmi
Roterodami, ad Reverendissimum dominum Petrum Thomitium Episcopum Cracovien-
sem, Regni Poloniae Vicecancellarium* (Cracow: Hieronym Wietor 1533). In 1922
the only known copy of the book, then in the collection of the Baworowski
Library at Lvov, was lent to the University Library at Cracow for the use of
P.S. Allen. For the surviving manuscript copies, which Allen judged to be of no
importance, see his introduction to the letter.

For Piotr Tomicki see Epp 1919, 1953. His answer to this letter is Ep 2861.

ERASMUS OF ROTTERDAM SENDS CORDIAL GREETINGS TO PIOTR
TOMICKI, THE BISHOP OF CRACOW

Justus Decius reproaches me because, although I had recently written to
many patrons and friends of mine in Poland who deserve to be honoured, I
did not send a letter to you,[1] though no one is more generous or friendly to 5
Erasmus than you. I know that what he says is absolutely true. But in fact
that is the very reason why, since I had no time to write to everyone, I passed
you over. For ordinary friendships must be cultivated so that they will not
grow cold. But just as your devotion to me is more attested and more confirmed than that it should require such ordinary obligations, so too I think 10
you perceive my feelings towards you so clearly that you do not expect the
stimulus of a letter, especially when no subject matter is at hand and the one
being reproached is extremely occupied with many important matters.

* * * * *

2 In a letter to Jacopo Sadoleto of 23 April 1533 Bonifacius states that he has sent
both works to him; see AK Ep 1742:1–4.

2776
1 Neither Decius' letter (cf lines 22–5) nor any recent letters of Erasmus to Poland
are extant. Erasmus' most recent surviving letter to Tomicki is Ep 2713.

For just as those who interrupt men exhausted by their duties are more truly troublesome than dutiful, so too it is often a duty not to write to someone unless something important makes it a duty to do so. What subject would I have chosen to write about? Would I have asked you to continue to be yourself in your relations with Erasmus? Of that I had no doubt. To offer my services? You knew that I was ready to do so at the merest nod from you. What if I cannot even write to all the friends I have in various regions? Return my love to all of them I can; write to all of them I cannot. 15 20

Nevertheless, the complaint of Justus, although it was unjust, was not unpleasant, because it let me know that he is concerned about my affairs. For when he writes that your most reverend Excellency is especially favourable to me, he is telling me something most gratifying to me, but not at all new. 25

This year was rather bleak for me, both because of some private troubles and because of the death of several friends, whose like I think I will never find for the rest of my life. In the month of August that greatest patron of my studies, William, archbishop of Canterbury, left us and departed to a better fate, and together with him perished whatever little fortune I had in England – I had almost two hundred florins. He often told me in letters that he wanted to set aside some kind of gift for me, because of the many vultures he had to maintain in his household because of his high rank; but at his death some tricksters made sure that he not only left me nothing as an inheritance but even the pension that had been owed to me for a year and a half was not paid.[2] In fact, my last letter to him, in which I reminded him of his old promise, was suppressed by the same tricksters. They say that vultures know three days in advance where the corpses will be, but these vultures of ours keep their beaks open for many years, waiting for someone to die. 30 35

He had already passed his eightieth year, and they say he used a cane,[3] but his health was good because of his sober life. And he did not die of old age, but was carried away by an unfortunate accident. He had got up one night, awakening his chamberlains. When bodily necessity once more pressed him, he got up without awakening them (such was the kindness of this great bishop) and while going back to his bed, he lost his footing and hit his side against some piece of wood. Apparently this ruptured some inner organ, and he began to spit up blood. After much torment he died within four days. His departure was not only a private loss to many but also a serious blow both to the realm and to the church. There was nothing more holy 40 45

* * * * *

2 On the death of Archbishop William Warham (22 August 1532) and its feared financial consequences for Erasmus, cf Epp 2761:20–4, 2783:6–9.
3 Literally 'a third foot'

or religious than his life. In giving counsel for the good of the realm he was   50
both forthright and prudent. I have not yet heard who is to be his successor.
Three other men have died, who I do not think were known to you but who
were very kind and close friends of mine.[4] But even in this mourning, which
is so great that I am afraid it might add me to their company, I have still not
interrupted my studies at all. The letters of St Jerome, with my revised com-   55
mentary, have been printed at Paris.[5] No one can easily imagine how much
work was expended on that. To the revised and augmented *Adagia* I have
added and published almost five groups of a hundred each.[6] I translated
eight homilies of Chrysostom which had never before been translated.[7] And
at the request of a man of high station, I wrote a dialogue explaining the   60
Apostles' Creed.[8] The other pieces are trifles.

During the winter my health was fairly good; towards the beginning of
March an unexpected cold spell affected my left foot. For three days the pain
kept me from eating or sleeping.[9] Now it is tolerable enough, though I limp
a little. This ailment has afflicted me three times within two years.[10] I suspect 65
the reason is that for twenty-five years now I have usually written standing up and I lean more on the left foot. My residence here threatens ruin.[11] I
have no friends left. I concentrate wholly on gaining an undying friend, who
never abandons anyone in life or in death.

I do not write you about the latest news, for if there is anything of im-   70
portance, you get a more accurate report than I do. Germany is calm enough
since, fortunately, the Turks have been driven back.[12] I only wish that the

* * * * *

4 In other letters of this period Erasmus lists as the trio of friends who, in addition to Warham, had recently died: Alfonso de Valdés, Krzysztof Szydłowiecki,
  and Zacharius Deiotarus; see Epp 2783:5, 2791:22–4 with n8, 2798:14–18,
  2800:27–30. But Szydłowiecki was obviously known to Tomicki, so the identity
  of the third member of this particular trio is not clear.
5 See Ep 2758.
6 See Ep 2773.
7 See Ep 2774.
8 See Ep 2772.
9 See Ep 2768 n11.
10 See Ep 2770 n3.
11 The Latin is *Domicilium hoc minitatur ruinam*. Since Erasmus' new house was in
   perfectly good shape, this appears to mean (in the context of the danger of religious war in Germany): 'My [continued] residence here [in Freiburg] threatens
   ruin [and that is why I have made plans to leave].'
12 The renewed Turkish invasion of Austria in April 1532 had been abandoned by
   the end of August. King Ferdinand and Sultan Suleiman concluded a truce in
   June 1533 (Ep 2780 n9).

conference of the emperor and the pope would have the same good fortune in restoring peace in the church,[13] which, as I see it, is in far greater danger than many think. The monks are in turmoil, the theologians write articles, but at the same time there is a species of men (I dare not say of what sort) who spread their roots and dig tunnels. May the Lord have mercy on us! I would be extremely pleased if I knew that things go well for your most revered Excellency. Farewell.

Given at Freiburg, 10 March in the year 1533 after the birth of Christ   80

2777 / From Juan Luis Vives to Gilbert Cousin   Oxford, 10 March [1533]

This letter was first published in Vives' *Opera omnia* (Basel: Nicolaus Episcopius, 1555) II 976. Because of its close connection to Erasmus, P.S. Allen decided to include it in his edition. Allen assigned the year-date on the basis of the reference to Quirinus Hagius (lines 5–6), who appears to have entered Erasmus' service in the spring of 1532 (Ep 2644 n2) and had left it by January 1534 (Allen 2896:20–1). Erasmus twice sent him to England: the first time not earlier than 29 August 1532 (Epp 2704:14–15, 2707:7, 2798:21–6), the second time in late April 1533 (Epp 2793:18–20, 2798:25–6). Since this letter is dated in March, it must refer to the earlier of the two visits. Apart from this letter there is no evidence that Vives was in England after 1528. On the other hand, the concluding greetings (lines 34–5) to Udalricus Zasius (professor of law at Freiburg) and Henricus Glareanus (since 1529 lecturer in poetry at Freiburg), point to the period of Erasmus' residence in Freiburg, 1529–35.

JUAN LUIS VIVES SENDS GREETINGS TO THE UNRIVALLED AND LEARNED YOUNG MAN GILBERT COUSIN OF NOZEROY, AMANUENSIS OF DESIDERIUS ERASMUS

From your two letters,[1] my dearest Cousin, the first of which Lieven Panagathus sent from Antwerp,[2] and the later one which was delivered by Quirinus, 5 a citizen of The Hague,[3] I have not been able to learn what I especially wanted

* * * * *

13 Ie the recent meeting of Clement VII and Charles V at Bologna: see Epp 2753 n13, 2767 n14.

2777
1 No other letters between Vives and Cousin have survived.
2 Lieven Algoet. 'Panagathus' is the Hellenized form of 'Algoet,' ie 'All-Good.'
3 Ie Quirinus Hagius (see introduction)

to know, whether the letters I sent from London to Erasmus and to you have
been delivered to you.[4] I strongly suspected they had not, because you made
no mention of them in your letter. I have the books that Quirinus delivered,
for which I am most grateful to you. I shall read them at my leisure. With   10
your letters I shall do what you ask; the other one I have already sent to
Charles Mountjoy.[5]

I have often begged you, my dear Cousin, to write to us more often,
especially concerning the health of our teacher Erasmus, and how things are
with him, whom I hold no less dear than myself, especially in order that we   15
may give no credence to rumours and may not be disquieted by them. I beg
and implore you most urgently to do this immediately. For I have had news
from Antwerp concerning his health that makes me shudder just to think of
it. But it is nothing new for us to hear such things, and we are less disturbed
by them because we have become inured to them. But the more we hear them,   20
the more we are frightened by the thought of the dangers men face and our
common mortality. Goclenius cheered me up when he told me that there was
a hostile rumour about Erasmus circulating in Brabant that would give pleasure only to evil-minded men,[6] and that otherwise he had discovered that everything was going well among you, for which I am deeply thankful to Christ.   25

When I arrived here the weather was bad – windy, sultry, and damp –
and the food here is much different from what I am used to. But otherwise
things go very well, thanks be to God. For the leading men are fond of me
and favourable, and they show it by their actions.[7] But I have decided to
return to Flanders in the month of June. Since I have told you in one of my   30
other letters what I hope for you, you are not unaware of my opinion and
my wishes. But whatever you decide, may God give you good fortune. You
will earn my sincerest gratitude if, in my name, you convey my greetings
to Master Erasmus, the teacher we have in common, and also Zasius and
Glareanus. Farewell again and again.   35

10 March. At Oxford

* * * * *

4 The letter to Erasmus is not extant.
5 Ie Charles Blount, fifth Baron Mountjoy (Ep 2726 introduction). The letter to
   him is not extant.
6 Rumour unidentified
7 For 'leading men' Vives uses the word *principes*.

2778 / To the City Council of Besançon   Freiburg, 12 March 1533

This letter was first published in the *Epistolae universae* page 1110. The surviving manuscript is a contemporary copy in the municipal archives at Besançon
(MS BB 15 folio 446). The letter is apparently one of thanks for the gift of wine
mentioned in Ep 2761:30–1, but it says nothing of the invitations to settle in
Besançon referred to in lines 29–30 of the same letter.

Cordial greetings. Magnificent and ever to be esteemed patrons, with my
whole heart I embrace and cherish your kindness (it is not the first time you
have offered it to me) in giving me a gift beyond anything I would have
dared to request. I have accepted this honorific gift with the greatest pleasure, but not without shame. For a gift spontaneously sent by such men to   5
someone who neither sought nor expected it could not but be most pleasing.
But a sense of shame is mingled with this feeling when I consider that I have
never deserved anything either from you or from the commonwealth over
which you preside, and I do not see what I can do in return. But I most faithfully promise that, if anyone can suggest how I, in turn, could do something   10
pleasing to my lords, to whom I am so indebted, I would strive with hands
and feet[1] to let them know that their protégé will not be lacking in ready motivation and good will. May the Lord preserve and advance your renowned
council and famous commonwealth in all things.

    Given at Freiburg im Breisgau. 12 March in the year 1533 after the birth   15
of Christ

    Your most devoted protégé Erasmus of Rotterdam (I have signed with
my own hand)

    To the most distinguished president and the most noble council, gover-
nors of the famous city of Besançon   20

2779 / To Andreas Silvius   Freiburg, 15 March 1533

First published by Allen, this letter survives only in a seventeenth-century copy
in the university library at Leiden made by J.F. Gronovius (MS Gronoviorum
105 folio 209). What little is known of Andreas Silvius of Bruges (documented
1533–70) at this stage of his life derives entirely from this letter. Later sources
indicate that he matriculated at Louvain in 1554, that at about the same time
he became active as a tutor, that by 1556 he had taken up a position of some

* * * * *

2778
1 Ie with all my might; see *Adagia* I iv 15.

authority in Italy, where he showed kindness to the son of Joachim Camerarius. In his preface to Girolamo Mercuriale's *Variarum lectionum libri quatuor* (1570) he thanked Cardinal Antoine Perrenot de Granvelle and other members of the Granvelle family for kindnesses shown him.

Greetings. I wrote to you via Claudius of Lorraine,[1] who delivered your letter. I wrote again via two other Frenchmen who said they were going to Paris.[2] They were pupils of Glareanus.[3] I sent a new preface to the Jerome,[4] which you will have them insert at the beginning, if it arrives in time. Now I am sending it again, in case the young men stopped off somewhere. That is   5
what happens with that German.[5]

Cajetanus has excerpted from my books several opinions that offended the theologians, but he expressed them in offensive language.[6] The bishop of Veroli, who is now the legate at Lucerne, wrote to me saying that he had seen to it that the pope impose silence.[7] I was surprised that the pope had   10
paid so much attention to me. Now I understand that he did so as a favour to Cajetanus. And yet I had complained about Béda in letters to Cardinals Campeggi, Cajetanus, and Veroli.[8] Cajetanus has already written again very kindly, saying that the pope is favourably disposed towards him, that he has shared my last letter to him with the pope, who looked it over very care-   15
fully, and that there was nothing he did not understand, including the Greek words I had added at the end.[9]

* * * * *

2779
1 Unidentified. Allen says 'possibly the Claudius of Epp 2412, 2433, 2434,' but if the description of this Claudius as 'from Lorraine' is accurate, that is untenable; see Ep 2412 n17.
2 Unidentified. None of these letters is extant.
3 Henricus Glareanus (Ep 2664 n2)
4 Ep 2758
5 Unidentified
6 This obscurely phrased sentence may possibly be related to Ep 2787:21–82, where Christoph von Stadion discusses certain 'errors of Cardinal Cajetanus' that had displeased the Paris theologians (Ep 2787 n6). Stadion twice cites Erasmus approvingly (Ep 2787 nn7, 11) against the theologians, but he gives no indication of any link between Cajetanus 'errors' and Erasmus' works. Cajetanus may have said something about this to Erasmus in a letter no longer extant.
7 The papal legate at Lucerne Ennio Filonardi, who in Ep 2738:1–12 promised to make an effort to get the pope to silence Erasmus' Paris critics
8 The letter to Campeggi is Ep 2579.
9 See Ep 2690 introduction.

I wrote to Brie to give you seven crowns on my behalf.[10] I would like
to know whether he did so. About the position with the bishop that Brie obtained for you,[11] I wrote that I regret that your present prospects are as slim   20
as you describe them. I am confident that you would preserve your integrity
even at court. But as a rule, courts customarily gobble a man up immediately,
that is, clip his wings so that he cannot fly away, and then, to keep him from
being discouraged, they nurse him sometimes with hopes and throw him a
scrap, so that once he has entered into the trap he can never get out. But I   25
think that this bishop of yours is a good man. And so strive as best you can to
preserve what you have and keep a lookout so as to change a stipend into a
benefice. For patrons are mortal, and even though nothing like that happens,
minds are wondrously mutable. I would not want you to grow old in that
sort of life. You can try it for a couple of years; if it does not go well, hasten to   30
get out of it. I thought it best to repeat this advice, in case the letter I entrusted
to others does not get through to you.

Omphalius (I am not sure which one, for I understand there are two
of this name) wrote that, when Carinus was laid up with a wound, you visited him and informed him that a courier had been engaged if he wanted to   35
write anything to me.[12] Nothing is more useless than to stir that Camarina.[13]
Recently a bundle of letters was delivered to me,[14] mixed in with which there
was one with the seal well intact addressed to Simon Grynaeus,[15] in which
another one seemed to be included. I did not recognize the hand of Carinus
well enough. And so, suspecting nothing, I sent the letter in good faith to   40
Grynaeus, adding in my own letter that I was sending it to him in more good

* * * * *

10 For Germain de Brie, see Ep 2727 introduction. The letter to him is not extant.
    The crown referred to was most likely the French écu au soleil, which was
    officially valued at 76d groot Flemish. Seven crowns were therefore equivalent
    to £2 4s 2d groot Flemish or fifty-six days' wages of an Antwerp master mason/
    carpenter at 9.05d per day (CWE 12 650 Table 3, 691 Table 13).
11 The bishop is unidentified.
12 The only Omphalius was Jacobus (Ep 2311 n14). No letters between him and
    Erasmus survive. Ludovicus Carinus, a one-time friend with whom Erasmus
    had had a terrible falling-out in 1528 (Ep 2111 n2), was at this time living at
    Paris with Johann Sturm (1507–89), who in 1537 would settle in Strasbourg,
    becoming the founding rector of its famous Gymnasium.
13 Ie stir up useless trouble; see Adagia 1 i 64.
14 Cf Ep 2788:18–36, where this same story is told in much the same words.
15 For Grynaeus see Ep 2659 n5.

faith than some Evangelicals did in handling my letters.[16] Grynaeus, suspecting from the letters of others that I was aware of the situation, gave himself
away and let it be known that it was a letter Carinus had written to me, but
that it had been left to his discretion whether he preferred to deliver it to me   45
or to throw it into the fire, and that he had thrown it into the fire because,
though the opening was mild enough, in the middle everything was full of
poison. I do not know whether those who get the man[17] so excited are from
there.[18] But if there are such people, I beg you to restrain them. The young
man is of an excessively melancholic temperament, absolutely at the mercy   50
of his emotions, which he cannot control. His language is most intemperate
if someone offends him, and on this point he is not a true follower of the gospel.[19] With men of such temperament I want neither friendship nor enmity.
To that end I would like the help of your prudence. And care must be taken
that he know nothing of my affairs. He writes about everything to fellow   55
initiates at Basel, and he adds his own strong feelings. He is a young man of
a dangerous temperament, especially when he has no reason to be afraid of
anything, since he has been cast out, as I hear, from his native land, his patri-
mony, and his prebend.[20] Keep me informed about this matter, if you learn of
anything that I should know about it.   60

Farewell. Freiburg, 15 March in the year 1533 after the birth of Christ
Yours truly, Erasmus of Rotterdam
I have written you via Anton Bletz.[21]

2780 / To Jan (II) Łaski   Freiburg, 21 March 1533

This letter, apparently the answer to one now lost, was first published in
Wierzbowski I 42. The manuscript, a contemporary copy, was in the same ill-
fated folio volume as that of Ep 1954. For Łaski see Ep 2746 introduction. His
answer to this letter is Ep 2862.

* * * * *

16 For Erasmus' enduring suspicion that Evangelicals were intercepting his correspondence see Ep 2487:3–6 with n2.
17 Carinus
18 Paris, where Carinus was now living
19 Carinus was by now a Strasbourg-style Evangelical.
20 In October 1531 Carinus had been deprived of his canonry at Beromünster.
21 The professional messenger who regularly carried letters between Basel,
Freiburg, and Paris; see Ep 1784 n1.

FROM ERASMUS TO THE MOST REVEREND MASTER PROVOST

I have no doubt that one day your fortune will match your outstanding merits, but I am sorry that it is taking so long. It was right that you should succeed your uncle, and I hoped that you would.[1] You used to tell me marvellous
things about him, and perhaps he was so to others; to me, however, he was   5
so parsimonious that for the dedication of the Ambrose he did not even send
me a thank-you note.[2] But to receive no rewards for dedications is nothing
new to me, so I am not the least bit offended. My library is already worth a
hundred crowns more than when you bought it.[3] So that you won't think
this incredible, the Galen alone, which Gianfrancesco Torresani gave me as   10
a gift, sold here just as it was for thirty gold florins. Imagine what the rest
would be worth.[4] But if you have no regrets about the contract, I will do what
is just. It seems to me, however, that you consider it abandoned. If that is the
case, I will repay you the two hundred florins (if you prefer to regard them
as a reward for the dedication of the Ambrose,[5] I will laud your generosity) 15
and I will look for another buyer.[6] The bishop of Vienna made overtures to
purchase it, but I answered that I was not at liberty to sell it.[7]

Fortunately the Turk has been put to flight – may he never come back![8]
There is a rumour concerning negotiations about a settlement between King

* * * * *

2780
1 On the death in 1531 of his uncle Jan (I) Łaski, archbishop of Gniezno and
   former royal chancellor of Poland (Ep 1855 introduction), Łaski renounced
   his share of the inheritance in favour of his two brothers. In 1530 he had been
   promised the succession to his uncle as archbishop, but he did not succeed in
   acquiring the office or its income.
2 See Ep 1855 introduction.
3 In 1526 Łaski had arranged to purchase Erasmus' library on terms that left
   Erasmus the use of it for the rest of his life. The price was '400 gold pieces,' 200
   of which were paid at the time, the other 200 of which were still owed. See CWE
   12 542:32–5 (Erasmus' first will) with n20.
4 Erasmus had said the same thing in almost identical terms in Ep 2033:19–21,
   but without mentioning Torresani, for whom see Ep 1989.
5 Erasmus' edition of the *Opera* of St Ambrose was dedicated to Jan (I) Łaski;
   see Ep 1855.
6 Łaski declined this offer to terminate the contract; see Allen Epp 2862:30–60,
   2911:8. In the end, following Erasmus' death, the terms of the contract were
   faithfully observed. On 28 September 1536 Łaski sent the 200 florins still owed
   (AK Ep 2072:12–17); the books were sent off to him at Christmas; and on 5 April
   1537 he acknowledged receipt of them (AK Ep 2130).
7 Nowhere in the correspondence is there any other reference to this inquiry by
   Johannes Fabri (Ep 2750).
8 See Ep 2776 n12.

Ferdinand and the voivode[9] – I hope that it also comes out to your advan-   20
tage.[10] Thomas More has put aside the packsaddles of the chancellorship,
with the good graces of the prince.[11] For the king more clearly showed his
affection for More by removing this burden than by imposing it. At the time
of the appointment he was a lover of his country, conferring this royal office
on the only man in the whole island who was equal to it; now he is a lover   25
of More, whose wish he granted. I can guess why More resigned from this
office. But this was an office which hardly anyone could fulfil without de-
viating from what is right and pious. The evangelicals rejoice, proclaiming
that More was deprived of the office by law and that he was succeeded by a
noble gentleman who immediately released twenty people whom More had   30
thrown into prison because they were members of sects. His successor was
Edward Lee's brother, who was a friend of mine in times past, so much so
that in the quarrel I had with Lee he openly stood on my side.[12] He does not
belong to the nobility, except that he is a lawyer, and that status among the
English is almost the only source of nobility. He was born in a village. But   35
More was born in London, which among the English constitutes a part of
nobility. His father was of patrician rank,[13] a doctor of British law who was

* * * * *

9 In June 1533 Ferdinand of Austria signed a truce with Suleiman I in which he
  recognized the Ottoman sultan as his 'father and suzerain,' agreed to pay an
  annual tribute, and abandoned all claims to rule beyond 'Royal Hungary,' the
  fragment of the kingdom over which he had managed to maintain control. This
  left Ferdinand's rival for the throne of Hungary, John Zápolyai, voivode of
  Transylvania, as the Ottoman puppet king with his capital at Buda. A personal
  settlement between Ferdinand and Zápolyai was not achieved until the treaty
  of Várad in February 1538.
10 Jan (I) Łaski and his nephews were members of the anti-Hapsburg party in
  Poland. Following the battle of Mohács (1526), Jan II's brother Hieronim had
  thrown in his lot with John Zápolyai. Gradually but surely this led to a decline
  in the family's fortunes and influence in Poland.
11 The encomium of More that follows is a shorter version of that found in Ep
  2750.
12 More's successor as chancellor was in fact Sir Thomas Audley. Erasmus somehow or other mistook him for Wilfred Lee, brother of Edward Lee (for whose
  controversy with Erasmus see Ep 765). Wilfred, whom Erasmus encountered
  several times at Louvain, acted as intermediary between Erasmus and his
  brother and attempted to mediate between them; see Ep 1053 n21.
13 The word for 'patrician rank' is *purpuratus*, a reference to Roman consuls,
  who wore a purple-hemmed toga, and senators, who had a purple stripe on
  their tunic.

himself preeminent among the twenty doctors of that category.[14] He held an honourable office in his city.[15] Then, drawn into the court, he showed his mettle in some embassies. Twelve years ago he was knighted.[16] But so far as 40 talent, learning, and eloquence are concerned, there is no comparison. The cardinal of York feared More rather than loved him.[17] Nevertheless, when he perceived that the king's anger was implacable, he declared that More was the only man in England equal to that office. My friend Mountjoy wrote me that he executed that office so well that everyone admits that no one had ever 45 done so more skilfully or with greater equity.[18]

Time and again the evangelicals have stirred up extremely dangerous unrest in England. In those circumstances, what is a judge of the kingdom to do? Oppose the view of the prince and the bishops by pouring oil on the fire? A sufficiently strong indication of More's mildness is that no one was 50 burned, beheaded, or hanged (which often happened in other regions).[19] I say nothing here about the teachings of Luther. Under this cloud a vicious kind of error is planted and spread abroad throughout the world – God knows where it will end!

What such people can do we learn from the slave war and the exam- 55 ple of the Templars.[20] The sects interpret any mercy from the princes as favour towards themselves; if the tiniest opening is given them they all rush through; and they teach the cities to fart in the face of princes. That is what happened to the duke of Cleves in a certain important city.[21] A Dominican is active as a preacher there who many years before had provided the perfect 60 example of an extraordinary scoundrel.[22] At Paris he persuaded a starving printer that he had the colloquies of Erasmus, revised by Erasmus himself. In the preface he makes me say that a child was taught Hebrew by Capito, was thoroughly instructed in Greek by Rhenanus, but was wrongly instructed by

* * * * *

14 Cf Ep 2750 n11.
15 Not John More but Thomas, who was undersheriff of London (1510–19)
16 The text says 'made a baron.' More was knighted in 1521.
17 Thomas Wolsey (Ep 284)
18 Letter not extant
19 Cf Ep 2750 n16.
20 To what does this refer? It can scarcely be the first-century Roman slave revolt, but 'slave war' (*servile bellum*) is hardly an apt description of the Peasants War of 1524–5. And what does either of them have to do with the example of the Templars, who were suppressed in the fourteenth century?
21 Soest; see Ep 2728:9 with n3.
22 For the rest of the story told in this paragraph, including Erasmus' misidentification of the Dominican preacher as Lambertus Campester, see Ep 2728:8–21.

me in the Christian religion.[23] And he corrupted all the colloquies with his   65
buffooneries. The case was instantly reported to me. When he found that out,
he rushed off to Lyon, where he became a wonderful lover of Erasmus. There
was nowhere he did not sing my praises. Thanks to this trickery he found
an archdeacon to be his patron, from whom in the end he ran away after
stealing three hundred crowns. He devised similar schemes in many places,   70
and sometimes his cowl was all that saved him from being executed. When
he was no longer safe anywhere, he resorted to his sheet anchor.[24] He threw
off his cowl and became an evangelical preacher, and not content to teach
Zwinglian or Lutheran doctrine, he teaches utter nonsense.[25] The duke wrote
to the city council that they should get rid of such a preacher. They replied   75
that the people could not do without their teacher.

        I learned this not from some vague rumour, but from a counsellor of
the duke.[26] But I have said far too much about it. I hope that you are in good
health. This March has put to the test every part of my poor body and continues to do so.[27] You will learn the rest from our mutual friend Justus.[28]   80

        Given at Freiburg, 21 March 1533
        You recognize, I think, the handwriting of your friend.

2781 / To Erasmus Schets   [Freiburg], 22 March 1533

        This letter was first published by Allen on the basis of the autograph in the
        British Library (ms Add 38512 folio 78).

Cordial greetings. In his last letter,[1] our Barbier accuses us of negligence
in not sending him a 'quittance,' as it is called, claiming that otherwise he
would have paid the pension, or at least part of it.[2] But how could I send

* * * * *

23 For this detail, missing from the account in Ep 2728; see Ep 1341A:318–22.
24 Ie his refuge of last resort; see *Adagia* I i 34.
25 Ie he had become an Anabaptist; see Ep 2728:18–21 with n6.
26 Probably Konrad Heresbach, who had visited Erasmus at Freiburg in September
   1532; see Ep 2728 n24.
27 See Ep 2768 n11.
28 Presumably Justus Lodovicus Decius (Ep 1341A n210)

   2781
 1 Not extant. The most recent surviving letter from Pierre Barbier is Ep 2404.
 2 On Barbier's role in the payment of Erasmus' Courtrai pension, see Ep 2704:22–3
   with n9.

a quittance, since he signified that he wouldn't send anything and it was
not clear how much he intended to send? I have no doubt that Laurinus is   5
trustworthy, but I am very doubtful about this.[3] You may find that few are
steadfast in their friendship to those who are absent. And to many the saying
'a Flemish skinflint' applies.[4]

Molendino has been the recipient of your hospitality – a marvellous admirer of Erasmus.[5] He has been running around Flanders, visiting my friends,   10
everywhere an Erasmian. But he is the one who laid down the warp for this
web of intercepting my pension; he did it together with Barbier, a Frenchman
with a Frenchman, a theologian with a theologian, a smooth talker with a
smooth talker.[6] When Barbier was active at Rome, trying to get his deanery,
he thought it preferable to intercept my money artfully in order to conduct   15
his lawsuit than to spend his own;[7] that is how much he loved Erasmus. The
trickiest of the tricksters. But I write this for you only. If Barbier did not send
anything, please have someone sent to Tournai, even at my expense, to give
to Barbier the letter included with this one.[8] I will write more shortly.

Farewell. 22 March 1533   20
Your Erasmus of Rotterdam
To the most honourable gentleman Master Erasmus Schets, business-
man of Antwerp, At Antwerp

2782 / To Georgius Agricola   [Freiburg], 24 March 1533

This letter was first published by Christian Gotthold Wilisch in his *Arcana bib-
liothecae Annaebergensis* (Leipzig: Lanckisch 1730) 169. In 1923, when P.S. Allen
was allowed to copy it, the autograph was in the private collection of Baroness

* * * * *

3 Cf Ep 2404:1–4, where Barbier excuses his delay in replying to a letter from
  Erasmus (not extant) on the grounds that Marcus Laurinus, dean of Bruges, had
  taken more than six weeks to forward it to him.
4 The saying is in Dutch: 'een Vlaemschen dayng,' which Allen in his note ren-
  ders as 'a Flemish good-for-nothing,' but the idea of being tight with money
  seems also to be involved. See Ari Wesseling 'Dutch Proverbs and Expressions
  in Erasmus' Adages, Colloquies, and Letters' *Renaissance Quarterly* 55 (2002) 126.
5 For Johannes de Molendino see Ep 371 introduction. On his hospitality from
  Schets, see Ep 2799:27–8.
6 See Epp 2763:5–6, 2799:28–31.
7 See Ep 2407:13–18.
8 Not extant, but answered by Ep 2842

James de Rothschild at Paris. The current location of the manuscript is unknown (cf Ep 2295 introduction). For Georgius Agricola, see Ep 1594 n23.

Cordial greetings. By some mistake it happened that I have not yet seen your
book,[1] but it is in a safe place. I will look at it soon. I am delighted that you
have partly kept your word. If I can do anything that will be of assistance to
you or will enhance your reputation, I will see to it that you will know I have
never failed in my duty.   5
    Plateanus found me both extremely occupied with writing letters and
struggling in various ways with the month of March, which never ceases to
scour all the recesses of my poor body:[2] it generated pleurisy in the left side
of my rib cage, and then a genuine and severe gout in my left foot, now a
stone in my right lower back, then with paralysis in my right arm. But even   10
so, it was not unpleasant to talk with him.
    Farewell. 24 March 1533
    Your Erasmus of Rotterdam, in my own hand
    To the very learned gentleman Master Georgius Agricola, physician

2783 / To Johann Henckel   Freiburg, 24 March 1533

> This letter was first published by Allen. The surviving manuscript, a sixteenth-
> century copy in the hand of Melchior Goldast, is in the Stadtbibliothek Bremen
> (msa 0011/061). For Johann Henckel, former preacher and confessor to Queen
> Mary of Hungary, now canon at Wrocław, see Ep 1672 introduction.

TO THE MOST DISTINGUISHED GENTLEMAN MASTER JOHANN
HENCKEL, CANON AT WROCŁAW
For many years none has been worse than this one, hugely troublesome be-
cause of domestic cares and fatal because of the deaths of so many great
friends, especially the archbishop of Canterbury and Alfonso de Valdés.[1]   5
Through the trickery of some false friends it was arranged that my pensions,

* * * * *

2782
1 *De mensuris et ponderibus*, which Erasmus had promised to read; see Ep 2529:21–
  2 and cf Allen Ep 2803:39–41. It was published by Froben in August 1533.
2 For Petrus Plateanus see Ep 2216 introduction. For the torments of March, see
  Ep 2768 n11.

2783
1 For William Warham, archbishop of Canterbury, cf Epp 2726:35–62, 2761:20–6,
  2776:28–51). For Valdés, see Epp 2776 n4, 2800:28–9.

that is, what little income I had in England, perished together with the arch-bishop.[2] They also suppressed the pension payments of the two preceding years.[3] For even then those vultures were hovering over the corpse. But the Lord will grant me more auspicious things instead of these, if he wishes.   10

In the autumn I was not ill, but I was weak. In the winter my health was all right. I revised the notes on Jerome, which were reprinted at Paris.[4] I revised the *Adages*, to which I added almost five hundred.[5] To the *Colloquies* I added two.[6] I translated eight homilies of Chrysostom that had never been translated before.[7] I wrote an explanation of the Apostles' Creed.[8] The rest   15 are of little importance. Towards the end of February, March sent out his advance troops, very nasty winds probing and reprobing all the nooks and crannies of this poor body. First it attacked my left shoulder blade, but with only moderate pain. From there it shifted to my left foot, with such excruciat-ing pain that for three days I could neither eat nor sleep. Slowly it went away.   20 It also tickled my right foot; at the end it invaded my stomach, and it still clings to my right and left shoulder bones, threatening to inflict now gout, now paralysis, now stones.[9] I am making plans to return to my native land, but without success.[10]

The queen triumphs there.[11] That is what the legation said that stopped   25 here on its way to the emperor, headed by a young man who is the brother of Cardinal Croy.[12] I rejoice that the Lord has given him this much consolation for his afflictions. If all goes well with you, I will be supremely delighted.

At Freiburg im Breisgau, 24 March 1533
Erasmus of Rotterdam, in my own hand   30

* * * * *

2 See Ep 2761:20–4 with nn9–10.
3 In Ep 2776:35–6 he says a year and a half.
4 Ep 2758
5 Ep 2773
6 In the edition of March 1533 (Basel: Froben and Episcopius): *Problema* 'A Problem' and *Epicureus* 'The Epicurean'
7 Ep 2774
8 Ep 2772
9 On Erasmus' ill health in the spring and summer of 1533 see Ep 2768 n11.
10 See Ep 2646:3–13.
11 Ie Queen Mary in the Netherlands; see Ep 2741:6–10.
12 Charles (II) de Croy, bishop of Tournai (Ep 1695 n2), brother of the late Cardinal Guillaume (II) de Croy (Ep 628:70n)

2784 / From Jean (II) de Carondelet   Brussels, 27 March 1533

This letter was first published in Ipolyi page 325. The manuscript is page 344
of the Olahus codex in the Hungarian National Archives at Budapest (Ep 2339
introduction). The letter conveys the invitation to return to the Netherlands
that Erasmus had requested in Ep 2762:16–20.

JEAN, THE ARCHBISHOP OF PALERMO, TO ERASMUS OF ROTTERDAM
Cordial greetings. Most renowned sir. Just as a few days ago my friend the
magnificent Master Nicolaus Olahus and I reported in our letters (which we
understand your Excellency did not receive),[1] that we have petitioned her
most serene Majesty, regent of the Netherlands,[2] to recall your Excellency   5
from the tumult in Germany to the peace and quiet of your native soil, paying thereafter the stipend formerly awarded, together with some ready money for the journey and for moving your furnishings here. But, though her
Serenity is most eager for this, nevertheless she does not want it to be done
without the consent of his sacred imperial Majesty. Therefore, at the com-   10
mand of her Serenity, I am now writing about this matter to Lord Granvelle,[3]
whom you will perhaps know by his good name, asking him to meet with
his imperial Majesty concerning that matter and to report to us with all diligence to what the emperor has in mind. In the meantime I hope that your
Excellency will, together with us, await patiently the response of his Majesty. 15
      Brussels, 27 March 1533

2785 / From Nicolaus Olahus   Brussels, 29 March 1533

This letter, Olahus' response to Ep 2762, was first published in Ipolyi page 328.
The manuscript is page 342 of the Olahus codex in the Hungarian National
Archives at Budapest (Ep 2339 introduction). Erasmus' reply is Ep 2792.

* * * * *

2784
1 Erasmus had evidently not responded to Epp 2689 and 2693, perhaps because
  he had not received them.
2 Carondelet calls them *patriae citeriores* 'the hither fatherlands.'
3 Nicolas Perrenot de Granvelle (d 1550), imperial chancellor for Netherlandish
  and German affairs; cf Ep 2785:60–5.

THE RESPONSE OF NICOLAUS OLAHUS TO ERASMUS OF ROTTERDAM
Recently I sent you a letter via the vicar of the lord bishop of Palermo, who is
at Besançon;[1] from which you would have understood that, because of your
long silence,[2] we almost despaired of your coming back here. For the reliable
rumour about your move to Besançon was spread abroad here, and we were   5
surprised by your sudden change of mind. Nevertheless, while we were in
this state of uncertainty, we were relieved by a letter from you that was delivered to me recently by some messenger or other from Antwerp,[3] in which
you amicably express to me your intention of returning to us and indicate the
manner and means by which you wish to do that, gently urging me to keep   10
your intention secret, not only from the Dane,[4] but from others as well. As for
me, most learned Erasmus, I congratulate you and am personally delighted,
for it will give me the opportunity of seeing you here, and because your presence will bring no little renown to your native land and joy to your friends,
who respect the honour and glory of your reputation. As you enjoined me, I   15
have taken all possible care to keep your decision secret; no one has learned
of it from me except the queen, Carondelet, his secretary Langhe (without
whom, as you can well imagine, the letter could not have been written),[5] and
I have also carefully warned all of them to remain silent. Moreover, you yourself mentioned your return in a letter to our friend Conradus Goclenius,[6] who   20
was recently at Louvain as well as with me here today. It was he, whom I always knew was a very close friend of yours, who on his own initiative made
mention of you. For my part, I kept the matter secret from him for some days,
and then, yesterday, when I was preparing to write back to you, I revealed
and reported to him what you had indicated to me, since he is a special and   25
trustworthy friend both to you and to me, admonishing him, however, to say
nothing about what I have done concerning your affairs.

* * * * *

2785
1 The letter was Ep 2759. It was the vicar in question who had relayed the rumour (see lines 4–5 below) that Erasmus was going to move to Besançon (Ep
  2759:17–21).
2 At the time Olahus wrote Ep 2759 (31 January 1533), he had not received an
  answer to Ep 2693, which he feared had not been delivered.
3 Ep 2762, which was presumably Erasmus' delayed answer to Ep 2693; cf Ep
  2759 n2.
4 Jakob Jespersen (Ep 2646 n9)
5 Jan de Langhe (d 1571), in the service of Carondelet as trusted secretary since
  at least 1524
6 Not extant

This is what I wanted you to know before I went on to the rest. In the presence of the queen I handled your case with the faithfulness, care, and devotion that I owe to you and that I would have exercised concerning my own affairs. The queen, as I wrote to you before, entertains special feelings of devotion and kindness towards you, both because your illustrious virtues require that from her but also because I, among others, have always been by no means the last to proclaim your praises to her, and always will be when the opportunity arises. She wishes and very much desires that you will return. But since earlier some mention was made of you when the emperor was here, she did not think it was prudent to recall you before she had taken care to suggest to him that perhaps you could be persuaded to return, if that should accord with his will. But consider that I advised that these things be done not merely for the sake of the emperor but to provide for the untroubled safety and tranquillity of your private circumstances. For, to speak to you more frankly, though it did not seem that you had informed me very thoroughly concerning your return, except concerning a letter and some fair travel expenses, nevertheless, being somewhat familiar with the character of people both there and here, and after receiving your letter and intervening on your behalf with the queen, I thought it was the duty of a true friend to oversee, provide for, and carry through the negotiations between friends, so that no insecurity or loss would befall them later. So on my own initiative I proposed to the queen that your recall would be more honourable and convenient if you could be certain about your security and about the present and future payment of the imperial pension. For you should not think that here too there is widespread prosperity.

Concerning your honourable invitation, the avoidance of the troubles of the court and of courtiers, and other matters that I thought pertained to you and seemed to be useful, honourable, and conducive to your peace of mind – all of this seemed right and proper to the queen as well. She wants you to live in safety and peace. But as I said previously, she wants your recall to be all the more honourable and safe if the emperor is also aware of it beforehand. She assigned this task to the lord bishop of Palermo, who holds you in high favour (unless he is, as you write, a smooth talker).[7] And indeed he wrote to Granvelle, who is now undertaking the duties of chancellor to the emperor (since he has no one else), asking him to say, not that this is your desire, but that you could perhaps be persuaded to return if conditions were favourable (if that were the emperor's will) and begging him therefore

* * * * *

7 Cf Epp 2762:13–15, 2784.

to bring the matter up with the emperor. For to use this pretext for writ- 65
ing seemed to me to be an approach more honourable to you. I sent this
letter today with courier. But you are quite aware that so much business is
transacted at the courts of princes that sometimes matters are neglected, and
since I know that Nicolaus,[8] the son of the president of Mechelen,[9] the successor to Valdés,[10] is most friendly to me and also a firm supporter of your 70
honour and reputation, I arranged that the lord bishop of Palermo put this
petition to Granvelle in the hands of Nicolaus. I also wrote to Nicolaus that
he should handle this business carefully, quickly, and secretly, and send back
a response. I think that he will do so. Therefore you must be patient for a little
while, and be assured that, God willing, you will return quite honourably 75
and safely. If I see that the matter is taking longer than we expect, I will see to
it that both Granvelle and Nicolaus are reminded about it again.

You know the general state of your affairs. If you think something
could be done better or more in keeping with your honour, status, and safety,
I would do nothing more willingly. As soon as have an answer, I will imme- 80
diately let you know. Together with this letter you will get the letter of our
friend Goclenius,[11] who has been here for two days conducting the suit for
his Antwerp canonry (he is returning to Louvain today),[12] and also the letter of a certain Spaniard who begged me very earnestly to send it to you.[13]
I would be pleased if you would inform the Spaniard, whoever he may be, 85
that you have received his letter. I have also sent you a letter of Carondelet.[14]
The bankers are at work. The president of the treasury is not in Flanders,[15]
and there has not been anyone at the court to whom I could have appealed. It
is more prudent, in my judgment, for us to wait for an answer. I understand

* * * * *

8 Nicolaus Grudius (1503/4–1570/1, son of Nicolaas Everaerts (see following
note), had studied at the Collegium Trilingue in his native city of Leiden, was
a Neo-Latin poet of merit who pursued a career in the imperial administration
of the Netherlands. At some point before May 1532 he was named secretary
to Charles v, which means that he cannot really have been the 'successor' of
Alfonso de Valdés, as Olahus here indicates; cf n10 below.
9 Nicolaas Everaerts (Ep 1092), president of the Grand Council at Mechelen
10 Alfonso de Valdés, the imperial secretary, who died in October 1532 (Ep 2776
n4)
11 Not extant
12 On the Antwerp canonry see Epp 1994A:69–72 with n17, 2573:58–65.
13 Possibly one of the Spaniards referred to in Ep 2802:19–21
14 Presumably Ep 2784
15 Presumably a reference to Pieter van Griboval, the treasurer of Flanders (Ep
2716 n39)

that your absence was the reason, whether true or fictitious, that your pen- 90
sion was not paid. When, God willing, you return, have no fear, the winnow-
ing basket of your body, as you wrote,[16] will be free of the court, except to the
degree you wish to be engaged there. And in your residence you will be able
to winnow to your heart's content. For I will take care of that. Farewell, be
happy, and continue to love me as I love you. 95

Brussels, 29 March 1533

2786 / From Georg Witzel   Vacha, 30 March 1533

The autograph of this letter was in the Burscher Collection of the University
Library at Leipzig (Ep 1254 introduction). Witzel himself revised the text for
publication in *Epistolarum ... libri quatuor Georgii Wicelii* (Leipzig: N. Wolrab
1537) folio Ee iv. Allen used the revised version. For Witzel, see Ep 2715 introduction. Having received no answer to that letter, Witzel tried again with this
one, once again without success.

I send cordial greetings. During the last fair I sent you a letter,[1] very loving
and quite loquacious, but for such a hero as you not only unworthy but completely unworthy. But my love knew no judgment, no bounds. I wrote what
I felt, with great simplicity, preferring to be audacious rather than timid. My
main preoccupation was an ecumenical council.[2] Good Lord, how my mind 5
was obsessed by endless thoughts about a matter of such great importance.
There is nothing now in my aspirations that takes precedence over this. For
I see there is no end to this enormous evil unless the issues are handled in
a lawful manner; they are exacerbated by war, not mitigated. Germany is
divided, to the great danger of the Roman Empire. If secular leaders sleep, 10
religion snores. And now where are the rhetoricians holding forth with their
customary oratory to goad the minds of leading men to matters of little
consequence and often to perpetrate world-wide calamities? Indeed, in our
times they strain every nerve, and from the very center of the citadel they in-
flame the cold hearts of those whose authority in this matter is said to be the 15

* * * * *

16 This Greek phrase does not appear in Ep 2762, only *corpusculum cribro rarius*
'my poor body, more porous than a sieve' (line 10).

2786
1 The autumn book fair at Frankfurt. Ep 2715 is dated 8 September 1532.
2 Cf Ep 2715:104–10.

2786 FROM GEORG WITZEL 1533

most valid. Oh, those deaf ears of yours, Rome! Oh hearts completely dead
to any thought about things that matter most, buried in worldly pursuits!
What does your title mean? What is your teaching? What is your duty? Have
we not waited long enough, we Catholics, for the help owed to us? Do you
care so little about the flock of the Lord Jesus, as the whole world has quickly   20
come to believe? Have minds not been moved even by good men who complain about your neglect of the vineyard of the Lord, and not simply by bad
men, who assail and condemn you in not very flattering terms? But there is
good hope that Emperor Charles will mollify the curia or simply wear it out
by disparaging it, so that out of shame at least they will not be able to reject   25
what is for their own good. What Luther's party will do I do not know. Some
think they will not consent to a just agreement. I think they will, if they are
summoned in a friendly way and treated courteously and if everything in
the gathering is conducted very benevolently. For it seems that some of them
are almost worn out. And I hear that some hardly attempt to conceal their   30
wish that their dogma had never been adopted, because of all the troubles it
has begotten and brought to birth. The fierceness of its founder, Luther, will
become gentler when he hears the judgment of the most learned men summoned from all over Europe; his arrogant crest will fall flat, his enormous
horns will fail him when he will have to render an account of yesterday's   35
opinions,[3] not on his own dungheap,[4] but in the clear public view of men.
You would be the last man in the world to be absent from such a useful
procedure. If I were the emperor I would not listen to 'I am suffering from
a gallstone,' 'I cannot come.' Indeed I would order Appius, both old and afflicted with the stone, to be brought in. For indeed there is no Hannibal at   40
the gates, we are not concerned in making peace with Pyrrhus,[5] but rather a
devil is striving desperately to overturn the Christian religion and we must
act to bring peace to the church. You stand for many: you will propose, dispute, you will respond, judge, advise, and consider like no one else. If we

* * * * *

3 The idea of Luther as someone with horns appears to have originated with
  Johannes Cochlaeus' *Adversus cucullatum Minotaurum Wittenbergensem* (Frankfurt:
  n p 1523). Cf Allen Ep 3111:178n.
4 *Adagia* IV iv 25
5 When, in the Samnite wars, Pyrrhus offered the Romans terms of peace, Appius
  Claudius, old, weak, and blind, was brought to the Senate and delivered an
  oration dissuading the Romans from accepting Pyrrhus' offer; Plutarch *Parallel
  Lives* Pyrrhus 18–19.

believe Plutarch, when factions arose in Athens, Solon was very careful not   45
to seem to favour any one party but rather made himself equally available to
all sides, working only to reconcile the discordant factions. For that reason,
by the common decision of all sides, by an extraordinary measure he was
proclaimed as both the lawgiver and the arbiter of disputes.[6] We hope that
you, great man that you are, will become our Solon, whose judgment would   50
take away something from each side and thus discord will be removed. For
the sake of concord everything must be tried. Even if the sword must be
thrust against certain established usages, discord can no longer be tolerated.
We must listen not to Luther, not to the sophists,[7] but to Erasmus and those
like him, that is, to those who do not advance either side but rather promote   55
Christianity sincerely and with their whole hearts. May the good Spirit of
Christ bring this about! Amen.

I sincerely desire that you always enjoy excellent health, and I hope
that as a ninety-year-old (if not older) you will live to see the church in good
condition. Likewise, I pray that you will regain the high regard that the envy   60
of this age has almost taken away from you. I hope that, once this dissension
has been put to rest, your fame, which is now overshadowed by those whom
you enlightened, will once more shine brightly. You know whom I mean. The
faction in Saxony is now stirred up against me because I have ceased to kiss
the feet of this misbegotten pope. Jonas, whom you once praised but who   65
is now your enemy,[8] has written lies and insults against me (since he had
nothing else to write about). I have responded but the volume is not yet published.[9] Besides him there is another worthless wretch who displays equal

* * * * *

6 Plutarch *Parallel Lives* Solon 14
7 Common derogatory term for scholastic theologians
8 Erasmus and Justus Jonas (Ep 876), Luther's colleague at Wittenberg, conducted a friendly correspondence until 1521, when the theological gulf between
   Erasmus and Luther became unbridgeable. But Jonas' admiration for Erasmus
   persisted at least until the controversy over free will in 1525–7.
9 Witzel and Jonas had for some time been engaged in an acrimonious controversy that is summarized in Kawerau II xxxviii–xlii. Jonas' most recent
   publication against Witzel was *Contra tres pagellas Agricolae Phagi, Georgii
   Witzel, quibus paene Lutheranismus prostratus et voratus esset, J. Jonae responsio*
   (Wittenberg: Georg Rhau 1532). Witzel responded with *Confutatio calumnio-
   sissimae responsionis Iustae Ionae ... per Georgium Vuicelium* (Leipzig: Nicolaus
   Faber, November 1533).

scurillity in tearing me to pieces,[10] but I care no more about the insults of such
a man than if a woman or a silly child threw a pebble at me, as the poet says.[11]   70

Farewell in Christ, from whom comes the remedy and the peace of the
church. Amen.

Given at Vacha, on Passion Sunday, in the year 1533

George Witzel, your disciple

To my previous letter you sent no reply, as far as I know. I only wish   75
that you would at least reply to this one, sending your letter to Fulda. Once
more, farewell.

To the very great gentleman Master Erasmus of Rotterdam, singular
protector of the Christian commonwealth, his most cherished master and
teacher. At Freiburg im Breisgau   80

2787 / From Christoph von Stadion   Dillingen, 4 April 1533

This letter was first published as Ep 20 in Horawitz I. The autograph is in the
Württembergische Landesbibliothek Stuttgart (MS Hist Fol 47 folio 7). For
Christoph von Stadion, bishop of Augsburg, see Ep 2029 introduction.

I send cordial greetings. I have received your letter, together with the Creed
and the new homilies of Chrysostom.[1] I will read them and then give you my
judgment about them; but what need is there for judgment, since nothing
comes from you but what is absolutely perfect? All learned men openly bear
witness to this, except for some recalcitrant theologians and monks; and in   5
this they do nothing but reveal their own stupidity.

It is rumoured that King Ferdinand has reached an agreement with his
adversary about coming to terms with the Turks.[2] We do not know for certain
what the conditions are, except that Hungary is to remain in the possession

* * * * *

10 Probably a reference to the Hessian pastor Balthasar Raida, who in January 1533
    published a polemic against Cochlaeus that bore the title *Widder das lester und
    lügen büchlein Agricole Phagi, genant Georg Witzel* (Wittenberg: Nickel Schirlentz)
    and had prefaces by Martin Luther and Justus Jonas. Jonas' preface is found in
    Kawerau I 188–9.
11 Homer *Iliad* 11.389

2787
 1 The letter is not extant. For the *Explanatio symboli* see Ep 2772; for the *Homiliae
    Chrysostomi* see Ep 2774.
 2 See Ep 2780 n9.

of Ferdinand. We expect at any moment to learn the entire content of the   10
agreement.

The Augsburgers have been consulting for a long time about the mass
and images, instigated by their preachers. It is to be feared that they will
throw out the mass and images, together with all the clergy.[3]

The Nürnbergers have changed the mass in this respect: they do not   15
celebrate it unless there are communicants present, nor do they display the
sacrament to the people as they used to.[4]

The pope has written to the German circles about calling a general
council, as in the leaflet enclosed with this letter. The emperor has written to
the same effect in German. But now I hear that this is nothing but verbiage.[5]   20

As far as the errors of Cardinal Cajetanus are concerned,[6] I would think
that the first proposition, namely, that if a man's wife commits fornication it

* * * * *

3 The religious situation in Augsburg was still much the same as that described
   in Ep 2430:11–35, with the city council hesitantly yielding to popular pressure
   to enact evangelical reform. In July 1534 the council would ban Catholic preaching and restrict the celebration of mass to the eight churches directly controlled
   by the bishop of Augsburg. It took until 1537 to achieve the complete expulsion
   from the city of all Catholic doctrine and ceremonies and the establishment of a
   church modelled on that of Strasbourg rather than Wittenberg. Cf Ep 2430 n8.
4 In 1525 the city council of Nürnberg had removed the city from the jurisdiction
   of the Catholic hierarchy, and in 1528 Catholic teaching and ceremonies were
   formally abolished and replaced by Lutheran doctrine and worship. At the beginning of 1533 Nürnberg and the neighbouring margraviate of Brandenburg-
   Ansbach proclaimed a common church order (ecclesiastical constitution) that
   included the prescribed order for the celebration of the Lord's Supper. Bishop
   Stadion's information about it is correct.
5 The pope and the emperor would have written in pursuit of their agreement
   to work together for the convocation of a church council (see Ep 2767 n14).
   The 'German circles' were the ten Reichskreise (imperial circles) into which
   the Holy Roman Empire was divided. They were administrative units, each
   headed by two princes (one secular, one ecclesiastical) and primarily concerned
   with the preservation of public peace, the organization of common defence, the
   collection of imperial taxes, and the enforcement of decisions of the Imperial
   Supreme Court (Reichskammergericht). Neither the leaflet nor the emperor's letter has been found. 'Nothing but verbiage' is an accurate description at least of
   the attitude of Pope Clement VII, who, though unable directly to say 'no' to the
   emperor's call for a council, was determined not to have one.
6 In a work that has not been found but that Stadion had before him, the Paris
   theologians had condemned a number of 'errors' in the works of Tommaso
   Cardinal Cajetanus. The five errors discussed here correspond to numbers 1, 5,
   8, 10, and 12 of the sixteen articles dealt with in Cajetanus' reply to the charges,

2787 FROM CHRISTOPH VON STADION 1533

is permissible for him to remarry, is perfectly true, according to the explicit
text of Matthew 19[:9], which states: 'If a man dismisses his wife, except because of adultery, and marries another, he commits adultery.' Therefore if he   25
dismisses her because of adultery and remarries, he does not commit adultery. I do not see how any other meaning can be derived from these words,
provided that this interpretation is not opposed by Paul in [1] Corinthians
7:[10–12], where he says 'not I but the Lord, etc' and seems to teach that there
is no cause that allows a man to put away his wife and take another, because   30
the words of Paul are to be understood according to the mind of Christ in the
previously cited passage from Matthew 19. Lawyers say that what a teacher
says is to be understood according to the law that he cites. But when Paul
adds 'it is not I but the Lord,' he is referring to the passage in Matthew 19, as
the theologians have claimed. It follows, therefore, that the words of Paul are   35
to be understood according to that same place. Christ makes an exception
for adultery, and therefore Paul also seems to make the same exception. This
is supported by the long and learned passage you wrote in the *Reckonings
against Noël Béda*.[7]

That auricular confession was not instituted by Christ, etc. The canon-   40
ists hold the same opinion in the chapter 'Everyone of both sexes, concerning penances and remissions,'[8] where Panormitanus[9] cites many who hold
the same opinion. In the chapter 'therefore concerning penance, distinction
1'[10] they support what you wrote at great length on this side in the apologia against Lee, commenting on a passage in Acts 19:[18]: 'declaring their   45

* * * * *

which he did not complete until December 1533: *Responsiones ad quosdam ar-
ticulos nomine theologorum Parisiensium editos*. No published text of it is known
earlier than that in the *Opuscula omnia Thomae de Vio Cajetani* (Lyon: Junta 1562)
298–9.

7 Ie the *Supputationes errorum in censuris Natalis Bedae adversus Natalem Bedam*;
see ASD IX-5 362–70.
8 *Decretales Gregorii* IX 5.38.12; Friedberg II 887–8
9 The text has 'Panormitanus Gratianus,' an unwarranted combination of the
names of two different canonists that Allen correctly rejected as an accident
possibly caused by the reference to Gratian's *Decretum* that immediately follows. Panormitanus (Nicolò de' Tedeschi, 1386–1445) was a renowned com-
mentator on canon law. Gratian was the compiler of the twelfth-century
Decretum Gratiani, the first of the six collections that together constitute the
Corpus iuris canonici.
10 *De poen* D 1; the *Tractatus de poenitentia* is causa 33, quaestio 3 of part II of
Gratian's *Decretum*; it consists of 7 distinctiones (Friedberg I 1159–90).

deeds.'[11] And all the authorities and arguments usually adduced on the other side, in my judgment, are weak and prove nothing.

That it is better that prayers in church be said in the vernacular rather than in Latin, I would think is quite true, since this increases and intensifies the devotion of those who are listening or are present there. For the word of God is not limited to one or another way of speaking. And so what can keep it from being recited in every language?

As for the celibacy of the clergy, I think it would be advantageous that they be permitted to enter into the contract of marriage, and I cannot see the slightest reason why they should not or cannot do so. This is the judgment of Panormitanus in the canon 'Since in the past, concerning married clergy,'[12] unless in that place Cajetanus has fallen into the same error now maintained by many, namely, that this act cannot be allowed to priests because of their vow, which is part of divine law. Nevertheless, this is no obstacle at all, in my opinion, since an oath is no less a part of divine law than a vow; and if someone takes ten oaths not to get married and he does in fact do so, the marriage would be valid, in spite of all the oaths. This is the way it is viewed in canon law. And why does the same law not apply if by marrying one breaks a vow, since a vow has no more force in divine law than an oath, and if it does, that comes only from man-made law? And therefore this law can be rescinded, since the one who established it can also rescind it. Why, then, does he not rescind it, since there are so many valid arguments at hand that those who refuse to do so can only with great difficulty be excused from slander?

Whether irreconcilable discord between such married partners is a reasonable cause for dispensing from the vow, that is, if each remarries with the previous consent of the other, I would not dare to assert, because of this saying: 'What God has joined together let no one put asunder.'[13] Nevertheless, if what the church claims for itself can be authorized by divine law, namely, when it dissolves a legitimately contracted marriage before subsequent copulation because one of the spouses enters a religious order, it seems to me that the same thing might be done according to the canon cited,[14] since there is a more valid reason for the dissolution. But I have some doubts about whether

* * * * *

11 See CWE 72 374–5 (*Responsio ad annotationes Eduardi Lei*). The reference to Acts is in Gratian; see Friedberg I 1176.
12 *Decretales Gregorii* IX 3.3.6; Friedberg II 458–9.
13 Matt 19:6
14 See n12 above.

the church can dissolve a legitimately contracted marriage so that someone can enter that sort of life, since nowhere can one find in Holy Scripture that 80 such a power was granted to the church. This is what I think about the errors of Cajetanus. Nevertheless, I submit all of this to your judgment, and I hope you are in good health.

Given at Dillingen, 4 April, in the year [15]33
Yours, Christoph, bishop of Augsburg   85

2788 / To Bonifacius Amerbach   Freiburg, 22 March, 10 April 1533

This letter (= AK Ep 1734) was first published in the *Epistolae familiares*. The autograph is in the Öffentliche Bibliothek of the University of Basel (MS AN III 15 47). The letter was written on 22 March, the long postscript on 10 April.

Cordial greetings. From what source you have learned about the favourable state of my health, I do not know.[1] To me it is certainly not yet clear whether I am to be numbered among the living or the dead. To such a degree does March assail me and scour through all the inner parts of my poor body! The new moon is upon us! Then comes that infamous tail of March,[2] which I am 5 afraid will stretch into the middle of April. May God look out for me. I am glad things go well with you.

If you have the chance, please see to it that my letter to Sadoleto gets through to him, and at the same time join to it my Creed, the eight homilies translated by me, and the same number by Brie.[3] If no one comes along 10 who is willing to carry the bag of books, send the letter by itself, promising the books if someone comes along who will not refuse to carry the small packages.

I have made my excuses to Herwagen, but gently.[4] I am resolved to do this with everyone from now on. Enough of slavery!   15

* * * * *

2788
1 Cf Ep 2770:1–6 with n3.
2 For the assaults of March 1533 in general, see Ep 2768 n11. We have not been able to trace the expression 'tail of March' (*cauda Martii*), but it seems clearly to express the idea that the end of March can easily be more like a lion than a lamb.
3 For the letter and the works of Erasmus to be included with it, see Ep 2775:5–6 with n2. For the work of Brie to be included, see Ep 2727 introduction. For Bonifacius' compliance with this request, see AK Ep 1742:1–4.
4 Ie his refusal of the request to write a preface for Herwagen's edition of Cicero; see Ep 2765 n5.

I congratulate your renowned university on being happily augmented by the accession of the new Doctor Brunsfeld.[5] But listen to this for a laugh!

In a certain bundle of letters to me, a letter was included with a double seal. There seemed to be another letter inside it. The form of address was high-flown: 'To that excellent, celebrated, but in fact even greater gentleman Simon Grynaeus, Professor of Platonic and Aristotelian Philosophy, etc.' I thought I had seen the handwriting before, but I did not recognize it. I was even further from guessing the truth because the letter was bundled together with some letters that had been sent from Italy.[6] I was surprised that admirers of Grynaeus were found there too. I sent it to Grynaeus wrapped up in an envelope of mine, in which I wrote that I was more trustworthy in sending the letter to him than some Evangelicals were in handling my letters. Thinking my remark was aimed at him, he immediately sent an angry reply, saying he wished that if I wanted to find fault with him, I would speak openly and tell him what it was that offended me. And, like a shrew-mouse giving itself away with its own squeaking,[7] he tells me that a letter to me from Carinus was included and that Carinus had left it up to him whether to throw it into the fire or to deliver it to me. He said that he had thrown it into the fire because, though the first part of the letter was mild, the middle contained the venom of long-standing enmity. Such a headstrong character, which no vengeance will satisfy! Other things can wait till I see you, which I hope will be in April. Best wishes to you.

Freiburg, 22 March 1533

Yours truly, Erasmus of Rotterdam

The letter of Anselmus' host,[8] which he sent a while ago by my thieving Jacobus,[9] got held up here for quite some time because no one came along to whom I could give it. But I have long since sent it by a reliable man to Johann

* * * * *

5 Erasmus means his old adversary Otto Brunfels (Ep 1405). Bonifacius had evidently informed him of Brunfels' doctoral promotion in medicine at Basel in 1532. Brunfels had not, however, joined the faculty of the university. He remained a schoolmaster in Strasbourg until October 1534, when he was called to be city physician in Bern, where he died in November 1534. See AK Ep 1734 n2.
6 This story is told in much the same language in Ep 2779:37–60.
7 *Adagia* I iii 65
8 Johann Gross, who had played host to Anselmus Ephorinus at Basel (Ep 2740 nn1–2). Nothing is known of the letter.
9 For Jacobus, see Ep 2652 n4.

Paumgartner.[10] He will take care of everything very carefully. Please let the
host know about this, whenever it is convenient, and please add greetings in
my name.   45

Herwagen is not doing anything. The bishops are calling on me for the
book on the method of preaching and other things.[11] I can hardly keep well,
and for many years now I have had no holidays. They are trying to get you as
an advocate, since they know I cannot refuse you anything. That is the way
Holbein extorted letters of introduction to England. But he lived at Antwerp   50
for more than a month, and would have stayed longer if he had found
dupes.[12] In England he deceived those to whom he had been recommended.[13]
I will let you plead for Herwagen, as long as you allow me to deny him. To
provide a preface about a noble author about whom I have written nothing
worthwhile[14] would be shameful and odious. Besides, I could not devote the   55
proper care to it, no matter how much I wanted to. Once more, farewell.

10 April

To the most renowned Master Amerbach, doctor of laws in the famous
University of Basel. At Basel

* * * * *

10 Presumably Johann (ii) Paumgartner at Augsburg (Ep 2774), who would send
   the letter on to Ephorinus at Padua, where Paumgartner's son, Johann Georg,
   was also studying at the time
11 The book was *Ecclesiastes sive de ratio concionandi*. Though it is beyond doubt
   that many of Erasmus' friends among the bishops looked forward to the publication of the work – it was written at the suggestion of John Fisher, bishop of
   Rochester, and dedicated to Christoph von Stadion, bishop of Augsburg – the
   context here indicates that Alfred Hartmann is probably correct in interpreting *episcopi* 'the bishops' as a reference to the publishers Nicolaus Episcopius
   (whose German name 'Bischoff' had been Latinized to *episcop[i]us* 'bishop') and
   Hieronymus Froben, who were business partners and lived in the same house.
   It was they who published the *Ecclesiastes* in August 1535.
12 Allusion to Juvenal 9.8, quoted in *Adagia* I vii 75: 'He goes the rounds and finds
   no dupes.' (For 'dupes' [*fatuos*] CWE 32 112 has 'innocents.')
13 In August 1526 Hans Holbein the Younger left Basel to seek his fortune in
   England, going first to Antwerp, bearing a letter to Pieter Gillis recommending him as a great artist (Ep 1740:20–5) He must have gone on to England
   fairly quickly, because in December Thomas More wrote to Erasmus singing
   Holbein's praises and offering to do everything possible to promote his fortunes in England (Ep 1770:77–9). Nothing is known of the deceptions of which
   Erasmus deemed Holbein to be guilty. It is scarcely likely that he would have
   been accused of poor quality work. But he might well have been accused of
   failing to execute commissions for which he had been paid, thus embarrassing
   Erasmus, who had recommended him.
14 Cicero

2789 / To Nicolas Bourbon   Freiburg, 10 April 1533

This letter was first published as an appendix to the second edition of Bourbon's *Nugae*, a volume of his poetic 'trifles' (Lyon: Gryphius 1538).

The son of a wealthy iron-founder, Nicolas Bourbon the Elder (c 1503–c 1550) was born at Vendeuvre, near Bar-sur-Aube. Educated at Troyes and then at Paris, where he studied Greek under Jacques Toussain (Ep 2119), he began writing poetry at an early age. By 1532 his search for wealthy patrons had led to his entering the service of Charles de Tournon, bishop of Viviers. The first edition of the *Nugae* (1533) gave ample evidence of his sympathy for religious reform (see n2 below), which probably accounts for his arrest and imprisonment on suspicion of heresy in 1534. He was released on the order of the king and, having already been appointed tutor to three young Englishmen, he spent the following year at the English court, where Hans Holbein the Younger painted his portrait. Returning to France, he lived at Lyon, continuing to publish poetry (*Paidagogeion*, 1536) and hunting for pupils and patrons. In about 1539 he became the tutor to Jeanne d'Albret, the daughter of Margaret of Angoulême (queen of Navarre and sister of Francis I). When his pupil married Antoine de Bourbon in 1548, Nicolas Bourbon celebrated the event with an *Epithalamion* (1549), and then retired to a benefice at Candé.

DESIDERIUS ERASMUS OF ROTTERDAM TO NICOLAS BOURBON
OF VENDEUVRE, POET CROWNED WITH LAUREL, GREETINGS
My most learned young Bourbon, I have read your letter and the odes and epigrams with which you have so happily amused yourself in Greek and Latin:[1] I cannot tell you how much pleasure I took in them.[2] For even though I have   5 now reached that stage in life when I know daily that death is either at hand or imminent, I was so delighted and refreshed by reading your poems that in the course of reading I almost forgot that I am Erasmus, that is, an old man with

* * * * *

2789
1 The letter is not extant. It accompanied a gift copy of the *Nugae*.
2 Erasmus had good reason to be pleased. The volume contains two sets of elegiac verse addressed to him, an epigram praising his translations of Lucian, and another epigram with a comparison of him and Guillaume Budé that is complimentary to both. Other friends of Erasmus addressed are Germain de Brie (Ep 2727), Andrea Alciati (Ep 1250), and Georges d'Armagnac (Ep 2569). There are also epigrams attacking Diego López Zúñiga (Ep 2637 n3), Noël Béda (Ep 2635 n4), and Pierre Cousturier (Ep 1943 n7). But the poems also bear witness to close connections with men whose religious views were suspect at best, including Lodovicus Carinus (Ep 2111 n2). See Allen's introduction to this letter.

one foot in the grave. Please do not think I am saying this just to please your ears. May our Lord Christ, at whose tribunal I must soon stand, so grant me 10 his favour, seeing that I speak from the heart. There is nothing more felicitous than your talent, nothing more copious than your creativity, nothing more elegant than your language. And I am confident that this judgment of mine will be approved by all who have come to know Bourbon as well as Erasmus has.

I would envy France her many bright lights, indeed pillars, of humane 15 learning, except that I think that not only France should be congratulated but also the whole commonwealth of letters because, before I depart from this life, I see rising in this age (otherwise the worst and most turbulent time) some vigorous defenders of refined literary study. Accordingly I am greatly pleased that a false rumour of my death gave you an occasion to write an epitaph for 20 me,[3] for such things delight me because I have long since reflected on taking flight from here. But nevertheless, I am not elated every time I am praised to the skies by you or men like you (who are very few indeed). I will deem myself abundantly celebrated and glorious if, after expending so much labour in restoring literary culture, I come one day, finally, to rest in Christ my Lord. 25

Farewell, O Bourbon, sweetest of poets, and make the Muses, who have granted you their favour with such kindness and intimacy, serve the glory not of men but of Christ. If the torments of this kidney stone allowed it, you would have a more extended letter. Return to the poet Salmon greetings in as many words as his.[4] 30

At Freiburg im Breisgau, 10 April, in the year of our salvation 1533

2790 / From Henricus Cornelius Agrippa   [Frankfurt], 10 April 1533

First published in the *Agrippae opera* II 1054, this is Agrippa's answer to Ep 2748.

AGRIPPA TO ERASMUS

I would have written to you concerning many important topics, thrice-great Erasmus, except that I expected more and greater things from you. For that is what you promise in your earlier letter: that when you had time you would

* * * * *

3 There is no such epitaph in the first edition of the *Nugae*, but there are two in the second edition.
4 Jean Salmon Macrin (1490–1557) of Loudun in Poitou studied at Paris under Jacques Lefèvre d'Etaples and Girolamo Aleandro, and with the help of influential friends became *valet-de-chambre* to Francis I (1530). A fertile Latin poet who took Catullus and Horace as his models, he included references to Erasmus and Thomas More in his *Carminum libri quatuor* (1530).

send me a long and personal letter.[1] But I do not dare to interrupt your oc-   5
cupations any further because I confess that I am not such a one as can give
in return what you deserve. Nevertheless, I wait for a letter from you with
the greatest eagerness and I beg you not to look down on your Agrippa, who
regards you with great affection. My little book against some theologians,
which I sent to be printed at Basel, was not printed and came back to me, be-   10
cause it had offended some people. Now it will be printed elsewhere.[2] I wrote
you at greater length about this matter, but I learned from your letter that my
letter was not delivered to you,[3] and I heard the same from Cratander.

But more about this at another time. Now, however, what it behooves
you to know is that the very reverend and most illustrious prince-elector-   15
archbishop of Cologne,[4] who is an enthusiastic devotee of your writings,
regards you with singular affection, devotion, esteem, and veneration, and
would like to strike up a friendship with you; he is eager see and hear you in
person, and he commanded me to write to you and to learn from you whether you would like to meet him sometime this summer at Bonn or Cologne to   20
gratify him by staying just a few days, and that he would make such a trip
very much worth your while. Please write back to me what you will do. One
thing I know, that if you do come you will meet a prince with a very Christian
outlook, one under whose patronage you would be able to confer and bestow
a great deal on the Christian commonwealth and on public tranquillity.   25
With the very best wishes, 10 April 1533. Written in haste

2791 / From Viglius Zuichemus   Padua, 17 April 1533

This letter was first published in Van Heussen 113, and then as Ep 44 in VZE. It
appears to be Viglius' response to one or more letters no longer extant (cf n2
below). Erasmus' answer is Ep 2810. For Viglius Zuichemus see Ep 2657.

* * * * *

2790
1 See Ep 2692:9–10.
2 The book was his *Apologia contra theologistas Lovanienses*, the text of which he
had sent to Basel to be published by Andreas Cratander; see Ep 2739 n2. It appeared later in 1533, with no indication of the place or the printer (not Basel:
Cratander but Cologne: Eucharius Cervicornus).
3 Ep 2748:5–6.
4 Hermann von Wied (Ep 1976). Erasmus' response to this latest overture from
Hermann was the decision to dedicate his edition of Origen to him (Ep 3128),
but he did not live to write the letter of dedication, which was supplied by
Beatus Rhenanus.

TO ERASMUS OF ROTTERDAM

From my latest letter,[1] my very learned Master Erasmus, you can see that
the bundle of your letters has been delivered to me.[2] Logau has not yet returned to us;[3] for a long time many have been waiting for him, not only our
countrymen but Bembo, Bonamico,[4] and other learned men with whom he   5
was acquainted and in whose financial records he left behind his name as a
reminder. But he sometimes writes about benefices, and lavish conditions,
and for the time being he cajoles his creditors with such smoke screens.

I am going to do what you advise concerning my studies, not to provide for my health but for my fortunes, and I will make use of the support   10
of my friends as long as they are able and willing to help me. This year was
somewhat troublesome for me. But still I think it has been not without considerable progress, especially in legal studies. I have put up with the enmity
and the attack of my antagonist, although in the beginning I found it difficult
to do, especially because I was not yet accustomed to Italian temperaments   15
and wiles.[5]

I hear that the man who has succeeded to the archbishopric of Canterbury functioned last year as ambassador to the emperor and that he is
commended by many for his kindness and learning.[6] I have no doubt that he
will see to it that your pension remains intact, provided he is informed about   20
it, for you can even claim it legally once an agent is named for it.[7] And it is
much better to gain some part of it through agents than to lose all of it. I did
not know Zacharias Deiotarus except from your letters. I hope that his place

* * * * *

2791
1 Ep 2767:1–7
2 Ie a bundle of letters (including Ep 2736) to all the people in Padua with whom
  Erasmus was in correspondence at the time. The several references to matters
  not mentioned in Epp 2736, 2767 – eg 'advice concerning my studies' (line 9),
  Deiotarus' death (lines 22–3), and Hoxwier in Erasmus' 'album' (line 29)
  – indicate that Viglius is responding to one or more letters of Erasmus no
  longer extant.
3 For Georg von Logau and his current absence from Padua, see Ep 2753:30–2.
  Viglius here turns the Latin form of 'von Logau' (a Logus) into Alogus, which is
  Latinized Greek for 'lacking in eloquence,' 'unreasonable,' 'stupid.'
4 Pietro Bembo (Ep 2106), Lazzaro Bonamico (Ep 2657 n18)
5 Antagonist unidentified
6 Thomas Cranmer, who succeeded William Warham as archbishop of Canterbury, had been ambassador to the imperial court in 1532; see Ep 2654 n8.
7 Cranmer did indeed continue the payment of Erasmus' pension; see Allen Epp
  2815:8–18, 2879:30–5).

will be taken by many Frisians who are as fond of you as he was,[8] for I think
it contributes to the honour of our country if it recognizes your merits and   25
shows itself to be worthy of your high regard.

Hoxwier is certainly not inferior to any of our countrymen in learning
and family, and he will rival me in integrity and, as I hope, in veneration
for you.[9] And I am delighted that he is enrolled in your album.[10] There are
many reasons for me to be well disposed towards him: native land, paren-   30
tal friendship, proximity, and friendship struck up during our studies. The
other one you mention has, I fear, contracted in Italy a disease not only of
the body but also of the mind.[11] Haio Cammingha begins to be a bit chilly
towards me because I did not recommend him elaborately enough when he
was staying with you.[12] But how could I be blamed, since I myself was still in   35
need of someone to recommend me to you, since I had just been admitted to
mutual friendship with you,? and since you also could perceive his virtues
well enough from daily living with him?

The son of the treasurer has high hopes about the payment of the
pension, and he has written to his father very diligently about that matter,   40
beseeching him earnestly to be energetic in supporting your case.[13] But as
winter approaches he himself will return to his country and there in person
he will devote his fullest energies to your cause. I am awaiting the arrival
of the other young man's father;[14] you will not lose the reward for the good
deed you have done for him.   45

For the enriched *Adages* all scholars are and will be indebted to you,[15]
for they find that collection incredibly fruitful. Girolamo Aleandro is now
the papal legate to the senate of Venice; he has received the office of judging
which books can be sold publicly.[16] Vida, the author of a poem on the art of

* * * * *

8 Deiotarus (Ep 1205 n1), member of the household of Archbishop William
    Warham, was one of the trio of 'kind and close friends' who had recently died;
    see Ep 2776 n4.
9 Viglius' kinsman and fellow Frisian, Hector van Hoxwier (Ep 2586 introduction)
10 Ie in the roster of those of whom you approve; see *Adagia* i vii 34.
11 Haio Herman; see Ep 2682 n24.
12 For Cammingha and his stay with Erasmus see Ep 2766 introduction.
13 For the treasurer of Flanders, Pieter van Griboval, and his son Florens, who was
    at this time living with Viglius at Padua, see Ep 2716 n39.
14 Johann Georg Hörmann, son of Georg Hörmann of Augsburg; see Ep 2716 n46.
15 See Ep 2773 introduction.
16 His term as papal legate to the imperial court having ended with the departure
    of the emperor from the Empire in the autumn of 1532, Aleandro was now the
    legate in Venice.

poetry, was made a bishop when he recently presented the six books of his   50
Christias to the supreme pontiff at Bologna.[17] Recently also Romolo Amaseo
has published Xenophon in Latin.[18] And at Venice there is in press a certain
work by Bartolomeo Ricci on elocution, which is marvellously extolled by
the Italians.[19] I am sending now the preface to the life of Chrysostom.[20] Canon
Zanchi gave me the sermons of Ambrose against the Arians and the Passion   55
of Cyprian,[21] both of which I will send you at another time. For he required
that I myself get them copied, and leave a copy with him. Bembo continues
to treat me in a very kind and friendly fashion. Recently I also received from
him permission to publish the *Institutiones* in Greek,[22] and I showed him the
preface, in which I expressed my thanks for his gift, thereby gaining access   60
to another book, the *Novellae constitutiones* of Justinian in a fuller and more

* * * * *

17 Marco Girolamo Vida (c 1485–1566) of Cremona was a member of the canons
regular of St John Lateran who from 1510 established a reputation as one of the
finest poets of sixteenth-century Italy. Among the works that established his
fame were the two mentioned here: *De arte poetica carmen,* published at Rome
in 1527, and the *Christiados libri sex,* a poem on the life of Christ modelled on
Virgil's *Aeneid.* Written before 1519 at the request of Pope Leo x, presented to
Pope Clement vII in 1532, and then published at Cremona in 1535, the *Christias*
earned Vida the name 'the Christian Virgil.' In 1533 he was made bishop of
Alba in Piedmont, where he proved himself a vigorous opponent of heresy.
Driven from Alba by French and Spanish armies in 1542, he retired to Cremona,
where he was appointed bishop in 1548. He had in the meantime (1545–7) visited Trent three times to participate in the council.
18 For Amaseo see Ep 2657 n20. His translation of Xenophon's *Anabasis* (*De Cyri
minoris expeditione*) was published at Bologna in March 1533.
19 A professor of rhetoric at Venice, Bartolomeo Ricci (1490–1569) was an avid
Ciceronian and the author of many works. The work on elocution mentioned
here was *Apparatus latinae locutionis,* published at Venice in 1533.
20 Presumably the edition of Helenopolitanus Palladius *De vita d. Johannis Chrysostomi archiepiscopi Constantinopolitani dialogus* published at Venice in 1533
(Bernardino Vitale)
21 For Giacomo Crisostomo Zanchi and the two works mentioned, see Ep 2716
nn35–6.
22 Pietro Bembo had placed at Viglius' disposal a thirteenth-century manuscript
of Theophilus Antecessor's Greek translation of the *Institutiones* of Justinian
(part 3 of the *Corpus iuris civilis*) owned by the library of St Mark's at Venice;
see Epp 2716:104–8, 2753:18–20. Together with another manuscript supplied
by Giambattista Egnazio (Ep 2657 n3), it was the basis of Viglius' edition of the
Greek text of the *Institutiones* published by Froben at Basel in 1534. For further
details see Allen Ep 2791:59n.

correct form than that which was published by Haloander.[23] And I conceived the hope that I would acquire other works from him. Farewell.

Padua, 17 April 1533

2792 / To Nicolaus Olahus   Freiburg, 19 April 1533

This letter, Erasmus' reply to Ep 2785, was first published in Ipolyi page 351.
The manuscript is page 345 of the Olahus codex in the Hungarian National
Archives at Budapest (Ep 2339 introduction). Olahus' reply is Ep 2828.

THE RESPONSE OF ERASMUS OF ROTTERDAM TO NICOLAUS OLAHUS
Read when you are alone.
I have received your last letter,[1] which gives ample testimony of your extraordinary prudence and a certain remarkable good will towards me. Would that
there were some favour I could do in return. I suspect that the consent of   5
the emperor is required for the pension to be claimed on firmer grounds. In
other respects, I am not banished from there; I left with full permission and
the facts themselves demonstrate that there was no lack of things to do in
Basel. Several years ago the emperor wrote to his aunt, the Lady Margaret,
that I should have a special pension (for the payment of other pensions was   10
suspended), so that I would have no reason to betake myself to any other
prince.[2] I was also courted with great promises by Francis, the king of France,
and that in a letter written in his own hand.[3] He had already destined for me
the provostship of Tongres, which brings a large income and much honour;[4]
but I valued above everything my leisure to write. When the matter had been   15
considered by the council, Lady Margaret sent a letter saying she was thankful I was not going to depart from the retinue of the emperor but that my

* * * * *

23 On Gregorius Haloander and his pioneering edition of the *Corpus iuris civi-*
lis, see Ep 2568 n9. The manuscript of the *Novellae constitutiones* (part 4 of the
Corpus) to which Viglius was given access had, like that of the *Institutiones*
mentioned in the preceding note, once belonged to Cardinal Bessarion. Viglius
made excerpts from it that were used by later scholars; see Allen Ep 2791:59n.

2792
1 Ep 2785
2 Ep 1380
3 Ep 1375
4 There was no such thing as a 'provostship at Tongres.' Erasmus clearly means
the treasurership at Tours, for which see Epp 1434:24–5 with n12, 1487:18–20.

absence was the reason my pension was not paid, and that if I wished to
return, not only my pension but also far greater recompense was in store
for me.[5] The main reason that I left is that some people had persuaded the   20
emperor to assign the Lutheran affair to me. The one who advised him to
do that was Jean Glapion.[6] I thought this was done in a spirit of friendship,
but because I was considered to be suspect (although with no grounds at all)
they wanted to involve me in that task either to make me the hangman of
some whom they thought I favoured, or else to make me betray myself and   25
be caught in their nets.

I regret many things, but I have never regretted my departure; and if
the dissension about religious devotion had not occurred, I think I could
have grown old there[7] quite comfortably. This city is cold,[8] the weather is
pestilential, the common people are inhospitable, and there is no place for   30
me to walk about without stirring up an immediate buzz of various rumours.
On the other hand, it would favour my health if I could somehow change
my location.[9] The Oecolampadians have an extraordinary hatred for me, and
the feeling is mutual. At Besançon there is serious dissension between the
clergy and the city council: the council invites me, the clergy hates the idea   35
of my coming.[10] Where you are, temperaments are more gentle. And an old
man can live nowhere more honourably than in his native country. There is
very little agreement among the princes in Germany. I am afraid that in the
absence of the emperor discord will spring up here; for it is already growing.[11] I am not so much concerned about my pension as about leaving here   40
in an honourable way. There is nothing more loquacious or more fatuous
than these Evangelicals. But I think I have made it quite clear to the monks
and theologians how little I agree with the founders of the sects, who pose
considerable danger to me here. For they never stop plotting and there is
nothing more vindictive than such men.   45

* * * * *

5 No letter of Margaret to Erasmus has survived.
6 The confessor of Charles v; see Ep 1275 introduction.
7 In this context 'there' has to mean Basel, from which Erasmus was driven in
   consequence of the stormy triumph of the Reformation.
8 Freiburg
9 Ie leave Freiburg but go somewhere other than Basel, which he had left in
   1529 after the victory of the Reformation under the leadership of Johannes
   Oecolampadius (see following sentence)
10 See Ep 2759 n3.
11 Charles v had left Germany for Spain via Italy in November 1532 (Ep 2753
   nn13, 16) and would not return until 1541.

I wish Lieven well,[12] but I am sorry that he is so frivolous: every time he has an opportunity he lets it slip through his fingers. He was born for intellectual pursuits, and it had been agreed that he should study medicine at Louvain. But he wasted his time there and did the same at Paris. Finally, after he had sold his books and spent everything, he took to begging, hunting jobs here and there. But he was not successful at that either. At Augsburg he found sufficient favour with the court.[13] He made a good deal of money and threw it all away. I advised him to follow the example of Schepper and hunt for a wife with a good dowry.[14] He married a girl with nothing. He never followed the advice of his friends in anything, and he himself is empty-headed by nature. What sort of life he is considering now, I have no idea. I have received the letter in which you describe the rashly contracted marriage,[15] but I deliberately concealed the marriage, for certain reasons. I also received the nonsense of the Dane; I wish he were a bishop in his Denmark![16] Perhaps he does not hate me, but he does more harm with his inopportune good will than an enemy would. What could be more useless than to tear Scaliger apart with inept verses and to stir up that Camarina, which it was better to leave untouched?[17]

I write about these things rather freely because, thanks to my completely trustworthy servant,[18] there is no danger that a rumour should arise there that I am doing this in order to be recalled honourably to Brabant. But it is better nonetheless that few know about it. Certainly I would not want

* * * * *

12 Lieven Algoet, the famulus whom Erasmus had urged to enter a learned profession but who instead had sought preferment at the imperial court. Erasmus had just managed, with the help of Olahus, to secure Lieven's appointment as a secretary at the court of Queen Mary (Ep 2693 n3), but was now greatly upset that he had entered into an unsuitable marriage (see below).
13 For Lieven's visit to Augsburg in 1530, see Ep 2278 n2.
14 Cf Ep 2799:19–21. At Bruges c 1528 the imperial diplomat Cornelis de Schepper (Ep 1747 n23) had married the wealthy widow Anna Isabella Donche.
15 Ep 2693
16 The Dane was Jakob Jespersen (Ep 2570 introduction), and his 'nonsense' was the 'inept verses' referred to below.
17 Jespersen had evidently taken aim at Julius Caesar Scaliger and his *Oratio pro Cicerone contra Erasmum* (for which see Ep 2635 introduction). To 'stir up the Camarina' means to stir up unnecessary trouble; see *Adagia* i i 64.
18 Quirinus Hagius (Ep 2704 n6), who was on his second journey to England in Erasmus' service. He doubtless carried this letter and Epp 2793–6, 2798–2800. The same endorsement of his trustworthiness is found in Epp 2799:14–16, 2800:100–1.

anyone to know or believe that this is my intention. Unless I am recalled
while it is still summer, undertaking the journey would not be without danger to my frail little body. But if everything goes according to my wishes, I   70
will not delay until the arrival of my Quirinus from England,[19] but will hasten there. If not, then I will have to pass the winter here, but with the will that
I established in Basel recognized here.[20] In that regard I have a letter of King
Ferdinand to the council of this city;[21] I have a public and general decree of
the emperor;[22] I have a papal brief.[23] But still, if I were to leave anything be-   75
hind, it would hardly be safe from the city council here, as I can predict from
many examples. They are a predatory breed of men. Farewell.

Freiburg, 19 April 1533

2793 / To Erasmus Schets   [Freiburg], 19 April 1533

This letter was first published by Allen on the basis of the autograph in the
British Library (MS Add 38512 folio 80).

Cordial greetings. I cannot understand from any of the three letters I have
received whether Peter, the public messenger of this city, has delivered any
letters to you.[1] One of the letters was to you, and included with it was a letter
to Barbier.[2] Another was to Karel Uutenhove,[3] and to that one was attached a
letter to the treasurer of Flanders.[4] A third was to Goclenius.[5] I see that some   5
were delivered, but I do not know, and would like to know, whether Peter
met you at Antwerp. Nowadays people are remarkably treacherous.

* * * * *

19 Quirinus was in the Netherlands on his return journey in early July 1533 (Allen
   Ep 2841:14), but not until November does Erasmus mention his presence in
   Freiburg (Allen Ep 2876:30).
20 Re Erasmus' will, see Ep 2754:7–12.
21 Ep 2317
22 Ep 2318
23 Ep 1588

2793
 1 None of the three letters is extant. No letters from Schets in the period March
   1532–February 1535 have survived.
 2 The letter to Schets is Ep 2781; the enclosed letter to Barbier does not survive
   but it was answered by Ep 2842 (cf Ep 2781:19 with n8).
 3 Not extant; cf Ep 2799:8–9.
 4 Not extant. The treasurer was Pieter Griboval (Ep 2716 n39).
 5 Not extant. The most recent surviving letter to him is Ep 2644.

Molendino congratulates me on coming to an agreement with Barbier. He says he learned about it from you.[6] Either I am completely mistaken or that courtier is making fun of me. But perhaps he will not get away with it unscathed.

I wrote to your Benedictine through this man.[7] If I had known that you were coming to Frankfurt,[8] I would have sent the letter to you. I would not want that good young man to do anything rash, especially in these times.

Make sure to keep to yourself the secret communicated to you by Olahus.[9] I do not know how highly I will be regarded there. It is enough if I will be safe.

If my plans are not successful,[10] I would like you to give to my servant Quirinus, when he returns from England, a brief written accounting of the money that you have. For on the basis of a letter I cannot ask anything from the heirs, though I have quite a few.[11]

Farewell. 19 April 1533

Yours truly, Erasmus of Rotterdam

To the outstanding gentleman, Master Erasmus Schets. At Antwerp

2794 / To Petrus Vulcanius   Freiburg, 20 April 1533

This letter, the response to one no longer extant, was first published in the *Vita Erasmi*. The autograph is in the University Library at Leiden (MS Vulc 109). For Petrus Vulcanius see Ep 2460 introduction.

For that sincerity of yours I am more grateful, my dear Vulcanius, than for your judgment about me, and no less grateful because you seek to alleviate my troubles by friendly consolation. What you write is true: this world is

* * * * *

6 See Ep 2763:4–5.

7 Quirinus Hagius; see Ep 2792 n19. For the Benedictine, see Ep 2763:14–23.

8 Presumably to the spring fair

9 Ie the plan to return to Brabant; see Ep 2785.

10 Presumably also the planned return to Brabant

11 The language here is bewilderingly vague. It is not at all clear what letter (*epistola*) is being referred to or who the heirs (*heredes*) were. (A *heres* could be the trustee of a will as well as one of its beneficiaries.) The gist of the passage seems to be that Erasmus, should he not return to Brabant, would need a written statement (*syngrapha*) of the money he had on deposit with Schets (not just a reference to it in a letter) in order to be able to leave binding instructions concerning its disposition in a will that would be executed in Freiburg (or, as it turned out, in Basel).

astoundingly ungrateful; it is in the other that we must seek a reward. Some
friends die; others change their minds. Christ can never refuse us.   5

I congratulate you on your good fortune,¹ no less than I do the commonwealth that has acquired for itself a man who possesses so many distinguished gifts. For I confess that I owe a great deal to your city.²

After your departure Charles Blount's style changed, but not for the
better. For his Theseus was gone.³   10

The inhabitants of Bruges are wise in wanting to put you into bond-
age – may the chains be pleasant and golden.⁴ I would pray that Vulcanius
should have a Venus except that I am terrified of a bad omen from Mars.⁵ But
all joking aside, if you happen to get a bride worthy of you – which I think
has already happened – I would not be unwilling to sing an epithalamium.   15
Nor is there any reason you should think of giving me a recompense. For I
am no Simonides, especially to learned and honourable friends.⁶

I have always been most fond of Leonard Casembroot, as he well deserves, and I think the feeling is mutual.⁷ I wonder why he has written nothing via my Quirinus.⁸ He is a most accomplished man, with many virtues. I   20
want to know if his fortune matches his merits.

Farewell. Freiburg, the octave of Easter in the year 1533

* * * * *

2794
1 Ie his appointment in September 1531 as a clerk in the government of his native
city of Bruges. He was not the 'pensionary' (chief counsellor in legal matters),
as Erasmus describes him in lines 24–5.
2 It is not clear why Erasmus would feel a particular debt to Bruges. Perhaps he
remembered it fondly as the city where his last-ever meetings with Thomas
More took place in 1520–1; see Epp 1106 introduction, 1233 introduction.
3 Before returning to his native city in 1531, Vulcanius had been the tutor of
Charles Blount, fifth Baron Mountjoy. Erasmus had praised Charles for his fine
style (Ep 2459:20–1), only to be confirmed later in his suspicion (Ep 2459:19)
that the praise really belonged to his tutor, here described as his 'Theseus,' ie
someone who provides outside help (see *Adagia* I v 27).
4 Cf Horace *Carmina* 4.11.23–4.
5 A play on the name of Vulcanius, who at this time got married. In mythology,
Vulcan married Venus, who then cuckolded him with Mars.
6 The Greek lyric poet Simonides of Ceos (556–468 BC) was allegedly the first poet
to demand fees rather than thanks for his compositions; cf *Adagia* II ix 12.
7 An old friend of Erasmus, Casembroot (Ep 1594 introduction) had since c 1527–
8 been a member of the civic administration of Bruges and would serve from
1535 to 1539 as pensionary.
8 Quirinus Hagius, who carried this letter; see Ep 2792 n19.

Erasmus of Rotterdam, in my own hand, extempore

To the very distinguished gentleman Master Petrus Vulcanius, pensionary of the renowned commonwealth of Bruges.[9] At Bruges in Flanders   25

2795 / To Guillaume de Horion   Freiburg, 21 April 1533

This letter was first published in the epistolary appendix to Erasmus' *De praeparatione ad mortem* (Basel: Froben 1534) 132–4.

Guillaume de Horion, lord of Ordingen, near St Truiden (documented 1530–
40), was the father of Michel de Horion, who in August 1530 became a student
of Conradus Goclenius at the Collegium Trilingue in Louvain. At Goclenius'
instigation (see lines 26–7) the father, who was known as a patron of scholars
and took an interest in Erasmus' works, had written to Erasmus a letter that
does not survive. This is Erasmus' reply to it. There is no other surviving trace
of correspondence between Erasmus and Horion. It seems that at some point,
perhaps as an accompaniment to this letter, Erasmus sent Horion the copy of
the *Explanatio symboli* (Ep 2772) that is now in the library of Trinity College,
Cambridge, inscribed and freely annotated in Horion's own hand.

DESIDERIUS ERASMUS OF ROTTERDAM TO THE RENOWNED MASTER
GUILLAUME DE HORION, GREETINGS

Most distinguished sir, in a calm sea it is not difficult to sail, but in a huge
storm it needs a skilled sailor to hold the rudder on course. In former times,
when pagans cruelly and barbarously tormented and murdered Christians,   5
there was a retreat to which they could retire: hidden away there they led a
quiet life as if they were in another world. Nowadays, when everything is
contaminated, to what harbour can one withdraw? I certainly don't see any,
unless one withdraws into oneself and seeks peace of mind in one's own
mind. For Christ alone truly calms the mind. He is within us, if we wish   10
it. Great solace is provided by books that breathe of Christ. What is more
pleasant or more salutary in this life than their words?

In that regard, I congratulate you on your good fortune: to your lot
has fallen leisure with dignity.[1] I, who have long sought the wooden sword,

* * * * *

9 Cf n1 above.

2795
1 The phrase 'dignified leisure' or 'leisure with dignity' (*otium cum dignitate*),
   coined by Cicero (see eg *De oratore* 1.1), was a favourite way of describing an
   honourable, well earned retirement from public life.

must die in the sands of the arena.[2] I have only one consolation: already I see 15
nearby that gate common to all, which, with the help of Christ, will bring an
end to everyone's labours and troubles.

Perhaps you are surprised that I, who am unknown to you, write these
things. You cannot say that I am altogether unknown to you since, as you say
in your letter,[3] I often speak to you, saying things that I hope are worthy of 20
you. Long ago at Louvain I knew a young man with the family name Horion.
But I don't think it was you. At any rate, I certainly desire to be enrolled as
your protégé, ready to obey you in every way, if there is any favour I can do
for you.[4] Farewell.

Given at Freiburg, 21 April 1533 25

After I had written this, I reread a certain letter of Goclenius in which
he asked that I send you a short greeting,[5] and I also discovered among my
disordered papers a letter from you that I had either not read or which, as
often happens in such a pile of letters, I had not read carefully. I was a bit
concerned that it might seem a little presumptuous for someone unknown to 30
you to bother you with a letter on his own initiative, but your letter relieved
me of that scruple. You were the first to urge friendship; it would have been
unkind not to reply. The matter of my return is still completely uncertain.[6]
This poor body of mine is falling to pieces – a long way from being up to long
journeys. And this court of ours is a leaky jar: it is always thirsty, but yields 35
nothing.[7] Some do nothing but detract,[8] and those who want to be taken for
great patrons do nothing but complain.[9] And that sort of thing just doubles

* * * * *

2 When a Roman gladiator retired he was presented with a wooden sword
   (*Adagia* I ix 24). On Erasmus' fondness for the image of gladiatorial combat to
   describe the many battles with his critics, see Ep 1934 n1.
3 Not extant
4 Horion was evidently a patron of scholars. Gerard Morinck (Ep 1994) dedicated to him his edition of Rudolf von Langen's *Historia Hierosolymae* (Louvain:
   R. Rescius 1539).
5 Goclenius' letter is not extant.
6 Ie his return to Brabant; see Ep 2785.
7 Cf *Adagia* i x 33: *Inexplebile dolium* 'A great jar that cannot be filled.' The meaning
   here seems to be that the court in the Netherlands is insatiable (for income) but
   perpetually short of funds (to pay Erasmus' pension).
8 It is not clear whether this is a reference to the court, or more generally to
   Erasmus' many detractors in the Netherlands.
9 This may be a swipe at Jean de Carondelet and Nicolaus Olahus, who were
   plainly impatient with Erasmus' dithering about his prospective return to the
   Netherlands and annoyed that he was considering Besançon instead; see especially Epp 2689, 2759:8–27, 2785:1–8.

the misery. 'At the bottom of the list?' you say. Should I enrol at the bottom
of the list of my friends such a renowned and remarkably upright man as
you? If so, I would truly be what they say the Batavians once were: crude and 40
far removed from the Graces.[10] Guillaume de Horion will be written down
as among my principal friends and patrons. And if you want my service in
any matter, put it to the test whether Erasmus is saying these things from his
heart. Once more, farewell, most renowned gentleman.

At Freiburg, on the same day and year 45

2796 / To Henricus Cornelius Agrippa   Freiburg, 21 April 1533

This letter was first published in the Agrippae opera II 1056. The day-date '21'
may be an error for '25.' In Ep 2800:56 Erasmus says that he has responded
'today' (25 April) to a letter from Agrippa. At all events, both letters were in the
packet carried by Quirinus Hagius (see Ep 2792 n18). For Agrippa see Ep 2692.

TO AGRIPPA FROM A FRIEND

Greetings. I wrote you briefly a while ago,[1] pointing out that the teaching in
that book of yours concerning the vanity of learning was warmly received by
the whole learned community here – for I had not yet read it.[2] A little later,
when I had acquired the book as a loan, I had my servant read it at dinner,[3] 5
for I had no other free time, and after dinner I myself am forced to refrain
from all study. I was pleased by its force and fullness, and I cannot see why
the monks are so upset about it. By attacking the bad, you praise the good,
but they love only to be praised. I repeat the advice I gave you then, that
if you can find a convenient way to do so, disentangle yourself from this 10
contention.[4] Remember the example of Louis Berquin, who was ruined by
nothing more than the free and straightforward way he treated the monks

* * * * *

10 Adagia IV vi 35

2796
1 The letter is not extant.
2 The book was De incertitudine et vanitate scientiarum atque artium declamatio
  (1530).
3 In Ep 2800:45–51 Erasmus adds that the lender wanted the book back without
  delay and that he only skimmed it.
4 For Agrippa's controversy with the Louvain theologians see Epp 2737:16–32,
  2739:13–14. For Erasmus' advice not to pursue the contention, see Ep 2748:7–9.

and theologians – in other respects he was a man of impeccable character.⁵ I
often tried to persuade him to use his skill to extricate himself from this situation. He was deceived by a hope of victory. But if you cannot escape from   15
experiencing the fortunes of war, see to it that you fight from a tower and
that you do not fall into their hands. Be especially careful not to involve me
in this matter. I am burdened by more than enough hatred, and your doing
so will both aggravate my troubles and be more of a hindrance than a help to
you. I made the same plea to Berquin, and he promised but failed me, trust-   20
ing his own opinion more than my advice. You see the outcome. Certainly
there would have been no trace of danger had he followed my advice. Over
and over I sang the same song to him, that neither the theologians nor the
monks can be conquered, even if he had a better case than St Paul had.⁶ If I
had any authority over you, I would advise you unceasingly to devote to the   25
promotion of liberal studies the effort that you would have spent on this
gladiatorial combat. At present I do not have time to say more. For I am
writing to many friends.

Farewell. At Freiburg, 21 April 1533

2797 / From Bernhard von Cles   Vienna, 21 April 1533

This letter was first published by Allen. The manuscript, an autograph rough
draft, is in the 'Corrispondenza clesiana' collection at Trent (Ep 2685 introduction). For Bernhard von Cles see Ep 2651 introduction.

TO ERASMUS

While I was devoting great deal of thought to you, about whom I had heard
nothing in detail for a long time (so help me God, this is the truth!), and
had decided to send you a letter to find out how you are faring, your letter
arrived,¹ most welcome as usual; it confirmed my intention even more, since   5
it offered a rich body of material to respond to. I will write a reply, not simply
as duty would require but indeed to make it very clear to you how deeply
grieved I am, out of fondness and good will towards you, that we have lost

* * * * *

5 For Erasmus' detailed account of the trial and execution of Louis Berquin at
  Paris in 1529, see Ep 2188.
6 Acts 26:1–32

2797
1 Not extant

so many choice friends,[2] who (in accordance with my wishes) truly took your part in words and deeds. But since this is the result of present circum-   10 stances, I will pass over this grief and address other matters, so as not to increase the pain of an old man so near his deathbed, whom everyone, in accord with my wishes, asserts and affirms to be most prudent; and we desire that the poor health from which you suffered last month, as we learned from this letter of yours, will be restored by diligent care to its former well-being   15 as soon as possible.

I am certain that peace with the Turkish tyrant will soon come about;[3] although this peace might perhaps have been freely offered, to the greater glory of all of Christendom (since we had an army drawn up against the enemy), nevertheless, under the present circumstances the more we see him   20 excel in warfare, especially in these stormy times, the more we will nod to his wishes. For our present status makes us desire most eagerly what we willingly reject when we have the power to do so.

We can hardly tolerate with equanimity this Lutheran defection, which spreads day after day. And although the ambassadors of the pope and the   25 emperor have been sent to the Christian princes to put an end to it in order to proclaim a council, and though they are at present here among us, nevertheless I am afraid their journey will be fruitless and that thus our plight will worsen day by day.[4]

I am no less grieved that the most flourishing kingdom of England has   30 now been subjected to the same kinds of heresy.[5] Even though we may think this has perhaps happened because of some particular error there, nevertheless it would be fitting that those who provide the cause of the errors should be the only ones to be punished.

Finally, seeing that at the end of your letter you firmly promise your   35 help if we should ever need it, we have thought that we will accept your

* * * * *

2 See Ep 2776 n4.
3 See Ep 2780 n9.
4 At the end of February 1533 a papal nuncio accompanied by an imperial ambassador departed for Germany to secure the support of the principal German princes for a church council. From 1 April to 13 May they were at the court of Ferdinand I in Vienna. There followed visits to all seven of the imperial electors and other princes as well. Similar delegations were dispatched to France and England. No consensus on the nature or the necessity of a council was achieved. See Pastor 10 223–7.
5 Erasmus must have reported what he learned from More (and others) about the incursions of heresy into England; see Ep 2659:98–112.

offer by asking you to do us a favour. We have constructed a building at Trent, more for the convenience of our successors than for our own, building it up from the foundations;[6] among others plans, we have a special desire to assemble a library (according to our station and our resources) including the   40
books of the best authors in every subject matter; and since we are not certain which ones are considered to be the best and which ones might be bought because of the printing or the beauty of the lettering, either in these regions or elsewhere, we would like to be instructed by you in this matter, and when you have the time for it please send us a little indication or list of them.[7] This   45
is our utmost desire. And, in return, if we can please you by doing some kind of favour, you will find us to be always quite willing.

Vienna, 21 April 1533

2798 / To Eustache Chapuys   Freiburg, 23 April 1533

This letter was first published in the epistolary appendix to Erasmus' *De praeparatione ad mortem* (Basel: Froben 1534) 134–8.

The early years of Eustache Chapuys of Annency (d 1556) are poorly documented. In the period 1507–15 he studied at Turin, Valence, and Rome, where he received a doctorate in law. At unspecified dates in the next two years he was ordained and made a canon of Geneva. In August 1517 he became the official (chief legal officer) of the diocese of Geneva. The bishop of Geneva, John of Savoy, was a close relative of Duke Charles III of Savoy, whose secretary and capable diplomat Chapuys soon became. In 1523 or 1524 the new bishop, Pierre de la Baume, lent Chapuy's services to Constable Charles de Bourbon, in whose company he visited Spain, where he attracted the attention of Charles v. Entering Charles' service, he was master of requests by July 1527, and in June 1529 he was appointed imperial ambassador to England, where he would remain for the next sixteen years, handling difficult matters, especially those arising from Henry VIII's divorce, with great diplomatic skill and keeping Charles v well informed concerning English affairs. In 1545 poor health led Chapuys to retire to Louvain, where he used his great wealth to found and endow the College of Savoy at Louvain (1548) and a secondary school at Annency to supply the college with well-prepared students (1556).

* * * * *

6 An enthusiastic builder, Cles had lavishly renovated the episcopal palace as well as the cathedral, in which the council of Trent would eventually meet.
7 There is no record of Erasmus ever having complied with this request.

During his long sojourn in England, Chapuys, who had always been a man of humanist sympathies, became the friend or acquaintance of most of Erasmus' English friends and patrons. But his friendship with Erasmus himself, whom he never met, came late. The present letter is the answer to what appears to have been one in which Chapuys sought to initiate contact. Though only two letters (this one and Ep 3090) from their correspondence survive, it is clear that it continued, both directly and via others, for the rest of Erasmus' life. Chapuys was an important source of news about developments in England, both personal and public, and he proved particularly useful in the delicate matter of the collection of the income from Erasmus' English livings, which had always been a source of trouble and anxiety. In 1535–6, in collaboration with the Antwerp banker Erasmus Schets, Chapuys made arrangements for the collection and remittance of the amounts due and assured Erasmus that he had the matter well in hand (Ep 3090).

DESIDERIUS ERASMUS OF ROTTERDAM TO EUSTACHE CHAPUYS,
IMPERIAL AMBASSADOR IN ENGLAND, GREETINGS

No possession is dearer or more precious than a genuine friend. But although in other respects I am not so different from Irus,[1] in this sort of wealth I think I am a veritable Lucullus,[2] since I discover day by day that I have more 5 friends than I thought I had. Believe me, you are wrong if you think that a rich benefice would please me more than the friendship of Eustache, whose portrait I have seen in your letter with the greatest pleasure.[3] It flows with such unadulterated frankness and sincerity that one can easily recognize in it a character entirely devoid of all dissimulation. 10

The addition (or, if you prefer, the recognition) of friends is especially pleasant to me at this time because during the past year I have lost some extraordinary ones: in England, the archbishop of Canterbury, one in a thousand; in the retinue of the emperor, Alfonso de Valdés; in Poland, Krzysztof Szydłowiecki, the supreme chancellor of that kingdom. Others I do not men- 15 tion, of lesser status but equal integrity, among whom is the Frisian Zacharias Deiotarus, who regularly received my servants most willingly and gladly when I occasionally was obliged to send them to England.[4] That service was

* * * * *

2798
1 Ie poor; see *Adagia* i vi 76: 'As poor as Irus or Codrus.'
2 Lucius Licinius Lucullus (c 116–57 BC) was a Roman general and consul proverbial for his wealth and luxurious banquets.
3 The letter is not extant.
4 For all these recent deaths see Ep 2776 nn2, 4.

Eustache Chapuys
Musée-Château d'Annecy

particularly gratifying because the ordinary inns offer little protection from
the accursed plague which recently spread into our territory from England, 20
where it has become all too familiar for more than forty years.[5] In the same
way, you took in my servant Quirinus there,[6] for which please know that
you have my full and heartfelt gratitude. And because at that time he did
something contrary to my wishes (through the efforts of some friends quite
unlike you), I have sent him there again to see if perhaps this time I may be 25
more fortunate.[7]

I do not know what image of me you find in my writings that leads you
to feel such warm and intense affection for me, since I am aware that that
all my qualities are less than mediocre. But the fewer the merits I recognize
in myself, the more I owe to your solicitude for me. Certainly there is noth- 30
ing left in Erasmus for you to deem worthy of your consideration. For you
would see not a person but the slough of a serpent, nothing but a miserable
wretch, unless we consider that when these remains are sloughed off, a new
creature, shining with youth, will emerge. Also you seem to know by what
waves I am battered, by what winds I am buffeted. But not far away the port 35
appears that will put an end to all our troubles, with the help of Christ. I have
a bad name, I am lacerated by tongues, and mostly by those who are most
deeply indebted to me. You could say: that is my fate. But even so, printers
say that hardly any name sells better than mine. I would think they are just
flattering me if they were not always pestering me for something – if nothing 40
else, just a little preface.[8]

I will add another proof. Nowadays the world is filled everywhere with
vagabonds, who have either deserted from their communities or have fled
for other reasons. Because these people are almost more empty than a snake's
slough, they have to get their travelling provisions by various schemes, for 45
the stomach is a marvellous schemer. From my writings some of them have
come to know my friends. They go to them and boast that they are my servants and disciples, even if they have never laid eyes on me. And by this
pretext they extort a not inconsiderable amount of money from them. When
they are afraid that their trick may be discovered, they change their pasture. 50

* * * * *

5 Ie the 'English sweat.' See Ep 2209 n31.
6 Quirinus Hagius, who was at this time on his second journey to England,
carrying this letter among others; see Ep 2792 n18.
7 Ie regarding the collection of monies owed him there
8 As, for example in Johann Herwagen's persistent requests that he provide the
preface for a new edition of Cicero; see Ep 2765 n5.

I did not want you to be unaware of this so that you would not lend credence to anyone unless he is recommended by name in a letter from me.[9]

But even going that far is not enough. I will tell you something to make you laugh. When Christophe de Longueil was staying with me at Louvain,[10] he told the story of how a young man whose name was Silvius (a fictitious 55 name, I imagine) had escaped from the Benedictines and had come to Rome; he had brought a letter written to Pope Leo in my name, in which he was highly recommended, for he had heard that I was then in the good graces of Leo, and I have no doubt that he had forged my handwriting. The pope embraced the man with both arms, promising him everything. But when he 60 had set out for somewhere else (I don't know where), Leo, of his own accord, asked why Silvius had not returned. But he had caught a fever and died. Wouldn't you call this humorous audacity?

But to come to an end, my extraordinary friend, although you surpass me in that you were the first to proclaim friendship, both by letter and by ser- 65 vice, nevertheless from now on I will strive not to seem unresponsive in our mutual exchange of good will. Thus, if there is anything in which I in turn can contribute something to your convenience or pleasure, you will learn that Erasmus does not lack a ready and friendly good will, though all else may be lacking. Other matters you will learn, if you wish, partly from the pages 70 of memoranda that I have given to my servant, and partly from what he reports to you, for I have found him to be trustworthy and not at all empty-headed. I am considerably grieved by the trouble the Scots are inflicting on the English.[11] For I think I owe more to that country, which has provided me with so many extraordinary friends, than I do to the country in which I was 75 born. But I am extremely distressed by the way Holland is treated nowadays, at times by the Danes (which is something new),[12] at times by Gelderland

* * * * *

9 Cf Allen Ep 2874:14–47.
10 Longueil (Ep 914 introduction) had spent two or three days with Erasmus at Louvain in October in 1519; see Ep 1011 n1. Erasmus tells this same tale in Allen Ep 2874:157–89.
11 There is nothing to indicate that the Scots were causing any major difficulties at this time.
12 Just at this time (April 1533) Holland was raising a war fleet in pursuit of its long-standing struggle with the Hanseatic city of Lübeck over access to trade in the Baltic. Denmark was involved because its current king, Frederick I, needed a war fleet that only Lübeck could supply to defend himself against the attempts of his deposed predecessor, Christian II (brother-in-law of Charles V), to regain the throne; cf Ep 2570 n14. Lübeck supplied the needed fleet in return for

(which is nothing new).[13] Hesiod made the oracular pronouncement that an evil neighbour is a mighty woe.[14] These are the shifty stratagems of rulers.[15] I hope all goes well with you, my very dear friend.

80

Given at Freiburg im Breisgau, 23 April 1533

2799 / To Karel Uutenhove   Freiburg, [c 24 April] 1533

This letter was first published in 1888 as Ep 10 in Horawitz II, on the basis of the original manuscript in the personal collection of the director of the Munich Hofbibliothek, Karl von Halm. Allen was unable to trace the original letter. Since it is clearly antecedent to Ep 2817 (see n21 below), in which Levinus Ammonius mentions that Quirinus Hagius had visited him on his way home from England (Allen Ep 2817:179–83) Allen concluded that this was one of the letters carried by Quirinus (Ep 2792 n18) and that a date near the end of April was 'certain.' As Allen observes, it is difficult to believe that the first sentence, beginning with 'but,' was the actual opening of the original letter, or that the postscript (lines 42–4) was as Horawitz had transcribed it.

Greetings. But we are so overwhelmed here by troubles that even cheerfulness itself could hardly be cheerful, and so I am all the more surprised that my letter brought you so much cheer.[1] Nevertheless, I am delighted, my dear

* * * * *

Frederick's undertaking to bar Hollanders from passage through the Oresund. See James D. Tracy *Holland Under Habsburg Rule, 1506–1566: The Formation of a Body Politic* (Berkeley 1990) 107–11.

13 There is no evidence of hostilities between Holland and Gelderland at this time; cf Ep 2645 n4. There are, however, documents in the Archives générales du Royaume at Brussels (Papiers de l'État et de l'Audience 1525) indicating that in April 1532 Charles v, writing from Regensburg, ordered the arrest of one Hendrik of Amsterdam, who was known to have travelled from Denmark to Amsterdam, and thence 'to the duke of Gelderland.' Hendrik was soon arrested and requested a trial to prove his innocence. It is not known who Hendrik of Amsterdam was or what his mission involved, but it is possible that one or more of Erasmus' correspondents in the Low Countries had heard reports that the Danes and the duke of Gelderland were up to no good. (Information kindly supplied by James D. Tracy.)

14 Cited in Greek. See *Adagia* I i 32:9, citing Hesiod *Works and Days* 344.

15 Greek in the text, though it is not clear why. The passage does not appear to be a quotation. Perhaps the intention was just to conceal a dangerous sentiment.

2799
1 Neither Erasmus' letter nor Uutenhove's reply to it is extant.

Karel, provided only that what you write is true. But if sometimes I do not
write to you as often as you would like, do not think that my kindly feelings 5
for you are even the least bit diminished. Among the *palaeonaeoi* is a quite
long letter to you.[2]

I wrote you a while ago via the public letter carrier of this city.[3] He says
he gave the letter to Schets. I do not know whether it reached you. At the
same time I wrote to the treasurer of Flanders,[4] whose son, named Florens, 10
is living at Padua.[5]

There was no need for you to be stripped of your silk.[6] Your sentiments
of loyalty act as a very great gift to me.

The news that is bruited about here you can learn partly from the pages
I have given to Quirinus, partly from what he tells you. He is a Hollander; he 15
could not lie even if he wanted to.[7] There are portentous tales flying around
here about a perjured man torn apart by two demons, a village burned down
by demons.[8] These well-endowed demons gave me a good laugh.

I advised Lieven either to hunt for a rich benefice or to marry a wife, but
one with a good dowry, as Schepper did.[9] I am amazed at how that young 20
man is debasing himself; I had entertained very high hopes for him.[10] But I
have not yet given up all hope.

Joachim Martens recently visited us, a remarkably learned young
man.[11] He seemed to be of two minds. Finally he said he intended to return
to Ghent, out of concern for the health of his aged mother. I would like to 25
know what he is doing.

Schets was recently visited by Johannes de Molendino, a wonderful
enthusiast for Erasmus, but at the same time he is colluding with Barbier,
who is misdirecting my pension.[12] I suspect that the matter is being plotted

* * * * *

2 Ep 2700, first published in the *Epistolae palaeonaeioi*
3 The letter carrier's name was Peter. The letters he carried 'a while ago' were
   those of 22 March; cf Ep 2793:1–5.
4 See Ep 2793:5.
5 See Ep 2716 n39.
6 Presumably a reference to some sort of gift
7 Cf Epp 2792:64–6, 2800:101–2.
8 The reference is to the town of Schiltach, near Basel; see Allen Ep 2846:124–52.
9 See Ep 2792 n14.
10 On Lieven's ill-advised marriage, see Ep 2693:26–99.
11 See Ep 2049 introduction. His visit to Erasmus in August 1532 is mentioned in
   Allen Ep 2817:186–7.
12 See Ep 2763 n2.

by Aleandro and Latomus.[13] They are French,[14] and it is now my lot (why I   30
don't know) to have the French set against me. The name of Germany is a
hindrance to me.

Glareanus returns your greetings, cordially wishing you well.[15] Amerbach is rarely here, since he has recently taken a wife.[16] You would hardly
believe how I mourn for Karel Sucket, a young man of the hightest hopes,   35
taken from us before his time.[17] I had some concern about him because of his
precocious abilities. I have higher hopes for you because you are climbing
gradually to the heights of glory. Give my cordial greetings to Master Willem
de Waele, a very honourable man.[18] For you, Karel, I pray for every[thing],
and at the same time I am preparing an epithalamium for you.[19]   40

Given at Freiburg im Breisgau, 1533

Ammonius' letter has been unwilling to arrive;[20] I have no idea
whether I have received it.[21] Please be sure to give my greetings to him and
to Edingen.[22]

Erasmus of Rotterdam, in my own hand   45

To the honourable and learned gentleman Master Karel Uutenhove at
Ghent

* * * * *

13 Girolamo Aleandro (Ep 2638) and Jacobus Latomus (Ep 934 introduction)
14 Cf Epp 2763:6, 2781:12–13. Latomus was a French-speaking Netherlander;
    Aleandro was Italian, but in earlier years (1508–13) he had taught at the
    University of Paris.
15 Henricus Glareanus (Ep 2664 n2)
16 Bonifacius Amerbach had been married to Martha Fuchs since February 1527.
    More recently his preoccupation had been the death of his infant daughter
    Ursula; see Ep 2684 introduction.
17 For Karel Sucket and his early death at Turin (3 November 1532), see Ep 2657
    n17.
18 Ep 301
19 Uutenhove had recently married Willem de Waele's niece; cf Ep 2700:152–3
    with n20.
20 For this unusual turn of phrase, cf Allen Ep 2911:1.
21 Levinus Ammonius (Ep 2016) had not yet answered Ep 2483, written two
    years earlier. He makes his excuses at length in Ep 2817. It makes no sense for
    Erasmus to say that he does not know whether he has received a letter that
    has just said he has not yet arrived. Allen concluded that the text was prob-
    ably faulty and that *quam omnino an acceperim nescio* might be an error for *meam
    omnino an acceperit nescio* 'I have no idea whether he received mine.'
22 For Omaar van Edingen see Ep 2060.

2800 / To Abel van Colster   Freiburg, 25 April 1533

This letter was first published in the epistolary appendix to Erasmus' *De praeparatione ad mortem* (Basel: Froben 1534) 138–43.

   Abel van Colster of Dordrecht (1477–1548), who studied at Cologne and
Orléans, was from 1506 until his death (with one brief intermission in 1515–16)
a member of the council of Holland at the Hague. This is the only surviving
letter in what was clearly a more ample correspondence between friends; see
Ep 2645:42.

ERASMUS OF ROTTERDAM TO THE MOST RENOWNED GENTLEMAN
MASTER ABEL VAN COLSTER, GREETINGS
Your letter,[1] bursting with Attic wit, not only cheered me up with such festive
turns of phrase but also gave me great pleasure because it tells me that you
are in good health and are enjoying yourself, which I pray will always be   5
the case, my very dear friend. I would be glad to engage in pleasantries with
you, except that at this time I have to write hundreds of letters.[2] I was very
amused when you wrote that my letter was so thirsty that it could suck up
a great deal of bile, so light that like cork it could buoy up such a great man
and keep him from drowning.[3]   10
   That great and wonderful Erasmus whom you claim to have seen is
completely unknown to me; I have neither seen nor heard of him. The worst
part of him now is merely the sloughed-off skin of a snake. I only wish that
the better part of him, even to some degree, could come up to that noble image that you depict for us in your letter. But I will not quarrel with you any   15
more on that subject. If there is anything good in me, it is a gift from God, and
I cannot properly be angry with you for seeing Erasmus through the cloud
of inordinate affection and singular benevolence of temperament that seems
to have obscured your vision. From the same source comes the satisfaction
you find in that much of your happiness consists in being enrolled in the   20
select group of Erasmus' friends. But I have more just reason to congratulate
myself in that I have happily had the effrontery and unabashed immodesty
to add such a splendid name to the list of my friends.
   And that is all the dearer to me because the past year, by the loss of
some of my special friends, has reduced me to an extraordinary poverty in   25

*   *   *   *   *

2800
1 Not extant
2 See Ep 2716 n38.
3 The letter is not extant.

Abel van Colster by Jan Mostaert
Musée d'Art Ancien, Brussels
Photo Patrimoine des Musées Royaux des Beaux-Arts

my most precious possession. To list only the most important: in England William Warham, archbishop of Canterbury passed away; in Vienna, in the retinue of the emperor, Alfonso de Valdés died, already a great man, but if he had lived, he would have been the very greatest; in Poland, Krzysztof Szydłowiecki, the supreme chancellor of that kingdom,[4] to whom I dedicated 30 *Lingua*.[5] Holland has done the right thing in placing you on a high watchtower, from which you can better survey the commonwealth, which now, from what I hear, has need of sagacious and vigilant sentinels. Who ever read or heard about, who ever saw, an age more turbulent or more wicked than this one? 35

But goodbye to such useless complaints! Since you are accustomed to betake yourself to my works, as if they were a pleasure garden, to refresh your spirits when you are exhausted by worrisome business matters, I only wish that in those gardens of mine there were something that could delight the eyes or the nostrils or the palate of Colster, a man of the most delicate 40 tastes. But they are sterile, or if they produce anything, it is beets, or mallows, or leeks[6] – and let's hope it has not come to hemlock and wolfsbane,[7] which are not lacking in the clamours of those whom you cleverly call venerable for their beards and their cloaks![8]

Concerning the man about whom you ask my opinion,[9] I rank him as so 45 brilliant that I could not tolerate any censure of his talents. I have not read his book, but I acquired it on loan. Since at that time I was so continuously engaged in working that I had no leisure to do anything else, a servant of mine read from it to me as I walked up and down at dinnertime, but in excerpts chosen from various chapters. The owner of the codex would not allow it to 50 remain with me any longer. From that taste, such as it was, I perceived him as a person of intense intelligence, varied reading, and a fine memory, but sometimes he is more copious than selective, and his language is more energetic than carefully composed. On all sorts of subjects he criticizes what is bad, praises what is good. But there are some who will not tolerate anything 55

* * * * *

4 For all these recent deaths see Ep 2776 nn2, 4.
5 Ep 1593
6 Ie things flat and insipid, with no taste
7 Both poisons
8 Beards and cloaks were the outward signs of those who professed themselves philosophers; see *Adagia* I ii 95, II viii 95. Presumably he means his opponents in the religious orders, 'the theologians and the monks,' as he says below.
9 Cornelius Agrippa, as is evident from the similar comments in Ep 2796

but praise. Today I answered a letter he sent to me;[10] I advised him to extricate himself from such mobs (for he threatens that he now wants to engage in a fair fight with the theologians), and if he cannot do this and is determined to roll the dice, he should keep his eye on two goals: on the one hand, to fight from a safe position, lest he fall into the hands of enemies who cannot be 60 conquered or placated, and on the other that he not get me mixed up in his exploit. For he writes that he will fight no less with my weapons than with his own; that part of his letter I found somewhat displeasing. Up to this point I have been fighting an undecided battle against a serpent that has not seven but innumerable heads,[11] and I can hardly hold out because of the *Folly* and 65 some other writings of mine that are rather unrestrained. But I am afraid that if he goes on in this way, he will revive all the hatred against me. What good he thinks he can get out of it, I do not know. But if he thinks that he can either correct or conquer the theologians and the monks, he is absolutely on the wrong track. What good does it do to stir up the hornets once more, now that 70 they are somewhat worn out, and to loose them at the heads of good men?

You know better than I what happened to Cornelis Hoen.[12] Louis de Berquin would have been in no danger if he had followed my advice.[13] He won the battle once. He prepared a triumph. I advised against it. He did not obey. He was a very good man, his circumstances were not of the lowest, 75 his temperament was straightforward, but his tongue was too unrestrained. When the king was absent in Spain,[14] he was thrown into prison once more. And he would have perished if the king's mother and soon afterwards the king himself (after he returned from Spain) had not supported him. Shortly thereafter he was released from prison and given a comfortable position at 80 the court; finally he was sent away with a genuine reprieve. I always sang the same tune to him: use your skill to get out of that affair. He promised himself a certain and splendid victory, even though he was acting against swarms of

* * * * *

10 Ep 2796, written a few days earlier but dispatched with the packet carried by Quirinus Hagius; see Ep 2792 n18.
11 See Ep 2639 n9.
12 Hoen (d 1524), a lawyer employed by the council of Holland, was twice arrested and prosecuted for heresy following the circulation of a treatise (1521) in which he rejected transubstantiation and interpreted the words 'this is my body' symbolically. Cf Ep 1358 n7.
13 This ensuing account of the case of Louis Berquin closely parallels that in Ep 2796:20–4.
14 Ie as the prisoner of Charles v, following the peace of Madrid in 1526

monks, against the theological faculty, against the noble parlement.[15] I got
nowhere with my advice. He flattered himself. What was the outcome? The   85
same thing happened to him as to Socrates: when the judges were about to
pronounce a rather light sentence on him and, according to custom, asked
the convicted man what punishment he considered to be fitting, he answered
'I should be maintained at public expense in the Pyrtaneum' – which among
the Athenians was considered to be the very highest honour. The judges   90
were so provoked by this arrogant reply that they condemned him to death.
So too, when they sentenced Berquin to prison, he said, with a resolute expression, 'I appeal to the king and the pope.' The judges were so irritated by
this statement that he was burned in the Place de Grève, a man of impeccable
character – about his teachings I have no certain knowledge.   95

But if none of this moves him,[16] at least let him not involve me in his
war. I often asked the same of Berquin, and he promised he would comply.
But he failed me, to his own doom and my grave misfortune. The theologians would never have published their censures of me if they had not been
harrassed by him.[17] So much for judgment. You will learn of the rest from my   100
faithful servant, who is delivering this letter.[18] Farewell. Cordial greetings to
the most renowned gentleman Assendelft.[19]

Given at Freiburg im Breisgau, 25 April 1533

* * * * *

15 Erasmus calls it the *senatus purpuratus*; cf Ep 2780 n13.
16 Agrippa
17 Erasmus exaggerates the connection between the case of Louis Berquin and the
Paris faculty's censure of his writings. The publication in 1525 of Berquin's unauthorized translations of some of Erasmus' works, into which he inserted passages taken from Luther and other reformers, did indeed draw the theologians'
attention to Erasmus, but by then they had already condemned new versions
of the Bible (1523) and censured errors in Erasmus' Paraphrase on Luke (1524).
The reference to harassment probably refers to the publication at Paris in 1527
of the anonymous pamphlet accusing Noël Béda of heresy, *Duodecim articuli in-
fidelitatis magistri Natalis Bedae*. Béda, who believed that Berquin was the author,
responded with his *Apologia adversus clandestinos Lutheranos* (1529), in which he
took the opportunity to assign Erasmus a leading place among the 'clandestine
Lutherans.' But by the time of the publication of the anonymous pamphlet,
Béda and his colleagues at the faculty of theology had already compiled the
list of Erasmus' errors that would eventually be published in their *Determinatio*
of 1531, and Béda did not require provocation from Louis Berquin to pursue
Erasmus as a heretic. See CWE 82 xiii–xiv, xxvii.
18 Quirinus Hagius; see n10 above.
19 Gerrit van Assendelft (Ep 2645 n9)

2801 / From Bernhard von Cles   Vienna, 27 April 1533

This letter was first published as Ep 21 in Horawitz I. The original letter, in a secretary's hand, is in the Württembergische Landesbibliothek Stuttgart (MS Hist
Fol 47 folio 11). There is also an autograph rough draft in the 'Corrispondenza
clesiana' collection at Trent (Ep 2685 introduction). For Bernhard von Cles, bishop of Trent and chancellor to King Ferdinand, see Ep 2651 introduction.

Dear sir, venerable in Christ, outstanding and truly beloved by us. What we
were not able to accomplish earlier because of our absence, now, at the urging of your last letter, we have obtained for your friend Glareanus fifty florins
and for yourself a gift of three times that much from his Royal Majesty.[1] But
since we were not satisfied with this alone, as a sign of the special affection   5
we have always had for you we send in addition to that, for you personally,
a gift of fifty florins on our own behalf, so that *in toto* you can rejoice in a gift
of two hundred florins;[2] and we do not wish that, because of that gift, you
should be persuaded that our former fondness for you will be diminished,
since from the bottom of our heart we intend to be willing to gratify you, in   10
whatever ways we can, in such a manner that our good offices may correspond to your expectations.
     Vienna, 27 April 1533

          * * * * *

2801
1 The most recent extant letter from Erasmus to Cles is Ep 2651 of 19 May 1532. If,
   as seems implied, Erasmus wrote a later letter to which this is the reply, it did
   not survive. The sequence of events is nonetheless clear. In Ep 2651 Erasmus
   said that he had nothing to ask for himself from King Ferdinand, but he commended to him Henricus Glareanus, who was sending a copy of his edition of
   Dionysius of Halicarnassus (lines 52–75). In his reply of 5 June (Ep 2655) Cles
   replied that he was unable to say whether the book had yet reached the king,
   but promised to do his best for Glareanus and Erasmus. A month later (Ep
   2685) Cles wrote again to say that the king's preoccupation with the Diet of
   Regensburg had delayed arrangements for the promised gift. The present letter
   announces that Cles had finally succeeded in his project.
2 In Ep 2808 (11 May 1533), Johann Löble, Ferdinand's treasurer, issued an order for the payment of the monies to Glareanus and Erasmus; the gifts were
   paid in Rhenish florins. The fifty florins for Glareanus were equivalent to £12
   5s 10d groot Flemish, which represented a year and three months' wages of an
   Antwerp master mason/carpenter (CWE 12 650 Table 3, 691 Table 13). The gifts
   to Erasmus amounted to 200 florins in total (150 florins from King Ferdinand
   and 50 florins from Cles), equivalent to £54 3s 4d groot Flemish, which represented five and a half years' wages of an Antwerp master mason/carpenter
   (CWE 12 650 Table 3, 691 Table 13).

Bernhard, by the mercy of God his most reverend Eminence, cardinal
and bishop of Trent   15
    To the venerable in Christ Master Erasmus of Rotterdam, outstanding
and truly beloved by us, professor of sacred theology. At Freiburg

2802 / From Chunradus Thuringus Saltzensis   Freiburg, [c April] 1533

> This letter was first published as Ep 198 in Förstemann / Günther. The writer
> identifies himself as Chunradus Thuringus Saltzensis, which could mean that
> he was from Langensalza in Thuringia, or perhaps that Thuring or Döring was
> his surname. He has never been identified. The letter states (lines 20–1) that he
> had just returned from Italy, where he had been with the emperor. Charles v
> had embarked from Genoa for Barcelona on 9 April 1533, hence the approxi-
> mate month-date assigned by Allen.

Greetings. I think I arrived here at a propitious moment, most learned sir,
because yesterday I happened to see you just once in a church, happily for
me, both because of your multifarious learning in in every kind of discipline,
and also because of your extraordinary and singular eloquence – in which
you felicitously dominate and surpass all the writers of our age to such a   5
degree that you can quite rightly be compared to, and even in a sense rival,
not only recent writers but also classical and ancient authors. What do your
Chiliads represent but an immense encyclopaedia of all subjects, a work that
is completely accurate and absolutely perfect in every detail? Is it not absolutely clear that your lucubrations give evidence of a pure and extremely rich 10
abundance of Latin eloquence, which delights the minds of readers with a
certain sweetness and elegance of style? O heart, brimming with all kinds of
learning, which could be called the habitation of the Muses and of all refined
literature! May almighty God, in his goodness and greatness, grant that you
live as long as possible in safety and health in this Germany of ours, worthy 15
in any case to live as long as Methuselah and Nestor.[1]
    Why should I delay you with distractions, engaged as you now are in
more serious affairs? Yesterday I had determined to meet you, but this intention of mine was obviated, partly by Spaniards, partly by some noblemen

* * * * *

2802
1 According to Genesis 5:27, Methuselah lived 969 years. Although Nestor only
  managed to live 'for three generations,' the expression 'as old as Nestor' was
  nonetheless proverbial, at least among those with a smattering of classical
  learning; see *Adagia* I vi 66 (citing Homer *Odyssey* 3.245).

who presented their most humble respects. But now, to put it very briefly, re- 20
turning as I am from his imperial Majesty in Italy, pressed by need and poverty, I have recourse to you as to the most helpful and unparalleled Maecenas
and refuge of those devoted to learning,[2] begging that you may be willing to
come to the aid of a little pauper like me with a few coins, so that I can set
out on my journey, since at the present time poorer than Codrus, as impov- 25
erished as Irus,[3] am I.

Live, fare happily, surpass even white-haired Nestor.

Given hastily at Freiburg in the year etc 33

Chunradus Thuringus Saltzensis

To the most learned and most eloquent gentleman Master Erasmus of 30
Rotterdam, his most favourably inclined Maecenas

* * * * *

2 For Maecenas, the proverbial name for a generous patron, see Ep 2716 n49.
3 For Codrus and Irus, see *Adagia* I vi 76 and cf Ep 2798:4.

TABLE OF CORRESPONDENTS

WORKS FREQUENTLY CITED

SHORT-TITLE FORMS
FOR ERASMUS' WORKS

CORRIGENDA FOR EARLIER VOLUMES

INDEX

TABLE OF CORRESPONDENTS

WORKS FREQUENTLY CITED

Agrippae Opera	*Agrippae ab Nettesheim ... Opera ...* (Lyon: Beringer Brothers [c 1580–1600]) 2 vols
AK	*Die Amerbach Korrespondenz* ed Alfred Hartmann and B.R. Jenny (Basel 1942–)
Allen	*Opus epistolarum Des. Erasmi Roterodami* ed P.S. Allen, H.M. Allen, and H.W. Garrod (Oxford 1906–58) 11 vols and index
ASD	*Opera omnia Desiderii Erasmi Roterodami* (Amsterdam 1969–)
Basler Chroniken	*Basler Chroniken* (Leipzig-Basel 1872–) 11 vols to date
Bellaria	Ambrosius Pelargus *Bellaria epistolarum Erasmi Rot. et Ambrosii Pelargi vicissim missarum* (Cologne: H. Fuchs 1539)
BRE	*Briefwechsel des Beatus Rhenanus* ed Adalbert Horawitz and Karl Hartfelder (Leipzig 1886; repr Hildesheim 1966)
CEBR	*Contemporaries of Erasmus: A Biographical Register of the Renaissance and Reformation* ed Peter G. Bietenholz and Thomas B. Deutscher (Toronto 1985–7) 3 vols
Chambers	R.W. Chambers *Thomas More* (London 1935)
CWE	*Collected Works of Erasmus* (Toronto 1974–)
Enthoven	*Briefe an Desiderius Erasmus von Rotterdam* ed L.K. Enthoven (Strasbourg 1906)
Epistolae familiares	*Des. Erasmi Roterodami ad Bonif. Amerbachium: cum nonnullis aliis ad Erasmum spectantibus* (Basel 1779)
Epistolae floridae	*Des. Erasmi Roterodami epistolarum floridarum liber unus antehac nunquam excusus* (Basel: J. Herwagen, September 1531)
Epistolae palaeonaeoi	*Desiderii Erasmi Roterodami epistolae palaeonaeoi* (Freiburg: J. Emmeus, September 1532)
Epistolae universae	*Des. Erasmi Rot. operum tertius tomus epistolas complectans universas* (Basel: Froben 1540)
Förstemann / Günther	*Briefe an Desiderius Erasmus von Rotterdam* ed J. Förstemann and O. Günther, XXVII. Beiheft zum *Zentralblatt für Bibliothekwesen* (Leipzig 1904)

Friedberg   *Corpus iuris canonici* ed Emil Friedberg et al (Leipzig 1879;
                          repr Graz 1959) 2 vols. Vol I = *Decretum Magistri Gratiani*;
                          vol II = *Decretalium collectiones*

Gerlo   *La correspondance d'Érasme traduite et annotée d'après l'Opus
                          epistolarum de P.S. Allen, H.M. Allen, et H.W. Garrod* ed and
                          trans Aloïs Gerlo and Paul Foriers (Brussels 1967–84)
                          12 vols

Horawitz   *Erasmiana* ed Adalbert Horawitz, Sitzungsberichte der
                          phil.-hist Classe der kaiserlichen Akademie der
                          Wissenschaften (Vienna 1878, 1880, 1883, 1885) 4 vols

Ipolyi   *Oláh Miklós Levelezése* ed Arnold Ipolyi, Monumenta
                          Hungariae historica: Diplomataria xxv (Budapest 1875)

Kawerau   *Der Briefwechsel des Justus Jonas* ed Gustav Kawerau (Halle
                          1884–5) 2 vols

LB   *Desiderii Erasmi opera omnia* ed J. Leclerc (Leiden 1703–6;
                          repr 1961–2) 10 vols

Major   Emil Major *Erasmus von Rotterdam* no 1 in the series *Virorum
                          illustrium reliquiae* (Basel 1927)

MBW   *Melanchthons Briefwechsel, kritische und kommentierte
                          Gesamtausgabe* ed Heinz Scheible et al (Stuttgart-Bad
                          Canstatt 1977–   ) 27 vols to date. The edition is published
                          in two series: *Regesten* (vols 1–12 in print); and *Texte* (vols
                          T1–T15 in print). The letter numbers are the same in both
                          series. In both series, the letters have identical sub-sections
                          marked by numbers in brackets.

Miaskowski   Casimir von Miaskowski 'Erasmiana. Beiträge zur
                          Korrespondenz des Erasmus von Rotterdam mit Polen. Teil
                          II' *Jahrbuch für Philosophie und spekulative Theologie* xv (1901)
                          195–226, 307–60.

OER   *The Oxford Encyclopedia of the Reformation* ed Hans J.
                          Hillerbrand et al (New York / Oxford 1996) 4 vols

Opuscula   *Erasmi opuscula: A Supplement to the Opera Omnia* ed Wallace
                          K. Ferguson (The Hague 1933)

Opus epistolarum   *Opus epistolarum Des. Erasmi Roterodami per autorem diligenter
                          recognitum et adjectis innumeris novis fere ad trientem auctum*
                          (Basel: Froben, Herwagen, and Episcopius 1529)

Pastor	Ludwig von Pastor *The History of the Popes from the Close of the Middle Ages* ed and trans R.F. Kerr et al, 6th ed (London 1938–53) 40 vols
PL	*Patrologiae cursus completus ... series Latina* ed J.-P. Migne, 1st ed (Paris 1844–55, 1862–5; repr Turnhout) 217 vols plus 4 vols indexes.
Pollet	Julius Pflug *Correspondance* ed J.V. Pollet (Leiden 1969–82) 5 vols in 6
RTA	*Deutsche Reichstagsakten, Jüngere Reihe* (Gotha-Stuttgart-Gottingen 1896–)
Sadoleti epistolae	*Iacobi Sadoleti, episcopi Carpentoracti, epistolarum libri sexdecim* (Lyon: Gryphius 1550)
Sepulvedae epistolae	*Io. Genesii Sepulvedae ... epistolarum libri septem in quibus cum alia multa quae legantur dignissima traduntur, tum varii loci graviorum doctrinarum eruditissime et elegantissime tractantur* ed Juan J. Valverde Abril (Salamanca: J.M. de Terranova and J. Archario 1557)
Sieber	Ludwig Sieber *Das Mobiliar des Erasmus: Verzeichnis vom 10. April 1534* (Basel 1891)
Van Heussen	*Historia episcopatuum foederati Belgii* ed Hugo Frans van Heussen (Leiden: Vermey 1719) vol 2 part 4: *Historia, seu notitia episcopatus leovardiensis*
Vita Erasmi	Paul Merula *Vita Desiderii Erasmi ... additi sunt epistolarum ipsius libri duo ...* (Leiden 1607)
VZE	*Viglii ab Aytta Zuichemi Epistolae selectae* = vol II/1 of C.P. Hoynck van Papendrecht *Analecta Belgica* (The Hague 1743) 3 vols in 6
WA	*D. Martin Luthers Werke, Kritische Gesamtausgabe* (Weimar 1883–1980) 60 vols
Wierzbowski	Teodor Wierzbowski *Materyały do dziejów piśmiennictwa polskiego I biografii pisarzów polskich* (Warsaw 1900) 2 vols

Titles following colons are longer versions of the same, or are alternative titles. Items entirely enclosed in square brackets are of doubtful authorship. For abbreviations, see Works Frequently Cited.

Acta: Academiae Lovaniensis contra Lutherum *Opuscula* / CWE 71

Adagia: Adagiorum chiliades 1508, etc (Adagiorum collectanea for the primitive form, when required) LB II / ASD II-1–9 / CWE 30–6

Admonitio adversus mendacium: Admonitio adversus mendacium et obtrectationem LB X / CWE 78

Annotationes in Novum Testamentum LB VI / ASD VI-5–10 / CWE 51–60

Antibarbari LB X / ASD I-1 / CWE 23

Apologia: D. Erasmi Roterodami apologia LB VI / CWE 41

Apologia ad annotationes Stunicae: Apologia respondens ad ea quae Iacobus Lopis Stunica taxaverat in prima duntaxat Novi Testamenti aeditione LB IX / ASD IX-2

Apologia ad Caranzam: Apologia ad Sanctium Caranzam, or Apologia de tribus locis, or Responsio ad annotationem Stunicae … a Sanctio Caranza defensam LB IX / ASD IX-8

Apologia ad Fabrum: Apologia ad Iacobum Fabrum Stapulensem LB IX / ASD IX-3 / CWE 83

Apologia ad prodromon Stunicae LB IX / ASD IX-8

Apologia ad Stunicae conclusiones LB IX / ASD IX-8

Apologia adversus monachos: Apologia adversus monachos quosdam Hispanos (Loca quaedam emendata in second edition, 1529) LB IX

Apologia adversus Petrum Sutorem: Apologia adversus debacchationes Petri Sutoris LB IX

Apologia adversus rhapsodias Alberti Pii: Apologia ad viginti et quattuor libros A. Pii LB IX / ASD IX-6 / CWE 84

Apologia adversus Stunicae Blasphemiae: Apologia adversus libellum Stunicae cui titulum fecit Blasphemiae et impietates Erasmi LB IX / ASD IX-8

Apologia contra Latomi dialogum: Apologia contra Iacobi Latomi dialogum de tribus linguis LB IX / CWE 71

Apologia de 'In principio erat sermo': Apologia palam refellens quorundam seditiosos clamores apud populum ac magnates quo in evangelio Ioannis verterit 'In principio erat sermo' (1520a); Apologia de 'In principio erat sermo' (1520b) LB IX / CWE 73

Apologia de laude matrimonii: Apologia pro declamatione de laude matrimonii LB IX / CWE 71

Apologia de loco 'Omnes quidem': Apologia de loco taxato in publica professione per Nicolaum Ecmondanum theologum et Carmelitanum Lovanii 'Omnes quidem resurgemus' LB IX / CWE 73

Apologia qua respondet invectivis Lei: Apologia qua respondet duabus invectivis Eduardi Lei *Opuscula* / ASD IX-4 / CWE 72

Apophthegmata LB IV / ASD IV-4 / CWE 37–8

Appendix de scriptis Clichtovei LB IX / CWE 83

Appendix respondens ad Sutorem: Appendix respondens ad quaedam Antapologiae Petri Sutoris LB IX

Argumenta: Argumenta in omnes epistolas apostolicas nova (with Paraphrases)
Axiomata pro causa Lutheri: Axiomata pro causa Martini Lutheri   *Opuscula* /
  CWE 71

Brevissima scholia: In Elenchum Alberti Pii brevissima scholia per eundem
  Erasmum Roterodamum   ASD IX-6 / CWE 84

Carmina   LB I, IV, V, VIII / ASD I-7 / CWE 85–6
Catalogus lucubrationum   LB I / CWE 9 (Ep 1341A)
Christiani hominis institutum, carmen   LB V / ASD I-7 / CWE 85–6
Ciceronianus: Dialogus Ciceronianus   LB I / ASD I-2 / CWE 28
Colloquia   LB I / ASD I-3 / CWE 39–40
Compendium vitae   Allen I / CWE 4
Conflictus: Conflictus Thaliae et Barbariei   LB I / ASD I-8
[Consilium: Consilium cuiusdam ex animo cupientis esse consultum]   *Opuscula* /
  CWE 71
Contra morosos: Capita argumentorum contra morosos quosdam ac indoctos   LB VI /
  CWE 41

De bello Turcico: Utilissima consultatio de bello Turcis inferendo, et obiter enarratus
  psalmus 28   LB V / ASD V-3 / CWE 64
De civilitate: De civilitate morum puerilium   LB I / ASD I-8 / CWE 25
Declamatio de morte   LB IV / ASD I-2 / CWE 25
Declamatiuncula   LB IV / ASD IV-7
Declarationes ad censuras Lutetiae vulgatas: Declarationes ad censuras Lutetiae
  vulgatas sub nomine facultatis theologiae Parisiensis   LB IX / ASD IX-7 / CWE 82
De concordia: De sarcienda ecclesiae concordia, or De amabili ecclesiae concordia
  [on Psalm 83]   LB V / ASD V-3 / CWE 65
De conscribendis epistolis   LB I / ASD I-2 / CWE 25
De constructione: De constructione octo partium orationis, or Syntaxis   LB I /
  ASD I-4
De contemptu mundi: Epistola de contemptu mundi   LB V / ASD V-1 / CWE 66
De copia: De duplici copia verborum ac rerum   LB I / ASD I-6 / CWE 24
De delectu ciborum scholia   ASD IX-1 / CWE 73
De esu carnium: Epistola apologetica ad Christophorum episcopum Basiliensem
  de interdicto esu carnium (published with scholia in a 1532 edition but not in
  the 1540 Opera)   LB IX / ASD IX-1 / CWE 73
De immensa Dei misericordia: Concio de immensa Dei misericordia   LB V / ASD V-7 /
  CWE 70
De libero arbitrio: De libero arbitrio diatribe   LB IX / CWE 76
De philosophia evangelica   LB VI / CWE 41
De praeparatione: De praeparatione ad mortem   LB V / ASD V-1 / CWE 70
De pueris instituendis: De pueris statim ac liberaliter instituendis   LB I / ASD I-2 /
  CWE 26
De puero Iesu: Concio de puero Iesu   LB V / ASD V-7 / CWE 29
De puritate tabernaculi: Enarratio psalmi 14 qui est de puritate tabernaculi sive
  ecclesiae christianae   LB V / ASD V-2 / CWE 65
De ratione studii   LB I / ASD I-2 / CWE 24

De recta pronuntiatione: De recta latini graecique sermonis pronuntiatione
  LB I / ASD I-4 / CWE 26
De taedio Iesu: Disputatiuncula de taedio, pavore, tristicia Iesu   LB V/ ASD V-7 /
  CWE 70
Detectio praestigiarum: Detectio praestigiarum cuiusdam libelli Germanice scripti
  LB X / ASD IX-1 / CWE 78
De vidua christiana   LB V / ASD V-6 / CWE 66
De virtute amplectenda: Oratio de virtute amplectenda   LB V / CWE 29
[Dialogus bilinguium ac trilinguium: Chonradi Nastadiensis dialogus bilinguium
  ac trilinguium]   Opuscula / CWE 7
Dilutio: Dilutio eorum quae Iodocus Clichtoveus scripsit adversus declamationem
  suasoriam matrimonii   Dilutio eorum quae Iodocus Clichtoveus scripsit ed Émile V.
  Telle (Paris 1968) / CWE 83
Divinationes ad notata Bedae: Divinationes ad notata per Bedam de Paraphrasi
  Erasmi in Matthaeum, et primo de duabus praemissis epistolis   LB IX / ASD IX-5

Ecclesiastes: Ecclesiastes sive de ratione concionandi   LB V / ASD V-4–5 / CWE 67–8
Elenchus in censuras Bedae: In N. Bedae censuras erroneas elenchus   LB IX / ASD IX-5
Enchiridion: Enchiridion militis christiani   LB V / ASD V-8 / CWE 66
Encomium matrimonii (in De conscribendis epistolis)
Encomium medicinae: Declamatio in laudem artis medicae   LB I / ASD I-4 / CWE 29
Epistola ad Dorpium   LB IX / CWE 3 (Ep 337) / CWE 71
Epistola ad fratres Inferioris Germaniae: Responsio ad fratres Germaniae Inferioris
  ad epistolam apologeticam incerto autore proditam   LB X / ASD IX-1 / CWE 78
Epistola ad gracculos: Epistola ad quosdam impudentissimos gracculos   LB X /
  CWE 16 (Ep 2275)
Epistola apologetica adversus Stunicam   LB IX / ASD IX-8 / CWE 15 (Ep 2172)
Epistola apologetica de Termino   LB X / CWE 14 (Ep 2018)
Epistola consolatoria: Epistola consolatoria virginibus sacris, or Epistola consolatoria
  in adversis   LB V / ASD IV-7 / CWE 69
Epistola contra pseudevangelicos: Epistola contra quosdam qui se falso iactant
  evangelicos   LB X / ASD IX-1 / CWE 78
Euripidis Hecuba   LB I / ASD I-1
Euripidis Iphigenia in Aulide   LB I / ASD I-1
Exomologesis: Exomologesis sive modus confitendi   LB V / ASD V-8 / CWE 67
Explanatio symboli: Explanatio symboli apostolorum sive catechismus   LB V /
  ASD V-1 / CWE 70
Ex Plutarcho versa   LB IV / ASD IV-2

Formula: Conficiendarum epistolarum formula (see De conscribendis epistolis)

Hyperaspistes   LB X / CWE 76–7

In Nucem Ovidii commentarius   LB I / ASD I-1 / CWE 29
In Prudentium: Commentarius in duos hymnos Prudentii   LB V / ASD V-7 /
  CWE 29
In psalmum 1: Enarratio primi psalmi, 'Beatus vir,' iuxta tropologiam potissimum
  LB V / ASD V-2 / CWE 63

In psalmum 2: Commentarius in psalmum 2, 'Quare fremuerunt gentes?' LB V /
ASD V-2 / CWE 63
In psalmum 3: Paraphrasis in tertium psalmum, 'Domine quid multiplicate'
LB V / ASD V-2 / CWE 63
In psalmum 4: In psalmum quartum concio LB V / ASD V-2 / CWE 63
In psalmum 22: In psalmum 22 enarratio triplex LB V / ASD V-2 / CWE 64
In psalmum 33: Enarratio psalmi 33 LB V / ASD V-3 / CWE 64
In psalmum 38: Enarratio psalmi 38 LB V / ASD V-3 / CWE 65
In psalmum 85: Concionalis interpretatio, plena pietatis, in psalmum 85 LB V /
ASD V-3 / CWE 64
Institutio christiani matrimonii LB V / ASD V-6 / CWE 69
Institutio principis christiani LB IV/ ASD IV-1 / CWE 27

Julius exclusus: Dialogus Julius exclusus e coelis Opuscula ASD I-8 / CWE 27

Lingua LB IV / ASD IV-1a / CWE 29
Liturgia Virginis Matris: Virginis Matris apud Lauretum cultae liturgia LB V /
ASD V-1 / CWE 69
Loca quaedam emendata: Loca quaedam in aliquot Erasmi lucubrationibus
per ipsum emendata (see Apologia adversus monachos)
Luciani dialogi LB I / ASD I-1

Manifesta mendacia ASD IX-4 / CWE 71
Methodus (see Ratio)
Modus orandi Deum LB V / ASD V-1 / CWE 70
Moria: Moriae encomium LB IV / ASD IV-3 / CWE 27

Notatiunculae: Notatiunculae quaedam extemporales ad naenias Bedaicas,
or Responsio ad notulas Bedaicas LB IX / ASD IX-5
Novum Testamentum: Novum instrumentum 1516; Novum Testamentum 1519 and
later (Greek and Latin editions and Latin only editions) LB VI / ASD VI-2, 3, 4

Obsecratio ad Virginem Mariam: Obsecratio sive oratio ad Virginem Mariam in
rebus adversis, or Obsecratio ad Virginem Matrem Mariam in rebus adversis
LB V / CWE 69
Oratio de pace: Oratio de pace et discordia LB VIII / ASD IV-7
Oratio funebris: Oratio funebris in funere Bertae de Heyen LB VIII / ASD IV-7 /
CWE 29

Paean Virgini Matri: Paean Virgini Matri dicendus LB V / CWE 69
Panegyricus: Panegyricus ad Philippum Austriae ducem LB IV / ASD IV-1 /
CWE 27
Parabolae: Parabolae sive similia LB I / ASD I-5 / CWE 23
Paraclesis LB V, VI / ASD V-7 / CWE 41
Paraphrasis in Elegantias Vallae: Paraphrasis in Elegantias Laurentii Vallae
LB I / ASD I-4
Paraphrasis in Matthaeum, etc LB VII / ASD VII-2, 5, 6 / CWE 42–50
Peregrinatio apostolorum: Peregrinatio apostolorum Petri et Pauli LB VI, VII / CWE 41

Precatio ad Virginis filium Iesum   LB V / CWE 69
Precatio dominica   LB V / CWE 69
Precationes: Precationes aliquot novae   LB V / CWE 69
Precatio pro pace ecclesiae: Precatio ad Dominum Iesum pro pace ecclesiae
    LB IV, V / CWE 69
Prologus supputationis: Prologus in supputationem calumniarum Natalis Bedae
    (1526), or Prologus supputationis errorum in censuris Bedae (1527)   LB IX /
    ASD IX-5
Purgatio adversus epistolam Lutheri: Purgatio adversus epistolam non sobriam
    Martini Lutheri   LB X / ASD IX-1 / CWE 78

Querela pacis   LB IV / ASD IV-2 / CWE 27

Ratio: Ratio seu Methodus compendio perveniendi ad veram theologiam (Methodus
    for the shorter version originally published in the Novum instrumentum of 1516)
    LB V, VI / CWE 41
Responsio ad annotationes Lei: Responsio ad annotationes Eduardi Lei   LB IX /
    ASD IX-4 / CWE 72
Responsio ad Collationes: Responsio ad Collationes cuiusdam iuvenis
    gerontodidascali   LB IX / CWE 73
Responsio ad disputationem de divortio: Responsio ad disputationem cuiusdam
    Phimostomi de divortio   LB IX / ASD IX-4 / CWE 83
Responsio ad epistolam Alberti Pii: Responsio ad epistolam paraeneticam Alberti
    Pii, or Responsio ad exhortationem Pii   LB IX / ASD IX-6 / CWE 84
Responsio ad notulas Bedaicas (see Notatiunculae)
Responsio ad Petri Cursii defensionem: Epistola de apologia Cursii   LB X / Ep 3032
Responsio adversus febricitantis cuiusdam libellum   LB X

Spongia: Spongia adversus aspergines Hutteni   LB X / ASD IX-1 / CWE 78
Supputatio: Supputatio errorum in censuris Bedae   LB IX
Supputationes: Supputationes errorum in censuris Natalis Bedae: contains
    Supputatio and reprints of Prologus supputationis; Divinationes ad notata Bedae;
    Elenchus in censuras Bedae; Appendix respondens ad Sutorem; Appendix de
    scriptis Clithovei   LB IX / ASD IX-5

Tyrannicida: Tyrannicida, declamatio Lucianicae respondens   LB I / ASD I-1 /
    CWE 29

Virginis et martyris comparatio   LB V / ASD V-7 / CWE 69
Vita Hieronymi: Vita divi Hieronymi Stridonensis   *Opuscula* / ASD VIII-1/ CWE 61

CORRIGENDA FOR EARLIER VOLUMES

CWE 9
Page xiii, in the sentence that ends with n25: insert 'which had' between 'cardinals,' and 'tried to prevent'

CWE 13
Ep 1810 n6, line 7 (page 62): for 'Ep 11825' read 'Ep 1825'

CWE 14
Ep 1989 n4, line 3: delete '2022:55–6'

CWE 15
Ep 2101 introduction, insert after first sentence: 'The surviving manuscript, a late sixteenth-century copy, is in the University Library at Ghent (MS 479 page 25).'

CWE 16
Ep 2352 n32: for 'William v (Ep 2234)' read 'John III'
Page 416 (Table of Correspondents), under Ep 2311: for '292' read '289'
Page 416 (Table of Correspondents), under Ep 2312: for '295' read '292'
Page 416 (Table of Correspondents), under Ep 2312A: for '307' read '295'
Page 416 (Table of Correspondents), under Ep 2313: for '309' read '307'
Page 416 (Table of Correspondents), under Ep 2314: for '311' read '309'

CWE 17
Ep 2383 n3, line 2: for 'n35' read 'n6'
Ep 2419 header: for 'Wolfgang Rem' read 'Wolfgang Andreas Rem'
Page 386 (Index), under 'Froben, Erasmius': for '224n' read '223n'

CWE 18
Ep 2490 n6, line 4: for '(Epp 2417–18)' read '(Epp 2317–18)'
Ep 2526:29: for 'Bartholemew' read 'Bartholomew'
Ep 2570:93: for 'Chemno' read 'Chełmno'
Page 410 (Index), under 'Aristotle, Aristotelian': for '131n' read '151n'
Page 410 (Index), under 'Bartolo of Sassoferrato': for '206n' read '296n'
Page 411 (Index), under 'Carondelet, Jean (II) de': for '31n' read '228n'
Page 416 (Index), under 'Homer': for '234n' read '235n'
Page 422 (Index), under 'Warham, William, Erasmus' pensions from: add '48n'; delete '286n'

Index

The design of
THE COLLECTED WORKS
OF ERASMUS
was created
by
ALLAN FLEMING
1929–1977
for
the University
of Toronto
Press